OBSCENE, INDECENT,
IMMORAL, AND OFFENSIVE

OBSCENE, INDECENT, IMMORAL, AND OFFENSIVE

100+ Years of Censored, Banned, and Controversial Films

STEPHEN TROPIANO

LIMELIGHT EDITIONS
An Imprint of Hal Leonard Corporation
New York

Published in 2009 by Limelight Editions
An Imprint of Hal Leonard Corporation
7777 West Bluemound Road
Milwaukee, WI 53213

Trade Book Division Editorial Offices
19 West 21st Street, New York, NY 10010

All interior photographs are courtesy of Photofest.

Printed in the United States of America

Book design by Publishers' Design and Production Services, Inc.

Library of Congress Cataloging-in-Publication Data

Tropiano, Stephen.
  Obscene, indecent, immoral, and offensive : 100+ years of censored, banned, and controversial films / Stephen Tropiano.
      p. cm.
  Includes bibliographical references and index.
  ISBN 978-0-87910-359-0 (alk. paper)
  1. Motion pictures—Censorship—United States—History. I. Title.
  PN1995.62T76 2009
  363.3'10973—dc22
                            2008052582

www.limelighteditions.com

CONTENTS

Contents

On the evening of June 25, 1997, three Oklahoma City police officers appeared at the doorstep of Michael Camfield, director of development for the American Civil Liberties Union (ACLU) in Oklahoma. They were there to confiscate a VHS copy of the German film, *Die Blechtrommel* (*The Tin Drum*—1979), which he had recently rented from his neighborhood Blockbuster. Camfield had heard of a local controversy brewing over the film, so he wanted to watch it in case he needed to prepare a formal response on behalf of the ACLU. The police informed him they were seizing all the copies of the tape because a judge had determined the film contained scenes of child pornography in violation of Okla. Stat. tit. 21, §1021.2. Camfield defended the artistic merits of the film to the police, but in the end he had no choice but to hand the tape over to the officers.

Based on the novel by Günter Grass, *The Tin Drum* is an allegorical tale set in Nazi Germany. Three-year-old Oskar is a defiant little boy who reacts against the hypocrisy, depravity, and complacency of adults, whom he blames for the Nazis' rise to power, by stunting his own physical growth. So as Oskar grows older, his body remains the same. The three scenes in question focus on Oskar's sexual awakening, all of which involve a young female character named Maria. In an affidavit, *Tin Drum* director Volker Schlöndorff confirmed that the actors playing Oskar and Maria, twelve-year-old David Bennent and twenty-four-year-old Katharina Thalbach, "displayed no frontal nudity" and did not engage in "any sexual conduct or any contact with the genitals or genital areas" in their scenes together.

It took several trials and numerous appeals over several years before justice prevailed. In two separate rulings, judges declared the police officers violated the Video Privacy Protection Act by obtaining customer records from Blockbuster without a prior search warrant, court order, or subpoena, and that *The Tin Drum* was not pornographic and therefore not in violation of the Oklahoma statute.

What happened in Oklahoma City may have been a rare occurrence, yet the self-generated hysteria, the Gestapo-like tactics, and the morality-based legal maneuverings are all strategies opponents of the cinema have been employing since audiences first laid eyes on "moving pictures." Since their inception, motion pictures and their content have been at the center of countless legal, political, social, moral, and religious battles between the people who make them (filmmakers, studios), those they are made for (the audience), and the institutions (local and state censorship boards, the Roman Catholic Church, etc.), who believe it is their God-given right to determine what movies can and cannot say and show.

Obscene, Indecent, Immoral, and Offensive aims to shed some light on the roles all of the above and others have played over the past ten decades in censoring and "regulating" (a gentler, kinder word for censorship) the content of movies. As the title suggests, the films discussed in the following pages were controversial at the time of their release and were deemed "obscene," "indecent," "immoral," or "offensive" (or any combination of the above).

The book is divided into six chapters. Chapter 1 offers a history lesson on the subject of film censorship and regulation in the United States, from the silent era through the creation of the Production Code Administration (PCA), which served as the film industry's official censor through the early 1960s. Chapter 2 takes a closer look at the PCA and two other organizations that played a significant role in determining what Americans could and should not see—the National Legion of Decency and the Classification and Ratings Administration (CARA), which oversees the current motion picture ratings system in the United States. The appendices include related documents, such as the 1930 Motion Picture Production Code (appendix D), the Legion of Decency Pledge (appendix F), and the original version of the Motion Picture Ratings System (appendix G).

The remaining four chapters focus on the content of motion pictures and the six major issues that have been the source of contention since the silent era: profanity, violence, sex, nudity, politics, and religion. Each chapter consists of case studies of specific films; many of them you have seen, though I have also included titles that you might not recognize, yet, at the time of their release, created quite a stir.

The most difficult part of writing this book was picking and choosing films. For every film discussed, there are two or three other titles that could have been included if space permitted. I acknowledge that the majority of films are American, though there are several imports included that could not be ignored, such as Roberto Rossellini's *Il miracolo* (*The Miracle*—1948), which was at the center of a landmark 1952 Supreme Court ruling protecting motion pictures as free speech (with the exception of obscenity) under the First and Fourteenth amendments.

One quick note: As film is a collaborative medium, I use the term *filmmakers* when referring to everyone involved in the making of a motion picture. The singular *filmmaker* refers to the director or writer/director of a film.

ACKNOWLEDGMENTS

For their assistance and support with the project, I would like to thank my agent, June Clark, and Michael Messina at Applause Books, who has been so patient and accommodating, even when I asked for the 310th time for "just a few more days." Thanks also to Jessica Burr and Joanna Dalin.

This book could not have been written without the wisdom and generosity of my friend Barbara Hall in the Special Collections Department of the Academy of Motion Picture Arts and Sciences' Margaret Herrick Library, which houses the Production Code Administration files.

I am also deeply indebted to my colleagues at the Ithaca College Los Angeles Program, Jon Bassinger-Flores and Holly Pietromonaco, who have both been so supportive during the process of writing this book. Thanks also to Holly for proofreading my manuscript; my research assistant, Anthony Bisalti, for all his hard work; and all my students at ICLA.

On a more personal note, thanks to my brother Joe and the rest of my family on the East Coast. Thanks also to Ray Morton and my West Coast family: Matthew Jon Beck, Linda Bobel, Faith Ginsberg, Gary Jones, Barry Sandler, Neil Spisak, Arnold Stiefel, and my friends at the Trevor Project (www.thetrevorproject.org).

This project was made possible in part by a James B. Pendleton Grant from the Roy H. Park School of Communications at Ithaca College. Thanks to Dianne Lynch, Elisabeth Nonas, and Patty Zimmermann for their continued support of all my academic endeavors.

Finally, this book is dedicated to Steven Ginsberg—here's to the next twenty.

CHAPTER 1

Censorship and Silent Cinema, or
Why a Kiss Is No Longer *Just* a Kiss

On April 23, 1896, Koster & Bial's Music Hall in New York City unveiled one of the first motion picture projection systems— Thomas Edison's "greatest marvel"—the Vitascope. According to a *New York Times* story, "the ingenious inventor's latest toy" was well received by the enthusiastic crowd, whose "vociferous cheering" started before the exhibition had even ended. Over the next three months, the Vitascope was exhibited in cities across America, where audiences were also reportedly captivated by the life-sized moving pictures of the rushing waters of New Jersey's Passaic Falls, a ferry boat leaving a New York dock, and a parade of bicyclists riding through the streets of Brooklyn.

The most popular film produced by the Edison Manufacturing Company in 1896 was *The May Irwin Kiss*, which featured two stage actors, May Irwin and John Rice, reenacting for the camera the climactic kiss from the final scene of their current hit Broadway musical comedy, *The Widow Jones*. More comical than titillating, the eighteen-second film (at thirty frames per second) consists of a single shot—a medium close-up of the romantic couple sitting closely together. As they talk, he moves his lips closer to hers. Irwin laughs as Rice, in preparation for the big moment, pulls his large handlebar moustache away from his lips. He then gently places his hands on her face and kisses her on the mouth.

In honor of the show's two hundredth performance, the *New York World* devoted an entire page to the filming of the kiss. The article, entitled "Anatomy of a Kiss," features four frame enlargements of key moments from the film with captions detailing the actors' actions leading up to the big moment: "A Perfect Gentleman Smooths His Mustache First," "This Is the Coy Moment—May Irwin Hesitates," "The Preliminary Snuggle Seems to Be a Good Thing," and "Climax—Long and Enthusiastic and Too Blissful for Adjectives."

When the Vitascope went "on the road," *The May Irwin Kiss* was a big hit with audiences. The film generated what the entertainment industry today calls a "pre-buzz" in most major cities, where the local press consistently singled it out as an audience favorite:

> Of the 10 pictures included in yesterday's programmes, it would be difficult to say which will leave the most lasting impression, but there is no shadow of a doubt as to which created the most laughter. That kissing scene in the *Widow Jones*, taken part in by May Irwin and John C. Rice, was reproduced on the screen, and the very evident delight of the actor and the undisguised pleasure of the actress were absolutely "too funny" for anything.
>
> —*Boston Herald* (5/19/1896)

> The famous kissing scene between May Irwin and John C. Rice in *The Widow Jones* is the most thoroughly successful reproduction in the list, and will make the hit of the exhibition.
>
> —*Chicago Tribune* (7/5/1896)

> In San Francisco and elsewhere, one of the most popular scenes was a reproduction of the famous bit of acting in which May Irwin is kissed by John C. Rush [*sic*]. The changing expression of their faces, their graceful movements, the play of hand and lip and eye, are said to be faultlessly reproduced.
>
> —*Los Angeles Times* (7/5/1896)

But everyone was not amused by Irwin and Rice's onscreen smooch. New York artist John Sloan wrote a scathing review of both the invention and the film, which was published in 1896 in a small arts journal, *Chap-Book*:

2

Now I want to smash the Vitascope. The name of the thing is in itself a horror. Its manifestations are worse. . . . In a recent play called *The Widow Jones* you may remember a famous kiss which Miss May Irwin bestowed on a certain John C. Rice, and *vice-versa*. Neither participant is physically attractive, and the spectacle of their prolonged pasturing on each other's lips was hard to bear. When only life size it was pronounced beastly. But that was nothing to the present sight. Magnified to Gargantuan proportions and repeated three times over it is absolutely disgusting. All delicacy or remnant of charm seems gone from Miss Irwin, and the performance comes near being indecent in its emphasized vulgarity. Such things call for police interference. . . . The immorality of living pictures and bronze statues is nothing to this. The Irwin kiss is no more than a lyric of the Stock Yards.

Sloan found the filmed kiss more objectionable than the live performance because of its duration (films were often shown repeatedly as a loop) and its lack of aesthetic appeal. He found Irwin and Rice unsightly to begin with, so the image of the couple locking lips, magnified by the Vitascope to "Gargantuan proportions," was by virtue of its size all the more "vulgar." The tone of Sloan's piece is also moralistic. One can safely assume he had "issues" about the public display of affection (even when captured on film), which he denounced as yet another example of the "recurring outrages to decency and good taste" that he continually encountered in books and on the legitimate stage.

The public's enthusiastic reception of *The May Irwin Kiss* versus Sloan's adverse reaction to the same fifty feet of film exemplifies how an individual's taste, values, and morals are all factors that shape and determine how an individual spectator responds to the flickering shadows up on the screen. It is these very differences that have fueled the hundred-plus-year culture war over the content of motion pictures and the ongoing debate over what is acceptable and what is obscene, indecent, immoral, and offensive.

Consequently, until the invention of television, no other form of entertainment had been subjected to the same intense public scrutiny as the cinema. Since pictures first started to move, they have been the source of contention between the people who make movies, those who watch them, and the individuals and organizations that regulate, censor, condemn, and ban them.

CENSORSHIP BY THE SEA

Motion picture censorship began in the United States in the 1890s with the introduction of the first film exhibition devices, Edison's Kinetoscope (1894) and the Mutoscope (1894). A customer simply dropped a few coins into a slot, peered through the viewfinder, and marveled at the physique of strongman Eugene Sandow (*Sandow* [1894, 1896]); the fancy footwork of dancing ladies (*Annabelle Butterfly Dance* [1895]; *Princess Ali* [1895]); performers from Buffalo Bill's Wild West Show (*Bucking Broncho* [1894]; *Annie Oakley* [1894]); historical reenactments (*The Execution of Mary, Queen of Scots* [1895]); and boxing matches between comical performers (*Glenroy Brothers* [1894]), professional boxers (*Corbett-Courtney Fight* [1894]), and animals (*The Boxing Cats* [1894]). The machines became a popular attraction in amusement parks and at seaside resorts, such as Asbury Park, Atlantic City, and Coney Island, where some of the earliest instances of film censorship on record occurred.

In July of 1894, Edison's Kinetoscope was put on exhibition at Asbury Park in the inventor's home state of New Jersey. On the evening of its debut, the town's founder, State Senator James A. Bradley, along with the city's mayor, Frank Ten Broeck, decided to have a look at Edison's latest invention. According to the *Newark Evening News*, the first film Bradley and Ten Broeck saw was a dramatization of a barroom fight. They were in agreement "that the supremacy of the law over the rougher elements had a good moral tone." The same could not be said for the next film, which the exhibitor insisted was one of the best pictures in the collection—a solo performance by professional Spanish dancer, Carmencita. The senator didn't approve of Carmencita's final move, in which "she gives the least little bit kick, which raises her silken draperies so that her well-turned ankles peep out and there is a background of white lace." Both men agreed the "picture was not fitted for the entertainment of the average summer boarder" and informed the exhibitor he would be shut down if he didn't find a replacement (he did—she was replaced by *The Boxing Cats*).

Historian Terry Ramsaye recounts a similar incident that occurred in Atlantic City, where male patrons were lined up at a Kinetoscope parlor to see the film *Dolorita in the Passion Dance* (1894). An "uplifter" (a person devoted to "uplifting" the morals of society) who happened to be passing by noticed the line. After having a look himself, he complained to the authorities, who forced the owner to bring the curtain down on Dolorita and put the film back in its can.

Unfortunately, these matters were not always handled in a quiet manner, particularly when they involved full-time moral reformers who, to make a name for themselves, raised their objections to indecent moving pictures publicly. In August 1896, F. J. Kane of the San Francisco chapter of the Society for the Suppression of Vice had Robert Klenck arrested for operating a Kinetoscope that allegedly showed an indecent film. A spokesman for Edison's company was confused about the allegations, stating that "we have always been careful not to take anything that would be in any way objectionable to the Authorities, although certain religious people might object to some of the characters introduced."

One man of the cloth who did object to the films being shown was Rev. Frederick Bruce Russell, President of the Law and Order Society of New York and part-time vigilante, who took matters into his own hands and raided several film parlors at Coney Island. According to the *Brooklyn Daily Eagle*, two films that "fell under the ban of the reformer's eye" both featured a group of young women having a bit of fun: *What the Girls Did with Willie's Hat* (1897) and *Fun in a Boarding School* (1897). The transcript of a British parliamentary debate over morality includes a short synopsis of *Willie's Hat*, in which "girls in short frocks engaged in kicking at a hat, there being at each attempt a liberal display of underclothing." Surviving stills of *Boarding School* also depict a group of girls frolicking as they enjoy each other's company.

Although these incidents seem like mere footnotes in American film history, they did foreshadow the attacks that would soon be launched by political, civil, and religious leaders, as well as the press, against motion picture exhibitors in New York City and Chicago.

MOVING PICTURES: "TOO VULGAR TO BE DESCRIBED"

One of the perils which threaten the moral development of young lives in this great city is the moving-picture machine. In the hands of vile men it has become a propagator of obscenity.

—Dr. John Josiah Munro (1899)
New York Evening Journal

By 1900, moving pictures had become a fixture in vaudeville houses, where they shared the bill with singers, dancers, comedians, and other variety performers. Edison was no longer manufacturing his Kinetoscope, but the American Mutoscope and Biograph Company continued to produce films for its invention, the Mutoscope, which remained a popular amusement at resorts, saloons, and rail stations; and its projection system, the Biograph, which was being used in theatres around the country. Over time, the Mutoscope and other peepshow devices started featuring more titillating films for adult male patrons. Their list of over 350 films released in 1899 included such "G-rated" fare as *Children Feeding Ducklings*, *Feeding the Pigeons*, and *Sunday School Parade*, as well as shorts with such provocative titles as *The Way French Bathing Girls Bathe*, *The Corset Model*, *Phillis Was Not Dressed to Receive Callers*, *Hazing Affair in a Girls' Boarding School*, *Her Morning Dip*, *A Burlesque Queen*, and *It's Dangerous to Tickle a Soubrette*.

In November of that same year, Mutoscope parlors were the target of a crusade launched by the *New York Evening Journal*, a daily tabloid owned by William Randolph Hearst and known for its sensationalistic headlines and yellow journalism. The *Journal* accused Mutoscope exhibitors of corrupting impressionable children by exposing them to images they considered "vulgar," "suggestive," "obscene," and "indecent." Some of these establishments also included live shows featuring female dancers or women in tights posing for the male clientele. With the cooperation of the police department, the *Journal* succeeded in shutting down several Mutoscope parlors and having the owners arrested. The paper also published the locations of the parlors, the names of their owners, and a list of schools "within the sphere of malignant influence." But as historian Dan Streible observes, the campaign was focused on the exhibitors as opposed to the Mutoscope and Biograph Company, the makers of the films that were corrupting America's youth. In fact, the stories in the *Journal* did not even include titles or descriptions of the films. One reporter chose instead to just simply state that what he saw in the "picture machines" was "too vulgar to be described." Streible believes the *Journal* didn't go after Biograph because the paper published illustrations from American Mutoscope and Biograph's films, including images from their film of the recent Jeffries-Sharkey fight (*Jeffries-Sharkey Contest* [1899]) in Coney Island on November 3, 1899. The film debuted on November 20, 1899, a little over a week before the *Journal*'s anti-Mutoscope campaign was launched.

CHICAGO: "NICKEL THEATRES CRIME BREEDERS"

In 1907, another newspaper launched a vicious attack against the movies that would have a more profound and lasting effect on the burgeoning motion picture industry. On April 10, the *Chicago Daily Tribune* ran an editorial entitled "The Five Cent Theatres," in which the newspaper expressed its support for the "war" being launched by various civic organizations against the "demoralizing influence" of the city's nickelodeons:

> Most of them are evil in their nature, without a single redeeming feature to warrant their existence. They minister to the lowest passions of childhood. They make schools of crime where murders, robberies, and holdups are illustrated. The outlaw life they portray in their cheap plays tends to the encouragement of wickedness. They manufacture criminals to infest the streets of the city. Not a single thing connected with them has influence for good.

The editorial proposed two solutions that would make it difficult for nickel theatres to stay open: charge the same licensing fees as stage theatres and restrict the entrance age to eighteen.

The *Tribune* continued its campaign with a headline that really summed up the whole situation: "Nickel Theatres Crime Breeders." As with the *Evening Journal* campaign, the Tribune *claimed* movie houses needed to be regulated to protect their most vulnerable patrons—the youth of Chicago. Likewise, the paper was critical of the films themselves and included a list of provocative titles, such as *The Bigamist* (1905), *An Old Man's Darling* (1906), *Female Highwayman* (1906), *Gaieties of Divorce* (1906), *Paris Slums* (1906), and *Seaside Flirtation* (1906). The article also contained a detailed synopsis of the most controversial film of the day, *The Unwritten Law: A Thrilling Drama Based on the Thaw-White Case* (see below), a 1907 docudrama based on the scandalous events surrounding "the crime of the century": the murder of architect Stanford White by millionaire Harry K. Thaw, who accused White of drugging and raping Thaw's future wife, chorus girl Evelyn Nesbit, when she was sixteen years old.

With its popularity on the rise, the cinema's potentially damaging effects on the minds and morals of America's youth was one of the many concerns shared by a group of social reformers known as the Progressives. Although they tackled a range of social problems plaguing urban America at the turn of the century—health issues, housing, child labor, prostitution—moving pictures were a priority because movie houses were frequented by children, and it was toward the "development of the child, by the most beneficial and constructive method possible, that much of progressive social activity was directed." As Michael G. Aronson explains, "Progressives recognized the medium as a double-edged sword: an instrument for education in the principles of human freedom and communal responsibility and, simultaneously, a weapon of indoctrination, capable of moving the masses to anarchy and socialism." Consequently, in a publicized meeting with law enforcement in May of 1907, many Progressives—social workers, clergymen, and settlement workers—supported the police's efforts to censor films and keep children out of theatres. Some supported an age limit for admission, which, like the current R rating, would require minors of a certain age to be accompanied by a parent or guardian. Another proposed ordinance would prohibit all children from attending—period. One dissenting voice belonged to Jane Addams, cofounder of Chicago's Hull House, one of the first settlement houses in the United States that offered social, cultural, and educational programs for children and adults. Addams supported the regulation of movie theatres, but she also believed the cinema could be "made instructive." She tried to prove her point by opening up what *Moving Picture World* dubbed an "uplift theatre," which screened "actualities and travel pictures, interspersed with lectures, and 'stories with moral lessons' and 'happy domestic situations.'" The theatre only lasted a few months before shutting its doors.

The controversy surrounding five-cent theatres in Chicago culminated with the passing of an ordinance on November 4, 1907, which established the city's police department as the country's first official censor. To prevent the "obscene and immoral films" from being shown in Chicago "in a public place or where the public is admitted," exhibitors and film exchanges had to first secure a permit from the city's chief of police. A print of the film was submitted and if approved, a permit was issued. If denied, an appeal could be made to the mayor. Historian Lee Grieveson regards the passing of this ordinance as an important moment in American film history because it signified "a shift from a literal policing of the cinema" (i.e., the closing of theatres by the police) to "a metaphorical policing that emerged in censorship institutions and self-regulatory strategies."

The constitutionality of the ordinance was put to the test in a case involving a Chicago exhibitor named Jake Block, who was denied a permit to screen a pair of films: *The James Boys in Missouri* (1908), the story of Western outlaws Frank and Jesse James, and *Night Riders* (1908), which according to court records centered around the "tobacco wars" and depicted scenes of "malicious mischief, and murder."

Block filed a complaint in the Cook County Superior Court claiming the ordinance deprived movie exhibitors their constitutional rights. He lost his case and appealed to the Illinois Supreme Court. His lawyers filed a brief claiming the ordinance was unconstitutional because it applied to only certain kinds of picture show exhibitors, and granted legislative and judicial powers to the chief of police whose decisions could not be appealed through the courts. Block's lawyers also claimed the police chief had the power to diminish the monetary value of a film without due process, and the law was unreasonable because the decisions of the police chief could cause injury to the exhibitor. Block lost his case, thereby making censorship boards constitutional. As John Wertheimer observes, the one issue that was never raised in relation to the case (nor in other theatre cases that preceded it) was whether motion pictures were protected speech under the Constitution, which would soon be determined.

NEW YORK CITY: "BAD MOVIES, BAD THEATRES"

Chicago was not the only city trying to drive the nickel theatres out of business. In 1907, a legal battle erupted in New York City when New York Supreme Court Justice James Aloysius O'Gorman revoked the license of a vaudeville house, the Victoria Theatre, for violating the Blue Laws, which prohibited "every possible form of entertainment" on Sundays. According to Section 1,481 of the Charter of the City of New York, it was unlawful

> to exhibit on . . . Sunday, to the public, in any building, garden, grounds, concert room, or other room or place within the City of New York, any interlude, tragedy, comedy, opera, ballet, play, farce, negro minstrelsy, negro, or other dancing, or any other entertainment of the stage, or any parts or parts therein, acrobats, or rope dancing.

Judge O'Gorman's decision upheld the legislature's authority to regulate the observance of the "Christian Sabbath . . . for the purpose of protecting the moral and physical well-being of the people and preserving the peace, quiet, and good order of society." In response to the ruling, the New York Police Commissioner had no choice but to enforce the law. On Sunday, December 8, 1907, regardless of the venue, "all performances" in New York City were banned. Religious leaders were jubilant over the news. A spokesman for the Inter-denominational Committee of the Clergy for Greater New York, which was formed specifically for the purpose of banning vaudeville on Sundays, called the judge's ruling a "triumph of law and order in Brooklyn." But penny arcades and vaudeville houses were not the only causalities. In the "Amusements" section of the *New York Times*, a listing for Carnegie Hall announced the cancellation of Sunday's concert, making it clear who was to blame for the last-minute schedule change: "On account of Justice O'Gorman's decision the Sunday Concert will not be given."

The *New York Times* reported the cancellation of another theatrical event—a sold-out production of Mark Twain's *The Prince and the Pauper* performed by children.

As for the movie theatres, the City Charter and the related statutes of the Penal Code never mentioned them because they were written decades before Edison threaded his first projector. The absence of moving pictures in the list of prohibited performances provided a loophole for exhibitors, who succeeded in getting an injunction to stay open. Their lawyers claimed that the phrase "or any other entertainment of the stage" did not apply to moving pictures because they do not require a stage. Over the course of the next few weeks, the Aldermanic Laws Committee worked to liberalize the law. The Duoll Ordinance, named after Alderman Reginald Duoll, stated that the performance of any tragedy, comedy, etc. was prohibited, yet permitted "sacred or educational, vocal or instrumental concerts, lectures, addresses, recitations, and singing, provided that such above-mentioned entertainments shall be given in such a manner as not to disturb the public peace or amount to a serious interruption to the repose and religious liberty of the community."

After a series of injunctions and legal battles, a judge ruled that the Sunday exhibition of moving pictures to the public was not illegal unless the peace of the day was disturbed or the exhibition was held outdoors. But the five-cent theatres and the images projected on their screens did not escape public scrutiny.

Approximately one year after the Blue Law crisis, movie exhibitors faced an even greater battle. On Christmas Eve, 1908, Mayor George B. McClellan gave the good people of New York City a very special Christmas gift and revoked the licenses of every moving picture house in the city, effective midnight on Christmas Eve. On the previous day, Mayor McScrooge presided over a public hearing at City Hall where community leaders, along with exhibitors, met to discuss the safety conditions of movie theatres and whether they should be permitted, despite the law, to keep their doors open on Sunday. The target of his campaign were the "five-cent theatres," which had a seating capacity of less than three hundred and were required to obtain a license from the Mayor's Marshal (a "concert-room license," issued by the police commissioner, was needed for larger theatres).

Religious leaders, who were adamant that movie theatres should be closed on the Lord's Day, demonized both the movies and their exhibitors. William C. Chase of the Christ Episcopal Church in Brooklyn stated, "I am not opposed to moving pictures shows or theatres; I am opposed to bad moving pictures shows and theatres. . . . These men who run these shows have no moral scruples whatever." Another man of the cloth condemned them outright, declaring exhibitors were "doomed to double damnation" (as opposed to single damnation?) for profiting from "the corruption of the minds of children." Episcopal Bishop David R. Greer blamed the city for not "safeguarding against degrading influences," which he found ironic considering New York was spending millions to educate and care for the city's children.

Representatives for the exhibitors responded by taking responsibility for the conditions of the theatres, which the mayor claimed posed a major public safety hazard because fire exits were blocked, locked, nonexistent, and/or poorly lit. They urged the city to keep their theatres open on Sunday, vowing to attend to all safety issues. Exhibitors also claimed that moving picture shows were the "poor man's theatres" and men were now patronizing them instead of the local saloon. Speaking on behalf of the film manufacturers, J. Stuart Blackton, founder of the Vitagraph Company, agreed to cease making "questionable films and to keep out importations of such films as far as possible." But the one concession made by the exhibitors that would certainly have a lasting impact on the industry and American film culture was their willingness to allow their films to be censored, as was being done in Chicago by the chief of police.

On Christmas Day, 1908, Mayor McClellan issued an official statement justifying the sudden shutdown of 550 five-cent theatres due to poor safety conditions, the potential fire danger posed by flammable film, and the lack of fire exits. He concluded by pledging that due to "serious opposition" of religious leaders as well as the Society for the Prevention of Cruelty to Children and the Society for the Prevention of Crime, licenses would only be reinstated if exhibitors signed a written agreement stating they would not open on Sunday. "I do further declare," the mayor added, "that I will revoke any of these moving-picture show licenses on evidence that pictures have been exhibited by the licensees which tend to degrade or injure the morals of the com-

12

munity." The mayor didn't elaborate on how it would be determined whether or not a film was a threat to the community's morals, nor did he identify the person or persons making those decisions.

Although community leaders had no hard evidence, those who advocated the regulation of movie houses and the censorship of motion pictures continued to assert that both could have potentially damaging physical and psychic effects on children. What evidence did exist was in the form of newspaper articles, which reported on studies of the harmful effects of moving pictures on the eyes and the opinions of experts on the link between motion pictures and crime. The *New York Times* featured a story (with the headline "Show Made Boy a Burglar") about a fifteen-year-old arraigned on a charge of grand larceny who told the judge a moving picture show inspired him to become a burglar. In July of 1910, twelve-year-old Ethel Allen admitted to setting fire to her apartment house and trying to extort fifty dollars from her father. She told police she got the idea from the movies (and even signed the note "Black Hand," which was also the criminal's name in the movie). An even more tragic tale involved the accidental shooting of a three-year-old by an eight-year-old whose mind was "seemingly warped by attending moving picture shows."

The annual report of the Executive Committee of the New York Society for the Prevention of Cruelty to Children, published in February 1909, confirmed the link between moving pictures and crime, claiming "children support the little picture shows at a cost to their little souls and bodies and minds. . . . The records of the Children's Court sadly prove that this new form of entertainment has gone far to blast the lives of girls and led many boys to criminal courts."

While exhibitors were obtaining court injunctions to reopen five-cent theatres, Mayor McClellan and the police seized the opportunity to make sure the larger theatres, which had concert or theatrical licenses, were following the Blue Laws and not featuring theatrical performances of any kind on Sundays. Play performances were prohibited as well as anything to suggest that a person standing on a stage was performing. Costumes, makeup, and the use of foreign accents were not allowed. Consequently, many vaudeville theatres eliminated moving pictures from their Sunday bills. Alleged violators were arrested, including a German immigrant for speaking onstage with an accent, and another man for wearing a black and brown spotted waistcoat, which the police claimed was a costume (the latter case was dismissed when the judge revealed he was wearing a similar coat). Moving pictures were only permitted on Sundays if they were used for illustrative purposes during a lecture. Historian Terry Ramsaye gives an example of how such a lecture became an exercise in sarcasm:

> At Hammerstein's Victoria the lecturer stood in the orchestra and watched the screen. When a train appeared he spoke up brightly. "These are railroad tracks." "More railroad tracks." "We are now passing a mountain." The lecture was the best act on the bill. It got a hand.

THE NATIONAL BOARD OF CENSORSHIP: "SELECTION NOT CENSORSHIP"

In March of 1909, the Motion Picture Exhibitors Association enlisted the help of the People's Institute of New York to organize a censorship board that would be responsible for prescreening films before they opened in New York City movie theatres. Founded in 1897, the institute was a progressive organization dedicated to social research that offered lectures, cultural enrichment programs, and adult education classes to the public. Charles Sprague Smith, the institute's director, and John Collier, a field investigator for the institute's "Committee on Cheap Amusements," were Progressives who recognized the important social role the cinema was playing in the lives of the working class. Collier was the author of a 1908 report, produced in conjunction with the Women's Municipal League, entitled "Cheap Amusement Shows in Manhattan," which acknowledged the cinema's role as "a new social force, perhaps the beginning of a true theatre of the people, and an instrument whose power can only be realized when social workers begin to use it." In addition to their pro-film stance, the Exhibitor's Association may have chosen the People's Institute because it had some experience in this area. Since 1907, its Dramatic Department had reviewed current theatrical productions and made recommendations based on their educational and artistic merit, as well as offered discount tickets to the public.

Established in March of 1909, the Committee on Censorship, which changed its name in June to the National Board of Censorship of Motion Pictures, was comprised of volunteers, the majority of whom were females and Progressives, including representatives from the Public Education Association, the Federation of Churches, the Society for the Prevention of Crime, the Board of Education, and the Women's Municipal League. At its first meeting, held on March 25, 1909, the committee met for five hours and reviewed eighteen thousand feet of film, four hundred of which were condemned, including *Every Lass a Queen* (1909), the story of a sailor with a girl in every port, "because it was inartistic!"

Distributors sent their films to the board on a voluntary basis. By August 1909, the board claimed to have inspected 75 percent of all films, with the exception of "special releases" and "secretly produced films." By 1910, that number rose to 90 percent, including films produced by both the major and the smaller film companies. In a letter to the *New York Times* clarifying its "methods and jurisdiction," the board explained that it was not "merely an advisory board," but "a body with power. This power is delegated by the manufacturers of pictures, and if a manufacturer refused to put into effect any verdict of the Board of Censorship the board would thenceforward decline to inspect any of his pictures and would so announce to the public."

The process of censoring films was the focus of a 1910 story for *World Today*. Journalist Charles V. Tevis sat in on a screening session with members of the board and observed their interaction as they cast their ballots, on which they gave their thumbs-up or -down by checking "Approved" or "Disapproved." If the censors did not agree, they were required to discuss the matter until there was a consensus. There was also room on the ballot to classify a film as educational if it was informative, which was the case with the undoubtedly provocative *The Sisal Industry in the Bahamas* (1910) and the equally captivating *Making Salt* (1910). Both films met with the board's approval.

The same could not be said for another film screened during the session entitled *Over the Cliff*, in which the villain kidnaps a little girl by throwing a sack over her head, nearly choking her to death. He is apprehended at the end, yet the board disapproved of the film because the violence was too graphic and "the scoundrel had scoundreled too

15

well. His acting had been so good that it hurt the drama." The censors' decision was then published in a bulletin that circulated around the country to exhibitors, who ultimately made the final decision regarding which films to book for their theatres. If they choose a film that had not been prescreened by the board of censors, they ran the risk of the police or local censorship board finding it objectionable and closing them down.

The board of censors had to answer to its critics as well. In 1909, the American Mutoscope and Biograph Company stopped submitting its films to the board because members of the censorship committee were claiming in interviews with the press that they were directly influencing the content of producers' films. The matter was eventually settled, though over the years other companies also withheld their films over disagreements with the board.

Some of the board's harshest critics were also members of the organization. In 1910, *Vogue* editor Josephine Redding resigned from the board because she felt it was approving violent films. The following year, even more serious charges were made by one of the board's original members, Mrs. Gilbert H. Montague, of the Women's Municipal League. Montague advocated the creation of a censorship board that would be independent of the industry and, as in Chicago, would have legal authority. She claimed that the decisions made by the board were compromised because it was subsidized by the industry, a fact it was allegedly keeping quiet. In addition, she charged it was not reviewing *all* films released in theatres, such as "special releases" (travel and historical films, Biblical pictures, fight films) and imports from other countries. She also believed the board was ineffective because the cuts manufacturers were ordered to make prior to the film's release were not always being carried out and it was difficult to track every film to determine if the cuts were made. The board fired back at Mrs. Montague, accusing her of misrepresenting the organization and its financial matters, which it claimed had never been kept a secret. It stated that the board reviewed 999 of every 1,000 films issued for the New York market and challenged its critics to name one European import shown in U.S. theaters it did not review or one instance in which the board had not followed up on a film that was not changed or altered.

Montague's criticisms were actually part of a larger campaign already in motion for the passage of an ordinance that would give the Bureau of Licenses the power to regulate all movie houses in New York City in regards to construction and ventilation. But one alderman named Ralph Folks added an amendment to the ordinance that would create an official board of censors in New York City under the jurisdiction of the Board of Education. ("Who in the Board of Education is going to act as censor?" another alderman asked, "The Professor of Mathematics or of Foreign Languages?) Folks convinced his fellow aldermen to pass the revised ordinance, which put the matter into the hands of New York City Mayor William Jay Gaynor, a former New York State Supreme Court Justice. On December 24, 1912, the fourth-year anniversary of the closing of the nickel theatres by Mayor McClellan, Mayor Gaynor held a hearing with religious leaders about the proposed amendment, during which he explained why he was planning to veto the measure:

> Our founders did away with censorship because it had been abused so much. They did not permit the censoring of religion. As the representatives of the various denominations have come before me today, I have thought each one of you has been under a censor at some time or another. That's the spirit in which I approached this. If this ordinance is legal here, it may be equally applicable to the press if the Aldermen choose to pass it.

Unfortunately, many lawmakers in other states did not share Mayor Gaynor's progressive views. They also believed the National Board of Censors was failing to provide the moral leadership necessary to keep films with objectionable content out of their local movie houses. Following Chicago's lead, several cities passed ordinances legalizing motion picture censorship. The majority of cities left the inspection of films to the police department, who, in many cases, also had the authority to enter a theatre at any time to ensure that the exhibitor was complying with the city ordinance. Several cities passed a local ordinance that created a censorship board or a moving picture censor. In some instances, the mayor was responsible for appointing an individual (Kansas City,

Missouri [1913]), an "advisory committee" (Seattle [1915]), or a board of censors (Houston [1915]). The commissioner of public affairs could also be assigned censorship duties (Spokane [1916]), or an individual was appointed by the city or elected by the city commission (Green Bay, WI [1917]) or board of commissioners (Memphis [1921]).

The residents of some cities were doubly protected from the immoral and corrupting forces of American cinema when their state legislature created a state censorship board, beginning with Pennsylvania (in 1911), followed by Ohio (1913), Kansas (1914), Maryland (1916), New York (1922), and Virginia (1922). In Ohio, Pennsylvania, and Maryland, the board's official name was the "Board of Censors." In Kansas, it was known as the "Board of Review." New York State referred to its board as the "Motion Picture Commission." One thing local and state censorship boards had in common was that they empowered a relatively small group of people (three to five) with the moral authority to decide if a film was "moral and proper" or "sacrilegious," "obscene," "indecent," and/or "immoral."

As their motto "Selection Not Censorship" states, the National Board of Censors deeply opposed the creation of state censorship boards because it believed motion pictures "were obviously a means whereby opinion is expressed, and as such are entitled to the same right of liberty as is accorded speech and press." It also objected to decisions about what an entire state could and could not see being left to three people who are "politically appointed and of inferior ability" and likely to confuse taste with morals. In an official statement on the issue of state censorship released in 1921, the board (renamed the National Board of Review in 1915) stated why it preferred local censors over state:

Awakened public opinion is the only ineffectual guaranty of safety and decency. Responsibility for public morals should therefore be put squarely up to the community and its constituted authorities. Any scheme which takes responsibility away from the community and vests them in a distant and small committee is plainly dangerous and vicious, particularly if such a board is clothed with arbitrary authority and is not directly responsible to the people.

The Pennsylvania State Board of Censors of Motion Pictures, the first state censorship board in the country, was approved by the state legislature in June of 1911, but due to legal maneuvering by Universal and the Mutual Film Corporation, it took four more years before the board got down to business. In the meantime, its original list of "Rules and Standards" had been revised (and approved by the Pennsylvania legislature in May 1915). According to state law, it was "unlawful to sell, lease, lend, exhibit, or use any motion-picture, reel, or view in Pennsylvania unless . . . [it] has been submitted by the exchange, owner, or lessee . . . and duly approved by the Pennsylvania State Board of Censors." To receive the board's approval, a print of the film, along with an application and fee, had to be delivered three days prior to its release. The board, comprised of one female and two male state residents appointed by the governor, reviewed the film within forty-eight hours of delivery. The applicant was immediately notified if the film was accepted, rejected, or accepted provided specific cuts were made. In addition, all advertising, which, according to Sec. 21 of the law could not contain "anything that is immoral or improper," also had to be submitted for the board's approval. Once the film was approved, four feet of footage containing the state seal and the message "Approved by Pennsylvania State Board of Censors" (along with the certificate number) was placed at the beginning of the film. To ensure that no unlicensed films were being shown to the public, Governor Brumbaugh asked approximately five to six thousand state employees to voluntarily monitor movie theatres. The governor also ordered the fire marshals of each town to inspect all films being shown in all movie houses to make sure they were board approved. In 1915, sixty-four exhibitors were fined for showing films not approved by the Pennsylvania State Board.

The list of "Standards" adopted by the Pennsylvania Board was extensive and specific, but also allowed the board some discretion in regards to subject matter related to sex and violence:

Barroom Scenes, Drinking, and Drunkenness: These have a legitimate place in the motion-picture drama. Objection to them may be found in the large proportion which they may bear to all other scenes. If a photoplay requires such scenes to give it realism and color, and if these scenes are not of undue length and are used with discretion, they may be approved.

Prolonged Passionate Love Scenes: If love scenes are treated truthfully, sympathetically, and artistically in plays no objection will be made to their being shown; provided that they be plays no objection will be made to their being shown; provided that they be not lengthened or otherwise cheapened to the extent of losing their significance.

Deeds of Violence: The board will require that violence be not degrading and the constant and undue use of weapons such as guns, revolvers, knives, clubs, etc., tending to a debasement of morals will be discouraged.

Crime: The board will not object to crime as such, but it will object to the display of crime being objective, instructive, and grewsome.

Vulgarity: Obscenity, immorality, or indecency in a picture are prohibited. Actions by the characters of a suggestive nature will be eliminated.

Under the heading "Suggestive and Vulgar Scenes," manufacturers and producers were warned about "scenes of a debasing and corrupting character" and actions and scenes involving the whole or parts of the male and/or female body:

The rough treatment of person by kicking, the use of pins, clubs, etc.

Excessive and suggestive wriggling of the body, whether of a man or a woman

Loose clothing not properly fastened or ready to fall

Making comedy of a woman's form and her clothing

Taking hold of a woman's limbs in a suggestive manner

Men looking lustfully at a woman's form in a way to attract attention

Spitting in another's face

Suggestive actions, while a woman sits on lap of a man or vice versa, or similar conduct

In a bulletin published by the Pennsylvania Board in December of 1916, some additions were made to the list of scenes that would be eliminated: safe cracking, tramps stealing watches, and people taking drugs. Among the list of films banned included *Harry K. Thaw's Fight for Freedom* (most likely *The Unwritten Law* under an alternative title), *Sappho* (1908), *The Human Beast* (mostly likely the French import *Une brute humaine* [1913]), *Lights and Shadows of Chinatown* (1908), along with thrillers with heroines tied to the train tracks, sixty films about white slavery, and twenty-five set in Mexico "whose manufacturers the censors have been unable to locate."

If an applicant did not agree with the board's decision, he or she was entitled to a reexamination before two or all members of the board and, finally, to an appeal to the court of common pleas. In their 1930 study of film censorship, Pare Lorentz and Morris L. Ernst demonstrate how each censorship board had its own issues and idiosyncrasies when it came to making cuts in films. They describe Pennsylvania as "the most arbitrary and severe." The efforts of the Pennsylvania Censors, which historian Terry Ramsaye characterizes as one of the world's "most entertaining of censorship boards," did not go unnoticed. In May of 1922, the *New York Times* featured a satirical piece entitled "Virtue Made in Pennsylvania," in which author Benjamin De Casseres rakes those "musnud of moralists"—those "Sanhendran [*sic*] of Sages"—over the coals for their recent hack job on *The Red Peacock* (1920), a German version of *Camille* starring Pola Negri. The author demonstrates how the absurd changes in the subtitles ordered by the censors, along with the elimination of all sense of Violette "embracing and kissing" her lovers, changed the meaning of the text:

> The board marries our Camille [renamed Violette] in the fourth reel. When the time comes they will marry Hamlet and Ophelia in the second reel. . . . It was fortunate for Shakespeare that he got Othello and Desdemona spliced. In Pennsylvania a man may smother his wife, but not his mistress.

Censorship in neighboring Ohio was legalized in the spring of 1913. The law created a censorship board composed of three individuals appointed by the Industrial Commission and approved by the governor for three years. The board had a legal obligation to examine all films that would be shown publicly for profit in the state and "only such films as are in the judgment and discretion of the board of censors of a moral, educational, amusing and harmless character shall be passed." Anyone who screened a film that was not approved by the board of censors could be arrested and fined. That's exactly what happened to the proprietor of a Columbus theatre who showed a film that had been rejected by the censors, a Charlie Chaplin comedy entitled *His Prehistoric Past* (1914), onto which he attached the official approval stamp of the Ohio censors from another film. When the Ohio Censorship Board started screening films in 1913, Maude Murray Miller, the only female in the original trio of censors, stated that the kinds of films that would be rejected were those containing "murders, suicides, drunken, or deathbed scenes, or pictures which are suggestive of immorality." "One thing is certain," she concluded, "no producer of motion picture films need have any fear of the Ohio board of censors so long as they send out the right kind of films, and they will soon learn just the kind which the Board will consider 'right'."

THE MUTUAL DECISION (1915): "A BUSINESS, PURE AND SIMPLE"

One distributor that was not interested in the board's opinion of its films was the Mutual Film Corporation, which purchased films and leased them to exhibitors in Ohio. Its headquarters was in Detroit, so if an exhibitor wanted to rent its films, Mutual would be forced to submit the film first to the censorship board and pay the required fee. In its lawsuit against the Industrial Commission of Ohio, Mutual contended that

1. The law violated the Ohio Constitution because it denied Mutual due process of law because the power to determine what films could be legally shown in the state was in the hands of the censorship board.
2. The standards stated in the 1913 censorship law (103 Ohio Laws 399) were too vague to be responsibly interpreted and thus were an unconstitutional delegation of legislative power.

3. The law violated the First and Fourteenth amendments of the U.S. Constitution and Article 1 of the Ohio Constitution ("Every citizen may freely speak, write, and publish his sentiments on all subjects . . . no law shall be passed to restrain or abridge the liberty of speech, or of the press.").

In the case of *Mutual Film Corporation v. Industrial Commission of Ohio*, 236 U.S. 230 (1915), the Supreme Court ruled—in a 9–0 decision— that motion pictures are not protected under the Constitution of Ohio. Writing on behalf of the court, Justice McKenna compared "moving pictures" to other "mediums of thought," such as "the theatre, the circus, and all other shows and spectacles," yet it is *not* protected speech under the U.S. Constitution:

It cannot be put out of view that the exhibition of moving pictures is a business, pure and simple, originated and conducted for profit, like other spectacles, not to be regarded, nor intended to be regarded by the Ohio Constitution, we think, as part of the press of the country, or as organs of public opinion. They are mere representations of events, of ideas, and sentiments published and known; vivid, useful, and entertaining, no doubt, but as we have said, capable of evil, having power for it, the greater because of their attractiveness and manner of exhibition.

One proposed solution for protecting the public from moving pictures that might corrupt its morals or incite violence and crime was the creation of a federal agency to censor and license all films distributed and imported into the United States. Although the multiple bills proposed over the years never garnered enough support to create such an agency, they did get people talking about what if any role the federal government should play in regulating the motion picture industry.

In December of 1915, Congressman D. M. Hughes of Georgia introduced a bill that would create the Federal Motion Picture Commission as a division of the Bureau of Education. The five-member commission would be appointed to a six-year term by the president. As outlined in the Hughes Bill, the commission's primary responsibility was to evaluate all films prior to their release. A film could be approved with or without cuts or flat-out rejected. Approved films would then receive a license (in the form of a certificate and an official seal), which all moving pictures screened in the country must have under penalty of law.

In addition to outlining the specifics of the commission, the Hughes Bill also explained its moral mission. The introduction to the bill states that the need for censorship is "beyond question" and has been acknowledged by both the public and "a large majority of the film manufacturers by their voluntary submission of their films to unofficial boards of censors for approval."

The bill contends that the Board of Censors [Review], which is "not a board of censorship, but a board of recommendation and approval," is inadequate because it has no legal authority, is paid for by "the leading motion-picture interests," and passes pictures "at the request of the manufacturers." Also, the Board of Censors [Review] only examines 95 percent of all films, leaving "5 percent which could be immoral and unfit to be shown." Consequently, the state and municipal boards were established "to prevent the exhibition of immoral, indecent, and obscene pictures." In the minds of Hughes and his supporters, the creation of the Federal Commission would make up for the Board of Censors' inadequacies and alleviate the burden on film distributors, who were forced to accommodate, at great expense, the requests of each censorship board.

On the surface it may appear as if the creation of the proposed Federal Commission was in the best interests of the motion picture industry. But Hughes also had a clear moral agenda, as stated in section 5 of the bill outlining the general criteria for granting a license:

> The commission shall license every film submitted to it and intended for entrance into interstate commerce, unless it finds that such film is obscene, indecent, immoral, inhuman, or depicts a bull fight or a prize fight, or is of such a character that its exhibition would tend to impair the health or corrupt the morals of children or adults or incite to crime.

There is nothing further in regards to how the commissioners would decide how a film qualifies as "obscene or indecent or immoral or inhuman" (*inhuman?*). Six days of hearings were held on Capitol Hill on January 13–15 and 17–19, 1916, during which a long line of witnesses spoke in support of (civic leaders, clergymen) and against (representatives of industry organizations, film companies, the press, etc.) censorship. Rev. Cranston Brenton, the current volunteer chairman of the National Board of Review, cleared up the misinformation he felt was out there about the censorship board concerning its relationship with the industry. He then made his argument against a federal board, which, he feared, would censor all films so they would be suitable for "the child of 12, 14, or 16," resulting in "a program of films that would be so insipid that it would be intolerable to the public."

From that point on, the motion picture industry—both manufacturers and exhibitors—remained vigilant about the goings-on in Washington. In response to the Hughes Bill, it rallied support from the public by launching a nationwide protest campaign in movie houses, where patrons were asked to sign a card stating "I, the undersigned, am in favor of retaining the National Board of Censorship as a national agency to criticise and pass final judgment on moving pictures. I am opposed to State and Federal boards of censorship because, in my opinion _____" (the blank line was for the reasons and a signature). In May of 1916, the Motion Picture Board of Trade sponsored the "First National Motion Picture Exposition" at Madison Square Garden. The president of the board, "veteran" movie man J. Stuart Blackton, opened the exposition with an impassioned speech against the proposed legislation:

> The greatest peril that menaces the photo play is the attempt by professional agitators, by hypocritical reformers, and office-seeking politicians to apply the muzzle of censorship to the motion picture, which, under the Constitution of the United States, should and must be as free and untrammeled as the press, the stage, and the right of free speech. The attempt to apply official and political censorship to the photodrama is equally an endeavor to deprive the public of the uninalienable [*sic*] right under the Constitution to decide for itself what it shall read and what it shall see. No group of paid officials has the right to decide what pictures 100,000,000 American citizens shall see.

Fortunately, the bill never received the required number of votes to land on President Wilson's desk for his signature, and if it had, it was likely he would have vetoed it. On a trip to Nebraska, Wilson stopped in Long Branch, New Jersey to meet with a delegation from the Motion Picture Exhibitors' League to discuss the Hughes Bill. Afterwards, the league released a public statement confirming that his "attitude and utterances . . . plainly indicated to his way of thinking the presumption was against the principle of censorship, and that an overwhelming strong case would have to be made out in favor of censorship before his support would be enlisted for it."

The case for federal regulation grew stronger in the 1920s when Hollywood was rocked by a series of scandals, four of which occurred in 1922 and involved major Hollywood stars (see inset). In the years that followed, several new bills were introduced in Congress to regulate the film industry. Senator Henry L. Myers (D-Montana) seized the opportunity to push his bill forward by denouncing the current state of Hollywood and its debauched, immoral, and overpaid denizens:

> The pictures are largely furnished by such characters as Fatty Arbuckle, of unsavory fame, notorious for his scandalous debauchery and drunken orgies, one of which, attended by many "stars," resulted in the death of Virginia Rappe, a star artist; William Desmond Taylor, deceased, murdered for some mysterious cause; one Valentino, now figuring as the star character in rape and divorce sensations. Many others of like character might be mentioned. At Hollywood, California, is a colony of these people, where debauchery, riotous living, drunkenness, ribaldry, dissipation, free love seem to be conspicuous. . . . From these sources our young people gain much of their views of life, inspiration, and education. Rather a poor source, is it not? Looks like there is some need for censorship, does it not?

Congressman William D. Upshaw (D-Georgia), a political ally of the temperance movement who ran for the presidency in 1932 as the Prohibition Party candidate, proposed an even more radical bill in 1923. The Upshaw Bill would create an even larger federal commission than the one proposed by Congressman Hughes, and would prohibit films that "emphasize and exaggerate sex," "[are] based upon white slavery," "making prominent an illicit love affair," "exhibit nakedness or personal scantily dressed," or contain "bedroom scenes," "passionate love," and "scenes which are vulgar." As Upshaw declared during the 1926 commission hearings, by regulating the industry, "we are simply proposing to stand at the door of our homes, our churches, and our schools and fight back the wolves of immorality, that are crouching to destroy the hope and strength of the Nation." The bill went as far as to turn the film industry into a police state, requiring anyone employed in the industry in any capacity to register with the commission.

THE GREAT HOLLYWOOD SCANDALS
OF 1922

Roscoe "Fatty" Arbuckle (1887–1933) was at the height of his popularity with a million-dollar contract with Paramount when he was accused of raping a twenty-four-year-old actress, Virginia Rappe, during a wild party on Labor Day, September 5, 1921, at San Francisco's St. Francis Hotel. Rappe died four days later of peritonitis and a ruptured bladder allegedly caused by a sexual assault by Arbuckle. After two hung juries, he was acquitted, with a written apology signed by the jurors stating, "acquittal is not enough for Roscoe Arbuckle; we feel that a great injustice had been done him." But the jurors' words fell on deaf ears. Despite the verdict, Will H. Hays, as part of his campaign to "clean-up" Hollywood, officially banned Arbuckle from the industry.

Rudolph Valentino (1895–1926) was convicted of bigamy and spent three days in jail and was fined $10,000 when he married costume designer Natacha Rambova in Mexicali, Mexico. At the time, he was legally separated but not divorced from his first wife, actress Jean Acker, who was a lesbian. They reportedly never consummated their marriage. According to her longtime friend, actress Patricia Neal, Acker locked Valentino out of their bedroom on their wedding night when he admitted to her that he had gonorrhea.

Wallace Reid (1891–1923) was a handsome, blue-eyed, all-American matinee idol known for his roles in D. W. Griffith's *Birth of a Nation* (1915) and *Intolerance* (1916) and as the star of Cecil B. DeMille's *Carmen* (1915). He also played a daredevil auto driver in a series of popular films for Paramount (*The Roaring Road* [1919], *Double Speed* [1920], *Excuse My Dust* [1920], *Too Much Speed* [1921]). While shooting *The Valley of the Giants* (1919), he was in a train wreck and treated with morphine, for which he developed an addiction. In October of 1922, his fans were told he suffered a nervous breakdown. By December he was fighting for his life in a sanitarium. His health deteriorated due to his drug addiction and alcoholism, and he died of influenza in a padded sanitarium cell on January 18, 1923, at the age of thirty-one.

William Desmond Taylor (1872–1922), motion picture director (*Anne of Green Gables* [1919], *Huckleberry Finn* [1920]), was murdered on February 1, 1922, in his Alvarado Street bungalow. The last person known to have seen him alive was comedian Mabel Normand, who visited him at his home in the early evening. Normand was questioned by the police, but she was not a suspect. She later denied being his lover ("Get it straight," she told reporters. "Our friendship was based on comradeship and understanding"). Taylor's lover was revealed to be the young starlet of several of his films, twenty-year-old Mary Miles Minter. Her involvement with forty-nine-year-old Taylor was a bona fide scandal that brought her promising career to a grinding halt. As for Normand, she battled alcohol and drug addiction and two years later became the focus of another scandal involving the shooting of her lover by her chauffeur with her gun.

Formed back in 1916, the National Association of the Motion Picture Industry (NAMPI), an organization comprised of producers, distributors, and some exhibitors, was stationed at the front line to combat the constant threat of federal and state legislation. Its strategy for blocking legislation was to convince lawmakers that it was taking action to purify the movies. In 1920, it succeeded in getting passed through the House and the Senate a revised version of section 245 of the U.S. Penal Code, which extended the existing law that had made the interstate shipment of any indecent or immoral book a misdemeanor to include motion pictures. However, it was unsuccessful in getting legislation passed that would provide motion pictures the same protection under the Constitution as the printed word.

In 1919, NAMPI President William A. Brady confirmed the organization's opposition to censorship by the federal government and its own plans to establish a system of self-censorship. It publicly condemned the exhibition of "all pictures which are obscene, immoral, salacious or tend to corrupt or debase morals." To prevent objectionable films from reaching the theatres, it devised a system similar to the National Board of Censorship, requiring NAMPI members to submit its films to a review board and agree to make any suggested eliminations and changes. NAMPI never followed through with the plans, though in March of 1921 the organization recommitted itself to cleaning up the movies by adopting a series of resolutions affirming its cooperation in assisting the authorities with prosecuting anyone producing, distributing, or exhibiting "any obscene, salacious, or immoral motion pictures in violation of the law." Known as "The Thirteen Points," the list included subject matter and themes that were frequently censored by current boards (see appendix A). In addition, a resolution was passed stating that members refusing to adhere to these resolutions would be expelled from the organization. Although NAMPI never created a governing body or a board of censors to enforce the "Thirteen Points," the specific issues it covered—sex, nudity, crime, vulgarity, religion, etc.— would one day be the focus of the dogma of the Hollywood studio system, the Motion Picture Production Code.

THE HAYS OFFICE

The history of the Hollywood Production Code begins with the appointment of Tinseltown's first czar, William Harrison Hays, Sr. Born in Sullivan, Indiana, Hays rose to prominence as chairman of the National Republican Committee and campaign manager for Warren G. Harding during his victorious bid for the presidency in 1920. While serving in the Harding Administration as postmaster general, he received an invitation from the newly formed Motion Picture Producers and Distributors of America (MPPDA) to serve as its first president and chairman of the board. A Washington insider from the Midwest seemed like a logical choice to appease the public and the motion picture industry's critics, who had not yet given up the fight for federal control of Hollywood. He became the voice of the industry, representing both the MPPDA and the Association of Motion Picture Producers (AMPP), which historian Ruth A. Inglis describes as the MPPDA's "alter ego" because each organization adopted the resolutions and policies of the other. Under Hays's leadership, the two organizations handled public relations for the industry, including working with civic, educational, and church groups in New York and in Hollywood; warning and protecting members against legal and legislative dangers; assisting with legal problems of foreign distribution; advising exhibitors on trade practices, settling disputes, and promoting fire safety in theatres; and most important of all, regulating film content of all features and shorts, film advertising, and film titles registered with the MPPDA.

When Hays started his tenure as head of the MPPDA in 1922, "legislative dangers" were at the top of his agenda. In the previous year, Governor Miller of New York signed a bill creating a state censorship board consisting of three newly appointed commissioners. Miller explained that he supported the bill after he "reached the conclusion that it was the only way to remedy what every one conceded had grown to be a very great evil." This was a major blow for the industry because New York is a major market. One year later, censorship bills were pending in thirty-two states, including Massachusetts, where, thanks to Hays's statewide anticensorship campaign, a referendum was defeated by a vote of 563,173 to 208,252. In an address to members of the industry in 1922, Hays spoke out against censorship:

> The principle of freedom upon which this nation was founded makes public censorship of press, pulpit, film or spoken word an impossibility. Statewide or nationwide censorship will fail in everything it undertakes. It hasn't been done successfully and never will be. Too many people who know nothing about the business are named on censorship boards. We are going to obviate the necessity of censorship.

Hays's plan to "obviate the necessity of censorship" was not spelled out in any detail, except to say that he hoped "to establish and maintain the highest moral and artistic standards and to develop the educational value and the general usefulness of the motion picture."

Despite the victory in Massachusetts, the threat of federal censorship continued to linger in Congress. The Upshaw Bill, which was defeated in 1923, gained supporters when it was reintroduced in 1926. The bill was once again defeated, thanks to Hays's friendship with President Coolidge, who stated that he favored state over federal censorship.

As he was keeping the federal government at bay, Hays worked toward developing a system of self-regulation that would satisfy the industry and the public, particularly the religious and civic groups that continued to voice their discontent over the content of motion pictures. The answer came in the form of a novel, *West of the Water Tower*, written by an anonymous author (later revealed to be Homer Croy), about hypocrisy in a small town. In 1923 the Famous Players-Lasky Company purchased the rights to the story, which contained elements—an illegitimate baby, a robbery, a dissolute preacher—that would definitely not meet the approval of certain politicians and critics of the film industry. To test the waters before bringing the story to the screen, the Hays Office decided to hand the novel over for review to members of the MPPDA's "Committee on Public Relations." Like the National Board of Review, the committee consisted of representatives of religious, public welfare, civic, professional, and fraternal organizations, including the National Congress of Parents and Teachers and the General Foundation of Women's Clubs, which both reviewed *West of the Water Tower* and gave it two thumbs down. When the Famous Players Company decided to ignore their recommendation and make the film, both organizations resigned and publicly condemned the Hays Office.

Will Hays realized the organization's credibility was slipping, so he disbanded the Committee on Public Relations in 1925 and devised a new strategy for reviewing potential properties for motion pictures, which became known as "The Formula" (see appendix B). Adopted on February 26, 1924 (a revised version was reaffirmed a few months later on June 19), "The Formula" required all film companies to submit a copy of each book, play, or story they wished to adapt. A member of the Hays office would then, in turn, review it and advise the studios if it was suitable material. Two years later, the MPPDA reached an agreement with the Authors League of America to allow books or plays that were deemed unacceptable to be rewritten, provided they were given new titles and the public was not made aware of the change. As Inglis points out, this did not seem to matter, because it was common for movie critics to point out the connection between the original and the film version.

Relations between what was by now referred to as the Hays Office and the studios improved when Hays made Colonel Jason S. Joy, who had worked in the War Department's PR office, director of the Public Relations Department and sent him to Hollywood, where he worked on building relationships with the studio executives. Over time, producers started submitting their scripts to Joy prior to shooting. He, in turn, advised them on how to treat certain subject matter and themes in order to avoid offending the public (and the industry's critics). Hays offered more producers additional guidance in the form of a list, known as the "Don'ts and Be Carefuls," which consisted of eleven things that should be avoided in films and twenty-five subjects that should be treated with "special care" (see appendix C), some of which were censored by local and state censorship boards. It was also strikingly similar to the "Thirteen Points" adopted, but never enforced, by NAMPI (see appendix A).

In January of 1929, Colonel Joy sent Will Hays a memo outlining what he believed were some of the problems with the current system. Joy was continuing to meet with executives and producers, but they were not required to take any of his suggestions, and they only represented 20 percent of the feature films being produced by their organization's members. Also, there was no way to know if the changes he was suggesting were even being incorporated into the final script. As for the "Don'ts and Be Carefuls." Joy felt they were "purely negative," had no philosophical base, and it was still "possible to produce the most outrageous offensive film while observing all of them." The transition to sound was also going to open the door for improvisation (or as Joy called it, "cheap wisecracking").

Sound did pose a problem for the film industry. While distributors could meet the demands of censorship boards by cutting a scene or a title card out of a silent film, sound film initially posed a much greater challenge because soundtracks were recorded on a separate record. The Vitagraph Company tried to prove in a Pennsylvania courtroom that a soundtrack could not be censored because it was not technically part of the film (ironically, the film in question was an early short starring comedian Polly Moran as *The Movie Chatterbox*). The state supreme court ruled in favor of the Pennsylvania Board of Censors in the "Chatterbox" case and another involving the Fox Film Company's refusal to submit its dialogue to the board.

The following year, Hays unveiled new rules to the MPPDA Board that would become the cornerstone of the industry's self-regulation of film content. The Motion Picture Production Code (1930) offered members of the MPPDA and the AMPP guidelines for the cinematic treatment of subject matter and themes involving crime and sex as well as most of the subjects prohibited under the list of "Don'ts and Be Carefuls" (sex perversion, white slavery, miscegenation, etc.). There were restrictions placed on vulgarity, obscenity (in any form), profanity (thirty-nine dirty words and expressions were included), dancing (sexually suggestive and indecent dances were a no-no), costumes (indecent or the lack thereof), religion (the clergy can neither be comical nor villainous), and nationalism. For Hays, the Production Code was the answer to how the industry could effectively regulate itself in order to keep the federal government, the censorship boards, and the public happy. As for studio executives, directors, writers, and others employed in the film industry, it would change the face of Hollywood filmmaking for the next three decades.

CONTROVERSIAL SILENT CINEMA

The Unwritten Law: A Thrilling Drama Based on the Thaw-White Case (1907): "The Trial of the Century"

On the night of June 25, 1906, on the roof garden of Madison Square Garden, millionaire Harry K. Thaw shot architect Stanford White in the head. When taken into custody, Thaw reportedly cried, "He has ruined my wife!" When Thaw's wife, Evelyn Nesbit Thaw, a former artist's model and chorus girl, took the stand in her husband's defense, she claimed White had drugged and deflowered her at the age of sixteen (the *Chicago Daily Tribune* called her testimony "one of the most shameful stories ever uttered by a girl"). What the newspapers were calling

"The Trial of the Century" (and it was only 1907!) ended on April 10 with a hung jury. Nine months later, Thaw was found not guilty by reason of insanity and sent to an asylum, where he remained until a judge declared him sane in 1915.

While the drama was unfolding in the courtroom, this torrid tale of love, jealousy, murder, and sexual depravity was also being played out on the big screen in *The Unwritten Law*. The title refers to the legal defense used by Thaw's lawyers based on the principle that a man has the right to avenge wrongs committed against a member of his family. As his defense attorney claimed in court, his client was suffering from "Dementia Americana . . . that species of insanity which makes every American believe . . . whoever stains the virtue of . . . [his] wife has forfeited the protection of human laws and must appeal to the eternal justice and mercy of God . . . for his protection."

In March of 1907, the Lubin Manufacturing Company released a dramatic recreation of the events leading up to the trial as well as the predicted outcome. The summary of the film supplied by Lubin states: "Almost everybody has read the Thaw-White Case which for many weeks filled the pages of all the daily papers throughout the country. Our film depicts in striking scenes the thrilling drama and thus gives a vivid interpretation of the dangers of a great city. The film contains absolutely nothing objectionable and may be shown in any theatre." *The Unwritten Law* also plays fast and loose with the facts, particularly the timeline of events. In the film, Nesbit, whose name is changed to Hudspeth, is a young, aspiring artist's model and chorus girl, who befriends a man named Mr. Black (Stanford White). In the film's most controversial sequence, Black has Hudspeth sit on a velvet swing in his studio (she's fully clothed, though the real Evelyn allegedly did it *au naturel*). Then, in what the press considered the most shocking scene in the film, she is led up a staircase to his "Boudoir of 1,000 Mirrors." He drugs her, she passes out, and he shields her body from the camera with a screen, which suggests he is going to take advantage of her. Cut to Hudspeth's wedding to Daw (Thaw), which is immediately followed by the shooting, a scene of Daw in jail, where he is visited by his wife and mother, and then the trial and Hudspeth's testimony on the stand. The trial was still going on at the time of the film's release, yet it was obvious the filmmaker's sympathies were clearly with Thaw and Nesbit when the jury found him not guilty. The Unwritten Law prevails!

The Unwritten Law was popular with audiences, but everyone who bought a ticket or put it on his or her "must see" list did not have the opportunity to see it thanks to local law enforcement, which decided the film, particularly the "Boudoir of 1,000 Mirrors" scene, was immoral. In 1907, the film was banned in several cities:

- In Houston, Texas, the police refused to allow an exhibitor to screen the film, despite his willingness "to cut out the mirrored bedroom scene."
- In Chicago, Lieutenant McDonald of the Chicago Police Department assured the public that "no pictures of the 'Thaw-White Case' will be allowed in any of the theatres. Places which have been advertising them must remove them at once."
- In Superior, Wisconsin, the chief of police closed down a screening by walking up to the stage just when the film had started and standing in front of the screen.
- In New York City, several nickel-show proprietors were arrested. George E. Watson's establishment at 477 Third Avenue was raided by the Children's Society. Upon discovering there were children in the audience, he was charged with "imperiling the morals of young boys" and fined $100. Henry Hemleb was arrested for showing the film on a Sunday with children in the audience and for including singing and dancing as part of the show, which was in violation of the city's Blue Laws.

In its review, *Variety* acknowledged that *The Unwritten Law* was a "fairly complete exposition" of Evelyn's testimony but objected to the film's premature dramatization of the trial's outcome, which the reviewer believed should have been a dream sequence. *Moving Picture World*, a trade publication, not only panned the film but published an editorial entitled "The Film Manufacturer and the Public" in its May 25, 1907, issue, demanding the filmmakers be held as accountable as a New York exhibitor named John E. Hauser who was fined $100 for "impairing the morals" of children. The editorial also stated the manufacturer of this "obnoxious film" should withdraw it from distribution, suggesting it alone was responsible for the downfall of the cinema:

> The exhibition of this one film alone, has been the cause of more adverse press criticism than all the films manufactured before, put together, have done. . . . If there was one redeeming feature in the film we would not write so strongly, but there is not one. There is nothing to elevate, nothing to entertain, or any good lesson to be gained in the exhibition.

But the film's harshest critic was Harry K. Thaw himself, who, despite the film's sympathetic portrayal of him, sent his lawyer to Hauser's trial and asked him to read a statement:

> Mr. Thaw has requested me to inform the court that the moving pictures which have just been under consideration are not what they purported to be. He wants it distinctly understood that the picture of his wife is not a good one, and that the other pictures do not show the marriage ceremony as it occurred, nor the principals in it. The same applies to the tragedy on the roof garden.

The story was also the subject of a play, *Millionaire's Revenge*, which was performed around the country, receiving rave reviews in Fort Wayne, Indiana ("the melodramatic sensation of the current season"); Lowell, Massachusetts ("one of the best plays of the melodramatic type"); and Washington, D.C. ("the most sensational play of its kind ever placed before the public"). A production at Newark's Columbia Theatre was not well received by the local police, who arrested the manager and the three actors, charging them with a "misdemeanor under the law which forbids the public representation of an improper scene."

More contemporary dramatizations of the Nesbit-Thaw-White tragedy included *The Girl in the Red Velvet Swing* (1955), starring Joan Collins in the title role (with the real Nesbit serving as a consultant), and director Milos Forman's 1981 film adaptation of E. L. Doctorow's *Ragtime* (1981) featuring Elizabeth McGovern in the Nesbit role, for which she received an Academy Award nomination. Doctorow's novel was also adapted into a stage musical version, which enjoyed a two-year run on Broadway (1998–2000).

Jeffries-Johnson World's Championship Boxing Contest, Held in Reno, Nevada, July 4, 1910 (1910): "The Fight of the Century"

On July 4, 1910 in Reno, Nevada, Jack Johnson knocked out heavyweight champ Jim Jeffries in the fifteenth round of what was billed as "The Fight of the Century." The fight was captured on film and scheduled for national release shortly after the bout. But both the fight and the film were embroiled in controversy due to the outcome: a Caucasian titleholder was defeated in the ring by an African American boxer.

The "fight film" genre dates back to 1894 when boxers were paid to come into Edison's Black Maria studio and go a few rounds for the camera (*Leonard-Cushing Fight*; *Corbett and Courtney Before the Kinetograph*, a.k.a. *The Corbett-Courtney Fight*). But it was difficult to film an actual match because prize fighting was illegal in every state (the matches that did take place were billed as "exhibitions"). The sport also faced serious opposition from some politicians and religious leaders. In response to news that James Corbett would once again face Peter Jackson in the ring (the rematch never happened), the Rev. S. Edwards Young declared from his pulpit that "brutal fisticuffs are a shame to our Christian Nation," and called for the formation of an "anti-prize fight league" in every state.

Prize fighting was illegal, but "fight films" were not. The most successful of the early fight films was a recording of the *Corbett-Fitzsimmons Fight* (1897), which was also one of the first feature films (ninety minutes in length) and the first to be shot in widescreen using a $2\frac{3}{16}$-inch-gauge film. According to historian Charles Musser, the film's popularity with both male and female patrons and the fact that the film was "an 'illustration' of a fight rather than a fight itself made the attraction not only legally but socially acceptable." As a testament to its popularity, the Lubin Company films produced several "reproductions" of several fights featuring performers resembling the boxers reenacting the fight (*Reproduction of the Ruhlin and Jeffries Fight* [1899], *Reproduction of the Corbett and Jeffries Fight* [1899], *Reproduction of the Jeffries-Corbett Fight* [1903]).

The film version of the Johnson-Jeffries fight was certain to score at the box office, but the film's release was jeopardized by the reported outbreaks of racial violence that erupted in several cities within a forty-eight hour period after the fight. On July 6, the *New York Times* reported ten deaths in seven cities resulting from fights "occasioned by the Johnson victory" in Reno. But that was only the beginning. In New Orleans, men of both races were beaten and killed. African Americans were nearly lynched by angry mobs in Wheeling, West Virginia and Charleston, Missouri.

Consequently, mayors and governors across the country immediately stopped the film from being exhibited in their city or state. The film was banned in Atlanta, Baltimore, Cincinnati, St. Louis, San Francisco, and Washington, D.C. By July 7, a total of twenty-two cities and seven states (Arkansas, Georgia, Iowa, Maine, Maryland, Texas, and Virginia) refused to allow the film to be exhibited in theatres. Although the rationale repeatedly offered for banning the film was the fear of violence, it was evident the decision was racially motivated. New York City Mayor William Gaynor, a former New York Supreme Court Justice (1893–1909), refused to ban the film because the Negro population was not as great in his city and he did not have the legal right to stop it.

But when the film finally opened in Brooklyn and Manhattan, the distributor refused to let the film be shown in theatres patronized by women and children. The film was also banned from "all houses in Negro districts," though the *New York Times* pointed out that the Orpheum in Brooklyn was "but a block or so from the so-called Hudson Avenue 'black belt.'" The *Times* also reported "popular prices would not prevail to 'discourage Negro attendance.'"

Before *Jeffries-Johnson* landed in theatres, several distributors and exhibitors attempted to cash in on the fight. A crowd assembled in a theatre advertising moving pictures of the fight, which turned out to be a fake. William Morris, proprietor of the theatre, who was in the balcony, ordered the film cut off immediately. Another theatre intentionally sold tickets to seven hundred patrons who were expecting to see moving pictures of the fights, but instead were shown still photographs. The proprietor claimed the signs in front read "Pictures of the Jeffries-Johnson Fight. First Time in New York Monday." The crowd was not interested in arguing semantics and proceeded to tear apart the lobby and the street signs outside the theatre.

In 1912, the controversy surrounding the Johnson-Jeffries fight culminated with the passage of federal legislation making it illegal to transport fight films over state lines. The law was not repealed until the 1940s. The following year, Johnson had his own run-in with the law when he was arrested under the Mann Act for transporting a woman, Belle Schreiber, from Pittsburgh to Chicago on October 15, 1910 for an "immoral purpose" and "in perpetration of a serious crime" (for more on the Mann Act, which was originally intended to prevent prostitution and human trafficking, see below). But it was difficult to prosecute Johnson for the crime because the woman, who had been a prostitute, had traveled by herself to Chicago. She also would not testify against Johnson, her future husband.

In 1913, while appealing his conviction, Johnson fled to France, only to return to the States in 1920. He was arrested and sentenced to one year in Leavenworth Penitentiary. Johnson died in a car crash in Raleigh, North Carolina, in 1946 at the age of forty-eight and was posthumously inducted into the Boxing Hall of Fame in 1954. His life served as the basis for Howard Sackler's 1968 stage drama, *The Great White Hope* starring James Earl Jones (as "Jack Jefferson") and Jane Alexander, who repeated their roles in the 1970 film version. Johnson's life was also the subject of a 2005 documentary by Ken Burns entitled *Unforgivable Blackness: The Rise and Fall of Jack Johnson*, based on the biography published in 2004 of the same name by Geoffrey C. Ward. More recently, an interview Johnson gave to a French sports magazine was translated and published in book form in 2007 under the title *My Life and Battles*.

D. W. Griffith's *The Birth of a Nation* (1915): "Mightiest Spectacle Ever Produced"

In the fall of 2004, the Silent Movie Theatre, a revival movie house in Los Angeles, scheduled a public screening of D. W. Griffith's *The Birth of a Nation*. Local civil rights leaders were outraged that Griffith's epic, set in the post–Civil War South during the Reconstruction period, was going to be shown. The film was controversial when it premiered in 1915 in Los Angeles for its valorization of the Ku Klux Klan and blatant racist stereotyping of African Americans (played mostly by white actors in blackface). On the morning of the 2004 screening, the theatre's owner, Charlie Lustman, gave in to pressure from local civil rights leaders (as well as anonymous threats) and canceled the screening. This was the second time Lustman pulled the film from the theatre's schedule within a four year-period (the first, which coincided with the National Democratic Convention in August 2000, was at the request of the National Association for the Advancement of Colored People [NAACP]).

The shelf life of most film controversies is relatively short because what society considers obscene, indecent, and/or immoral changes with the times. *Birth of a Nation* is one exception (another is Leni Riefenstahl's cinematic valentine to Hitler and the Third Reich, *Triumph of the Will* [1935]). At the time of its release, some Americans considered the film racist, while others considered it a masterpiece—a groundbreaking cinematic work due, in part, to Griffith's innovative directorial style. The issue today is not whether it's a racist film (I want to believe that in 2008 only a very, very small segment of the population would disagree) but whether it should be exhibited publicly. From a legal standpoint, there was nothing stopping Lustman from going ahead with the screening. But deciding whether or not to show *The Birth of a Nation* is a modern-day moral dilemma. Does the film deserve to be hailed as a "cinematic masterpiece" if it distorts and perverts nineteenth-century American history for the purpose of promoting its racist agenda?

In the tradition of American melodrama, *The Birth of a Nation* displaces political issues onto personal conflicts, in this case the effects of the Civil War on two families—the Stonemans from the North and the Camerons from the South. Austin Stoneman is an abolitionist with a daughter, Elsie, and two sons. The Camerons are Southern plantation owners with two daughters, Margaret and Flora, and three sons. When the war breaks out, the sons in each family fight for their respective sides. Ben, the only surviving Cameron, is seriously injured in a Northern hospital, where Elsie Stoneman nurses him back to health. Cameron is sentenced to death, but Elsie and his mother intercede by appealing to Abraham Lincoln, who is then assassinated.

The second part of the story focuses on Austin Stoneman and his protégé, a mulatto named Silas Lynch, who travels to South Carolina to get African Americans to vote. Lynch becomes lieutenant governor and presides over a mostly black legislature, which motivates Ben Cameron and others to protect their interests by forming the Ku Klux Klan. Out of loyalty to her father, Elsie objects to Ben's involvement with the KKK, but she eventually supports him. Meanwhile, Gus, a former slave, sees innocent Flora Cameron walking through the woods. When he attempts to molest her, she jumps to her death to escape from him. Ben and the Klan capture Gus, hang him, and leave his dead body on Silas's doorstep. Silas orders the local black militia to hunt down and kill Klan members. He tries to get Elsie to marry him and become queen of his Black Empire, but she resists. The Klan arrives and rescues Elsie, and then succeeds in disarming the black militia. The KKK later celebrates its victory by riding through the streets to the cheers of the white townspeople. When the town's black citizens see this, they run away in fear.

On Election Day, the Klan prevents the blacks from voting. The film ends on a happy note with a "double honeymoon" (Ben Cameron and Elise Stoneman, and Phil Stoneman and Margaret Cameron). The film's epilogue begins with the title: "Dare we dream of a golden day when the bestial War shall rule no more. But instead—the gentle Prince in the Hall of Brotherly Love in the City of Peace." An image of tortured souls under the control of the ruthless "God of War" appears and then fades out. A shot of a happier and peaceful world, presided over by Jesus Christ, takes its place. Ben and Elsie, very much in love, sit at the top of a hill looking toward the celestial city. The final title reads: "Liberty and union, one and inseparable, now and forever!"

The Birth of a Nation is based on Thomas Dixon Jr.'s *The Clansman: An Historical Romance of the Ku Klux Klan* (1905), and Dixon's play version of his novel. Griffith also reportedly used material from another one of Dixon's books, *The Leopard's Spots: A Romance of the White Man's Burden, 1865–1900* (1902). But Griffith's interest in the Civil War probably had more to do with his father, a colonel in the Confederate Army who later served in the Kentucky General Assembly. In a rather bizarre prologue to the film shot in 1930, actor Walter Huston sits in a study with a gray-haired Griffith and presents him a gift—a genuine Confederate sword. A sedate Griffith thanks Huston, who then asks him if he based the story of *Birth of a Nation* on "his father's story," Griffith says, "No, no, I didn't—" but then chuckles and says, "Well, after you mention it, perhaps I did." Just as President George W. Bush seemed to be working through his own Oedipal issues by finishing what his dad started back in the early 1990s with Operation Desert Storm by invading Iraq, Griffith seized the opportunity to rewrite Civil and post–Civil War history.

Griffith's historical drama about the Civil War could not end with the South defeating the North. So he gives former Confederate soldiers dressed in white sheets and hoods a second chance to emerge as the victors by riding to the rescue and taking back control of the South from the villainous African Americans and Northerners through intimidation and violence. Griffith believed his film was an accurate portrayal of the events that occurred in the South during the Reconstruction period. As historian V. F. Calverton points out, the film presents a distorted view of the Reconstruction Period by subscribing to the legend that African Americans dominated legislatures in the Southern states when they only had a majority in two states and it was for a brief period in time.

Griffith once drew a comparison between the work produced by historians and filmmakers: "It is right for historians to write history, then by similar and unanswerable reasons it is right for us to tell the truth of the historic past in motion pictures." He believed that motion pictures would one day replace history books:

> The time will come, and in less than ten years, . . . when the children in the public schools will be taught practically everything by moving pictures. Certainly they will never be obliged to read history again. . . .
>
> Instead of consulting all the authorities, wading laboriously through a host of books, and ending bewildered, without a clear idea of what exactly did happen and confused at every point by conflicting opinions of what did happen, you will merely seat yourself at a properly adjusted window, in a scientifically prepared room, press the button, and actually see what happened.
>
> There will be no opinions expressed. You will merely be present at the making of history. All the work of writing, revising, collating, and reproducing, will have been carefully attended to by a corps of recognized experts, and you will have received a vivid and complete expression.

As Robert Lang observes, Griffith's "grasp of historiography was astonishingly naïve," as he failed to understand that a historical drama is in itself a "construction" (as opposed to actually seeing "what happened") and certainly not, as his film proves, ideology-free.

The film was previewed (under the title *The Clansman*) on January 1 and 2, 1915, at the Loring Opera House in Riverside, California. A little over a month later, on February 8, 1915, it was screened under the same title at Clune's Auditorium, Los Angeles. The film premiered under its permanent title, *The Birth of a Nation*, on March 3, 1915, at the Liberty Theatre in New York. Admission prices were set at an all-time high— two dollars. At the time, the price of admission for an evening show ranged from twenty-five cents to a dollar.

While the majority of critics recognized the epic as a technical achievement, they were divided over the historical accuracy of the events depicted and the misrepresentation of the "Negro" characters. In her analysis of approximately sixty reviews and articles, historian Janet Staiger concluded that "no extrinsic reasons for alignment with one position or another were discernible; for example, there were no consistencies from a regional perspective."

The NAACP denounced the film for its unfavorable depiction of Negroes and its graphic and dramatic depiction of historical events that in the name of racial harmony were best forgotten. Before the film opened in New York, they launched a nationwide campaign to get its members and allies to petition the powers that be to ban the film. Its efforts had mixed results.

In Los Angeles, the NAACP put pressure on the city's board of censors to ban the film before its February 8 premiere. But the board approved the film once the exhibitor agreed to cut four "objectionable parts" from it. Rev. Charles Edward Locke of the Los Angeles Methodist Episcopal Church was critical of the board of censors' decision:

> I am hot with indignation against it. . . . It is a libel against the white people of the South and it is a positive blackmail against the negro. It exhibits the negro character in such perfidy and diabolism as to do a crying injustice to a large portion of our fellow-citizens, who, with great odds against them, are trying to make good. . . . I resent the imputations and falsehoods of the pictures and regard them as wholly reprehensible.

W. H. Clune, the exhibitor whose auditorium would be the site of the film's L.A. premiere, was pleased with the decision and released a statement to the *Los Angeles Times* that offered readers an explanation for the "unexpected opposition" to the film:

> The unexpected opposition to the exhibition of this film has been due to a misunderstanding of the great historical purpose of the picture, which is not an attack on any race or section of the country. It is a most powerful sermon against war and in favor of brotherly love of all sections and nations.

The NAACP turned next to the Los Angeles City Council and requested it take action and have the chief of police suppress the film, but a court injunction was obtained and the film opened on the scheduled date.

The film was approved by the National Board of Censors and the New York Board of Censors (though cuts were required) and opened in New York on March 3, 1915, despite the NAACP's pleas to New York City Mayor John Purroy Mitchel to ban the film on the grounds that it was an insult to the Negro race and that it would do untold damage.

The Birth of a Nation also received an endorsement from a former college classmate of Dixon's—President Woodrow Wilson, who did not have a good track record when it came to race relations. When Wilson was president of Princeton University, he discouraged African Americans from applying for admission. He later instituted segregation within the federal government and became defensive when William Monroe Trotter, an African American delegate from the National Independence Equal Rights League, challenged his policy. According to the *New York Times*, the president claimed "the policy of segregation had been enforced for the comfort and the best interests of both races in order to overcome friction." Wilson also insisted that politics should be left out of racial issues.

In February of 1915, President Wilson had a chance to see *Birth of a Nation*, which constructs the same grim vision of the South during the Reconstruction Period as Wilson's pro-Klan book *History of the American People*, a quote from which appears in the second part of the film: "The white men were roused by a mere instinct of self-preservation . . . until at last there had sprung into existence a great Ku Klux Klan, a veritable empire of the South, to protect the Southern country." Upon seeing the film, Wilson reportedly stated, "It is like writing history with lightening. . . . And my only regret is that it is all so terribly true," though over the years historians have questioned whether he actually made that statement or it was invented by a publicist, or by Griffith himself.

The NAACP next moved its campaign to Boston, where Griffith already planted in the local papers a statement encouraging people to see the film and make up their own minds: "You must see this picture if for no other reason than that your mental machinery—in whatever line it may be working—must of necessity be stimulated to an amazing degree." The demonstrations did not necessarily stop once the film opened. On the fiftieth anniversary of Lincoln's assassination, a screening in a New York theatre was disrupted by the shouts of patrons; one man even threw rotten eggs at the screen. In Boston there was an even more dramatic disruption when five hundred African Americans, headed by William Monroe Trotter, reportedly tried to buy tickets to see the film, only to be told at the box office that they needed to be purchased in advance. There was a confrontation between Trotter, the theatre manager, and the police, which ended with Trotter's arrest when he refused to leave the premises.

The Birth of a Nation did not play in all parts of the country. The film was banned in Denver, Pittsburgh, and Ohio. The governor of Ohio supported the recommendation of the state censorship board to ban the film. The film was rejected by the Kansas State Board of Review and the appeals board. The ban remained in effect until 1923. In Minneapolis, Mayor W. G. Nye used his legal authority under the city charter to revoke the film's license. He challenged the film's historical inaccuracies, which "prejudiced the public mind," and believed the film "tended to bring reproach upon the Negro race" and "would invite race hatred and riots." His reading of the film was supported by an independent panel and the Supreme Court of Minnesota.

But this was only the beginning of this controversial film's long history. Nearly every subsequent re-release and public screening has been met with opposition. Perhaps the legacy of a classic like *The Birth of a Nation* is how it continues to this day to serve as a powerful reminder of the extent to which racism was once socially acceptable (even in the name of art) in the United States.

On a personal note: Having never read Dixon's *The Clansman*, I bought a copy online from a used bookseller in Milwaukee. When I unwrapped the package, I was shocked to see a photograph of William Wilkinson, former Imperial Wizard (1975–83), on the cover staring back at me. Dressed in complete KKK regalia, he stands with his arms folded in front of a burning cross. Published by the KKK (circa late 1970s/early 1980s), the edition includes a brief history of the organization and a bio of Wilkinson.

I'm sure Dixon, who died in 1946, would have been proud.

THE CINEMA OF "DON'TS AND BE CAREFULS": CONTROVERSIAL SUBJECT MATTER

In 1927, the Board of the MPPDA adopted the list of "Don'ts and Be Carefuls," which was comprised of eleven subjects and themes considered unsuitable for American audiences by most state and local license boards (see appendix C). MPPDA members agreed to ban the eleven "Don'ts" from appearing in their films "irrespective of the manner in which they are treated."

Prior to that time, some of the topics that made the list—birth control, social diseases, drugs, white slave trade, etc.—had been the subject of a series of "social problem films," which aimed to educate audiences about the issues Progressives were addressing in their efforts to improve the quality of urban life in America. In fact, some Progressives were even directly involved in the making of these films both in front of and behind the camera.

The White Slave Trade: *Traffic in Souls* (1913) and *The Inside of the White Slave Traffic* (1913)

During the Progressive Era, the widespread belief that women and girls were being coerced into prostitution or "white slavery" at an alarming rate generated a "white slave" panic in many cities. However, there was no hard evidence to support this claim. In fact, in 1910 John Rockefeller, Jr., served as the foreman of a special grand jury charged with investigating New York's white slave trade. Their report found no evidence of a formal white-slave trade ring in New York. Still, in that same year, Congress passed the White-Slave Trade Act, also known as the Mann Act, which stated that any person who knowingly aids or entices a woman or girl to travel in interstate commerce "for the purpose of prostitution or debauchery, or for any other immoral purpose," was guilty of a felony and could be fined up to $5,000 or imprisoned for up to five years. Although the law was designed to protect women and girls from exploitation, social critics have since interpreted both the Mann Act and white-slavery panic as mechanisms for controlling sexual behavior in an age of increased mobility via interstate trains, trolley services, and now the Model-T.

Young women living in the big city were warned about the dangers white-slave traders posed in two films released in 1913, *Traffic in Souls* and *The Inside of the White Slave Traffic*.

In *Traffic in Souls*, Mary Barton (Jane Gail) enlists the help of her boyfriend, a police officer named Burke (Matt Moore), to help find her sister, Lorna (Ethel Grandin), who has been kidnapped by white-slave traders. When Mary loses her job at the candy store, she is hired as a secretary to William Trubus, the head of the citizen's league, who is actually a member of a white-slave trade ring. With her help, the police are able to rescue Lorna and close down the trade operation.

The film was passed by the National Board of Censors after being reviewed by representatives from the Camp Fire Girls, the District Attorney's Office, the City Vigilance Committee, and the Sanitary and Moral Prophylaxis Society. As the white-slave trade was associated with prostitution, the board also consulted with "experts" before passing the film with some deletions and modifications. In its final analysis, the board described the film as "a high-grade picture capable of real moral teaching and dramatic entertainment, yet stripped of all questionable features, such as suggestiveness and allurement, that such a subject might carry." The film, which opened in New York on November 24, 1913, was publicized as a "dramatization" of the Rockefeller grand jury report on white slavery.

The Inside of the White Slave Traffic, which opened the same month as *Traffic in Souls*, was an even bigger moneymaker. The film was written and produced by Samuel H. London, who participated in the Rockefeller Commission. Only fragments of the film survive, but it's clear from what remains, as well as the reviews, that it took a more sensationalistic approach. The story revolves around an innocent young woman named Annie who is drugged by a man named George, who has sex with her. Her father throws her out of the house for being promiscuous, so she returns to George, who passes her off to a white-slave trader. She escapes, but winds up back in the trader's hands. In the end, we are told she ends up "an outcast in Potter's field." While the film was a hit with audiences, London and the managers of two theatres in New York City showing the film ended up in court on a morals charge. London was convicted, but the judge let him off. During the trial, the film was screened in its entirety in the courtroom. According to the *New York Times*, it was the first time a motion picture was presented as evidence in a trial.

Birth Control: *Where Are My Children?* (1916), *Birth Control* (1917), and *The Hand That Rocks the Cradle* (1917)

In 1916, Margaret Sanger opened a birth control and family planning clinic in Brooklyn. The circular for her clinic (printed in English, Yiddish, and Italian) read:

MOTHERS!

Can you afford to have a large family?

Do you want any more children?

If not, why do you have them?

DO NOT KILL, DO NOT TAKE LIFE, BUT PREVENT

Safe, Harmless Information can be obtained of trained

Nurses at

46 AMBOY STREET

Nine days later she was arrested and imprisoned for thirty days for disseminating information about birth control, which at the time was illegal. As part of her mission to educate the public about contraception, Sanger wrote and starred in *Birth Control* (a term she coined). The film was based on a true story that sparked Sanger's personal commitment to the cause: the tragic suicide of a poor woman who did not want to have more children. The National Board of Censors passed *Birth Control*, commending its handling of the subject "with deft touch and intelligence." But the film's opening was postponed when the New York City

License Commissioner condemned the film as "immoral, indecent, and directly contrary to public welfare" and in violation of the state's law "forbidding the dissemination of contraceptive knowledge." The film's distributor argued in court that the purpose of the film was to gain public support to repeal the law. A judge ruled in the distributor's favor, claiming the license commissioner violated the filmmakers' right of free speech. A New York State appellate court reversed the judge's decision by evoking the U.S. Supreme Court's 1915 decision in the *Mutual v. Ohio* case, which stated that motion pictures were a business "pure and simple" and not protected speech.

The judge's ruling then served as the basis for the court's decision to deny a license for another version of Sanger's story, *The Hand That Rocks the Cradle*, written, produced, and directed by wife-and-husband team Lois Weber and Phillips Smalley. Under the law, *Birth Control* and *Hand That Rocks* could not be publicly screened until the U.S. Supreme Court decriminalized the dissemination of information regarding contraception to unmarried individuals and couples.

One of eight female directors working at Universal Studios, Lois Weber was also one of their highest paid because many of her films, which dealt with current and inherently sensationalistic topics such as capital punishment (*The People vs. John Doe* [1916]), child labor (*Shoes* [1916]), and opium addiction (*Hop—The Devil's Brew* [1916]), were moneymakers. One of her most successful films, *Where Are My Children?*, advocates the legalization of birth control, while at the same time condemns illegal abortions. The title refers to a question posed at the end of the film by a district attorney, who has learned that his wife and her bourgeois friends have had multiple abortions. According to historian Kevin Brownlow, most attempts by state boards to ban the film failed, except for Pennsylvania, where censor Dr. Ellis P. Oberholtzer declared he would permit this "mess of filth" to pass the board in his state over his dead body.

Venereal Disease: *Fit to Win* (1919)

This film was a modified version of an army training film entitled *Fit to Fight*, produced by the American Social Hygiene Association, the Medical Department of the Army, the U.S. Public Health Service, and the

War Department Commission on Training Camp Activities. The story opens with an explicit lecture on the dangers of venereal diseases, which apparently falls on deaf ears when four newly enlisted soldiers visit a brothel. Two of them contract syphilis, which prevents them from being shipped overseas to die for their country. Their buddy, a famous college football quarterback, who decided to save himself for his girlfriend, becomes a captain and returns home to marry the girl he loves.

When *Fit to Win* opened at the Grand Opera House in Brooklyn, boys under sixteen and girls under eighteen were not admitted, customers were informed of the film's subject matter, and a percentage of the proceeds went to the Social Hygiene Association. Once again, New York's license commissioner decided the film was immoral, indecent, and obscene, and threatened to take the exhibitor's license away if he didn't pull the film. The newly formed censorship committee of the National Association of the Motion Picture Industry (NAMPI) also condemned the film, contending that if exhibited commercially, it would open the door to the exhibition of similar films.

A U.S. circuit court of appeals upheld the decision of the commissioner, who used "fair and honest judgment" and "honestly concluded that the exhibition of the film to mixed audiences will be injurious to decency and morality."

Apparently there were some subjects Americans were still not ready for.

CHAPTER 2

Movies, Morality, and the (Self-)Regulation of the Hollywood Film Industry

What makes a controversial film controversial? The word *contro-versy* is derived from the Latin word *controversia*, from *controver-sus*, which means "turned in the opposite direction" (*contra* [against] + *versus* [to turn]). During the studio era (1930s–1960s), the "controversial" label was affixed onto films that turned in the opposite direction of what was generally considered at the time to be decent, moral, and inoffensive. Moviegoers, who were believed to be easy prey for the forces of evil and subversion, were shielded from the images and sounds the censors believed posed an immediate threat to the viewing public's morals, values, and principles. Keeping the country's movie screens free of sex and violence, these dedicated, all-knowing human barometers of morality, empowered by the film industry (or in the case of the Legion of Decency, a "Higher Power"), determined for the rest of America what was "acceptable" and what was obscene, indecent, immoral, and offensive.

Consider for a moment Miss Emma Viets of Gerard, Kansas. As chair of her home state's censorship board for six years (1924–30), it was her duty to protect the good people of Kansas from any "questionable" con-tent, which according to the board's guidelines included the "display of nude human figures," "crimes and deeds of violence," "passionate love scenes," and "bar-room scenes with drinking, gambling, and loose con-duct between men and women." "It is our job," she explained, "to help the moving picture fulfill its avowed purpose—to amuse the public in a clean, wholesome way." As for her qualifications, Miss Viets was a former movie theatre house owner, who, during the time she served on the board, was a member of the world's largest fraternal organization, the Order of the Eastern Star, and held the title "Right Worthy Association Grand Matron of the Eastern Star of the World."

So Grand Matron Viets was not only qualified (at least in her mind) to censor films, but on occasion she took it upon herself to "fix" them if there was a problem with the plotline or if a film ran too long. For instance, she did not like the climactic scene of the 1927 drama *Sorrell and Son*, in which a doctor ends his dying father's suffering by giving him poison. She decided the film should end with an earlier scene in which the father collapses in the garden because it is "more artistic, deeper in pathos, [and] less shocking in many minds . . . [and] the film was long anyway and could stand cutting." So with her scissors in hand, Miss Viets eliminated the ending, which could not have pleased Herbert Brenon, who received an Academy Award nomination for his direction.

In addition to state and local censorship boards, three organizations have wielded the most power, at various times and to varying degrees, in regards to censoring, banning, condemning, and regulating the content of motion pictures in the United States: The Production Code Administration (PCA; 1934–68), the Legion of Decency (1934–65), and the Classification and Ratings Administration (CARA; 1968–present day).

The PCA and the Legion of Decency were both founded in 1934 in response to the perceived steady decline of moral standards in motion pictures. A branch of the Motion Picture Producers and Distributors Association (which changed its name in 1945 to the Motion Picture Association of America [MPAA]), the PCA regulated the content of motion pictures through the enforcement of the Production Code, a set of guidelines governing the treatment of crime, violence, sex, profanity, and other questionable subject matter in motion pictures. The members of the MPAA were not permitted to release a film until it received the PCA's official "Seal of Approval." Although the PCA was a secular organization, religion and, more specifically, Roman Catholicism strongly influenced the conception, application, and enforcement of the Code. The moral mission of the PCA is clearly stated in the beginning of the Code under the heading "General Principles": "No picture shall be produced which will lower the moral standards of those who see it. Hence the sympathy of the audience shall never be thrown to the side of crime, wrong-doing, evil or sin." (For the entire text of the 1930 Code, see appendices D and E.)

Throughout most of its history, the PCA had strong ties with the Legion of Decency, a group formed by Catholic bishops who believed "the pest hole [Hollywood] that infects the entire country with its obscene and lascivious moving pictures must be cleaned and disinfected." The Legion did not censor films per se, but reviewed and rated films prior to their release to determine from a moral standpoint the suitability of their content for Roman Catholics. Films that did not subscribe to the teachings of the Catholic Church were deemed morally objectionable or, in some instances, outright condemned. The rating the Legion assigned to a film mattered not only to its members but to the filmmakers, the production company and/or studio that produced it, the distributor, and the exhibitor, all of whom were well aware of the negative impact the Legion's boycott of a film could have on box-office receipts.

Although what you can and can't do and say on the silver screen has changed over the years, morality—what's acceptable and what's not by current standards—has been and, to some extent, still is a primary consideration when a rating is assigned to a film. Unlike the Production Code Administration, the Classification and Ratings Administration (also known as CARA) does not technically censor film content, but just as the Legion of Decency rated films for Catholic moviegoers, CARA assigns a rating to a completed film to inform parents about the suitability of its content for children and teenagers in regards to profanity, nudity, sex, violence, subject matter, and themes. A film's rating can affect the box-office receipts and, in the case of NC-17 films, restrict how and where one can advertise a film. Since replacing the Production Code in 1968, the Motion Picture Ratings System has been criticized for its lack of consistency in assigning ratings to films, particularly when it comes to nudity, sex, and violence and its biased treatment toward films produced by the major studios (the heads of which sit on the MPAA's Board of Directors) over independently produced films.

The studios, filmmakers, special interest groups, and moviegoers have certainly not always agreed with the decisions these organizations have made over the years about the "suitability" of film content. To gain some insight into why certain films were controversial, it's important to first understand how these organizations operate(d) and the extent of their influence and power over what Americans could and could not watch on the big screen.

It is also imperative to remember that *economics*, not morality, was and still is the primary motivation for the major film studios to self-regulate their own industry. Of course, there have always been dedicated and talented professionals on both the creative and business ends of the Hollywood film industry who regard filmmaking as an artistic endeavor. At the same time, since its infancy, the film industry has operated within a capitalist system, and it doesn't matter if a studio is a family business owned by four brothers, or part of the largest media conglomerate in the universe, the bottom line in Hollywood is you have to make money to make movies. Self-regulation—in the form of a Production Code and the current ratings system—continues to be the most effective way the industry can show the U.S. government, its critics, and the public that the industry has a conscience and is genuinely concerned that children are not watching films made for adult eyes only. Since the 1920s, the threat of government interference has loomed over the industry, and it is that threat (be it real or, as some claim, imaginary) that continues to serve as the motion picture industry's primary incentive for keeping a close eye on its own backyard.

THE MOTION PICTURE PRODUCTION CODE

After 1934, state censors could not begin "fixing" a film until it was approved by the Production Code Administration. Under the direction of Joseph Breen, the PCA performed some of the same duties as the Studio Relations Committee. Before a film went into production, the studio was required to submit a plot synopsis, a treatment, and all drafts of the screenplay to the PCA office for approval. Members of the PCA staff read the material and reported on it the following day at their daily morning staff meeting. If two members were not in complete agreement, another reader or the PCA director would read it. The PCA then responded by letter to the studio or production company stating whether or not the material as a whole was acceptable under the provisions of the Code, along with specific notes on the parts of the script that were unacceptable and why. All subsequent script revisions needed to be approved, along with song lyrics and costume designs (to ensure they were not too revealing). In addition, distributors were required to submit all advertising materials to the MPPDA's Advertising Advisory Council for its approval.

Once the editing was completed, a final print was submitted to the PCA. If additional cuts were required, the reedited version needed to be resubmitted. Upon approval, the PCA issued the film an official certificate and number, which had to appear along with the MPPDA's seal on every print of the film. The certificate was a contract between the PCA and the studio stating that all future prints in release would be exact copies of the version approved and would follow the PCA's rules pertaining to advertising.

The correspondence between the PCA and the studios and production companies, which is now housed in the Special Collections Department of the Academy of Motion Picture Arts and Sciences Library in Beverly Hills, reveals the efficiency of the PCA Office when it came to reading scripts and generating a response, which was often done within a forty-eight hour period. In 1946, the PCA reviewed a total of 397 feature films, plus 549 short subjects and 28 imported films. They read over 900 scripts (plus all the revised and additional pages) and wrote over 3,500 opinions on feature and short-subject scripts.

In addition to screenplays, treatments (summaries or outlines of a screenplay), and story synopses, a production company or studio could also submit a novel or play before purchasing the film rights to make sure the material was acceptable under the provisions of the Code. If all or part of the property violated the Code, the filmmakers needed to change these objectionable elements so they would comply.

For example, in June of 1955, independent producer Hal Wallis submitted a copy of Tennessee Williams's stage play *Cat on a Hot Tin Roof* to the PCA for its approval. The play was currently running on Broadway and had just earned Williams his second Pulitzer Prize for Drama (his first was for *A Streetcar Named Desire* back in 1948). In the play, Brick, a repressed homosexual, was in love with his best friend, Skipper, who committed suicide. Brick won't sleep with his wife, Maggie, who knows she must produce an heir in order to get her hands on Brick's dying father's fortune. After reading the play, Geoffrey Shurlock, who succeeded Joe Breen as head of the PCA in 1955, informed Wallis's associate, Paul Nathan, "it would be necessary to remove every inference or implication of sex perversion and to substitute some other problem for the young husband" (in 1950s America, "sex perversion" was a "polite" term for homosexuality). When Wallis decided not to purchase the play, MGM President Dore Schary became interested, but before securing the rights, he asked the PCA for its opinion on his suggestions for changing the play to make it Production Code–friendly. In Schary's proposed version, Brick's feelings for Skipper were not homosexual but a severe case of hero-worship (though in the film the gay subtext is obvious). This change, which was incorporated into the 1958 film, radically altered the meaning of the play—a change the PCA and the studio felt was completely justifiable (see below for other examples of PCA-induced endings to the film versions of stage plays).

The rationale for the changes in Williams's play, and, at least on paper, every change dictated by the PCA, goes back to the Code, which was adopted in 1930 but not fully enforced until 1934. Under its provisions, members of the MPPDA agreed not to distribute, release, or exhibit any film, whether produced by the company or not, until approved by the PCA and issued a certificate signed by the PCA director. If an MPPDA member did not comply with these provisions (or perhaps was tempted to change the content of a film after receiving a seal), the studio would be fined $25,000 "for liquidated damages" because its actions would "disrupt the stability of the industry and would cause serious damage to all members."

The Code is divided into two parts. The first half (appendix D) consists of the "General Principles" that establish the Code's moral foundation, followed by the "Particular Applications," a list of subjects and themes, similar to those on the list of "Don'ts and Be Carefuls," which are "forbidden" or require careful, respectful, or tasteful treatment. The second half (appendix E) is the underlying rationale for the "Preamble" of the Code, the "General Principles," and the "Particular Applications."

As stated in the "Reasons Supporting the Preamble" (appendix E), the Code is based on a fundamental assumption that the cinema, as a form of artistic expression and mass entertainment, can be "helpful or harmful to the human race," because art has the potential to be "morally good" and "morally evil." The power of motion pictures also lies in its unique characteristics that distinguish it from other forms of cultural expression. Literature is limited to printed words and images, while the physical space of a theatre restricts the audience's proximity to the actors. But the cinema can bring the audience, via the camera, closer to the actors, which the Code suggests is the reason why audiences are so enamored with film actors and are more sympathetic toward the characters they play. For this reason, and the nature of the medium itself, filmmakers have a moral obligation to their audience:

> In general, the mobility, popularity, accessibility, emotional appeal, vividness, straightforward presentation of fact in the film make for intimate contact with a larger audience and for greater emotional appeal. Hence the larger moral responsibilities of the motion pictures.

Consequently, the Code was conceived based on the assumption that the influence motion pictures can exert over the minds of moviegoers, particularly those of America's youth, is so profound it is imperative that any violation of God's or man's law is not condoned. The authors of the Code were, of course, naïve to think the minds and morals of spectators are so malleable and so easily influenced by the cinema that they would be inspired to commit a crime or adultery (or both) by watching a film.

Consequently, the decision of what was and what was not acceptable under the Code was really a *moral* question. Joseph Breen, the keeper of the Code, served as the director of the PCA from 1934 to 1941 and 1942 to 1954 (in between he had a brief stint as a studio executive for RKO). Breen was also a conservative Irish Catholic who was very active in church affairs. As he explained in a letter to a member of the MPPDA, he believed in the Code and the moral mission of the PCA:

> Motion pictures, I need not remind you, constitute a peculiar and a powerful influence, for good or evil, upon all those who see it. Because of their widespread popularity, the vividness of their

presentation and the facility with which they never fail to impress and to stimulate, too much emphasis cannot be placed upon the need for the exercise of the greatest possible care in the construction of the pictures, and, at the same time, the likely effect the picture may have upon the minds of those who see it. . . . To really understand the Code, one should study it. . . . This Code is a *moral Code*. Its principles, for the most part, are built upon the basic concepts of Natural Law. No other industry, so far as I know, has undertaken to pattern its products in conformity with the basic tenets of *decency* and *morality*.

The Natural Law, which provides the moral foundation of the Code, is based on the teachings of St. Thomas Aquinas, who states that the first precept of law is that "good is to be done and pursued, and evil is to be avoided." Breen believed that through the application of the Code, the PCA was protecting the public from sin and vice and providing them with the moral guidance that motion pictures, an instrument with a capacity for good and evil, obviously demand.

But unlike the Ten Commandments, the Production Code was not written in stone, and like the Bible, it was open to interpretation. If a filmmaker and the studio disagreed with a decision made by Breen and his staff, they could appeal to the MPPDA's board of directors, which had the power to reverse any decision. The board usually sided with the PCA, but on some occasions an appeal was sustained.

One such case was over the inclusion of the word *hell* in Otto Preminger's film adaptation of the hit Broadway musical *Carmen Jones* (1954). This modern version of Georges Bizet's 1875 opera *Carmen* featured new lyrics by Oscar Hammerstein II sung by an African American cast. The most recognizable song in Bizet's score, the "Toreador Song," belongs to Escamillo, the matador, who describes his experiences in the bullfighting ring. In *Carmen Jones*, prizefighter Husky Miller (Joe Adams) sings Hammerstein's version, a rousing anthem entitled "Stan' Up an' Fight," to express to the crowd what it feels like to be in a boxing ring. The song contains the line "Until you hear that bell, that final bell, stand up and fight like hell!" Unfortunately, *hell* was still on the list of forbidden words. In a letter to director Preminger, Joseph Breen outlined the problems with the script ("lack of any voice of morality . . . an over emphasis on lustfulness"). He also objected to the line "fight like hell," which under the profanity clause of the Code needed to be changed. Preminger spoke to Hammerstein, who did agree to rewrite some of the sexually suggestive lyrics (one line in question was "Would like slice o' sumpin' nice, yore savin' up for Joey"), but would not alter the line "fight like hell." As Preminger explained, "Apart from the fact that this is today a colloquialism that can be heard everyday in every type of society, this particular song has actually become a classic since he wrote it." Consequently, Twentieth Century Fox appealed to the board of directors, which reversed the PCA's decision.

The PCA's position on making an exception for one film was just that—an exception—and did not signal a major change in the Code (which required an amendment passed by the board of directors). As to be expected, there were problems with consistency when it came to enforcing the Code. In April of 1954—the same year "Fight like hell!" got the green light from the PCA—the MPAA Board of Directors approved the phrase "go to hell," which is uttered twice by Terry Moran (Marlon Brando) in *On the Waterfront*. Although it was in violation of the Code, Breen supported its inclusion because it "is not used in a casual manner, as a vulgarism, or as a flippant profanity. It is used seriously with intrinsic validity." Breen's decision angered many producers, particularly those who had made a similar request to use the h-word.

Prior to producing the film version of *Cat on a Hot Tin Roof*, Hal Wallis battled the censors over the use of some questionable language in *Cease Fire* (1953), a docudrama in which American soldiers reenact a mission during the Korean War. Wallis was forced to delete the words *hell* and *damn* in three lines: "To hell with all this rice" (a line sung by the soldiers), "To hell with that," and "I hate those damn things." His studio, Paramount, argued that the use of the words in the context of the film are neither profane nor harmful, but add a dimension of realism. The board of directors refused to overturn the PCA's decision. As Wallis explained in a letter to Clifford Forster, executive secretary of the National Council on Freedom from Censorship, the MPAA acknowledged the use of the words in the film as "normal and natural but felt that to permit them to remain in the picture would set a 'bad precedent.' This ground for ordering the elimination of words seems to me to be

FROM THE PCA FILES: SCRIPT NOTES ON ACADEMY AWARD WINNERS FOR BEST PICTURE

The PCA staff provided the studios with notes on script submissions detailing the elements that were unacceptable under the Production Code or likely to be censored by state or local censorship boards. Here are some examples from screenplays for films that would go on to win the Academy Award for Best Picture.

Gone with the Wind (1939, U.S., dir. Victor Fleming)
"Political censor boards almost invariably delete the word 'diapers.' Consequently, we recommend that you delete the word from Mammy's speech toward the bottom of page 168."

Casablanca (1943, U.S., dir. Michael Curtiz)
"The suggestion that Ilsa was married all the time she was having her love affair with Rick in Paris seems unacceptable, and could not be approved in the finished picture. Hence, we request the deletion of Ilsa's line, 'Even when I knew you in Paris.'"

The Best Years of Our Lives (1946, U.S., dir. William Wyler)
"Page 122: We presume in the scene of the 'old-fashioned bathroom,' there will be no toilet."

West Side Story (1961, U.S., dirs. Robert Wise and Jerome Robbins)
"With regard to the lyrics of the Jet Song ["Gee, Office Krupke"], we would like to urge that you eliminate the reference to social disease. We feel that that could be considered offensive by many people, and certainly is vulnerable to the charge of being in bad taste."

Lawrence of Arabia (1962, U.K., dir. David Lean)
"Page 43: In scene 53, we suggest not having the boy raise the camel's tail before prodding it."

Tom Jones (1963, U.K., dir. Tony Richardson)
"Granted that this is a classic of English literature, nevertheless, the present script seems to us to utilize an unacceptable amount of very coarse language, and to be told with altogether too much emphasis on scenes of physical sexual promiscuity."

particularly oppressive and unjustified and constitutes the most unbridled form of censorship."

Some producers did more than express their outrage over the PCA's control over film content. The first major challenge to the system occurred in the early 1940s with producer/director Howard Hughes's sex western, *The Outlaw*.

THE OUTLAW (1943): "HOW WOULD YOU LIKE TO TUSSLE WITH RUSSELL?"

The title character of producer/director Howard Hughes's sex Western, *The Outlaw*, is none other than legendary gunslinger Billy the Kid (Jack Buetel). The film opens with the arrival of another Western legend, gambler Doc Holliday (Walter Huston), to Lincoln, New Mexico in search of his horse, Red, which is now owned by Billy, who claims he bought it from a stranger. Doc takes a liking to Billy and stops his old friend and current sheriff of Lincoln County, Pat Garrett (Thomas Mitchell), from arresting him. Meanwhile, Doc's girlfriend, Rio McDonald (Jane Russell), tries to shoot Billy to avenge the murder of her brother, whom Billy claims he killed in a fair fight over a woman.

Sheriff Garrett, who is jealous of Doc's friendship with Billy, shoots the Kid, who is saved by Doc and brought to Rio's house. Unaware of her confrontation with Billy, Doc asks Rio to nurse him back to health. While Billy recovers from his gunshot wounds, Rio considers killing him, but she falls in love with him instead. While he is delirious from fever, she sleeps with him (and to make it legal, she marries him without him knowing it). When Doc discovers the truth, Billy gives him a choice: Rio or Red (he chooses the horse). The love triangle (it actually has four sides if you count Red) and Garrett's relentless pursuit of Billy are interrupted by an Indian attack. In the end, Garrett is so consumed with jealousy over Doc and Billy's friendship that he kills Doc. Garrett later feels guilty about what he's done, but then turns on Billy, who outsmarts him. The Kid ties up Garrett, and he and Rio ride off together to start a new life.

The behind-the-scenes story of *The Outlaw* is far more interesting than what happens on the screen. As a Western, *The Outlaw* is more talk than action, and the film suffers from the miscasting of an unknown, Jack Buetel (his real name was often misspelled as Beutel), as Billy. Buetel is handsome, but his inexperience in front of the camera, particularly alongside veteran character actors Mitchell and Huston, is made painfully obvious by his wooden performance and flat line delivery, which do little to help the corny dialogue. Despite his lack of talent, Buetel turned out to be one of the luckiest nonworking actors in Hollywood. In 1940, at the age of twenty-two, he signed a contract with Howard Hughes, who paid him a salary for the next ten years because he didn't want him or Russell working on any other film until *The Outlaw* was in theatres (Russell was allowed to make a few films, but they were not released until after *The Outlaw*).

Although *The Outlaw* also marked her film debut, Russell, a former model whom Hughes supposedly discovered when she was working as a receptionist for his doctor, is by far the more talented of the two. But the display of her curvaceous figure or, more specifically, her 36D size breasts, was only one of the many reasons for Hughes's ongoing battle with the censors.

The story behind *The Outlaw* began in April of 1940 when director Howard Hawks, who would eventually quit the project after two weeks into shooting, shared the plotline of the film with the PCA. Joseph Breen told him a film about Billy the Kid must end with the outlaw being punished for his crimes. As Hawks explained, Billy is not "a hero or sympathetic character" and is never shown committing any crimes. Breen was optimistic they could work it out, yet eight months later he was surprised to read that the shooting of the film had begun without Hughes submitting the script to the PCA for approval.

The shooting script was eventually reviewed by the PCA. In a five-page letter to Howard Hughes, Joseph Breen offered a detailed analysis of the script, which he found unacceptable for three reasons. Firstly, although Billy is never shown committing a crime, it is made clear through the dialogue and a "Wanted Dead or Alive" poster that Billy is a killer. Secondly, despite the fact that a preacher marries Rio and Billy (offscreen), their sexual affair is still illicit because Billy did not consent to the marriage. Thirdly, the script contains "undue brutality and unnecessary killing" (much of which is not in the final film). Breen also warned there would be complaints from the public if the film glorified a well-known criminal.

When the film was screened for Breen the following March, he was horrified by what he saw. He informed Hughes the film was in violation of the Production Code and could not be approved based on the following two objections: 1) the inescapable suggestion of an illicit relationship between Doc and Rio, and between Billy and Rio; and 2) the countless shots of Rio in which her breasts are not fully covered. As expressed in an interoffice memo to Will Hays, Breen was clearly unnerved by the display of Russell's cleavage:

> In my more than ten years of critical examination of motion pictures, I have never seen anything quite so unacceptable as the shots of the breasts of the character of Rio. This is the young girl whom Mr. Hughes recently picked up and who has never before according to my information appeared on the motion picture screen. Through almost half the picture the girl's breasts, which are quite large and prominent, are shockingly emphasized and, in almost every instance, are very substantially uncovered. So far as we know there is no possible way to bring this picture within the provisions of the Production Code except either by a large number of re-takes. . . . Many of these breast shots cannot be eliminated without destroying the continuity of the story.

The following day Breen sent a follow-up memo to Hays in which discussed the recent trend in breast shots:

> In recent months we have noted a marked tendency on the part of the studios to more and more undraped women's breasts. In recent weeks the practice has become so prevalent as to make it necessary for us, almost every day, to hold up a picture which contains these unacceptable breast shots. . . . In the last few days we have again had to hold up a Universal picture, in which there was a shocking display of women's breasts. We also found it necessary to withhold approval of a Columbia picture, in which scattered throughout the entire production there were a large number of "sweater shots"—shots which emphasize women's breasts by way of tight, close-fitting garments.

Howard Hughes believed the first of the two issues Breen identified ("the illicit relationship") could be solved by changing two lines. As for the breast shots, there was simply no extra footage to replace them, so they had no choice but to appeal the PCA's denial of a seal, which was upheld by the board of directors. The notification letter from the board also included a summary of a meeting between Hughes's representatives and the board. The letter states that a seal would be issued if specific changes were made that would total forty feet of footage. The deletions consisted mostly of shots of Rio's breasts as well as sexually suggestive dialogue (like the expression "Tit for tat!"). The censors also objected to Garrett's final line as he watches Billy ride away ("Some kid!"), which the Board felt constituted the "glorification of a criminal by this officer of the law." Hughes made the required cuts, but then tried to sidestep the PCA by submitting unedited versions of the film to the state censors. The film was approved without eliminations in Kansas, while the cuts in Pennsylvania and Ohio were even more extensive than those demanded by the PCA.

When the U.S. entered World War II, Hughes turned his attention to the war effort and let the *The Outlaw* sit on the shelf for the next two years. During that time, his publicity machine, headed by Hollywood's top publicist Russell Birdwell, best known for orchestrating the publicity behind MGM's search for an actress to play *Gone with the Wind*'s Scarlett O'Hara, was hard at work promoting Jane Russell (and to a lesser extent Jack Buetel), which was definitely a challenge considering the public had never actually seen the pair up on the screen—a fact magazine and newspaper articles repeatedly pointed out. Russell graced the magazine pages of *Life* (1/26/42), *Look* (9/8/42), and *Esquire* (6/42), which featured a two-page, full-color photo of Russell lying in a haystack by famed photographer George Hurrell. Articles with titles like "Publicity's Lucky Star," "Provocative Poser Muffled to Calm Censors," and "Will Hollywood's Jane Russell Be a Dark-Haired Harlow?" accompanied by stills of Russell not only played up the trouble the film was running into with the Hays Office, but addressed the ongoing publicity campaign itself. "Jane, as publicity material, is a dream," observed one journalist, "Forms such as hers, have set men gasping for centuries. . . . For a publicist like Russell Birdwell, press agent for years for some of Hollywood's top talent, she was ideal clay."

The public finally had a chance to see Russell on screen when *The Outlaw* premiered at San Francisco's Geary Theatre on Friday, February

5, 1943. Hughes transported via train forty-eight Hollywood reporters, columnists, and fan magazine writers to San Francisco for a four-day press junket. The film was preceded by a live performance by Russell and Buetel of a scene presumably censored from the film. The critics and columnists wasted no time weighing in on this highly anticipated (and publicized) production.

They were not kind.

Time magazine described *The Outlaw* as "obvious, corny, overdrawn, melodramatic" and "a strong candidate for the floppero of all time." The review also described the audience's reaction at the premiere: "The audience, politely embarrassed, sat quietly for some time, the critics exchanging incredulous stares as the picture grew steadily cornier. Finally the audience broke down utterly, laughing at serious scenes, groaning at funny ones." Syndicated Hollywood columnist Erskine Johnson said that if you take the film as a "straight drama, which Hughes insists it is, *The Outlaw* is unbelievably bad," but as a "burlesque of western bad men, it's great fun." Fellow columnist Robbin Coons offered a similar reading of the film: "I think it is a picture so incredibly bad that it is excellent entertainment. . . . The picture is best taken as a burlesque of all western pictures past and future. So considered, it has many earmarks of a master work."

Wood Soanes of the *Oakland Tribune* said that the "worst sin of *The Outlaw* is not the one that brought blushes to the faces of Hays' boys . . . its greatest offenses are the dullness of the theme and the ineptitude of its exposition." The *Los Angeles Times*'s Edwin Schallert dubbed *The Outlaw* as one of the "weirdest western pictures that ever unreeled before the public" and, like his fellow critics, he thought the film at times "rated a burlesque" with "the repartee exchanged between its leading characters . . . as funny as any ever heard in a picture."

The advertising campaign for the film, which consisted of billboards plastered around the city, also raised a few eyebrows, including those of the ladies who were members of the San Francisco Motion Picture Council, one of the many councils based in cities around the country affiliated with the National Board of Review. A letter addressed personally to Will Hays from the council's corresponding secretary expressed its disapproval of the billboards advertising the film featuring "a very disgusting portrayal of the feminine star" and demanded to know,

"Why was such a picture allowed to pass your Board of Censorship?" The image Birdwell chose to advertise the film is the now iconic shot of Russell sitting in a haystack with the caption "How would you like to tussle with Russell?" Another featured the tagline "Mean . . . Moody . . . Magnificent." Apparently word about the billboards and the film traveled down the West Coast to Los Angeles's Motion Picture Council, which made it clear to Sergeant Fulton of the Los Angeles Police force that they were not going to allow "objectionable advertising" and a film with "certain objectionable scenes" in their city. Three years later, when *The Outlaw* was finally released in theatres nationwide, the film returned to San Francisco for a run at the United Artists' theatre. The run was cut short when the theatre's manager, Al Dunn, was arrested on charges of exhibiting a movie "offensive to decency." A complaint was filed under Section 711 of the Police Code banning motion pictures that "excite vicious or lewd thoughts, which is lewd or obscene or vulgar . . . so suggestive as to be offensive in the moral sense." The charges were later dropped. The judge in the case said, "I cannot bring myself to the legal conclusion that the picture . . . has left you ladies and gentlemen of the jury in a state of moral suspense, or of mental lewdness and licentiousness, bewitched, and seduced." To illustrate his point, the judge spoke directly to the female jurors describing the controversial scene in which Rio gets into bed with Billy to help him break his fever:

> I cannot bring myself to the legal conclusion . . . that you would at some opportune and clandestine future abandon your hearths, your children and your husbands to lie in the bed of some invalidated or dying man for one last moment of carnal or lustful experience.

The advertising campaign was also a factor in the Legion of Decency's decision to slap the film with a C rating (Condemned!) because it "presents glorification of crime and immoral actions" and "a very considerable portion of its length is indecent in costuming." Hughes never provided the Legion's review board with a print, so the film had to be screened and evaluated in San Francisco, where the reviewers were apparently influenced by the "salacious advertising" and the "suggestiveness and salacious character" of the stage show before the film.

The reaction of the audience and the critics prompted Hughes to tinker with the film, putting scenes in and taking scenes out to test the audience's reaction. The PCA also encouraged Hughes to take advantage of this opportunity to make the necessary cuts so the Legion would reconsider its C rating. The major objections raised by the members of the Legion's review board over the film focused on the same areas that had been raised by the PCA: the breast shots, the glorification of a criminal, and the scenes suggesting sexual intimacy between Rio and Billy. But judging from some of the individual comments of the board members, which included both clergymen and laymen (nonclergy), it seemed unlikely that the film could be salvaged from the Legion's perspective. Here are summaries of its responses to the question, "What modifications, if any, would improve the rating of this picture?"

- Stupid; no changes could cure it.
- Impossible to classify this picture; unites badly two things: criminal glorification and worn out western which was shot to make red hot with a sex theme; devoid of any elements except animal passion. If the objectionable parts were cut there would be nothing left.
- It flaunts trickery and degradation. It makes women chattel equal in value to a horse. Scenes terminate with definite indication of morality. It ridicules justice. The costumes of the heroine are vulgar.
- Heroine indecently clad; no coherent story; could not be revised.

The second chapter of *The Outlaw* saga begins in 1946 when Hughes decided to move forward with releasing the film.

As in San Francisco, the advertising was once again pure exploitation featuring sexually charged images of Rio (photos and drawings) with her breasts, as always, prominently displayed. The captions were as sensationalistic (and suggestive):

Bold—With Primitive Emotion
Who wouldn't fight for a woman like this?
The Music Halls [the name of a LA theatre chain] *get the big ones!*
How Would You Like to Tussle with Russell?

Here They Are!
That Girl, Tall, Terrific . . . and Trouble!
That Story! Real, Ruthless . . . Rugged!
That Picture Not for Faint Heart
They made their own rules . . . then broke them!
Savage, barbaric drama of ruthless men and a woman with a heart
    of dry ice . . .
What are the two great reasons for Jane Russell's rise to stardom?

The advertising campaign also highlighted the film's censorship history by including such phrases as "Exactly as it was filmed!" and "Not a Scene Cut!" The most original ad was an eight-panel comic strip entitled "*The Outlaw*: Here's Why This Thrilling New Picture Has Been Kept Off the Screen for Two Years!" The story begins with Howard Hughes ("World Famous Flyer and Motion Picture Producer") completing the film that will introduce his new discovery—Jane Russell. The film opens in San Francisco, where it breaks every existing recording during its eight-week run. "Then," one panel reads, "*The Outlaw* is banned by the Censors! But rather than cut a single scene from the film, Howard Hughes withdraws it from the theatres of the world." The next panel features a drawing of Hughes in front of a theater (with a "Closed by Censor" sign in front of it) where he tells reporters, "I'm going to fight this battle to the finish and make sure that the public sees my picture as I made it!" Hughes's efforts obviously paid off: "Now at last . . . After a two years' fight with the censors . . . Howard Hughes brings you his daring production . . . *The Outlaw*! Exactly as it was filmed! Not a scene cut! And introducing a new star, Jane Russell!" Perhaps the lowest point of his campaign involved a skywriting plane, which flew over Los Angeles and drew two circles with two dots in the middle.

Darryl F. Zanuck, Vice President in Charge of Production at Twentieth Century Fox, was so outraged by these ads that he sent a letter to Joseph Breen expressing his disapproval: "The whole campaign on this picture is a disgrace to the industry. . . . The major companies make many mistakes but I have never seen any major company resort to such cheap vulgarity as this." Zanuck was certainly not the only member of the MPAA to disapprove, and while the film may have been granted a seal, Hughes violated article 14 of the association's bylaws pertaining to "the observation and maintenance of standards of fair representation and good taste in the advertising of motion pictures." The advertising in question also included newspaper ads in Chicago, Los Angeles, and Salt Lake City; billboards in Los Angeles and those used in San Francisco back in 1943; and advertisements furnished to Loews Theatre in Richmond, Virginia. Hughes filed a lawsuit against the MPAA (from which he resigned), claiming the requirement to submit advertising materials for approval exercises coercion over 90 percent of the exhibitors in the United States and constitutes an unlawful system of private censorship. Hughes lost the case (and his subsequent appeal). In between trials, the MPAA revoked the film's seal. Hughes's request for an injunction was denied, and he was ordered to remove the MPAA Seal of Approval from the prints of his films.

The removal of the seal should have translated into the removal of *The Outlaw* from any theatres owned by the members of the MPAA. Surprisingly, Eric Johnston, who succeeded Will Hays as president in September of 1945 (and was responsible for changing the organization's name three months later) issued a statement essentially assuring MPAA members that despite the revocation of the film's certificate, they were free to show the film and they would not be punished if they did so. Since 1934 it was understood that MPAA members would have to pay a $25,000 fine for showing a film that did not carry a PCA seal. As historian Ruth Inglis points out, an amendment to this rule was quietly enacted in 1942 stating "member companies are no longer in an agreement not to present in their theatres films that do not bear a 'Code Certification.' Member companies, however, are pledged to maintain in their theatres moral and policy standards as exemplified in the Production Code and accompanying regulations." The change had not become known until *The Outlaw*, which continued to play in theatres affiliated with the MPAA.

While Hughes's legal team was battling the MPAA, *The Outlaw* fell victim to state and local censors. In most cases, the film was banned due to its sexual content (except in Memphis, where the board thought there was "too much shooting"). Baltimore Judge E. Paul Mason upheld the ban by Maryland's board because Russell's breasts "hung like a thunderstorm over a summer landscape." The film was also banned in Massachusetts and Ohio. New York State granted the film licenses and it was set to open in New York City until the police commissioner, Arthur W. Wallander, and Benjamin F. Fielding, commissioner of licenses, declared the film "obscene" and threatened theatre owners with criminal prosecution and revocation of their licenses. A judge refused to lift the ban, claiming Wallander and Fielding did not act "arbitrarily or capriciously or maliciously" when informing owners that violation of the law would result in criminal proceedings. The three-way battle between Hughes, New York City officials, and New York State officials played out in the courts, with the city officials emerging as the victors when a court upheld their right to ban the showing. After losing in court, Hughes finally conceded and edited the film down so it could be shown in New York City. The film opened on September 11, 1947, at the Broadway Theater, though as the *New York Times*'s review observed, it was obvious the film was severely edited, particularly the "torrid love scenes" which have "enough cuts to leave them hanging pretty much in mid-air."

In 1948, Hughes decided to get the Legion of Decency to reclassify his film from a C rating to a B ("morally objectionable in part for all"), which required 147 cuts totaling 20 minutes of footage, thereby reducing the film's running time from 116 to 96 minutes. Most of the shots of Rio bending over were removed from the film, along with the scene in which she gets into bed to "warm up" the feverish Billy. Narration was also added to the end of the film to appease those who believed audiences needed to be reminded at the end that Billy the Kid was a very, very bad man: "History is vague concerning Billy the Kid. Some say he was a cold-blooded killer. But there are other legendary stories which describe him as a young boy who was a victim of circumstance and the wild, lawless surroundings of the untamed West."

The Outlaw will always be best remembered for the drama it generated offscreen for nearly a decade. The film was widely panned by the critics, yet in the end, the "controversial" label—imposed by the MPAA and the Legion of Decency, and exploited by the filmmakers—certainly paid off at the box office, where it took in over $5 million and became United Artists' highest grossing film for the decade.

HOLLYWOOD ENDINGS: FROM STAGE TO SCREEN VIA THE PRODUCTION CODE

According to "The Reasons Supporting Preamble of Code" (see appendix E), "everything possible in a *play* is not possible in a film." Film audiences, compared to theatre audiences, are larger and more heterogeneous and therefore have a lower "moral mass resistance to suggestion." Also, by virtue of the size of the image, film audiences are in closer proximity to the fiction than a theatre audience, so it was believed they were more likely to be influenced by immorality in terms of plot and characters. In the 1950s, the American theatre was not under the same restrictions as motion pictures, so stage plays were able to address more provocative subject matter and mature themes. Consequently, this made the adaptation of some plays difficult, sometimes requiring an entirely new ending.

The Bad Seed (1956) is a dark psychological thriller (or a black comedy, depending on your point of view) about a precocious, pigtailed eight-year-old named Rhoda Penmark (Patty McCormack), who will stop at nothing to get what she wants, including murder. Little Rhoda is all smiles and hugs, but beneath her "sugar and spice" exterior is a cold-blooded psychotic with no conscience and no empathy for others. She has everyone fooled, even her mother, Christine (Nancy Kelly), until one of Rhoda's classmates mysteriously drowns during a school outing after winning the school's penmanship medal. When Christine finds the dead boy's medal in Rhoda's room, she realizes her daughter is a monster—"a bad seed"—who inherited murderous tendencies from her own mother (Rhoda's grandmother), a serial killer who was sent to the electric chair. Rhoda eventually admits to "accidentally" killing her classmate and the Penmarks' former neighbor, whom she pushed down the stairs. Her third victim is their handyman, Leroy. When he discovers what the little tyke has been up to, she locks him in the cellar and sets it on fire.

At the end of Maxwell Anderson's play, adapted from a novel by William March, little Rhoda gets away with her crimes. But that would be a violation of the Production Code, so the film ends with Rhoda trying to retrieve the penmanship medal her mother threw into the bay

71

earlier to protect her. All of a sudden, Rhoda is struck by lightning and disappears in a puff of smoke. Then, before the final credits role, a voice (director Mervyn LeRoy) says, "One moment please—and now our wonderful cast." In the style of a theatrical curtain call, the voice introduces each cast member by his or her real name and role in the story. When Nancy Kelly is introduced at the end, she runs over to the couch where McCormack is sitting and puts her over her knee and spanks her as the two actresses giggle. The Brechtian device, which signals to the audience "this was only a movie," coupled with Rhoda's *deus ex machina* demise, were both added to please the censors. By comparison, the ending of the play is far more chilling because it suggests that little Rhoda, along with God knows how many more like her, is still out there.

Like *The Bad Seed*, the hit Broadway stage play *Tea and Sympathy* (1956) seemed like an unlikely candidate for the big screen due to its treatment of two themes prohibited under the Production Code— adultery and sexual perversion. Despite warnings by the Hays office, MGM bought the rights and hired Robert Anderson to adapt his play. Geoffrey Shurlock rejected each draft because "the problem of the boy is still fear that he may be homo-sexual and the wife's giving herself to him in adultery still appears to violate the Code."

In the play, Tom Lee, a shy, introvert prep student, is accused of being a homosexual when he is seen skinny-dipping with a gay music teacher. Tom's only true friend is Laura Reynolds, the wife of Tom's headmaster, Bill Reynolds, a man's man who believes Tom should get kicked out of school. Laura, whose relationship with the boys is limited to offering them "tea and sympathy," thinks her husband despises Tom because he represents "what he fears in himself." There is also friction between the adult couple due to Bill's inability to return Laura's affection, which seems to have more to do with her inability to be the kind of wife he wants. Meanwhile, Tom, in an effort to change his reputation, tries to have sex with a local girl, but his plan backfires and he is thrown out of school. In the final scene, Laura, who has affections for Tom because, like her first husband, he is "kind and gentle, and lonely," gives herself to him. As the curtain comes down she utters that now classic line, "Years from now when you talk about this—and you will—be kind."

In the film version, the gay teacher is eliminated, as are all other direct references or inferences to homosexuality, including Laura (Deborah Kerr)'s implication that her husband (Leif Erickson)'s dislike of Tom (John Kerr) is due to his own latent homosexuality. Yet there is still something unsettling in the film, as there is in the play, about Bill's animosity towards Tom and his rejection of Laura. Although she doesn't diagnose her husband's fears in the film, his "symptoms" remain. As for Tom, he is a nonconformist who is different from the other guys, though there are still plenty of "signifiers" to suggest he's queer (he walks a little funny, knows how to sew, and wants to be a folksinger). His affection for Laura is genuine, though his attraction toward her seems more Oedipal (she is a substitute for his absent mother) than overtly sexual.

If any damage was done to *Tea and Sympathy* during its transition from stage to screen, it was the addition of a framing story in which an adult Tom, a married (sigh of relief), successful writer, returns to Chilton Prep for his ten-year reunion, which essentially turns the play into one very long flashback. To abide by the PCA's insistence that Laura's adultery not go unpunished, the film doesn't end with Laura telling young Tom to "be kind," but with an adult Tom visiting Bill, who gives him an unsent letter from Laura, who left Bill many years ago. In the letter, she tells Tom that their sexual encounter was wrong and that by sleeping with him, she sacrificed her marriage. She adds that he was wrong to romanticize his relationship with her in his novel. In some respects, the inclusion of the "unsent letter" as a device to tell Tom he should not have romanticized the past, which the film had just done, seems to be Anderson's way of suggesting that perhaps the letter's "implied author" was not Laura, but the Production Code Administration.

The Code would not accommodate the subject of "sex perversion" until 1961 when the ban was finally lifted in anticipation of the release of the film adaptation of another play, Lillian Hellman's *The Children's Hour* (1961), in which two schoolteachers are accused of lesbianism, and *Advise and Consent* (1962), a political drama that gave American audiences its first glimpse into a gay bar.

Another taboo topic in Hollywood was abortion, which was added in 1951 to the list of subjects, alongside "sex hygiene" and "venereal disease," considered improper for motion pictures. This posed a problem for the producers of the film version of *Blue Denim* (1959), James Leo Herlihy and William Noble's play about the lack of communication between parents and their children—in this case a teenager named Arthur (Brandon De Wilde)—who struggles to tell his self-involved mother and father he got a girl, Janet (Carol Lynley), pregnant. In the play, Janet has the abortion (which was, of course, illegal at the time), but that's not the primary focus of the story. Of course this was not possible in the film, which ends with the girl being rescued at the eleventh hour from an abortion clinic that looks like something out of a German horror movie and sent off to have her baby. There's actually a double happy ending when Arthur lives up to his adult responsibilities and joins Janet on a bus out of town, where they will presumably start a new life together.

The altered endings of these plays when they made the transition from stage to screen illustrate just how behind the times Hollywood was when it came to the treatment of mature subject matter and themes. At various points in its history, certain sections of the Production Code were tightened or loosened in response to pressure from both inside and outside the industry to either update the Code in accordance with the changing times or put an end to recent trends in the treatment of certain subjects and themes. For example, the board of directors approved "special regulations" (see appendix I) on the treatment of crime and criminals (1938) and animals (1940). In 1951, significant additions were made to the Code prohibiting drug addiction (section 1), abortion (section 2), and suicide (Special Regulation on Crime, paragraph 5).

But some producers felt the changes were not happening fast enough. In the early 1950s, producer Samuel Goldwyn advocated a major overhaul of the Production Code. In a letter written in December of 1953 to MPAA President Eric Johnston, Goldwyn explained the necessity of changing the Code, which had been in existence for the past twenty-five years:

I believe the time has come when it is imperative to bring the Production Code up to date. As one of the initiators of the Code, I have never for a moment wavered in my belief—nor do I now—that the principle of the Code is essential to the well being of our industry. . . .

Nevertheless, we must realize that in the almost quarter of a century since the Code's adoption the world has moved on. But the Code has stood still. Today there is a far greater maturity among audiences than there was 25 years ago—and this is true of the young people as well as of the older ones.

Goldwyn also believed that not updating the Code would be dangerous for the industry because more companies would try to bypass it.

In December of 1956, the MPAA Board approved the first major revision of the Production Code. In a press release, MPAA President Eric Johnston emphasized his philosophy that the Code is "a flexible, living document—not a dead hand laid on artistic and creative endeavors." He claimed the Code's underlying moral principles had not changed, yet revisions were made that strengthened some provisions, while "certain subjects, now prohibited, are made permissive under conditions which assure restrained and careful treatment." Although there were still some restrictions on their treatment, certain subjects and themes—drug addiction, kidnapping of children, abortion, and nudity—were now permitted. Blasphemy, venereal disease, and sex perversion were still forbidden.

The loosening of the Code and the decline in power of the PCA can be attributed to several factors: the shifting social and moral climate of post–World War II America; the box-office success of films released without a seal, such as *The Outlaw* (1943), *The Moon Is Blue* (1953—see chapter 3), and *The Man with the Golden Arm* (1955); and the influx of Code-defying art films from Western Europe, Scandinavia, and Japan.

In the 1950s, the industry also felt the pressure to keep up with the changing times, as film attendance was on the decline compared to the previous decade. In 1945, an average of 82 million Americans attended the movies on a weekly basis. That number dipped to 55 million in 1950 and to 30 million in 1960. The introduction of television in American homes was certainly one factor, but as historian Dorothy Hamilton points out, blaming television for "siphoning off the movie audience . . . is too simplistic" because the decline in the box office occurred before most American families owned a set. Hamilton suggests that other changes in the post-war era, such as the economic boom, which allowed more time for leisure activities, were also a factor.

In addition to the decline in attendance, studio profits sharply declined beginning in 1952 due to a 1948 Supreme Court ruling known as the "Paramount decision." During the studio era (1930s–1960s), the five major studios—MGM, Paramount, RKO, Twentieth Century Fox, and Warner Brothers—produced, distributed, as well as owned the first-run theatres where their films were exhibited. The three minor studios—Columbia, United Artists, and Universal—produced and distributed films. They did not own theatres, but they had an agreement with the major studios to exhibit their films. Meanwhile, independently produced films were shut out of first-run theatres, while independent exhibitors were unable to book first-run movies from the major and minor studios. In the case of *United States v. Paramount, Inc.*, 334 U.S. 131 (1948), the Supreme Court ruled, in an 8–0 decision, that the current distribution system, under the control of the major and minor studios, along with their other business practices, violated antitrust laws, thereby forcing the major studios to sell off their theatres, which they did over the next five years.

Another Supreme Court decision, in the case of *Burstyn v. Wilson*, 343 U.S. 495 (1952), also known as the *Miracle* case, would have a more direct and profound effect on censorship in the United States. It also marked the beginning of the end for the Legion of Decency, which, since the 1930s, also played a significant role in regulating the content of motion pictures.

THE LEGION OF DECENCY: THE PURIFICATION OF THE AMERICAN CINEMA

The Legion of Decency was born out of the criticism Catholic leaders launched in the early 1930s toward Will Hays and his office's ineffectiveness in stopping the alleged evil and immorality that continued to permeate Hollywood movies. The fact that movies could now "talk" only seemed to have made matters worse in the minds of moralists and clergymen, who did not approve of what they heard coming out of the mouths of fallen women and gun-toting gangsters. Sex—or at least what qualified as sex in the movies in the 1930s—and violence seemed all the more real when sound was added to the image.

Catholic leaders had two powerful allies with direct ties to the industry: Joseph Breen, who was appointed the first head of the Production Code Administration in December of 1933; and Martin Quigley, publisher of the *Motion Picture Herald*, who coauthored the General Principles of the Production Code with Father Daniel Lord. Breen and Quigley offered advice and participated in discussions about the most effective way for Catholics to send a message to Hollywood filmmakers and put pressure on them to clean up their act. Both men believed the constant threats of a boycott and the "blacklisting" of films would force Hays to be more rigid in enforcing the Code.

The Catholic campaign against Hollywood was launched by an outsider—an apostolic delegate from the Vatican named Monsignor Amleto Giovanni Cicognani. On October 1, 1933, he delivered a speech to four thousand Catholics at a Catholic Charities Convention in New York, in which he encouraged the crowd to do their share to help others combat poverty during these hard economic times. He also addressed the "forces of evil" that the church believed were interfering with its "divine mission of saving souls":

An example in our day is moving pictures, with its incalculable influence for evil. What a massacre of the innocence of youth is taking place hour by hour! How shall the crimes that have their direct source in immoral motion pictures be measured? Catholics are called by God, the Pope, the Bishops and the priests to a united and vigorous campaign for the purification of the cinema, which has become a deadly menace to morals.

Cicognani's words were interpreted by Catholics as not merely a suggestion from their Holy Father in Rome, but a directive to all Catholics. The statement was, in fact, written by Joe Breen and inserted, with the apostolic delegate's approval, into the speech. As a result of Cicognani's criticism of the films coming out of Hollywood, the Catholic Legion of Decency was formed. Their mission was the purification of Hollywood cinema. Their strategy was a three-prong approach: create a pressure group, organize boycotts against objectionable films, and support the self-regulation of the industry through the Production Code.

When the Catholic Legion of Decency opened its doors in April of 1934, it changed its name to the National Legion of Decency, a more inclusive and appropriate name considering they were encouraging non-Catholics to join and were getting support from organizations like the Federal Council of the Churches of Christ in America and the Central Conference of American Rabbis. In July of 1934, representatives of the Catholic, Protestant, and Jewish clergy converged in New York and voted in favor of cooperating in the nationwide Legion of Decency campaign.

Meanwhile, the Legion's campaign was picking up steam in cities around the country. Cardinal Denis Dougherty of Philadelphia solicited the support of Catholics in his diocese in a high-profile boycott against the film industry. Pledge cards for both adults and children to sign were sent to each parish, along with a letter from Dougherty, informing Catholics that a "vicious and insidious attack" was being made "on the very foundations of our Christian civilization" by Hollywood movies.

> A very great proportion of the silver screen productions deal largely with sex or crime. The usual theme of these moving pictures is divorce, free love, marital infidelity, and the exploits of gangsters and racketeers. . . . This sinister influence is especially devastating among our children and youth. Experience has shown that one hour spent in the darkened recesses of a moving picture theatre will often undo years of careful training on the part of the school, the church, and the home.

Once again, the harmful effect of movies on innocent, vulnerable young spectators was the justification for regulating film content. Historian Gregory D. Black argues that the idea for the boycott actually came from Joseph Breen, who wanted to get back at Warner Brothers, which controlled the Philadelphia market, for his three-month battle with them over the sex comedy *Madame DuBarry* (1934), which would be condemned by the Legion of Decency. In his correspondence with the cardinal, Breen suggested enlisting the help of civic leaders to protest immorality in the movies because "Jewish boys" (the studio heads) are easily "impressed—and terrified." He also suggested putting pressure on the district manager for Warner Brothers, whom Breen, an anti-Semite, referred to as "a kike Jew of the very lowest type." Similar action was taken in cities around the country. In New York, an interfaith committee of Catholics, Jews, and Protestants announced their plans to enlist volunteers to go door-to-door in the five boroughs to collect signatures. Chicago's Michigan Boulevard was the site of a protest staged by fifty thousand Catholic school children, who were no doubt encouraged by adults, considering they were carrying banners with slogans like "Decency the death-knell of depravity" and "Chicago youth shall boycott evil films."

On December 10, 1934, the Legion of Decency reached out to America's 22 million Roman Catholics in the United States to pledge their allegiance to the Legion by taking an oath in church and filling out pledge cards. Archbishop John T. McNicholas, who wrote the original two-hundred-word pledge (see appendix F for the original and revised versions of the pledge), told Catholics that "millions of Americans, pledging themselves individually, can rid the country of its greatest menace—the salacious motion picture." In reciting the pledge, a member of the Legion vowed not to see "indecent and immoral pictures and those which glorify crime or criminals" and to support the organization's efforts.

Catholics were given the opportunity to take the pledge each year on the Sunday after the Feast of the Immaculate Conception (December 8), when it would be read from the pulpit at Mass. One theologian claimed "one of the most attractive features" of the Legion was the voluntary character of the pledge, which "does not itself impose obligations under pain of sin." Yet one wonders if anyone would dare not stand in church and recite the oath in front of his or her fellow parishioners.

To keep Catholics on the straight and moral path, the Legion of Decency created a ratings system to measure a film's moral content (see appendix F). The Legion's team of raters assigned an A-1 rating to films with no objectionable content and suitable for "general patronage" (much like the G rating in the MPAA's current ratings system). Films with content that required "maturity and experience if one is to witness them without danger" received an A-2 ("Morally Unobjectionable for Adults"). The A-2 rating did not set an age limit, but left the decision to parents, pastors, and teachers.

The more questionable films received a B or C rating. The B rating ("morally objectionable in part for all") was assigned to films containing "elements dangerous to Christian morals or moral standards." The big C (Condemned) was reserved for films "because of theme or treatment . . . described by the Holy Father as 'positively bad.'" The ratings and a short rationale were made public (the more controversial decisions were covered by the trade papers [*Variety, Hollywood Reporter*] and the *New York Times*). Beginning in 1936, members of the International Federation of Catholic Alumnae (IFCA) became the official film reviewers for the Legion of Decency. In 1939, the IFCA had five hundred branches with over one hundred thousand Catholic female members. The group consisted of female graduates of parochial high schools, Catholic academies, and liberal arts colleges, which qualified them to pass judgment on films in terms of the church's teachings and philosophy.

The Legion of Decency did not directly censor films à la Miss Emma Viets, but it did have considerable influence over producers and studio

"POSITIVELY BAD": FILMS CONDEMNED BY THE LEGION OF DECENCY

Between the years 1937 and 1968, the National Legion of Decency reviewed over thirteen thousand films, 2 percent of which received a C (Condemned) rating at the time. While the list of condemned films includes many obscure films that received little if any critical attention at the time of their release, there were also many imported films that are regarded today as classics and/or have gained cult film status. Here is a partial list, with the Legion's rationale for condemning each film:

Black Narcissus (1947, U.K., dirs. Michael Powell and Emeric Pressburger)
"The character of this film and the attitude displayed therein create an impression that constitutes an affront to religion and religious life. It ignores the spiritual motivation which is the foundation of and safeguard of religious life and it offensively tends to characterize such life as an escape for the abnormal, the neurotic, and frustrated."

Rififi (1955, France, dir. Jules Dassin)
"The film is of low moral tone throughout. It overemphasizes and glamorizes criminals and criminal activities in such a way as to arouse undue sympathy. Furthermore, it contains material morally unsuitable for entertainment in motion-picture theatres and seriously offends Christians and traditional standards of morality and decency."

Sommarnattens leende (*Smiles of a Summer Night*—1955, Sweden, dir. Ingmar Bergman)
"Both in theme and treatment this film seriously violates Christian and traditional standards of morality and decency by reason of an unmitigated emphasis on illicit loves and sensuality. Suggestive costuming, dialogue, and situations."

À bout de souffle (*Breathless*—1960, France, dir. Jean-Luc Godard)
"The grossly indecent and salacious treatment of this film in costuming, dialogue and situations make it completely unacceptable from a moral point of view for a mass medium of entertainment."

L'avventura (*The Adventure*—1960, Italy, dir. Michelangelo Antonioni)
"The theme of this film is developed in an atmosphere of complete moral ambiguity. The treatment is grossly suggestive and pornographic in intent. It is totally unacceptable in a mass medium of entertainment."

Blowup (1966, U.K./Italy/U.S.A., dir. Michelangelo Antonioni)
"Brilliance of camera technique and beauty of image composition do not justify a sexual treatment, which, in certain sequences, will impress viewers as going beyond reasonable limits of moral acceptability for a public entertainment medium."

Barbarella (1968, France/Italy, dir. Roger Vadim)
"This science fiction film, presumably intended as a 'comic strip' for adults, is basically structured around repeated sexual encounters involving the heroine. As a sick, heavy-handed fantasy, it relies for its appeal on a crass exploitation of nudity and graphic presentations of sadism rather than sophisticated wit and imagination."

executives, who were well aware of the financial impact a B or C rating could have on a film's box-office receipts. The Legion screened a film prior to its release, which allowed the studios a sufficient amount of time to make any necessary changes that could, for example, bump a film rating up from a B to an A-2. But as historian Frank Walsh points out, "despite the Legion's assertion that it was simply advising Catholics on what films they should avoid, the result was a national classification system that affected what all Americans saw and didn't see on the screen." Just as the PCA sometimes required filmmakers to cut a film in order to conform to the Code, the Legion of Decency interfered with the creative process by threatening to give a film the dreaded C rating if the studio did not make the specific cuts it recommended.

For example, David O. Selznick's $6 million sex Western *Duel in the Sun* (1947), starring Jennifer Jones and Gregory Peck, opened in Los Angeles on New Year's Eve prior to its national release in order to qualify for the Academy Awards (it received two nominations—for Jones and supporting actress Lillian Gish). The film was passed by the PCA, but Selznick was not able to submit a print to the Legion of Decency due to a strike at the Technicolor plant. Meanwhile, William Mooring, film critic for the Los Angeles Catholic paper *Tidings* and other Catholic publications, found the film (which he called "plush pornography") more objectionable than *The Outlaw* due to its sympathetic portrayal of a pair of sinners (Jones and Peck), a scene of seduction, and Jones's sexy attire. He also accused the filmmakers of making fun of religion through the character of Jubal Crabbe, a.k.a. the Sinkiller (Walter Huston), whose prayers for Jones's soul garnered unintentional laughs. From his pulpit, Most Reverend John J. Cantwell, Roman Catholic Archbishop of Los Angeles, warned Catholics that "pending classification by the Legion of Decency they may not, with a free conscience, attend the motion picture *Duel in the Sun* . . . [which] appears to be morally offensive and spiritually depressing." In order to raise the film's classification from an inevitable C to a B, Selznick was forced to make forty-six cuts, though the Legion took issue with the newspaper ads for the film, which included the statement "The picture has been passed by the New York Board of Censorship and the Legion of Decency." The Legion issued a statement clarifying that it had not "passed" the film, but rated it B due to "immodestly suggestive sequences" and the "glorification of illicit love."

Selznick was forced to cooperate to protect his investment, though like most creative personnel who fell under the wrath of the Legion, resented its interference and did not necessarily hide it, particularly when the cuts it demanded were absurd. For example, the comedy *And Baby Makes Three* (1949), which was passed by the PCA, contained the line "There hasn't been a miracle since the thirteenth century" (the same line had been used in *Knock on Any Door* [1949] without any problems). In his response to Columbia Pictures' request to cut the line, producer Robert Lord sent a telegram stating, "Make cut if you have to, but Legion's objection seems really preposterous and absurd." He also added that the industry must take a stand against the threat of censorship and boycotts.

When asked by the *New York Times* to comment on his reported conflict with Warner Brothers over cuts made to *A Streetcar Named Desire* (1951), director Elia Kazan responded by writing an article detailing the reasons why cuts were made to his film prior to its release. According to Kazan, Warner Brothers panicked when they learned the Legion of Decency intended to condemn the film, because Catholics would boycott it and prevent others from going to see it by picketing the theatres. So the studio hired a Catholic layman independent of the Legion of Decency who recommended a total of twelve cuts totaling approximately three to four minutes of footage. After the film was cut, it was shown to Kazan:

> As the director of the picture, I see the deleted film somewhat differently. It does make a difference. I see it as small but necessary bits that built mood or motivation as I needed them, and whose rough excision leaves small holes or unprepared climaxes that make my work appear cruder than it was. I see it as lost fragments of a subtly told story, whose omission leaves the characters less fully explained than the author intended and than the actors, before, conveyed.

As Kazan candidly points out, what the Legion was advocating by putting pressure on the studios was essentially another code, which, unlike the Production Code, he felt he was under no obligation to follow. "My picture had been cut to fit the specifications of a code which is not my code," wrote Kazan, "is not the recognized code of the picture industry, and is not the code of the great majority of the audience."

Like that of the PCA, the influence of the Legion of Decency diminished in the 1950s due to the changes in the social climate in the post-Kinsey era, particularly around society's attitude toward sex, marriage, and divorce. The close bond between the PCA and the Legion was also severed over disagreements over certain films, such as *Baby Doll* (1956—see chapter 5), and the loosening of the Code in 1956 under the PCA's new director, Geoffrey Shurlock.

The Legion did revise its own ratings system the following year (see appendix F). A-2 now read "Morally Unobjectionable for Adults *and Adolescents*" (emphasis mine), while films with an A-3 rating were "Morally Unobjectionable for Adults." In its rationale for the changes, the Legion explained that the A-2 rating was designed to provide moral guidance to adolescents who might be seeking films with "more adult content and orientation," while A-3 was their attempt "to provide for truly adult subject matter . . . provided that the themes in question and their treatment be constant." The Legion also believed the addition of the A-3 would send a clear message that when a film was rated B and C (which remained unchanged), they meant business (see appendix F). In 1962, another category, A-4, "morally acceptable for adults with reservations," replaced the "Special Classification" rating, which had been given to certain films that were not morally offensive, but required some explanation or analysis because they could potentially be wrongly interpreted. But as the Production Code continued to be chipped away, the Legion of Decency had outlived its initial purpose. In 1965, its name was changed to the National Catholic Office for Motion Pictures.

Today the "Office for Film and Broadcasting," which is under the jurisdiction of the United States Conference of Catholic Bishops, continues to evaluate films. The A-1, A-2, and A-3 classifications remain, but A-4 has been replaced by L ("Limited adult audience, film whose problematic content many adults will find trouble"). Movies are no longer "Condemned," but are labeled O for "Morally Offensive." Among the list of recent films classified as O are *Borat* (2006—"going for shock laughs over wit"), *The Da Vinci Code* (2006—"the obvious falsehoods about Opus Dei are deeply abhorrent"), and *Superbad* (2007—"unremittingly low-minded and vulgar"). Ratings and reviews are posted on its website at http://www.catholicbishops.org/movies/weekly.shtml.

IL MIRACOLO (THE MIRACLE—1948): "A DESPICABLE AFFRONT TO EVERY CHRISTIAN"

The most controversial film of the 1950s was *The Miracle*, an Italian import directed by Roberto Rossellini and starring Anna Magnani. Ironically, despite the film's controversial treatment of religious themes, *The Miracle* is best remembered for what happened offscreen when the film debuted in the United States in November of 1950 and the 1952 landmark Supreme Court decision bearing its name. The *Miracle* decision reversed the 1915 Mutual decision, in which the Supreme Court ruled that motion pictures are not protected speech under the Constitution, thereby opening the floodgates for censoring and banning films. In the case of *Burstyn v. Wilson*, 343 U.S. 495 (1952), the Supreme Court ruled "expression by means of motion pictures is included within the free speech and free press guarantees of the First and Fourteenth Amendments." The decision struck down all but one criterion—obscenity—for censorship. Consequently, the *Miracle* decision had a direct impact on cases involving five other films: *La Ronde* (1950; banned in New York), a remake of *M* (1951; banned in Ohio), *Pinky* (1949; banned in Marshall, Texas); *The Moon is Blue* (1953; banned in Kansas, Maryland, Ohio, Jersey City, and Milwaukee); and *Native Son* (1951; banned in Ohio).

With a running time of forty-one minutes, *The Miracle* was paired with another Rossellini-Magnani short, a film version of Jean Cocteau's *The Human Voice*, when it premiered under the title *L'amore* at the 1948 Venice Film Festival. Joseph Burstyn and his partner Arthur Mayer, who distributed Rossellini's *Roma, città aperta* (*Rome, Open City*—1945) and De Sica's *Ladri di biciclette* (*The Bicycle Thief*—1948), secured the rights to *The Miracle* and packaged it with two older French shorts, Jean Renoir's *Partie de campagne* (*A Day in the Country*—1936) and Marcel Pagnol's *Jofroi* (1933) under the title *Ways of Love* (1950).

Less than one month later, Cardinal Spellman read a statement from his pulpit in St. Patrick's Cathedral calling every Catholic in the United States (estimated at around 26 million) to boycott the film:

> *The Miracle* is a despicable affront to every Christian. It is a mockery of our faith. . . . This picture blasphemously and sacrilegiously implies a subversion to the very inspired word of God. Satan alone would dare such perversion. . . . In a secondary way, *The Miracle* is a vicious insult to Italian womanhood. It presents the Italian woman as moronic and neurotic and, in matters of religion, fanatical. Only a perverted mind could so misrepresent so noble a race of women.

The film Spellman declared war on is the story of what we might call today a "mentally challenged" peasant woman (she is neither moronic or neurotic) named Nanni who encounters a handsome stranger while herding her goats on a mountainside. She thinks the bearded man (played by director Federico Fellini, who collaborated on the screenplay) is St. Joseph. He remains silent as she begins to talk nonstop, pausing only to sip from the bottle of wine he shares with her. She falls asleep and when she awakens he is gone. When Nanni returns to her village and shares the news, no one believes her. Weeks later, she passes out and the villagers discover she's pregnant; they mock her for thinking she's pregnant by the grace of God (like the Virgin Mary). The younger villagers follow her through the streets, throw cabbages at her, and put a basin on her head as if she is wearing a halo. She leaves the village and goes up into the hills to live alone. When it's time for her to give birth, she goes into a church, where she delivers her baby. Overjoyed by the sight of her child, she cries out, "My son! My love! My flesh!"

When *The Miracle* was imported to the U.S. by Joseph Burstyn, it arrived with some critical baggage. The film flopped with Italian audiences, which reportedly found it boring. The Catholic Cinematographic Center, the Legion of Decency's Italian cousin, blacklisted the film, dubbing it "an abominable profanation." A review that appeared in the Vatican newspaper, *Osservatore Romano*, acknowledged that the film was objectionable from a "religious viewpoint," yet it does contain "scenes of undoubted screen value." Rossellini did not fall out of favor with the

Catholic Church over the film. In fact, in 1949, Rossellini was granted approval by the Church to make a film about the life of St. Francis (*Francesco, giullare di Dio* [*Francis, God's Jester*—1950]), released in the U.S. in 1952 as *The Flowers of St. Francis*.

The objection to Rossellini's film in Italy was subdued compared to the religious and legal powder keg this simple tale ignited when it opened in New York. Burstyn could never have imagined the film would become front-page news, especially after making it through the Customs Bureau, getting the approval of the National Board of Review, and being passed by the New York Censor Board, which was now part of the New York State Department of Education, without deletions not once but twice (the first as an individual work on March 2, 1949, and again on November 28, 1950, in *Ways of Love*). The film had been running for less than two weeks when Lillian Gerard, the managing director of the Paris Theatre, received a letter from Edward T. McCaffrey, New York City's Commissioner of Licenses, informing her that he found the film "officially and personally blasphemous" and threatened to revoke the license if she did not pull the film. It was certainly no coincidence the newspaper broke this story on Christmas Eve—the same day the Legion of Decency condemned *Ways of Love* (all three films) as "a sacrilegious and blasphemous mockery of Christian and religious truth."

The banning was denounced by the National Council of Freedom from Censorship, the New York Civil Liberties Committee, the ACLU, and thirteen of the sixteen members of the New York Critics Circle, which voted *Ways of Love* the Best Foreign film of 1950. Although appeals were made to New York Mayor Vincent Impellitteri to lift the ban, he decided to let the court decide—and it did. New York Supreme Court Justice Henry Clay Greenberg reportedly only took five minutes to lift the ban. Greenberg considered McCaffrey's decision "arbitrary" because the state's official censorship board had approved the film. One week later, a second New York Supreme Court Justice, Aron Steuer, based his decision to grant a temporary injunction restraining the city from enforcing the ban on the same rationale: "The right to determine whether a motion picture is indecent, immoral, or sacrilegious is vested solely and exclusively in the Education Department of the State."

But the courts certainly could not prevent Cardinal Spellman from rallying Catholics to boycott the film, which sparked a series of protests (to chants of "This is the kind of picture the Communists want!") and bomb scares (in both the Paris Theatre and St. Patrick's Cathedral). Martin Quigley fanned the flame with an editorial that tried to make a case that the film—the work of leftists Rossellini and Magnani—was part of the Communist conspiracy "to destroy religious belief . . . because the spread or containment of Communism depends entirely on their success or failure in this regard." Compare Quigley's reading of the film to that of Rossellini, who, amidst all the controversy, contacted Cardinal Spellman via telegram to express his "profound sorrow" that Catholics were boycotting his film and offer an explanation of the film's intended message:

> In *The Miracle*, men are still without pity because they have not gone back to God. But God is already present in the faith, however confused, of the poor, persecuted woman and since God is forever, a human being suffers and is misunderstood. "The Miracle" occurs when, with the birth of the child, the poor demented woman regains sanity in her maternal love. They were my intentions and I hope Your Eminence will deign to consider them with paternal benevolence.

Although the independently released film was not required to go through the PCA's channels, Joseph Breen considered "Burstyn's latest attempt to stir up trouble" to be "very portentous" (they had clashed over cuts in *The Bicycle Thief*). But Breen was optimistic that political changes in New York, including "the favorable disposal of Governor Dewey," would "completely re-arrange, and re-set the business of film censors in New York State," which was generally regarded as "a farce, and completely ineffective."

When the State Board of Regents scheduled a hearing for the purpose of deciding whether the film's license should be revoked, several religious and civic organizations submitted petitions, including the American Civil Liberties Union, the Authors League of America, academics from several major universities, as well as clergymen, rabbis, and religious leaders from New York, New Jersey, and Connecticut. Despite their efforts, the Board of Regents reevaluated the film and on February 16, 1951 issued a statement that included a rationale for its decision to revoke both licenses the film had received (as a single film and as part of *Ways of Love*):

> In this country where we enjoy the priceless heritage of religious freedom, the law recognizes that men and women of all faiths respect the religious beliefs held by others. The mockery or profaning of these beliefs that are sacred to any portion of our citizenship is abhorrent to the laws of this great state. . . . This picture takes the concept so sacred to them set forth in both the Protestant and Catholic versions of the Bible . . . and associates it with drunkenness, seduction, mockery, and lewdness.

As expected, the response to those opposing the ban was swift and direct. A *New York Times* editorial challenging the decision raised a very important question concerning the power of the Board of Regents to deny a license to a film on the grounds that it is "sacrilegious." While there is general agreement over what is obscene or immoral, "that which is sacrilegious to one religion may not be sacrilegious to another." This argument and the question of whether the Board of Regents had the power to revoke a license were raised when Burstyn took the Board of Regents to court. The ban was upheld in the appellate division of the State Supreme Court, which ruled that it was in the board's power to revoke a license, and as motion pictures are not free speech, the ban "is not a denial of religious freedom." After losing an appeal in the New York Court of Appeals, Burstyn turned to the Supreme Court, which rendered a decision on May 26, 1952, overturning the ban by ruling that motion pictures were no longer "business pure and simple," but entitled to the guarantees of free speech and free press.

The *Miracle* decision marked the beginning of the end for film censorship, though it would take more than a decade before all state and local censorship boards would be completely dismantled and the Production Code would be replaced by the current ratings system.

THE MOTION PICTURE RATINGS SYSTEM

In 1966, three years after the death of MPAA President Eric Johnston, the organization finally hired his successor. Like Will Hays, Jack Valenti was a Washington insider who had no prior experience working in Hollywood (at the time of his hire, he was a "special assistant" to President Lyndon Johnson). As a lobbyist for the film industry, his political connections and knowledge of how things worked in Washington were considered an asset, particularly at a time when the Hollywood Production Code was on its last legs.

Valenti arrived in Hollywood when the industry was going through what journalist Peter Bart referred to as a "frantic change." The movie moguls who controlled the town were out of the picture and the major studios were either warding off corporate raiders or already in the hands of large, diversified corporations like Gulf and Western, which bought Paramount in 1966, and the Transamerica Corporation, which acquired United Artists the following year. Rising production costs and a decline in weekly attendance posed a major challenge for the studios' new management teams, many of whom knew little about the film industry (as much as actors and directors did not appreciate the "micro-management" style of Louis B. Mayer, Jack Warner, Darryl Zanuck, and Sam Cohn, at least they knew how to make movies).

In an effort to ensure that the regulation of motion pictures remained out of the government's hands, Valenti made the outdated Code his first priority. In September of 1966, he introduced a revised version ("The Motion Picture Code of Self-Regulation"), which, as the Code stated, was "designed to keep in closer harmony with the mores, the culture, the moral sense and the expectations of our society." A precursor to the motion picture ratings system, the revised Code took a clear position against censorship ("an odious enterprise"). At the same time, the Code retained a list of "Standards for Production," which prohibited or restricted the treatment of the same subjects and themes as the previous versions of the Code (evil, sin, crime, nudity, illicit sex, obscenity, profanity, religious and racial slurs, and cruelty to animals). But like the list of "Don'ts and Be Carefuls" from 1927, the language is a bit loose and at times vague. For example, it stated that "special restraint" should be used in the portrayal of criminals, and their crimes

90

and "sex aberrations" (homosexuality) should be presented with "restraint and care." "Undue" profanity is not permitted. While the whole concept of a Production Code was "so thirty years ago," this was the best the industry could do to stay in step with the times and compete with the influx of foreign-produced "art films" that were being released without a seal, some of them through newly created subsidiaries of the major studios.

The 1966 Code also stated that in order to help parents make more informed choices about what films their children should see, some films would carry a "Suggested for Mature Audiences" label. Among the list of films carrying the SMA label in 1966–67 included *A Funny Thing Happened on the Way to the Forum* (1966), *Georgy Girl* (1966), *Two for the Road* (1967), and *Reflections in a Golden Eye* (1967). Certain films would also still be required to carry an age limit if they contained unsuitable content, which had been the case since the early 1960s with films such as *Elmer Gantry* (1960) and *Splendor in the Grass* (1961), both of which required children sixteen and under to be accompanied by a parent. The film version of Edward Albee's play *Who's Afraid of Virginia Woolf?* (1966—see chapter 3) carried an even higher age limit: "No one under 18 will be admitted unless accompanied by his parent." All of these changes were significant because rather than attempting, like the earlier versions of the Code, to level the moral playing field for the entire viewing audiences, the 1966 Code recognized that there are motion pictures made by responsible filmmakers for mature audiences.

But the new Code would remain in effect for only two years until it was replaced by an entirely new system, a variation of which is still in effect today. According to Jack Valenti's first-person account of the birth of the ratings system posted on MPAA's official website, his first move in creating the motion picture ratings system was "to abolish the old and decaying Hays Production Code." This is simply not true. The original version of the revised "MPAA Code of Self-Regulation" published in *Variety* on October 8, 1968 (see appendix G), not only introduced the original four letter-ratings to be assigned to films (G, M, R, X), but included the same list of "Standards for Production" as the 1966 Code. Furthermore, the word *Code* was retained, appearing in the title of the document and name of the newly formed branch of the MPAA, CARA (Code and Ratings Administration; *Code* was replaced in 1977 by

TABLE A EVOLUTION OF MOTION PICTURE RATINGS SYSTEM (1968–2007)

RATING	1968*	1969–2006	2007**
G	**G: SUGGESTED FOR GENERAL AUDIENCES** "This category includes motion pictures . . . acceptable for all audiences, without consideration of age."		**G: GENERAL AUDIENCES** **All Ages Admitted**
M	**M: SUGGESTED FOR MATURE AUDIENCES—ADULTS & MATURE YOUNG PEOPLE** "This category includes motion pictures which . . . because of their theme, content, and treatment, might require more mature judgment by viewers, and about which parents should exercise their discretion."	1970: M replaced by GP	
GP		1970: GP replaces M **GP: ALL AGES ADMITTED PARENTAL GUIDANCE SUGGESTED** 1972: GP replaced by PG	
PG		1972: PG replaces GP **PG: PARENTAL GUIDANCE SUGGESTED—Some material may not be suitable for pre-teens.**	**PG: PARENTAL GUIDANCE SUGGESTED** **Some material may not be suitable for children.**
PG-13		1984: PG-13 added **PG-13: Parents are strongly cautioned to give special guidance for attendance of children under 13. Some material may be inappropriate for young children.**	**PG-13: PARENTS STRONGLY WARNED** **Some material may be inappropriate for children under 13.**

TABLE A Continued

RATING	1968*	1969–2006	2007**
R	**R: RESTRICTED—PERSONS UNDER 16 NOT ADMITTED, UNLESS ACCOMPANIED BY PARENT OR ADULT GUARDIAN** "This category includes motion pictures which . . . because of their theme, content or treatment, should not be presented to persons under 16 unless accompanied by a parent or adult guardian."	1970: minimum age changed from 16 to 17. **R: RESTRICTED— PERSONS UNDER 17 NOT ADMITTED, UNLESS ACCOMPANIED BY PARENT OR ADULT GUARDIAN**	**R: RESTRICTED UNDER 17 REQUIRES ACCOMPANYING PARENT OR ADULT GUARDIAN**
X	**X: PERSONS UNDER 16 NOT ADMITTED** "This category includes motion pictures . . . which in the opinion of the Code and Rating Administration are rated X because of the treatment of sex, violence, crime or profanity. Pictures rated X do not qualify for a Code Seal. Pictures rated X should not be presented to persons under 16."	1970: minimum age of 16 changes to 17 and 18 "in accordance with exhibitors and various local and state ordinances." 1990: X replaced by NC-17	
NC-17		1990: NC-17 replaces X **NC-17: NO CHILDREN UNDER 17 ADMITTED**	**NC-17: NO ONE 17 AND UNDER ADMITTED**

*Source: *Variety,* 8 October 1968, 6.

**Source: Motion Picture Association of America's official website
<http://www.mpaa.org/FlmRat_Ratings.asp>.

the word *Classification*), which replaced the PCA. More importantly, some of the practices of the PCA continued as well, including holding script conferences with producers and studio executives, and instructing writers and directors on how to get the desired rating for their film in both the preproduction and postproduction stages.

The rating system started with four letters, each designating the suitability of a film's content for children: G (General audiences), M (Mature audiences—Adults and mature young people), R (Restricted—Persons under 16 not admitted unless accompanied by parent or adult guardian), X (Persons under 16 not admitted). As table A reveals, major changes have been made to the Code over the past forty years, including the age restrictions of certain ratings.

Overseeing the newly formed Code and Ratings Administration (CARA) was seventy-four-year-old Geoffrey Shurlock, who had been working for the PCA since 1932 and for the past fourteen of those years served as its director. His staff of five Los Angeles–based raters, who were all forty-nine years old or over, included a former Associate Press reporter and a graduate of Harvard School of Business Administration (a sixth staff member, with a background in psychology and law, represented CARA on the East Coast). Only members of the MPAA were required to submit their film. As with the PCA, filmmakers who did not agree with CARA's decision could appear in front of an appeals board. The appeal cases were originally heard in New York and required a majority vote, but Valenti later allowed appeals to be heard in California, and two-thirds was eventually required to overturn an appeal.

The initial response both inside and outside the industry was generally positive, yet cautious. The *New York Times* and the *Los Angeles Times* used the exact same phrase ("a worthwhile attempt") in their editorials expressing their support for the new ratings system, though both papers also emphasized that the responsibility ultimately falls on the parents to decide which films are suitable for their children. By its first birthday, CARA had rated approximately 435 films, the majority of which received an M (170), followed by G (139), R (101), and X (25). By its third birthday, major changes had been made to the ratings system due to criticism launched against CARA, Valenti, and the system he devised.

A joint report issued in May of 1970 by the Protestant film board, the Broadcasting and Film Commission of the National Council of

Churches, and the National Catholic Office for Motion Pictures criticized the rating system for its lack of "sufficient independence of judgment and enforcement teeth to maintain its public credibility." Their report claimed the film industry had failed to educate the public about the ratings system and suggested CARA be more autonomous from the industry. In regards to the ratings, the report concluded that films were being rated based on "language and visual elements" rather than "their general treatment and theme" and believed a clearer distinction needed to be made between the R and X categories. One year later, both groups officially withdrew their support of the ratings system over the GP rating (which replaced M in 1970) because GP was becoming a "catch-all category" for films that should have been rated R, which they believed was the case with *Ryan's Daughter* (1970—see below), *Valdez Is Coming* (1971), and the Woody Allen comedy *Bananas* (1971). Jack Valenti disputed their claims by insisting no other medium had regulated itself so closely as the motion picture industry, and public opinion, according to a poll taken by the Opinion Research Corporation, was on their side (64 percent found the ratings system useful).

In response to criticism and confusion over the Code, some changes were implemented in January of 1970. The age restrictions for R were changed (from sixteen to seventeen) as well as those for X (from no one under sixteen admitted to seventeen or eighteen, depending on the exhibitor and local and state ordinances). The change in the age limits was an attempt to broaden the R category so films containing a "shock" element (such as full frontal nudity), profanity (such as *fuck*), and strong sexual content would not automatically receive an X. In addition, the M (Mature) rating was replaced by GP (all ages admitted, parental guidance suggested) due to the misperception that an M (for Mature) rating automatically meant the film was not suitable for children of any age.

But the harshest criticism came from the inside the organization. Future *Movieline* film critic Stephen Farber had just received his M.A. in film history from UCLA when he was hired as a fellow, along with Estelle Changas, to the Code and Rating Administration Board, where they both participated in the rating process. In 1972, Farber chronicled his experiences on the board in his controversial book *The Movie Ratings Game*, in which he candidly identified the problems with the system: "overly harsh restrictions for sex, surprising leniency in rating violence;

the fact that ratings so often seemed determined by minor elements in a film, a bit of nudity or a four letter word." But the practice he found most disturbing, which contradicted Valenti's insistent claims that the ratings board was not a censorship board and their primary purpose was to provide information to parents, was the role board members of CARA were taking in reediting films and reshaping scripts. As in the old days, studios still submitted scripts to the ratings board, which responded with a list of recommended changes and deletions that should be made in order to achieve a desired rating. A similar process occurred when the film was submitted to the ratings board. Last-minute edits were being made at the suggestion of board members in order to insure the film received an R instead of an X or an M/GP/PG instead of an R.

Since its inception, the ratings system has been the source of controversy for many films, some of which have brought to light the faults of a system, especially the lack of consistency in assigning ratings and the board's leniency when it comes to violence as opposed to nudity and sex, particularly female sexuality.

RATINGS CONTROVERSIES

Ryan's Daughter (1970)

After their success with *Lawrence of Arabia* and *Doctor Zhivago*, director David Lean and writer Robert Bolt collaborated on this big-screen epic loosely based on Flaubert's *Madame Bovary*. Set in a small Irish village during World War I, *Ryan's Daughter* is the story of a schoolmaster's wife (Sarah Miles) who has an affair with a shell-shocked British officer (Christopher Jones) and is shunned for being an adulteress and wrongly accused of informing on the IRA. Unfortunately, the story doesn't warrant such an expensive and lavish production, beautifully shot by Freddie Young, who picked up his third Oscar (the first two were for *Lawrence* and *Zhivago*).

MGM, which was having financial problems, had a lot riding on *Ryan's Daughter* ($14 million to be exact), so when the film received an R instead of a GP from CARA, the studio announced its plans to market the film nationally with no mention of its rating. The R rating was reportedly due to the nude love scene between Miles and Jones, although according to Stephen Farber, the problem was not with the flash of her breast, but the suggestion that she was having an orgasm (see *Ecstasy* in chapter 5). The appeals board examined the five-minute scene in the context of the film and agreed that the themes it addressed were too "universal" to impose an R rating. At the same time, Farber suggests it was also known that MGM's financial future rested on the success of the film "and unless the rating was changed from R to GP, then MGM was going to die."

All the President's Men (1976): The "F" Word

Robert Redford and Dustin Hoffman star in this docudrama based on investigative reporters Bob Woodward and Carl Bernstein's account of how they uncovered the Watergate scandal, which led to the resignation of President Richard Nixon. The film has no sex or violence, but when it was submitted to the MPAA ratings board, it was slapped with an R rating due to the inclusion of the word *fuck* (and variations thereof). Under the "automatic language rule," which the Policy Review Committee had passed in April of 1976, all films with "sexually connotative language" would receive an R or X rating. Redford, whose Wildwood Productions produced the film, and Warner Brothers were not pleased with the decision. As part of their campaign to convince the appeals board to change the R to a PG, they submitted over two hundred affidavits from educators, social scientists, and religious representatives.

CARA Chairman Richard D. Heffner did not support the rating board's decision. In an apologetic letter to Redford, he praised the film ("a most important motion picture that surpasses in historical significance even the innovative reportorial book on which it is based") and explained the rationale for the language rule ("around this country too many ordinary parents will consider these words inappropriate for younger children . . . to classify any film that uses them as PG"). Heffner, who had a vote on the appeals committee, supported the reversal (which passed by a 19–2 vote), marking a significant change in CARA's policy governing language. But Jack Valenti claimed the appeals board decisions had no precedent value. "This judgment applies to this specific film only," Valenti told *Variety*, "*President's Men* contains no violence, no sex, and if it weren't for the language factor, it would be a G picture."

However, according to Heffner, a total of fifty-five films rated R based on the automatic language rule were subsequently reversed on appeal.

The Birth of PG-13: *Poltergeist* (1982), *Indiana Jones and the Temple of Doom* (1984), and *Gremlins* (1984)

The PG (Parental Guidance Suggested) rating was under fire from parents, critics, and movie theatre owners in the early 1980s due to a series of big studio releases that contained scenes that some felt were unsuitable for younger children. But the studios and the MPAA did not spring immediately into action. They were hesitant about tampering with the Code, particularly the PG rating, because 70 percent of the top ten highest-grossing films between the years 1980 and 1984 were rated PG; the remaining 30 percent were R (no G-rated films made the list).

One of the first films to raise questions about the suitability of film content in a PG-rated film was *Poltergeist*, a modern ghost story directed by Tobe Hooper and produced by Steven Spielberg. The plot revolves around a family's battle with ghosts who are trying to drive them out of their new home, which they discover was built over a graveyard, from which the headstones were removed, yet the coffins remain. The film includes several *very* intense scenes in which children are being terrorized by spirits (the scariest involving a clown doll and a tree that comes to life). In the film's climax, dozens of coffins and decaying corpses spring out of the ground. All in all, the film contains some pretty scary stuff (and not just for young kids). When *Poltergeist* was submitted to the ratings board, it received an R rating. The film's distributor, MGM/UA, appealed its decision and won (a rarity, considering in the past three years, only three of sixteen appeals were overturned). A PG rating for *Poltergeist* meant that a five-year-old could go see the film without a parent or guardian.

Two years later, Paramount anticipated it might get a similar reaction from parents over its upcoming release of another Spielberg production, the long-awaited sequel to *Raiders of the Lost Ark*, *Indiana Jones and the Temple of Doom*. Paramount included a warning in the ad ("This film may be too intense for younger children"), because parents who attended preview screenings with their kids complained about scenes of a living man's heart being torn out of his chest, children being flogged, and a caged man being immersed in a pit of boiling lava. Even Spielberg admitted in a television interview there were scenes in the film he would not allow his ten-year-old child to see. Aware their film contained scenes that were not suitable for all children, Spielberg and executive producer George Lucas issued a statement: "*Indy* is less violent than *Raiders*, but it's more intense. A story with children in jeopardy is going to get a more emotional reaction than a story with Indiana Jones battling Nazis."

Acknowledging there were PG-rated films that required a more restrictive rating, as well as R-rated films that could have carried a less restrictive rating, the MPAA started to consider the creation of a new rating that would fall somewhere between a PG and an R. Barry Diller, chairman of Paramount, was initially the only studio head advocating a change in the system. He believed a new category, R-13, should be added, which would lift the restriction on teenagers thirteen and over, but require children thirteen and under to be accompanied by a parent. In addition, he believed descriptive language should also be included to explain why a movie was being given a particular rating.

Gremlins, another PG-rated Spielberg production, was also criticized for graphic violence. Vincent Canby found the film more disorienting than *Poltergeist* and *Indiana Jones* because principal characters in the film are stabbed, run down, and killed violently. A film buyer in the Midwest reported that the violence prompted fifty people to walk out of a screening of *Gremlins.*

The new PG-13 rating went into effect on July 1, 1984. Among the first films to receive a PG-13 included *Red Dawn* (1984), in which teenage renegades defend America against Russian invaders; *Dreamscape* (1984), a sci-fi flick about people who can invade each other's dreams; and *The Woman in Red* (1984), an American remake of a French sex comedy.

Ironically, the decision to amend the ratings system did not receive the support of its creator, Jack Valenti, whose favorite saying was "If it ain't broke, don't fix it." However, Valenti succeeded, with the support of the theatre owners, to make the rating nonrestrictive because children do not carry IDs and it is difficult to tell the difference between a thirteen-year-old and someone younger.

The Birth of NC-17: *The Cook, The Thief, His Wife and Her Lover* (1989); *¡Átame! (Tie Me Up! Tie Me Down!*—1990), *Henry: Portrait of a Serial Killer* (1986), and *Henry & June* (1990)

The NC-17 was created in the early 1990s when a series of serious, non-pornographic films intended for an adult audience were given an X rating due to graphic violence and/or explicit sexual content. This time the complaints came from filmmakers, independent production companies, and some critics, who objected to the X rating, which had become synonymous with pornography and would severely limit both the marketing (many newspapers refused to run ads) and distribution of the film (many theatres had a "No X-film" policy).

Between the years 1989 and 1990, several films received an X from the MPAA, three of which appealed and lost: Peter Greenaway's delightfully perverse *The Cook, The Thief, His Wife and Her Lover*, Pedro Almodóvar's oddly romantic *¡Átame! (Tie Me Up! Tie Me Down)*, and John McNaughton's disturbing *Henry: Portrait of a Serial Killer*. Consequently, the distributors of all three films optioned to release their films without a rating. Almodóvar and *Tie Me Up!*'s U.S. distributor, Miramax Films, and Maljack Productions, producers of *Henry*, both filed lawsuits against the MPAA—the first since 1970, when director Joseph Strick sued over the X rating he received for his film adaptation of Henry Miller's *Tropic of Cancer*.

Miramax's counsel, William Kunstler, called the X rating "arbitrary, capricious and unreasonable" under Article 278 of the New York State Civil Practice Law and Rules. He also claimed there had been many other films with more explicit sex and violence that had not been given an X rating. But New York State Judge Charles E. Ramos disagreed, ruling that Kunstler failed to prove his case (he also inferred that Miramax brought the suit on for publicity purposes). In his thirteen-page decision, Judge Ramos also criticized the integrity of the MPAA in the way it rated movies, its lenient policy toward violence, and the make-up of the ratings board: "The industry that profits from scenes of mass murder, dismemberment and the portrayal of war as noble and glamorous apparently has no interest in the opinions of professionals, only the opinions of its consumers. There are no physicians, child psychiatrists or child care professionals on the board." Of course Valenti denied its leniency toward violence and defended the board, claiming "only parents have the authority and the responsibility to set value standards for their children."

Members of the Hollywood film community agreed that the present system needed to be overhauled. Over thirty Hollywood directors, including Francis Coppola, Jonathan Demme, Ron Howard, Spike Lee, Barry Levinson, Sydney Pollack, Rob Reiner, John Sayles, and John Schlesinger signed a petition, and met with Valenti to discuss the matter. In September of 1990, the MPAA agreed to nail the coffin shut on the X rating and replaced it with NC-17 (No Children Under 17). In addition, R ratings would now be accompanied by a brief explanation specifying why the film has been given an R—because of sex, violence, or other reasons. While the industry may have welcomed the changes, the National Council of Churches and the United States Catholic Conference were not pleased. In a joint statement, they accused the MPAA of having "caved in to the commercial interests of those who are attempting to get sexually exploitative material into general theatrical release. It is an arrogant and ill advised decision which deeply affects the public good."

The first film released with the new rating was director Phillip Kaufman's *Henry & June*, which chronicled the ménage à trois involving writer Henry Miller (Fred Ward), his wife June Miller (Uma Thurman), and French author Anaïs Nin (Maria de Medeiros). Although the critics seemed to agree it was not a perfect film, they praised Kaufman for taking a serious, intelligent, and uncompromising approach to the subject of eroticism. The film opened to sellout crowds, though moviegoers in conservative Orange County were greeted by protestors, who equated the film with pornography (despite the fact that the majority of them had not seen it). In Bedham, Massachusetts, a middle-class suburb located ten miles south of Boston, a movie theatre bowed to pressure from town officials and canceled the film (once again, the two officials admitted to not having seen the film). Meanwhile, Kaufman seemed to have the public's reaction to his film in perspective. "There are two sides that aren't going to like the film," he told an interviewer, "the prudish people and the prurient side. The prudish people I would suggest not see it. And the prurient, who want to see pornography or nudity beyond the nudity of this film, well I'm sorry. In a way, the real nudity lies in Anaïs' soul stripped bare, if I can be a little flowery about it."

Unfortunately, *Henry & June* did not open the studio doors for more NC-17 films made for and about consenting adults.

Clerks (1994): Potty Mouths

Kevin Smith's slacker comedy, *Clerks*, was shot after hours in a convenience store over three weeks for a mere $27,575. After taking home trophies from the 1994 Sundance and Cannes film festivals, Smith became the toast of the American indie scene and the inspiration for anyone with a camera to follow their dream and make a film. *Clerks* was picked up for distribution by Miramax, which hired defense attorney Alan Dershowitz when the film came back from the MPAA with an NC-17 rating based on profanity and frank sexual talk (like *All the President's Men*, there was no sex or violence). Miramax owner Harvey Weinstein claimed the MPAA had a clear double standard when it came to independent films vs. studio movies (case in point: *Natural Born Killers*, which Stone managed to trim down to get an R rating). Smith was shocked by the NC-17 rating. "It's a first-amendment issue," Smith explained. "You see *True Lies* and Arnold Schwarzenegger blows away over 100 people and it gets an R. There's not a frame of violence or nudity in my movie. What are they afraid of, a little language? Hang out in any convenience store or anyplace where there are young people and you'll hear that language."

At its hearing, Miramax submitted a petition supporting its appeal signed by screenwriter Callie Khouri (*Thelma & Louise* [1991]), filmmaker Cameron Crowe, and Stacey Sher and Danny DeVito, executive producers of another Miramax release, *Pulp Fiction* (1994). The appeal was overturned, which pleased Smith, who said, "Justice was done today. But you don't feel too celebratory when the film finally receives the rating it deserved all along."

CHAPTER 3

%@!%#@#—A Few Choice Words About Bad Language

In his autobiography, Will H. Hays recalls the discussions that took place at the MPPDA during the advent of the "talkies," regarding the challenge that the addition of sound, particularly dialogue, was going to pose to the industry's self-regulation of motion pictures:

> Still, I declared that as a matter of policy we ought to avoid expressions that would rub any notable section of the public the wrong way. And it is amusing to record that when we were ready for the Code and the Producers Committee went to work in 1930, this subject received more attention than any other. The use or non-use of profanity was discussed—incidentally, with plenty of profanity—at many meetings and until far into many a night.

When the Production Code was adopted in 1930, the censoring of obscene, profane, and blasphemous words, phrases, and expressions was hardly a new concept. Since ancient times, censors have believed it is their moral duty to protect the public from indecent language. But what exactly are censors protecting us from? What damage or harm can come from hearing an actor utter the word *hell* or *goddamn* or *asshole* or *motherfucker*?

Plenty!—at least according to Aristotle, who advocated legislation restricting the use of "improper language" in the theatre. The philosopher believed "the light utterance of shameful words leads to shameful acts," particularly for youth, who are apt to repeat the words they have heard. Over 2,000 years later, lawmakers debated the same issue when an ordinance was proposed in 1911 prohibiting the use of profanity on the New York stage. What constituted profanity was still a matter of opinion (one alderman insisted *darn* and *devil* should be included on the list), as was the necessity for a law that one politician claimed would "prevent God-fearing Christian people from having their sensibilities shocked."

Before shocking your sensibilities, it is necessary at this point to distinguish between three general types of indecent language: *profanity*, *blasphemy*, and *obscenity*:

- *Profanity* literally means "temporal, unholy, lacking sanctity . . . to be godless, to treat holy things in an irreverent manner." But in the present day, the term is no longer limited to exclamations like "Christ!" or "Go to hell!" but includes "secular" dirty words related to sex, excrement, and certain "naughty parts" of the body.
- *Blasphemy* expresses contempt for religion, religious doctrine, or authority, or the church as a whole (as in "To hell with your God!" or "To hell with the Pope!")
- *Obscenity* is a legal term defined as "disgusting to the senses . . . abhorrent to morality or virtue, designed to incite lust or depravity." Obscenities are often sexual in nature (i.e., *fuck, motherfucker, cocksucker, cunt, tits,* etc.). The FCC also uses the term "indecent language," which includes "milder obscenities and unsavory references through euphemism or circumlocution."

CURSING IN SILENCE: BEFORE THE CODE (PRE-1930)

Profanity and blasphemy could be "heard" in American films before pictures even started talking. Words and expressions like *hell, damn,* and *goddamn* were included in the titles of films and in dialogue for both dramatic effect and as part of everyday speech. For example, *hell* not only appears in the title of the western *Hell's Hinges* (1916), it adds an extra touch of sacrilege to the film's climactic scene in which the villain's henchmen decide to torch the town church, exclaiming, "TO HELL WITH THE CHURCH! Let's burn her down!" In *Foolish Wives* (1922), a scoundrel named Count Karamzin (Erich von Stroheim) seduces the wife of a U.S. diplomat who afterwards tells him to "Go to hell!" When Johnny Sims (James Murray) abruptly quits his position at the Atlas Insurance Company in King Vidor's *The Crowd* (1928), he exclaims, "To hell with this job! I'm through!" In wartime, *hell* is used in a colloquial sense in exchanges between two doughboys in *The Big Parade* (1925) ("Aw, they're making this a helluva army!") and two World War I fighter pilots who share a platonic kiss in *Wings* (1927) ("Friendship means a hell of a lot to you.")

As in *Hell's Hinges*, *hell* appeared in the titles of many films, such as *Hell Hath No Fury* (1917), *The Hell Ship* (1920), and the film adaptation of Hatcher Hughes's Pulitzer Prize–winning play, *Hell-Bent for Heaven* (1926). The word was particularly popular in the titles of Westerns, usually in reference to the film's setting: *The Passing of Hell's Crown* (1916), *The Hell Cat* (1918), *Hell Roarin' Reform* (1919), *Hell's Fury Gordon* (1919), *Hell's Oasis* (1920), *The Man From Hell's River* (1922), *Hell's Border* (1922), and *The Valley of Hell* (1927). One "*hell* title" that didn't make it past the Ohio Censorship Board belonged to an early John Ford western, *Hell Bent* (1918), which was changed to the far less menacing *Three Bad Men*. Sometimes a "*hell* title" could also be part of a title character's nickname, such as a lumberjack in *Hell-to-Pay Austin* (1916), a saloon owner in *Hell Morgan's Girl* (1917), and in the sound era, rodeo-rider *Hell-Fire Austin* (1932). In some instances, *hell* literally meant *hell*, as in the place where Satan and his demons like to party in the early animated Disney short, *Hell's Bells* (1929).

Other popular exclamations in silent films were *damn* and *goddamn*. In the climactic scene of *The Big Parade* (1925), soldier Jim (John Gilbert) loses it on the battlefield when his friend Slim (Karl Dane) is shot. "They got him! They got him!" he cries, "GOD DAMN THEIR SOULS!" In *Dr. Jekyll and Mr. Hyde* (1931), the disapproving Dr. Lanyon (Charles Lane) tells Dr. Jekyll (John Barrymore) that he doesn't approve of his experiments: "Damn it, I don't like it! You're tampering with the supernatural!" When Douglas Fairbanks's swashbuckling *Robin Hood* (1923) discovers Lady Marian Fitzwalter (Enid Bennett) is being held prisoner, he rushes to her rescue, but not before cursing her captors and shouting "Damn their black hides! I'll lash them 'til they bleat!"

Not all profane expressions appeared on title cards, yet sometimes it's obvious when an actor is mouthing a certain word or expression.

For example, in a dramatic moment in D. W. Griffith's *The Birth of a Nation*, Silas Lynch (George Siegmann) sees the dead body of "renegade negro" Gus (Walter Long). Raising his clenched fists, he cries out "Son of a bitch!" In a much lighter moment, a soldier mouths the same expression in *The Big Parade* when he is ordered to shovel manure.

The use of profanity in director Raoul Walsh's 1926 screen version of Maxwell Anderson and Laurence Stallings's hit stage play *What Price Glory* (1926) immediately caught the attention of critics. Set against the harsh realities of World War I, the character comedy revolves around the romantic rivalry of two military officers, a sergeant and a captain. When it debuted on Broadway in September of 1924, local censors targeted the play due to a complaint over its profane dialogue. On the evening of September 24, a New York City inspector, along with thirty-five plainclothes special service men, were stationed in and around the theatre, ready to shut the play down. But playwrights Anderson and Stallings, a veteran who lost his leg in World War I, had already deleted some of the words said in conjunction with *damn*, while other "rough epithets were omitted or softened." Consequently, no arrests were made that night or the following year in Boston, where all of the strong language was eliminated (Mayor Curley insisted the Marines speak in the stage trenches as if they were before their mothers and sisters). The profanity was also omitted from the titles of the screen version, but as British critic G. A. Atkinson observed, "There is nothing to prevent the actor from saying what he is obviously thinking, and experienced lip readers are frequently aware of strange screen confidences." *Variety* predicted that those who see the picture "are going to start tipping off on the cuss words used, words that can only be gotten by lip-reading, but the bunch that goes to see the picture will watch for that rough stuff." *The Hollywood Spectator* was less than enthusiastic: "Wherein does it profit us to photograph a man's lips so that the audience knows that he is uttering profanity not uttered in the presence of women?"

THE PRE-CODE ERA (1930–34)

The transition into sound coincided with the adoption of the Motion Picture Production Code in 1930, which prohibited obscenity (part 4) as well as profanity (part 5—see appendix H). The Code prohibited specific words ("God, Lord, Jesus, Christ—unless used reverently, Hell, S.O.B., damn, Gawd") and, to no doubt cover their bases, there was also an all-inclusive clause prohibiting "every other profane or vulgar expression." Still, in the so-called Pre-Code Era (between 1930 and 1934, when the Code was not fully enforced), films were not necessarily profanity or obscenity free.

For example, in *The Miracle Woman* (1931), Barbara Stanwyck stars as Florence Fallon, a preacher's daughter who loses faith and teams up with a con man named Hornsby (Sam Hardy). At one point Hornsby threatens to fire her chauffeur, who, when Hornsby's back is turned, gives him the middle finger.

On a much lighter note, MGM's "Flip the Frog" was a cartoon character created by Ub Iwerks Studio who appeared in a series of animated shorts in the Pre-Code Era. Even by today's standards, Flip's onscreen antics are a bit risqué, and his vocabulary, which included words like *hell* and *damn*, would certainly not have made it past the censors after 1934. For example, in *Room Runners* (1932), he tries to avoid his landlady because he owes back rent. He attracts attention to himself by falling down a flight of stairs. At that moment he turns to the audience and says, "Damn." In *The Milkman* (1932), a cow joins Flip and a little boy in a rendition of "Hail, Hail, the Gang's All Here." When the cow sings the second line, "What the hell do we care," Flip and the kid scold him by telling him, "You mustn't say the naughty word!"

Between the introduction of the Production Code in 1930 and its enforcement in 1934, *hell* continued to appear in the titles of Westerns (*Hell's Heroes* [1930], *The Man From Hell* [1934]), gangster films (*The Doorway to Hell* [1930]), screen adaptations of stage plays (*Guilty as Hell* [1932], *From Heaven to Hell* [1933]), dramatic stories of the Foreign Legion (*Hell's Island* [1930]), and prison chain gangs (*Hell's Highway* [1932]). *Hell* was also used to accentuate the bravery of butch American aviators in *Hell's Angels* (1930), directed by Howard Hughes; *Hell Divers* (1932), starring a young Clark Gable as a navy pilot; and *Hell in the Heavens* (1934), based on Herman Rossman's play *The Ace*.

Once the Production Code was fully enforced in 1934, it was more difficult to get "hell titles" approved by the censors. The producers of *Hell Diggers*, a 1938 drama about miners, were forced to change the title to *Fury Below* (1938—another miner film, *Black Hell* [1935], was released under the title *Black Fury* [1935]). One of the more absurd changes was to the title of a 1946 Roy Rogers film, *Heldorado*. Rogers plays a Nevada state ranger captain named Roy Rogers (coincidence?), who travels with his horse, Trigger (playing himself), to the annual Helldorado (that's with a double *l*) Frontier Days Festival in Las Vegas. Helldorado is actually the nickname given to Tombstone, Arizona by a disgruntled miner, who was expecting to be living in a boomtown brimming with gold (like the mythical Spanish city "El Dorado"), but instead found himself, like many others, doing menial work (thus the name "Helldorado"). The PCA apparently cringed at the thought of the letters *h-e-l-l* appearing on movie marquees, so one "l" was subtracted from the title.

One notable exception was *Hell-Ship Morgan* (1936), the story of a sea captain, Ira Morgan (George Bancroft), whose bride, Mary (Ann Sothern), falls in love with his best friend and crew member, Jim (Victor Jory). Mary tells Captain Morgan the truth, but their conversation is interrupted by a ravaging storm that hits the ship. When Jim falls overboard, Morgan rescues his friend and rival, but the captain is crippled for life in the process. In the end, he decides to commit suicide by jumping overboard into shark-infested waters.

The PCA had strong objections to Morgan's suicide: "It is our impression that it [suicide] always leaves a definitely unpleasant flavor in the minds of the spectator," wrote Joe Breen, "and is bound to have an unfavorable audience reaction." Will Hays did have to justify the inclusion of *Hell* in the title to Nicholas M. Schenck, a MPPDA board member who at the time was the head of MGM's parent company, Loews Inc. Schenck wanted to register the title *Hell's Heroes*, prompting Hays to remind him of a board meeting back in 1932 when they discussed the overwhelming number of titles "incorporating the term" and the criticism they were receiving "from all directions including censor boards, church, and civic leaders." Hays also listed several titles that were rejected and explained that *Hell-Ship Morgan* was the only exception because "Columbia called attention to the fact that the term 'hell-ship' had a very definite usage to describe a ship where cruelty towards the crew was the rule. . . . The decision [by the board] that its usage should be allowed . . . should not be considered a precedent or in any way a letting down of the policy in this regard."

Although studios did not adhere to the Code during the Pre-Code Era, the Studio Relations Committee, under the leadership of Colonel Jason Joy, did its best to exert its influence over the content of scripts. While some filmmakers simply disregarded the Code, others directly challenged it when they were instructed to delete objectionable words. For example, the screen version of Sinclair Lewis's novel *Arrowsmith* (1931) contains four *hells*—all of which are uttered by the film's title character, a dedicated medical researcher (Ronald Colman) who has developed an experimental serum to prevent the spread of a deadly plague. He travels to the West Indies with his devoted wife, Leora (Helen Hayes), who is exposed to the plague and dies. Arrowsmith decides to abandon his experiment and distribute the serum to all who need it. In a drunken stupor, the grieving scientist denounces his work and his mentor (Gottlieb) and cries, "To hell with the experiment! To hell with science! To hell with Gottlieb!"

Colonel Jason Joy was pleased with the film, but reminded producer Samuel S. Goldwyn that the lines containing "hell" were in violation of the Code. Joy and Will Hays eventually decided to make an exception and proposed an amendment to the Code, stating, "Only where they are required for development of plot or where their use is essential to the realistic presentation, are the less offensive expletives permitted." The statement was approved by the Hays Office but voted down by the board of directors, who had the final say regarding any proposed changes to the Code.

Two years later, the inclusion of two *hells* and one *damn* posed a similar problem for *Cavalcade* (1933), the saga of two British families whose lives are forever changed over the course of three decades by a series of personal tragedies and historical events, including the sinking of the *Titanic* and World War I. The film, based on a play by Noel Coward, was well received by critics and won three Oscars—Best Picture, Best Director (Frank Lloyd), and Best Art Direction. After seeing the film, James Wingate, who took over for Colonel Joy in 1933 as the head of the Studio Relations Committee, informed Will Hays that he did not consider the inclusion of the word *hell* to be pointed profanity because it is spoken by "a fine type of cultured English gentleman and his son" during a discussion about the war:

FATHER: Any idea what a war costs?

SON: Hell of a lot, I suppose.

FATHER: Hell of a lot. And the Germans can afford it even less than we can.

While Hays believed the word *hell* in this case was neither "required for the development of the plot" nor was even "essential to the realistic presentation of the subject," its use was justified when it related to war. His only concern was setting another precedent, as *Arrowsmith* had done, to make an exception to the policy. "Each time this is done, of course," he warned, "it is harder for you to avoid it in cases less justifiable." After seeing the film ("It is a very great picture—a very great picture. . . . I was deeply moved"), Hays concluded that *hell* is not "pointed profanity" and will probably go unnoticed by the audience, yet he was still convinced that someone in the future would use it to justify the use of the word in another film. He did not feel the same way about the word *damn*, which he considered "pointed profanity" and would come back to haunt them in the future:

Here again it is a case where it will probably bring no bad audience reaction but inter-company-wise it will be pointed to, and in some later sequence in another picture you will be told that it was used here and recognition will not then be given to the circumstances in *Cavalcade* in which it is used nor to the glory of the picture.

Ironically, the first major controversy to erupt over the profanity clause and the Production Code Administration was over the inclusion of the word *damn* in the dramatic conclusion of *Gone with the Wind* (1933). In Sidney Howard's screenplay, Rhett Butler (Clark Gable) walks out on his wife, Scarlett O'Hara (Vivien Leigh), who cries, "Rhett, Rhett . . . Rhett, if you go, where shall I go? What shall I do?" His reply is one of the most famous lines in American film history: "Frankly, my dear, I don't give a damn." (In Margaret Mitchell's bestselling novel, the line is "My dear, I don't give a damn.") Joseph Breen repeatedly reminded producer David O. Selznick that the line had to be changed because *damn* violated the Code. As Breen explained to Will Hays, Selznick was adamant about including the line:

David seems to think that because this picture is a screen dramatization of a really great American novel, it is a sort of classic and that, as such, should be permitted to use this line from the book, which is so well known to millions of readers, and he is quite set in his thought. So much so he tells us that he proposes to appeal from our decision to you.

In a letter dated October 20, 1939, Selznick informed Hays that he intended to keep the film's "punch line" and stated his case for its inclusion:

It is my contention that this word as used in the picture is not an oath or a curse. The worst that could be said against it is that it is a vulgarism, and it is so described in the Oxford English Dictionary. . . . A canvass of the popular magazines shows that even such moral publications as *Woman's Home Companion*, *Saturday Evening Post*, *Collier's*, and the *Atlantic Monthly*, use this word freely. I understand the difference, as outlined in the code, between the written word and the word spoken from the screen, but at the same time I think the attitude of these magazines toward "damn" gives an indication that the word itself is not considered abhorrent or shocking to audiences.

Although Selznick doesn't mention it in his letter, there was a precedent for the inclusion of the word in a film based on a literary source. In 1937, Warner Brothers released a short based on the Edward Everett Hale's novel *The Man Without a Country*. First published anonymously as a short story back in 1863, *Country* is the story of a U.S. army lieutenant, Philip Nolan (John Litel), who is accused of treason and renounces his country at his trial by declaring, "Damn the United States! I wish I may never hear of the United States again!" His wish is granted and he is exiled from his homeland and confined to a ship at sea where he will never hear or read a single word about the United States again (the infamous line—cuss word and all—was quoted by a little boy who recites the Hale story in another film, *Pride of the Marines* [1936]). The PCA justified the inclusion of the line in both films, as in *Arrowsmith*, because it was a "technical violation" and did not "violate the *intent*, or *spirit*, of the Code." But apparently everyone did not agree: the line was cut from all prints by the Massachusetts Film Censor Board.

Of course Selznick appealed the PCA's decision regarding *Gone with the Wind*, and the film was granted a seal in October of 1939. The offscreen saga resulted in the adoption of an amendment to the Code on November 1, 1939 (see appendix H). The amendment contained two major revisions. First, a clause was added allowing *hell* and *damn* if they are "essential and required, in proper historical context," in a scene or dialogue based on historical fact or folklore, the Bible, or a literary work provided it's not objectionable and in good taste. Second, thirty additional words (see table B) were added to the list, along with an obscene gesture (the finger) and a sound (listed twice as the "Bronx Cheer" and "the razzberry"). In addition, three types of jokes/gags were forbidden under the Code: "toilet gags," "Farmer's Daughter jokes," and "Traveling Salesman jokes." The forbidden words and phrases are mostly slang—and the majority of them are derogatory names for promiscuous women and effeminate men.

In *Hollywood's Movie Commandments*, a handbook for motion picture writers and reviewers published two years prior to the 1939 Amendment, author Olga J. Martin, a former secretary to Joseph Breen, gives wannabe writers tips on how to approach and/or avoid certain topics and themes related to crime, sex, marriage, prostitution, and religion. In a chapter entitled "Vulgarity," Martin offers an even more extensive list of forbidden words, including several racial epithets: *Chink* (Chinese), *Dago* (Italian/Spanish), *Frog* (French), *Hun* (Eastern European), *Kike* (Jewish), *Nigger* (African American), and *Wop* (Italian). Immediately after the end of World War II, the MPAA approved an amendment prohibiting the use of racial epithets—words and phrases "obviously offensive" to American audiences "and more particularly to the patrons of motion pictures in foreign countries" (see appendix H). The Production Code list included all of the epithets listed above (along with *Hunkie* for *Hun*), which, with the exception of the terms for Jews and African Americans, were derogatory names for our allies during World War II. Missing from the list were racist terms for the two major Axis powers, which explains why in World War II films produced during the war (*Air Force* [1943], *Journey* [1943], *Destination Tokyo* [1943], *Thirty Seconds over*

TABLE B Forbidden Words/Expressions/Sounds/Gestures & Their Meanings

1939 Amendment to Motion Picture Production Code

Note: The 1939 Amendment lists the words, but not their meanings.

Word/Expression/ Sound/Gesture	Meaning
Alley cat	Promiscuous woman; a prostitute
Bat (applied to a woman)	Streetwalker, prostitute
Broad	Promiscuous woman
Bronx Cheer (the sound)	Verbal expression of derision
Chippie	Promiscuous young woman; a prostitute
Cocotte	Female prostitute
Fairy (in a vulgar sense)	Effeminate man
Fanny	Buttocks
The Finger	"F—k you!"
Cries of "Fire!"	A character can not yell "Fire!" in a movie because someone might misinterpret it as real and the crowd might panic
Goose (in a vulgar sense)	To pinch or poke someone in the buttocks
Hold your hat(s)	Be prepared for something shocking
Hot	Sexually promiscuous woman
In your hat	Dismissive response
Louse	Mean, contemptible person
Lousy	Anything or anyone causing an unfavorable impression
Madam (relating to prostitution)	Woman running a house of prostitution
Nance	Effeminate man
Nerts	Exclamation of incredulity or disgust
Nuts (expect when meaning crazy)	Expression of disdain, disgust, or derision
Pansy	Effeminate man
Razzberry (the sound)	Expression of derision
Slut	Promiscuous woman
SOB	Son-of-a-Bitch
Son-of-a	You could not use the phrase son-of-a even if it is cut off before the speaker says bitch
Tart	Promiscuous woman; prostitute
Tomcat (applied to a man)	Man on the prowl for sexual conquests
Whore	Promiscuous woman; a prostitute

Tokyo [1944]) as well as after (*Sands of Iwo Jima* [1949], *Battleground* [1949], *Stalag 17* [1953], *Run Silent Run Deep* [1958]), our fighting boys referred to the Japanese as *Japs* and *Nips*, and the Germans as *Krauts*.

BASTARDS: AT HOME AND ABROAD

Bastard was not one of the eight words forbidden by the 1930 Production Code, nor did it appear on the longer list of "profane" and "vulgar" words or expressions added to the Code in the 1939 amendment. But both versions of the Code state that the list is not exclusive and the rule applies to all profanity, which justified its deletion beginning in the early 1940s from screenplays and the final cuts of narrative features and documentary films submitted to the PCA.

For instance, the PCA's handiwork is evident in the screen adaptation of Joseph Kesserling's hit Broadway comedy *Arsenic and Old Lace* (1944). The film stars Cary Grant as drama critic Mortimer Brewster, who discovers his two sweet old spinster aunts (Josephine Hull, Jean Adair) have been murdering their elderly male tenants and burying their bodies in the cellar. In the final scene of both the play and the film, Mortimer, afraid that insanity runs in his family, is relieved to learn he is not related by blood to his crazy aunts and lunatic uncle. But the censors forced the filmmakers to alter the "big reveal" about Mortimer's lineage and, in the process, changed the play's memorable punch line.

In the play, Mortimer's Aunt Abby explains that when his mother came to work for them as a cook, she was pregnant and unmarried. They didn't want to lose her, so their brother married her. Upon hearing the news, an overjoyed Mortimer turns to his bride and declares, "Elaine! Did you hear? Do you understand? I'm a bastard!" When Columbia Pictures studio chief Harry Cohen submitted the play to the Hays Office for their approval, the PCA report stated that "the indication that Mortimer is a bastard is, of course, unacceptable, and must be changed." Consequently, screenwriters Julius J. and Philip G. Epstein changed Mortimer's back story to imply that his mother was a widow and his father a "chef on a trapped steamer." He breaks the news to Elaine by declaring, "I'm not a Brewster. I'm the son of a sea cook!" On paper the substitution, a euphemism for "son-of-a-bitch," makes sense, though it's hardly the comical equivalent to someone declaring he's a "bastard." The change did not go unnoticed by the critic for the *Hollywood Reporter*, who acknowledged "those who saw the play will miss the terrific tag which, unfortunately, is barred from films by the Production Code."

The fact that the change received little if any attention is surprising considering the negative press the Hays Office had recently received over the deletion of the word from two films about the current war. *Bastard* (along with *hell*, *God*, and *lousy*) was deleted from the soundtrack of the British import *In Which We Serve* (1942). The military drama is loosely based on the true story of the British Navy destroyer the H.M.S. Kelly, which was sunk by German planes in the Battle of Crete. Directors David Lean and Noel Coward (who penned the screenplay and plays the ship's captain) aimed to offer a realistic depiction of Navy life, including some salty language (at least by 1940s standards). The word *bastard* is uttered at two separate points in the film—both times in reference to the enemy. The first time comes after the ship has been destroyed and German planes continue to shoot at the British crew as they float helplessly in the water ("Look out, here comes the bastards again!" warns one of the crew). The second time is when they are standing on the deck of the rescue ship and German bombs can still be heard going off in the distance ("Of all the persistent bastards—you'd think they'd get tired").

The Hays Office was attacked on both sides of the Atlantic. An editorial in the *New York Herald Tribune* called it a "preposterous decision," pointing out that the film was seen by King George VI and Queen Elizabeth, Winston Churchill, and Eleanor Roosevelt. While the word might offend American audiences if "used indiscriminately or in one of the Hollywood's versions of what life is like," in *In Which We Serve* it is "natural and unobtrusive." One British government official even resorted to name calling (but no profanity). On the floor of the British House of Commons, Information Minister Brendan Bracket denounced the Hollywood censors for their "squeamishness and old maiden aunt–like apprehensions."

The film's producers appealed the PCA decision on the grounds that the filmmakers' intentions were to make an honest and realistic film about national war heroes. Furthermore, there is "nothing profane, indecent, or wrong in the use of the word." As evidence, their written appeal included a passage of a speech delivered over shortwave radio to the people of Italy by New York Mayor LaGuardia, in which he described Mussolini and his government as "bastards of Fascisti."

As its denial of their appeal explains, the PCA was not interested in patriotism or realism:

> The function of the Production Code is not to be patriotic, it is to be moral. The function of the Production Code is not create authenticity nor realism. The Code cannot be sufficiently elastic to accommodate itself to the impulse of the individual to be any of these things. The Code is the chart. It is the frame of our society. It is the collateral which guarantees our public trust.

The appeal continued by explaining that one can be patriotic without being profane, and there is nothing dignified (even if it's Mayor LaGuardia) about publicly calling someone a "bastard." (When it comes to name calling, is there a "dignified" name for a fascist dictator?)

The PCA allowed some of the other choice words to remain but granted a seal provided United Artists dubbed the word *bastard*, which they reportedly did without putting anything in its place (apparently it was clear from watching the actor's lips what he was saying). Despite the omission of a few words, *In Which We Serve* was praised by critics. The New York Film Critics and the National Board of Review both voted the film Best Picture. In addition to receiving two Academy Awards nominations (Best Picture and Screenplay) in 1943, Noel Coward received an Honorary Award the previous year ("for his outstanding production achievement").

The PCA apparently didn't discriminate when it came to patriotism. Around the same time *In Which We Serve* reached theatres, another battle was being waged between the PCA and Twentieth Century Fox over *We Are the Marines*, a feature-length documentary about the U.S. Marines, which is part of the studio's *March of Time* series. The PCA informed the production company that it must remove the words *hell*, *damn*, and *bastard*, which once again refers to the enemy ("Okay boys, blow the bastards out of the water. Commence firing."). In appealing the decision, the producers also claimed that the words were included to give "a realistic and accurate portrayal of the Marine Corps" and therefore could "in no way be considered intrinsically objectionable or offensive to good taste." More specifically, in regards to the word *bastard*, the appeal notes that the word is not expressly prohibited in the Code or the Production Code Administration's "Words and Phrases," and then notes "an exception must be read into the Code similar to that relating to the words *damn* and *hell*, and that's where it is essential to a realistic and accurate portrayal of an historical event to use the word, then its use should not be prohibited."

In its response, the PCA contended, as they had done in the past, that realism was not a legitimate reason for offensive language. They also addressed the word *bastard* and the word's literal meaning in more specific terms:

> *Bastard* as a word has a single valuation. It indicates birth out of wedlock. It does not reflect upon the person to whom it is addressed but upon his parentage; some of our greatest personages are known to have been bastards. Thousands of our justly respected people are bastards. It is not difficult to realize the poignant hurt use of that word gives these defenseless people. So the truth is we have no authenticity calling all Japanese bastards. Colloquially, the use of the word is vulgar. It is offensive. It is cheap. It reflects nothing but a limitation upon the author's power of expression.

In other words, *bastard* is prohibited because it is offensive to anyone who was born out of wedlock. (Does that mean *bitch* is offensive to female dogs and their owners?)

Bastard eventually made it past the censors, first in written form in the opening crawl of another war film, *Battleground* (1949). The drama recounts the events surrounding the Battle of Bastogne, in which the American 101st Airborne Division and the U.S. 10th Armored Division occupied the town of Bastogne, Belgium in an effort to stop the Germans who were advancing from all directions. After the opening titles, the crawl reads: "This story is about, and dedicated to, those Americans who met General Heinrich von Luttwitz and his 47 Panzer Corps and won for themselves the honored and immortal name 'The Battered Bastards of Bastogne.'"

Although *bastard* was censored (along with the word *tart*) from the screenplay of the British crime drama *The Blue Lamp* (1950), it's a mystery how it was allowed to remain in the print released in July of 1950. In its report on the script, the PCA instructed the producers, the J. Arthur Rank Organisation, to eliminate the words *tart* (in reference to a girl) and *bastard* and the expression "For God's Sake." Seven months later, producer Sir Michael Balcon sent a wire to the PCA describing the "American version" of the film, which included the substitution of *rat* for the word *bastard* in reel 10. The film received a seal, yet documents in the PCA film indicate that the word *bastard* remained, because the Massachusetts Censor Board required the word be deleted from reel 10.

The word's literal meaning added an air of historical authenticity to Otto Preminger's long-awaited screen version of George Bernard Shaw's *Saint Joan* (1923). The play was first submitted by producer Joseph Schenck back in 1935, but Will Hays rejected it on the basis that Shaw's "satiric and ironic" treatment of St. Joan and the various religious characters "will be found dangerous and objectionable from the point of view of the Catholic Church." When the play was submitted again in 1943, Joseph I. Breen's response to Gabriel Pascal, who produced the film versions of Shaw's *Pygmalion* (1938), *Major Barbara* (1941), *Caesar and Cleopatra* (1945), and *Androcles and the Lion* (1952), stated that *bastard*, along with *damn, damned, goddamn,* and *by God,* must be eliminated. The 1957 Preminger version did contain language that one reviewer referred to as "startling," particularly the reference to Count Jean de Dunois as "the Bastard" (of Orleans—played by Richard Todd).

By the 1960s, *bastard* was uttered more frequently, but in a more colloquial sense. *Bastard* along with *bloody* and *bleedin'* added to the "kitchen sink" realist style of the 1960 film version of Alan Sillitoe's 1958 novel *Saturday Night and Sunday Morning.* Borrowing an expression popularized by U.S. General Joseph W. Stilwell in World War II, a rebellious factory worker named Arthur Seaton (Albert Finney) declares, "Don't let the bastards grind you down!" Female characters also started using the word for dramatic effect when expressing their disgust toward men of questionable character. In *Hud* (1963), Alma (Patricia Neal) wards off the advances of the amoral, cocky, and sexy Hud Bannon (Paul Newman) by equating him with her ex-husband. ("No thanks," she tells him. "I've done my time with one cold-blooded bastard. I'm not looking for another.") In the final scene of director John Ford's final film, *7 Women*, Dr. Cartwright (Anne Bancroft) spikes the wine of evil Chinese warlord Tunga Khan (Mike Mazurki) with poison, and then joins him in a toast ("So long, ya bastard!"). The British comedy *I'll Never Forget What's'isname* (1967), which is cited as one of the earliest films released in the United States containing the word *fuck*, includes a scene in which actor/singer Marianne Faithfull screams "You fucking bastard!" at ex-boyfriend Jonathan Lute (Oliver Reed). Lute, an advertising executive, catches the moment on film and includes it in a commercial for a home movie camera, which he turns into an autobiographical piece about his failed relationships.

When it comes to men and women, the term *bastard* can also serve a dual purpose as a "putdown" and a pseudo–term of endearment. In the closing lines of *Two for the Road*, husband Mark (Albert Finney) and wife Joanna (Audrey Hepburn) exchange pleasantries by calling each other a *bitch* and a *bastard*, respectively. In the Code-breaking film version of *Who's Afraid of Virginia Woolf?*, Martha (Elizabeth Taylor) laughs up a storm and cries "You bastard!" when George surprises their horrified guests by shooting a rifle at her, which opens up into an umbrella. Of course, some men admitted to being a *bastard*. In *The Night They Raided Minsky's* (1968), Raymond Paine (Jason Robards) explains to a younger, love-stricken Chick Williams (Norman Wisdom) that "women love bastards" and that he is a "BFC—Bastard First Class." In *Cactus Flower* (1969), dentist Julian Winston (Walter Matthau) takes it one step higher and admits to girlfriend Toni Simmons (Goldie Hawn) that he's "the biggest bastard in the whole world!"

Now that *bastard* is widely used in both films and on television, it's necessary to combine it with another word. For example, *fucking bastard*, *rat bastard*, and *stupid bastard* are often the insult of choice, particularly among the testosterone-charged characters that populate the testosterone-driven films of Guy Ritchie, Robert Rodriguez, Martin Scorsese, and Quentin Tarantino.

THE BRONX CHEER, A.K.A. THE RAZZBERRY

Dating back to the late 1920s, the "Bronx Cheer" is verbal expression popular among New York Yankee fans to relay their displeasure with the umpire and/or the opposing team. An April, 1928 *Time* magazine story about another sporting event—the Stanley Cup finals—attributed the New York Rangers' surprise victory over the Montreal Marions to New York's goalie, Joe Miller, who had replaced the team's injured starter. His lack of skill made him unpopular with fans, who, according to *Time* magazine, gave him "what's locally known as the Bronx Cheer, a huzzah of sarcastic intention." Miller reportedly "begged to be sent back to the minor leagues 'where they wouldn't razz him.'" *Razz* is short for *razzberry*, another word for the same sound that appeared alongside "Bronx Cheer" when both were added to the PCA's list of profane words and phrases in 1939.

In the early 1930s, "talkies" incorporated the Bronx Cheer into movie dialogue in creative ways. In *Pardon Us* (1931), prisoners Laurel and Hardy win the respect of a tough inmate known as "The Tiger" (Walter Long), who mistakes the sound made by Laurel's loose tooth as a "razzberry." "Put'er there," he says, "You're the first guy who had the nerve to razzberry the Tiger." A waitress named Mary (Joan Blondell) sends one from offscreen to her boyfriend Bill (Grant Withers) when she breaks up with him for refusing to marry her in *Other Men's Women* (1931). Mickey Mouse's motorcycle makes a razzberry sound when he starts it up in *The Dog Napper* (1934), and although the Hays Office did not censor it, the Kansas Censorship Board did. In the Van Beuren Studio's animated *Circus Capers* (1930), a mouse dressed as a clown (who could easily be mistaken for Mickey) attracts the attention of a female mouse (a dead ringer for Minnie). When she puckers up for a kiss, he gives her the razzberry, which causes her bloomers to fall as she spins through the air and faints. As in other films, the razzberry was soon banned from animated films. A 1939 article that appeared in *Look* magazine entitled "Hollywood Censors Its Animated Cartoons" offered illustrated examples of the impact the Hays Code had on the way cartoon characters looked (cartoon animals were now required to wear clothes) and behaved (bad guys must be punished). Among the illustrations is a picture of a little boy blowing the razzberry with the caption: "A nice little boy doesn't stick out his tongue and doesn't give the 'razzberry,' so scenes (and sounds) like this are eliminated in animated cartoons."

Around the same time, the Bronx Cheer was also making newspaper headlines. In November of 1933, the *New York Times* reported that a witness in a Toledo murder trial of mobster Serafino Sinatra (a.k.a. Joseph "Wop" English) demonstrated the Bronx Cheer in open court. The violence was apparently sparked when local night club owner and bootlegger Jack Kennedy was driving by a downtown intersection when mobster John Mirabella, who was standing on the corner with Sinatra and another associate, greeted him with a Bronx Cheer. A fight broke out, ending with Kennedy's death by gunfire. According to the *New York Times*, the witness "demonstrated by contorting his lips, protruding his tongue slightly, and exhaling vigorously through his mouth." A second demonstration of what another witness called a "razzberry" was reportedly "far more elegant and refined." As for the judge—he was "unable to devise a method of incorporating a Bronx Cheer into the trial record."

Five years later, the Bronx Cheer itself would go on trial when a man sitting in a movie theatre watching *Mutiny on the Bounty* became increasingly annoyed at the woman sitting behind him, who kept telling her friend what was going to happen next. He turned around and gave her the Bronx Cheer, which, according to a judge, was perfectly legal and justified. The judge stated that he "had considerable experience with the Bronx Cheer" because he was formerly the counsel for the Brooklyn Dodgers. The Bronx Cheer was also part of a major international news story in August of 1936 when a debate erupted over the reception of the American athletes during the opening ceremony of the Olympic Games in Nazi Berlin. The *New York Times* reported that some witnesses believed that some German spectators gave the Americans 'the German equivalent of the 'Bronx Cheer'," which was described as "whistling," though it remained unclear whether it actually came from "enthusiastic American spectators" or from the Germans in response to the United States' refusal to dip its flag, which is never done in accordance with the United States Flag Code.

By the late 1930s, the PCA requested the removal of all Bronx Cheers, from both "A list" productions, such as Lillian Hellman's adaptation of Sidney Kingsley's hit Broadway play *Dead End* (1937), and B-films, like the Joe Penny comedy *The Day the Bookies Wept* (1939).

Two animated shorts managed to get around the censors. In 1942, Walt Disney Studios produced the Academy Award winning animated short *Der Fuehrer's Face*, starring Donald Duck as a factory worker loyally serving the Fuehrer in Nazi Germany. Fortunately, it's only a nightmare, and at the end Donald is relieved to wake up in the "good ole USA." The short is based on a novelty song popularized by Spike Jones and his City Slickers that mocks Hitler and the Third Reich:

Ven der Fuehrer says, "Ve iss der master race,"

Ve HEIL! [sound] HEIL! [sound] Right in der Fuehrer's face!

In Jones's version of the song, the "razzberry" follows each "HEIL," therefore sounding as if one is breaking wind "right in der Fuehrer's face!" Disney used the song for the basis of its cartoon, though due to the Code's "no razzberry rule," the sound after each "HEIL," is a sousaphone played by Japanese Emperor Hirohito, who is part of a marching band (with Italian dictator Mussolini on the bass drum) that marches through a German town. The music wakes up Donald Duck, who has his breakfast (a piece of stale bread) and reports to the factory, where he screws the caps onto the top of artillery shells as they pass on a conveyor belt, along with photos of the Fuehrer's face. He must *Heil!* each photo as it passes by. As the pace quickens, he becomes disoriented, but eventually wakes up and discovers it was all a dream. He sees a small replica of the Statue of Liberty and gives it a hug. The cartoon ends with the image of Hitler's face and the song's closing line: "Not to love the Fuehrer is a great disgrace. So we Heil! Heil! Right in the Feuhrer's face." At that point, a tomato is thrown into his face and a "razzberry" is heard on the soundtrack. One of the cartoon's writers, Joe Grant, claimed that only because it was wartime, the Hays Office reluctantly let it stay in.

Two years later, the Hays Office allowed a silent razzberry pass the censors in the MGM cartoon *Screwball Squirrel* (1944). Legendary animator Tex Avery introduced a new cartoon character, Screwy Squirrel, an off-the-wall, somewhat anarchistic squirrel who spends most of his time torturing and committing acts of cartoon violence on a pedigree birddog named Meathead. At one point he is at a phone booth talking to Meathead, teasing the dog by telling him he is incapable of chasing squirrels. He turns to the audience and says "Pardon me," and then closes the phone booth door. You then see (but don't hear) Screwy giving a Bronx Cheer into the phone. The soundtrack resumes once he exits the phone booth, where he is confronted by an angry hound.

There is evidence that the PCA was still enforcing the gag order on the razzberry through the mid-1950s. The producers of both *Blackboard Jungle* (1955), a gritty drama about juvenile delinquency in an urban public school, and *Guys and Dolls* (1955), the big-screen adaptation of the long-running Broadway musical, were reminded when they submitted early drafts of their respective scripts that the Bronx Cheer is forbidden under the Code.

The spirit of the razzberry lives on in Hollywood in the form of "The Razzies," the annual awards given each year to honor the worst of Hollywood (visit www.razzies.com). Among the Worst Films that have received the coveted Razzie statue (it's a golden raspberry [as in the fruit] on a pedestal) over the years have included *Basic Instinct 2* (2006), *Battlefield Earth* (2000), *Gigli* (2003), *Hudson Hawk* (1991), *Showgirls* (1995), *Striptease* (1996), and *Swept Away* (2002).

BREAKING THE CODE

The Moon Is Blue (1953): "Affection, but No Passion"

The Moon Is Blue is a sex comedy minus the sex. While the film's romantic leads—architect Don Gresham (William Holden) and struggling actress Patty O'Neill (Maggie McNamara)—do share a kiss or two, they never hit the sheets. In fact, they never make it into the bedroom (at least at the same time). Still, in light of all the controversy that swirled around *The Moon Is Blue*—the first film by a Hollywood studio to be released without a seal from the Production Code Administration—audiences in 1953 were probably thinking the screen version of the successful Broadway play was going to be provocative, racy, and maybe even a little lascivious. But what they got instead was a chaste, conventional, and very moral romantic comedy about two modern New Yorkers in love.

The plot, which takes place within a twenty-four hour period, begins on the top of the Empire State Building, where Don puts the moves on Patty. That very same morning, Don had broken off his pseudo-engagement with his ex-fiancée (and neighbor), Cynthia Slater (Dawn Addams), who becomes insanely jealous when she sees Patty going into Don's apartment. While Don is forced to meet his manipulative ex-fiancée for a drink, Cynthia's father, David (David Niven), a charming, wealthy rogue, moves in on the virtuous Patty. She kisses him when he offers her a $600 gift (no strings attached), which is interrupted by Cynthia and Don. The chances of Don and Patty's future as a couple is further complicated by the sudden appearance of her father, who gives Don a black eye and drags his daughter away. By morning, the misunderstandings are cleared up and the couple reunites where they met the previous day—on the top of the Empire State Building.

The Moon Is Blue bears a slight resemblance to the screwball/romantic comedies of the 1930s/early 1940s (*It Happened One Night* [1934], *Bringing Up Baby* [1938], *The Lady Eve* [1941]) in which the female characters defy their traditional gender roles by having the upper hand over the males (at one point Don even calls Patty a "screwball"). Patty can hold her own when she squares off with a long-time bachelor like Don, whose confidence begins to dissipate as she continually surprises him with her forward demeanor when it comes to sexual matters. Apparently she was also a bit too forward for the PCA, which rejected both the screenplay and the final cut of the film for two reasons.

First, there was the provocative language, more specifically, the words *seduce, virgin, mistress,* and *pregnant,* all of which are the topic of conversation. But what makes the use of these words all the more provocative is they are uttered by Patty as a means of establishing her character as a modern girl (at least on the surface) who talks openly about sex (but hasn't necessarily lost her virginity). She catches Don off guard when she asks him point blank, "Will you try to seduce me?" and "Do you have a mistress?" The filmmakers are obviously aware that the audience may be shocked by what they are hearing during the "seduction discussion," which most likely accounts for the presence of a cab driver (played by Gregory Ratoff, who was Max Fabian in *All About Eve*

[1950]), who, as a sort of stand-in for the audience, reacts to their conversation and even becomes protective of Patty (he has three daughters) as he drops them off in front of his apartment. Patty may talk like a modern woman, yet deep down she is an old-fashioned girl, who is not career driven, but "dying" to get married and have children (preferably with someone who is rich and has already been married before). Don promises to be on his best behavior, promising "affection—but no passion. My word of honor." She is impressed by his motto and suggests that he could "run for president with that."

But the four "dirty words" were not the sole or even the main reason why the PCA refused to approve the script and grant the completed film a seal. The real issue is morality or rather what the PCA perceived as a *lack* of morality, as expressed in PCA Director Joseph Breen's rejection letter to producer/director Otto Preminger, in which he states the screenplay "is unapprovable under the requirements of the Production Code. . . . [I]t contains an unacceptably light attitude towards seduction, illicit sex, chastity and virginity." The list of "unacceptable material" includes specific lines (i.e., "Men are usually bored with virgins") and makes reference to dialogue exchanges (about *seduction, mistresses, pregnancy,* etc.). To Preminger and screenwriter Herbert's credit, two bits of dialogue from the script do not appear in the final film: "the broken expression 'son of a . . . '" and a reference to marijuana. According to Jack Vizzard, who was employed at the PCA at the time, the comedy violated the clause of the Code stating, "Pictures shall not infer that low forms of sex relationship are the accepted or common thing." From the perspective of the PCA, "the story was saying that 'free love' was something outside the scope of morality altogether, was a matter of moral indifference." The character who is guilty of moral indifference is Cynthia's father David, who considers inviting a woman (actually a "dame") over for sex and gets upset with Don for not making a pass at his daughter. Among the lines the PCA found problematic are the occasional quips David makes about his own character: "I always feel uncomfortable on a high moral plane," "Godliness does not appeal to me. . . . Steaks, liquor, and sex—in that order."

In his response, Preminger, writing on behalf of himself and Herbert, took personal offense at Breen's criticism of the script's treatment of sexual matters:

Not only as craftsmen who have served the industry for many years, but as members of the community who have never been connected with anything shady, dishonorable, salacious, or illicit, we must object to this unwarranted and unjustifiable attack. Our picture does not have a light attitude toward "seduction, illicit sex, chastity and virginity."

Preminger also defended the morality of Don and Patty and the film's treatment of sex:

On the contrary, it is a harmless story of a very virtuous girl, who works for a living, who neither smokes nor drinks, who is completely honest and outspoken, who resists temptation and whose aim in life is to get married and have children. She achieves this aim in our picture when she meets a young, upright, typical American boy who shares her views and ethics. . . . There are no scenes of passion in our picture, no scenes of crime and vice. We concede there is a discussion of sex—a topic of somewhat universal interest—but we are both deeply convinced that it is handled in such a way that it cannot conceivably harm those whom the Code was created to protect.

Preminger, who had directed the Broadway production, was so confident in the material that he simultaneously directed a version in English and a second in German with two different sets of actors (Don and Patty's German alter egos are played by Hardy Krueger and Johanna Matz, who appear as the young tourist couple in the English version's final scene).

But Don's declaration of "affection, but no passion" was apparently not enough for Breen and the MPAA Board, who refused to reverse the decision. The film's distributor, United Artists, resigned from the MPAA, and Preminger—in an unprecedented move—continued with his plans to open the film in New York, Chicago, Los Angeles, and San Francisco without a seal from the PCA (the film was passed by the New York State Censorship Board and given the green light in Pennsylvania, Illinois, and Massachusetts). The director also criticized the

MPAA, claiming its decision was unfair if you compared his film to others that were passed that year: "We will humbly submit to judgment this audience—judgment reached by their standard of good taste. By their instinct for wholesome entertainment—not by standards of a group of competitors, based on hypocritical interpretation of an antiquated code."

A second blow to the film came in the form of a condemnation by the Legion of Decency. It gave the film a C rating: "The subject matter of the picture in its substance and manner of presentation seriously offends and tends to deny or ignore Christian and traditional standards of morality and dwells hardly without variation upon suggestiveness in situations and dialogue." If the C weren't enough, Cardinal Spellman of New York put in his two cents via a letter that priests within his archdiocese were instructed to read at Sunday Mass:

This picture is condemned because the subject matter and its substance and manner of presentation seriously violates standards of morality and decency and dwells, hardly without variation, upon suggestiveness in situations and dialogue. Because this picture bears a serious potential influence for evil, especially endangering our youth, tempting them to entertain ideas of behavior conflicting ideas with the moral law, inciting to juvenile delinquency, I am gravely concerned about its presentation. . . . Since this picture is an occasion of sin, I remind our Catholic people of their obligation to avoid it.

Meanwhile, out on the West Coast, Cardinal James Francis McIntyre required all churches within the Archdiocese of Los Angeles to read a similar letter warning Catholics that seeing the film "is hazardous and in violation of good moral conduct." Ironically, the film was given a rave review from *St. Joseph's* magazine, a Catholic publication. Critic Richard Hayes called the film a "delicious adaptation" that will "surely figure in any moviegoer's 'favorite' list as the brightest and most originally charming light comedy of the year."

There were attempts to censor the film on the local level. The film was almost banned from Minneapolis when *St. Paul Dispatch* film critic

Bill Diehl denounced *The Moon Is Blue* as "smut" and "filth." Diehl had not even seen the film—only a production of the play in Minneapolis a few seasons back. Diehl accompanied the mayor and members of the City Council to a special screening arranged by United Artists. Afterwards, they offered their reactions. The mayor didn't think the film was "family entertainment." One of the commissioners stated, "The picture stinks—it isn't good entertainment." Another commissioner said the whole controversy surrounding the film was a "shining example of making a mountain out of a molehill." As for Diehl, he was on the next train to Chicago to see the film again to make sure that the print they received was not edited.

In Birmingham, Alabama, Chief of Police E. H. Brown took a two-pronged approach to protecting the morals of the inhabitants of "The Magic City." He limited admission to adults over twenty-one and censored the taxicab scene, during which Patty asks Don if he intends to seduce her and discloses that she is a virgin (the dialogue had recently been published in a *Life* magazine pictorial). Unfortunately, Brown was a one-man censor whose decisions couldn't be appealed. The management of the Empire, a 950-seat theatre where the film was playing to capacity, invited a local women's club to see the film. They told Chief Brown that the film taught "a good moral lesson to teenagers." The theatre manager decided to let his customers in on what they were missing (and the reason why) by hanging a copy of the *Life* spread in the lobby with a sign reading "This Is What the Chief of Police Censored." The dialogue was also reprinted in the local paper, the *Birmingham Post-Herald*. According to *Variety*, Chief Brown admitted that he had not seen the film. When asked about his educational qualifications as the city's censor, he became defensive and replied, "That's personal; it's not of your business" (his personnel file revealed he had an eighth-grade education). As a result of the bad publicity, City Hall passed an ordinance to create a censorship board made up of eighteen "club women" and one gentleman. When the public safety commissioner, who appointed the board, asked why he chose so many women, he explained, "they had more time to see the movies and would be more conscientious about the job."

Meanwhile, as the film was playing to packed houses (the film's box-office receipts totaled $3.5 million by the end of 1953), one controversy continued to mount, culminating in a court case involving the constitutionality of the Kansas Censorship Board to prohibit the exhibition of the film based on the following: "Sex theme throughout, too frank bedroom dialogue: many sexy words; both dialogue and action have sex as their theme." The film's production company, Holmby Productions, Inc., challenged the censor's decision, which reevaluated the film, and this time, citing the words of the Kansas statute, concluded it was "obscene, indecent and immoral and such as to tend to debase or corrupt public morals." But Holmby Productions won the first round in Wyandotte County District Court, where Judge Miller ruled that the statute creating the board was "repugnant" to the First and Fourteenth amendments (under which motion pictures were now protected speech) and its meaning "so broad and vague as to be unconstitutional." The board appealed to the Supreme Court of Kansas, which overturned Judge Miller's decision. Holmby Productions appealed to the U.S. Supreme Court, which, standing on its ruling in the 1952 *"Miracle* decision," reversed the Kansas court's decision. On April 7, 1955—between Judge Miller's ruling and the Kansas court's reversal—Kansas Governor Fred Hall abolished the Kansas Board of Review. "Every believer in freedom of expression will rejoice that Kansas has repealed its ancient censorship law," Governor Hall said, "It is to be hoped that the lead of Kansas will be followed by her sister states that still have anachronistic censorship statutes on the book." Hall's sendoff was premature; a legal technicality kept the Kansas board in operation for eleven more years.

Eight years after its release, a period in which the Production Code was revised and loosened in regards to language and adult themes, *The Moon Is Blue* finally received a PCA seal. However, the film continued to carry a C rating from the Catholic Church.

This is the legacy of *The Moon Is Blue*, an innocuous romantic comedy—its contribution to the genre forever upstaged by four little words.

Anatomy of a Murder (1959): Keeping It Real

Six years after *The Moon Is Blue* was released without a PCA seal (which it did eventually receive in 1961, though the film continued to carry a

"Condemned" rating from the Legion of Decency), Otto Preminger once again broken new ground with his critically acclaimed adaptation of Robert Traver's bestselling novel *Anatomy of a Murder*. The courtroom drama stars James Stewart as a small-town lawyer, Paul Biegler, who is hired to defend Lieutenant Frederick Manion (Ben Gazzara), who is standing trial for murdering a local bar owner, Barney Quill, after he allegedly raped Manion's wife, Laura (Lee Remick). Paul decides to argue that the Lieutenant was suffering from a "dissociative reaction" and was therefore unable to control his actions. The prosecuting attorney, Claude Dancer (George C. Scott), tries to discredit Laura and her story by painting her as a loose woman and suggesting, through the testimony of one of the Lieutenant's fellow inmates, that he fooled the psychiatrist and Biegler into believing his actions were impulsive. The decision is left to the jury, who must decide whether he was powerless when he murdered Barney Quill.

The making of *Anatomy of Murder* was the subject of a book, *Anatomy of a Motion Picture*, written by Richard Griffith, film curator at the Museum of Modern Art. According to Griffith, Preminger was set to shoot the film's interiors at the actual location where the story is set—the Upper Peninsula of Michigan (known as U.P. to its inhabitants), near the Canadian border, and the exteriors back in Hollywood. But he decided to shoot the entire film—both the interiors and exteriors—on location in the Michigan towns of Ishpeming and Marquette, which together would become the fictional town of Iron City. He explained to Griffith why it was so essential to move the entire production to Michigan:

> It's not only the *look* of the place that I want to get on the screen. I want the actors to *feel* it, to absorb a sense of what it's like to live here—to smell it. In a Hollywood-made picture, even when you shoot exteriors on location, the core of the film is the studio-made scenes; the exteriors are just hung on it to achieve a surface realism. But *Anatomy* is a story which requires reality. I'm going to bring the whole cast and crew up here and install them in Ishpeming. We'll live through it together and that will help to make the film more "real" than any single thing I could do.

In addition to shooting in an actual jail and hospital, Preminger kept it "real" by using the Marquette County Courthouse as the principal set. Locals were hired as extras and to sit on the jury. Robert Traver—the pen name of John D. Voelker, a former justice of the Michigan Supreme Court—was on hand to serve as a technical adviser for the courtroom scenes.

Adding an air of authenticity to the trial scenes was the casting of Joseph N. Welch as the trial judge. Welch, an experienced attorney, was best known for his exchange with Senator Joseph McCarthy during the Army-McCarthy hearings of 1954. Welch was the head attorney for the U.S. Army, which was under investigation for espionage and subversion by McCarthy and his closeted gay chief counsel, Roy Cohn. During the proceedings, McCarthy intentionally revealed publicly for the record that a member of Welch's firm, Fred Fisher, had once been a member of the National Lawyers Guild, which had been linked to the Communist Party. Welch explained that Fisher had disclosed his former association to him, but the senator would not leave the matter alone, prompting Welch, in a manner befitting a dignified New England lawyer, to ask McCarthy the rhetorical question, "Have you no sense of decency, sir, at long last? Have you left no sense of decency?" As for his performance, Welch holds his own alongside a seasoned pro like Stewart and up-and-coming young "actor's actors" like Scott and Gazzara, though from a lawyer's perspective, "Judge Weaver appears too kindly to be a courtroom disciplinarian."

While the location shooting, along with the participation of Voelker and Welch, certainly contributed to the realistic look and feel of the film, it was the graphic language Biegler uses as he recounts the details of Barney Quill's alleged rape of Laura Manion that separated *Anatomy* from other courtroom dramas. When Otto Preminger submitted Wendell Mayes's screenplay to the Production Code Administration for its approval, Geoffrey Shurlock responded that while the "basic story meets the requirements of the Code, the present version contains two scenes of such clinical nature, discussing rape, that we fear they would prove unacceptable when we came to review the finished picture." Shurlock pointed out that the words *sperm, sexual climax*, and *penetration* seemed "hardly suitable for a picture to be released indiscriminately for mixed audiences." He also complained that there was an "overemphasis on the words *rape* and *panties* to the point where this element possibly becomes offensive."

Preminger did eventually agree to change the expression *knocked up* and a line pertaining to the rape ("he was going to tear all my clothes off and take me again" to "he was going to tear all my clothes off and attack me again"). He also reduced the number of *panties* and *rapes*, but on the advice of Traver, he refused to change the word *penetration* to *violation* because the former is actually used in the Michigan statute. "He does not understand why *violation* should be less censorable than *penetration*," Preminger wrote, "Besides, to his legal mind at least, the substitution of *penetration* with *violation* does not make sense at all." However, Shurlock did not share Preminger's concern for authenticity in regards to use of language, but rather insisted that what is and is not acceptable should be measured by his acceptability "for discussion before mixed audiences in a movie theatre." He also reminded Preminger that censors boards, which "would feel entitled to delete it . . . are still empowered by the Supreme Court to delete anything that they think comes under the head of obscenity."

The word did remain in the script and the final cut of the film, which was issued a PCA seal on June 18, 1959. The film was both commended and criticized for—to borrow an adjective repeatedly used by critics—the "frankest" dialogue heard on the silver screen. Echoing Shurlock's objections to the script, *Variety* called the inclusion of such words "bold but foolhardy" because "they are likely to be startling and distasteful to general audiences." Perhaps even more surprising was their assertion that the words are not "strictly germane to the narrative" and their inclusion was simply a matter of "realism for its own sake, rather than the good of the story." An editorial in the *Richmond News Ledger* (entitled "Too Much Anatomy") described the film as "in disgracefully bad taste, offensive, indecent, and far beyond the bounds of propriety. . . . [W]e believe the average Richmonder, considering the movie as a whole, would be offended by the prurient theme of the material."

In a moment of levity, the film is comically self-conscious (and no doubt making fun of the censors) about the inclusion of what is perhaps the least controversial of the questionable words: *panties*. During the testimony by Detective Sergeant James Durgo, Judge Weaver calls all the lawyers to the bench to discuss the "undergarment" referred to in his testimony. "There's a certain light connotation attached to the word *panties*," the judge says. "Can we find another word for them?" Dist. Attorney Mitch Lodwick (Brooks West) claims that's what his wife calls them. Biegler pleads ignorance ("I'm a bachelor"). Dancer says he knows a French word for them, bit it's "slightly suggestive." "Most French words are," quips the judge.

But it was the graphic language used during the cross-examination of the medical examiner, Dr. Raschid (Ned Wever), which contains the words *spermatogenesis, intercourse, contraceptive,* and *sexual climax,* that served as the basis for the Chicago Censor Board's decision to ban the film on the grounds that it was obscene. The board, composed of six women, initially objected to five scenes, but the number was reduced to two (Raschid's testimony and Laura's description of the rape) by Police Commissioner Timothy J. O'Connor. The presiding judge over the case, Federal Judge Julius H. Miner, reportedly watched the film with his wife, seventeen-year-old son, and fifteen-year-old daughter. His decision in the case of *Columbia Pictures v. City of Chicago,* 184 F. Supp. 817 (1959) upholds the power of the city of Chicago to censor films, yet states the city ordinance is not applicable in this case:

> Taken as a whole, the film cannot be placed in the category of the obscene or the immoral because its dominant effect does not tend to excite sexual passion or undermine public morals. In fact, the criminal assault on the murderer's wife has an effect of arousing pity and revulsion, rather than desire or sexual impure thoughts. Furthermore, under present-day standards, neither of these two words [*rape* and *contraceptive*] offends the common conscience of the general public.

As authors Edward De Grazia and Roger K. Newman point out, Judge Miner applied the rule "generally followed in the Federal and State courts" that "a book or play is to be judged as a whole in terms of its effect on the average, normal reader or viewer." The rule was applied by the Supreme Court in the landmark obscenity case, *Roth v. United States,* 354 U.S. 476 (1957), which narrowed down the definition of obscenity as material "whose dominant theme take as a whole appeals to the prurient interest."

Six years later, Otto Preminger found himself in court once again when he filed an injunction against Columbia Pictures and its subsidiary, Screen Gems, to prevent them from distributing an edited version of the film, which was scheduled to air on ABC. Preminger's contract guaranteed him approval of all cuts made of his film. But the injunction was denied because the clause in his contract applied only to theatrical distribution, not subsequent airings on television. During the trial, director Elia Kazan took the stand as an expert witness on Preminger's behalf and testified that cutting a minute out of a film can change the meaning of a picture. Later that same year, Preminger enjoyed a minor victory when ABC agreed to let Preminger make all of the deletions and select the places for commercial interruptions for the television airing of *The Man with the Golden Arm*.

Ironically, Preminger had used the medium of television to promote *Anatomy of a Murder* while the film was still in production. On March 29, 1959, the director allowed scenes shot on the first day of filming to be shown on *The Ed Sullivan Show*. The footage no doubt did not contain any words the PCA deemed offensive to the ears of America.

The Connection (1961): "The *Shit* That Will Do You In . . . "

In July of 1959, Jack Gelber's provocative play, *The Connection*, premiered at the Living Theatre, an off-Broadway theatre group known for its productions of modernist and experimental works. The drama focuses on a group of junkies badly in need of their next heroin fix sitting in a tenement apartment impatiently waiting for their dealer to arrive. As in *Waiting for Godot*, the characters spend much of their time on stage waiting, yet unlike the title character of Beckett's absurdist, existential play, the "connection"—a hipster known only as Cowboy (Carl Lee)—does finally arrive. He is accompanied by an unlikely companion: an elderly woman in a Salvation Army uniform named Sister Salvation (Barbara Winchester), who has no idea she has just walked into a drug den. To avoid his play becoming sentimental or overly melodramatic, Gelber uses a "play-within-a-play" structure to remind the audience they are watching a theatrical presentation. The performers break the "fourth wall" by acknowledging the audience (one actor even screams at them, "Why are you here, stupid?") The drama is also interrupted by the entrance of two characters who are identified as the playwright and the producer of the drama that is unfolding onstage. Adding to the realism of the theatrical experience is the use of adult language, particularly one four-letter word that was a euphemism for heroin—*shit*. In a piece for the *New York Times* entitled "Rinse Its Mouth," Chief Drama Critic Howard Taubman stated that he is not (and hopes never to be) ready for censorship. He understands Gelber's reason for using the word, yet he wonders whether "its mood and character would be portrayed if some other hard, brilliant word were substituted?"

The film version of *The Connection* (1962) was shot in nineteen days on a minuscule budget ($150,000). The filmmaker, Shirley Clarke, was a New York–based director and a member of the New American Cinema Group, a new generation of filmmakers that included Peter Bogdanovich, Robert Frank, and Alfred Leslie, who signed a public statement (dated September 30, 1960) denouncing the "official cinema" (meaning commercial, Hollywood cinema) as "morally corrupt, aesthetically obsolete, thematically superficial, [and] temperamentally boring." They believed filmmaking, like the other arts, was a form of "personal expression" and therefore rejected all forms of censorship. Their manifesto posed basic yet very pertinent questions: "Who are the censors? Who chooses them, and what are their qualifications? What's the legal basis for censorship? These are the questions that need answers."

In adapting his play for the screen, Gelber substituted the "play-within-the-play" device with a "film-within-the-film." Clarke's camera doubles for that of a pretentious and very square documentary filmmaker, Jim Dunn (William Redfield), who is paying for the junkies' fix in exchange for allowing them to be filmed. He grows increasingly more frustrated with the inactivity of his uncooperative (and paid) subjects. Both Clarke and the fictional Dunn employ a realist filmmaking style complete with long takes and a moving camera (including some hand-held camera work) that tries to compensate for the characters' limited mobility (as on stage, the mood is set by a jazz combo, which plays intermittently while waiting with the others for their next fix). The characters often look directly into the camera as they are talking to Dunn, yet it seems as if they are talking directly to us, cluing the audience in about the life of a junkie, and explaining "it isn't the shit that will do you in, it's the lack of it."

The device operates on two interrelated levels. First, it reminds us that despite the naturalistic acting and dialogue, and the "realistic" set (complete with cockroaches, etc.), the film we are watching (*The Connection*), is just that—a film. Second, the concepts of "realism" and "truth" in the cinema are called into question when the filmmaker-within-the-film soon violates one of the cardinal rules of *cinéma vérité* documentary by coming out from behind the camera to "direct" his subjects. As Solly (Jerome Raphael), the smartest junkie in the room, warns, "You came here to make a movie and now you are getting involved." After Cowboy arrives, the filmmaker reluctantly agrees to become a subject in his own film and shoots up on camera, which makes him sick and unable to finish his project. This explains the statement by the filmmaker's rarely seen cameraman, J. J. Burden (Roscoe Brown), which appears at the start of the film. Burden claims the disillusioned Dunn turned all the footage over to him. "The responsibility of putting the material together is fully mine," Burden declares, "I did it as honestly as I could."

The Connection was the surprise hit of the 1961 Cannes Film Festival, where it had its world premiere at an out-of-competition screening. It was slated to open in New York in the fall of 1961, but the state's censor, Lewis M. Pesce, refused to license the film for public showing unless the repeated use of the word *shit* was deleted. Under Section 122 of the Education Law, a license can be withheld if a film is "obscene, indecent, immoral, inhuman, sacrilegious, or is of a character that its exhibition would tend to corrupt morals or incite to crime." Upon the distributor's request, Pesce reviewed the film again, and once again refused to grant the film a license. An appeals board supported Pesce's decision, leaving the distributor no alternative but to take the censors, who were a division of the New York Board of Regents, to court. In July of 1962, the Appellate Division of the State Supreme Court overruled the censorship board's denial of a license on the grounds of obscenity. From a legal standpoint, the Appellate Court's decision is significant because it was not based on the meaning of the word itself, but its meaning in the context of the film. The decision stated: "In most instances, the word is not used in its usual connotation but as a definite expression of the language of the narcotic. At most, the word may be classified as vulgar, but it is not obscene."

Knowing the Board of Regents had the right to appeal the court's decision, the distributors moved forward and booked the film in the D. W. Griffith, a New York City "art house" theatre, where it played two shows on October 3, 1962. Pesce reportedly showed up at the theatre with reporters (he insisted on buying a ticket). Once inside, he warned the management that he was committing a misdemeanor if he showed *The Connection* without a license. The theatrics continued upstairs in the projection booth, where Pesce issued the same warning to the projectionist, who stated that he was assigned to this theatre by his union, which later issued a statement supporting the distributors' fight against censorship in New York State and criticizing the local papers for refusing to run ads for the film. Before the third show, the distributor's attorney, Ephraim London, who won the landmark *Miracle* case, was served with an injunction to halt all future screenings. The case was heard in the New York Court of Appeals, which upheld the Appellate Court's decision, thus allowing the film to at last to be screened—legally—in a public theatre.

Film critic Stanley Kauffman put the absurdity of the whole situation in perspective. His review, one of the few to actually print the word in question, appeared in the *New Republic* soon after the film's one-day run at the Griffith Theatre. Kauffman observed how the censors and their motives were years behind the times:

> The controversy is over the use of the word *shit* which recurs in the drug addict's sense. . . . No reader of contemporary novels (including many of the finest), no viewer of French films whose vocabulary goes as far as merde [shit], no visitor to the off-Broadway theatre, is likely to be offended by the word. . . . Films must be more strict, presumably, because more minors go to films than plays. So the censors are safeguarding minors from that word. Haven't they any idea at all of what young people know? Don't they think adolescents read paperback novels, hear the vulgate, are alive. As always, the biggest difficulty in the struggle against

censorship is to keep from doubling up with laughter the whole time.

The effects of the court's decision would not be felt immediately, though it certainly paved the way for the inclusion of the word *Variety* called (in 1968) "a four-letter vulgarism for defecation." Up to that time, the word was heard in another independently released film, a screen adaptation of James Joyce's *Ulysses* (1967) (which is also remembered for introducing the word *fuck* into the American cinematic lexicon). But in 1968, two films released by studios that were members of the MPAA—*Rosemary's Baby* (Paramount) and *Boom!* (Universal)—contained the word. In *Boom!*, the big floppola screen version of Tennessee Williams's *The Milk Train Doesn't Stop Here Anymore*, Elizabeth Taylor (as Flora "Sissy" Goforth), delivers that immortal line, "Shit on your mother!" The PCA tried to excise John Cassavetes's throwaway line, "Oh, shit," from the final cut of *Rosemary's Baby*, but the studio stood by the director (the film carried a "Suggested for Mature Audience Label" at the time of release). *Bullitt*, released that same year, is one of the first (if not the first) Hollywood films to use a popular variation of the word. When the corrupt politician Walter Chalmers (Robert Vaughn) tells San Francisco Police Lt. Frank Bullitt (Steve McQueen) "We all have to compromise," the no-nonsense Bullitt replies, "Bullshit!" Once the Motion Picture Ratings System was in full swing by 1968, the number of times per film a character said *shit* rose steadily from one to four (*Midnight Cowboy* [1969]) to nine (*Love Story* [1970], *Five Easy Pieces* [1970]), to eleven (*Shaft* [1971]).

Who's Afraid of Virginia Woolf? (1966): "Some Goddamn Warner Brothers Epic . . . "

In March of 1963, Warner Brothers submitted a copy of Edward Albee's play *Who's Afraid of Virginia Woolf?*, which the studio had purchased for a half a million dollars, to the Production Code Administration for its review. After reviewing the play, Geoffrey Shurlock phoned Jack Warner and then sent him a short letter summarizing their conversation:

As discussed over the phone, in order to bring this material within Code requirements it would be necessary to remove all the profanity and the very blunt sexual dialogue. This of course would considerably reduce the impact of this very highly regarded play. We regret having to report unfavorably on this material, but under the circumstances it is the only judgment we can render.

Five days later, Warner received a five-page memo consisting of a page-by-page list of every profane word and "blunt sexual dialogue." The word *goddamn* topped the list (at 22 times), followed by *Jesus* (12), *bastard* (9), *S.O.B./son-of-a-bitch* (9), *bugger* (8), *for Christ's sake* (7), *screw* (5), *scrotum* (2), *Up yours!* (2), *ass* (1), *frigging* (1) (these numbers include variations of certain words, such as *Jesus God*, *Jesus Christ*, and *"Jesus H. Christ"*). Interestingly, the memo only addresses the profanity and suggestive language (like *Hump the hostess*, *monkey nipples*, and *angel tits*) with no mention of the play's other elements (characters, story, theme, etc.), including the offstage adulterous "quickie" between Martha and Nick.

Virginia Woolf is set in the home of George, a history professor at a small New England college, and his wife, Martha, the college president's daughter. Late one Saturday evening, George and Martha return home from a faculty party at her father's house to play host to Nick, a handsome new addition to the biology department, and his mousy wife, Honey. Over the course of the evening, which ends at the crack of dawn, George and Martha drink, argue, call each other names, and then drink some more. At first, Nick and Honey sit on the sidelines like spectators, watching George and Martha go at each other. But the young couple is soon pulled into their "fun and games" (the title of the play's first act), which climaxes in the early morning when George gets back at Martha by breaking the news to her that their teenage son has died in a car accident. But it is soon revealed that their son does not exist; he is a mutual fantasy in the minds of the childless couple.

Albee's play is a biting critique of marriage and relationships. As the playwright explains, it is "about people of more than average intelligence getting to the point where they can't any longer exist with a whole series of games, tricks, and false illusions, and then knocking down the entire tenable superstructure." The title, a variation of the children's song "Who's Afraid of the Big Bad Wolf?" poses the question "Who's afraid of living life without delusions?" "I am, George, I am," replies Martha just before the final curtain goes down. Ironically, the song was sung in the play to the melody of "Here We Go 'Round the Mulberry Bush," rather than "Who's Afraid of the Big Bad Wolf?" from the 1933 animated Disney short, *Three Little Pigs*. Disney wanted $200 a week for the rights for the song, so the producers went with "Mulberry Bush" instead because it was in the public domain.

The Broadway production was generally praised by critics and received both the New York Drama Critics Award for Best Play and five Tony Awards, including Best Play. It was also expected to win the coveted Pulitzer Prize for Drama. In fact, *Virginia Woolf* was the only play submitted by the two critics on the drama jury. But the final decision was made by the Advisory Board of Journalists, not all of whom had seen the play (W. D. Maxwell, editor of the *Chicago Tribune*, called it a "filthy play"). The vote was split, so no award was given in the drama category. The *New York Times* did not approve of the omission and questioned the board's decision:

> Could Edward Albee's play have been too gamy for the Pulitzer advisory board? Could this off-beat account of the home life of college faculty members have seemed unacceptable simply because the board met on Columbia's campus? Whatever the explanation, the decision was so irksome to the two distinguished critics whose advice the board disregard, that they have resigned as jurors.

The reviews for Albee's first Broadway production ranged from raves for both Albee's writing and the production to critical lambasting from two local critics, the *Daily Mirror*'s Robert Coleman ("a sick play for sick people") and John Chapman of the *New York Daily News*, who described the play as "three and a half hours long, four characters wide and a cesspool deep."

The PCA was more cordial when communicating to director Mike Nichols its objections to the final cut of his film. Once again, Geoffrey Shurlock spoke to Jack Warner on the phone and then confirmed in writing the PCA's refusal to grant *Virginia Woolf* a certificate of approval "due to the presence of a good deal of profanity, blunt sexual references, and coarse and sometimes vulgar language." Rather than cutting the film, which would certainly not have gone unnoticed by the critics and those familiar with the play, or resigning from the MPAA, Warner exercised his right to appeal the decision to the MPAA Board. On Friday, June 10, 1965, the MPAA granted an "exemption from existing Code regulations" to *Virginia Woolf*, as permitted under Section 6, Paragraph (i) of the MPAA's bylaws. Although exercising the exemption rule was by no means a common occurrence, the appeals board had overturned the PCA's refusal to grant *The Pawnbroker* (1965) a seal because it included partial female nudity. A statement released by the MPAA explained the rationale for granting the exemption to *Virginia Woolf*:

1. The film is not designed to be prurient. This film document, dealing with a tragic realism of life, is largely a reproduction of the Edward Albee play which won the New York Drama Critics Award in 1963, and has played throughout the country.
2. Warner Bros. has taken the position that no persons under 18 will be admitted unless accompanied by a parent.
3. This Exemption means exactly that—approval of material in a specific, important film which would not be approved for a film of lesser quality, or a film determined to exploit language for language's sake. This Exemption does not mean that the floodgates are open for language or other material. Indeed Exemption means precisely the opposite. We desire to allow excellence to be displayed and we insist that films, under whatever guise, which go beyond rationale measure of community standards will *not* bear a Seal of Approval.

Meanwhile, Jack Warner had already announced that the studio was imposing an "adults only" policy in the form of a clause in exhibitors' contracts prohibiting theatres from admitting anyone under the age of 18 unless accompanied by parents:

The play was undoubtedly a play for adults and we have gone ahead to make *Virginia Woolf* a film for adults, because it has something important to say to adults. We do not think it is a film for children, nor do we think every film should be for all ages. After all, not all subjects discussed by parents are fit for their children; for that matter, much entertainment for children is not appropriate for their parents. . . . I don't believe a controversial, mature subject should be watered down.

Theatres were prohibited from admitting anyone "under the age of 18 unless accompanied by his parent." Despite the restrictions, the film was a major hit at the box office for Warner Brothers, earning $14.5 million (the studio's #1 film for the year). *Virginia Woolf* received thirteen Academy Award nominations and won five, including Best Actress (Elizabeth Taylor) and Best Supporting Actress (Sandy Dennis).

CHAPTER 4

Guns, Gangs, and Random Acts of Ultra-Violence

In the silent era, the cinematic treatment of crime and criminals was a major point of contention for those who believed there was a direct cause-and-effect link between the depiction of murder, rape, and violence and real crimes committed by real people in the real world. They were particularly concerned about the negative effects of screen violence on impressionable youth, who were supposedly prone to imitate the bad behavior they might witness in a dark movie theatre one sunny Saturday afternoon.

Consequently, when the Production Code was drafted in 1930, it explicitly prohibited the portrayal of criminals as sympathetic or heroic and crime films from serving as "how-to manuals" for wannabe law-breakers ("And now, ladies and gentlemen, here's how to blow up a train . . ."). The MPPDA believed these restrictions were necessary due to the growing popularity of a genre that introduced audiences to the crime-ridden underworld of the American movie gangster.

LITTLE CAESAR (1931), THE PUBLIC ENEMY (1931), AND SCARFACE: THE SHAME OF THE NATION (1932): GANGLAND, ILLINOIS

On September 28, 1928, the *Chicago Daily Tribune* featured a front-page story entitled "Well, Pupils, Tell Us What Is a *Racket*?" After explaining how the word *racket* had only until recently taken on a whole new meaning in certain circles, the article answers the question posed by the title in the form of a definition, which at the time could not be found in the pages of *Webster's International Dictionary*:

Racket: An apparently legitimate enterprise carried on by a habitual criminal or criminals who extort money from respectable citizens by means of intimidation, bombing, or murder.

But *racket* was only one in a litany of gangster-inspired words that were splattered across the front page of Chicago newspapers in the 1920s and 1930s. In the same month as the *Tribune* article, syndicated journalist James P. Kirby began an eight-part series about the birth and growth of *racketeering*, which he claimed was America's "new big business," with annual profits in Chicago alone totaling between $50 and $70 million (a lot of *dough* in 1928!) His first article offered readers a rundown of the latest gangster slang, such as *racketeer*, *mob*, *mobster*, *muscling* (as in *muscling in* on another's *racket*), and *muscleman* (the guy who does the *heavy work*, a.k.a. a *hitman*). It also included an artist's rendering of the city's most powerful mobster—"The Beer Baron of Chicago"— "Scarface" Al Capone.

During the Prohibition Era, Americans were fascinated by the headline-making exploits of Capone, Hymie Weiss, Bugs Moran, and other Chicago mobsters as they battled for control of the city's illegal liquor and beer trade. But gangsters were not the only ones breaking the law. Corruption in Chicago's City Hall was not a well-kept secret, starting with the city's crooked mayor, William "Big Bill" Thompson, who was elected to two consecutive terms (1915–23) and an additional four more years (1927–31) thanks to a generous campaign contribution from Capone. Thompson vowed to clean up Chicago, yet organized crime thrived under his watch. According to statistics released in the fall of 1928 by the Illinois Association for Criminal Justice, 215 murders related to beer-running privileges, racketeering, and election disputes were committed over a two-year period—without a single conviction for a gangland murder.

One year later, on St. Valentine's Day, the Chicago mob wars were front-page news when five members of George "Bugs" Moran's gang, along with two others, were machine-gunned to death, execution style, by Capone's men in a North Side garage. Still, despite the blood, carnage, and negative publicity, mobsters did perform a "public service" by supplying nonteetotalers with beer and bootleg gin and an out-of-the-way place (a speakeasy) where they could enjoy a glass (or twelve).

"Mobspeak" was also all the rage in Hollywood in a cycle of gangster films produced between 1927 and 1933, a six-year period that coincided with the film industry's transition to sound. A silent shootout between the cops and a gangster armed with a Tommy gun left plenty to the audience's imagination. But it was the addition of sound, namely the urban slang spoken by tough-talking gangsters and dramatic sound effects (machine-gun fire, police sirens, shouts and screams, city noises, etc.) that brought an added sense of realism and brutality to the genre.

Newspaper stories were the primary source material for silent and early sound gangster films, so when the characters and plotlines hit too close to home, the studios ran into problems with state and local censorship boards. In *The Racket* (1928), based on Bartlett Cormack's successful stage play, an honest Chicago police captain (Thomas Meighan) pursues public enemy #1 Nick Scarsi (Louis Wolheim), who has the mayor on his payroll. The censor boards in Philadelphia and New York did not appreciate director Lewis Milestone's realistic depiction of Chicago's underworld and demanded that the film's violent moments be cut, along with any inferences that Chicago's judges and politicians were in bed with the mob. Cormack's play, which "named names" (including Mayor Thompson), had already been banned by the Illinois State Attorney's Office, while Chicago's film censor board, under the jurisdiction of the police, prevented *The Racket* from being shown in the city dubbed "Gangland."

Film historians generally agree the gangster genre was established in the early 1930s with the release of three films by Warner Brothers: *Little Caesar*, *The Public Enemy*, and *Scarface*. All three films trace the rise and tragic fall of their title characters, who are born to poor immigrant parents, but refuse to allow their low social status prevent them from fulfilling the "American Dream." Through racketeering and bootlegging, they attain wealth and power, yet it is their unyielding hunger for control that also eventually leads to their downfall. In the end, the gangster meets his maker with some help from either a rival gang or the police as part of their ongoing effort to maintain order in the urban jungle.

At a time when the country was in the throes of the Great Depression, movie audiences lived vicariously through the dirty dealings of *Caesar*'s Rico (Edward G. Robinson), *Enemy*'s Tom Powers (James Cagney), and *Scarface*'s Tony Camonte (Paul Muni). Critics of the genre believed gangster films were harmful because unlike the other testosterone-driven genres, such as the detective film and the Western, they focused on the "bad guys." Since the first "General Principle" of the Production Code prohibited the audience's sympathy being thrown "to the side of crime, wrong-doing, evil, or sin," gangster films also featured law enforcement officers (the police or FBI) who served as the voice of morality and were on hand to ensure justice was being served.

Still, during the peak of its popularity, the genre faced harsh criticism from some lawmakers, justices, journalists, and social scientists, who were convinced gangster films were turning America's youth into juvenile delinquents. As in the nickelodeon era when moral reformers waged a battle to close theatres due to the so-called harmful effects of moving pictures on young people, newspapers once again ran stories about gun-toting kids and teenagers who were negatively influenced by big-screen gangsters. In 1931, two eighteen-year-olds charged with second-degree robbery admitted they were inspired by gangster films to try the "easy money racket" for themselves. Before sending them to a reformatory, the presiding judge had some harsh words for the film industry:

> The moving picture industry is complaining about poor business, but it only has itself to blame. Gangster and sex pictures, which seem to predominate, are killing the goose that lays the golden eggs. No responsible parent cares to take children to these pictures. Maybe some day the industry will again become respectable; but until then it will not be a financial success.

One tragic incident that launched a formal campaign against the genre and Hollywood occurred on June 23, 1931, in Montclair, New Jersey. While sixteen-year-old Harold Gamble was describing a scene from a gangster film to twelve-year-old Winslow Elliot, he pulled out an automatic pistol from his hip pocket. The gun accidentally went off, killing Elliot. Local and neighboring community leaders were outraged and demanded gangster films be banned from local theatres. The mayor of East Orange, New Jersey, Charles H. Martens, sent a protest letter to Will Hays, who pointed out in his reply that a "system of self-regulation is shown on many screens in the words 'Crime does not pay.'" Hays also added that "unanimous scientific judgment" accepts gangster films as a deterrent to crime and the real culprit was the gangster himself, not the *gangster film*.

Mayor Martens was not alone in voicing his objections. Italian-American organizations, such as the NYC Federation of Italian-American County Democratic Organizations and *Il Progresso Italo-Americano*, objected to gangster films because of their negative portrayal of Italian Americans. The Patrolmen's Benevolent Association also adopted a resolution urging Hollywood to stop making films that "glorify the lives of gangsters, gunmen and racketeers."

The influence of crime films on youth was addressed in a four-year study (1928–32) commissioned by the Motion Picture Research Council. The "Payne Fund Studies," so named after its benefactor, the Payne Study and Experiment Fund, examined theatre attendance, the content of films, and the effects of motion pictures on children's behavior, attitudes, emotions, and sleep patterns. The results were published in nine volumes and summarized by Henry James Forman in his controversial bestseller *Our Movie Made Children* (1933). An indictment of motion pictures for their negative effects on children, Forman's opus makes up for the Payne Fund Study's lack of scientific evidence with hyperbole and inflammatory statements directly linking juvenile crime with motion pictures. The author claims that in addition to teaching juvenile delinquents specific criminal methods and techniques (e.g., how to open a safe, jimmy a door or window, pick a pocket), they propel spectators toward criminal behavior by stimulating their confidence and "desires for ease, luxury, easy money as obtainable through criminal or illegitimate enterprise." In November of 1933, representatives of the Motion Picture Research Council appeared before a U.S. Senate Subcommittee on Crime Control to present their evidence. Testifying on behalf of the film industry, MPPDA secretary Carl E. Milliken disputed the validity of the Payne Studies, which he charged had employed improper research techniques, such as asking young subjects leading questions when collecting their data.

While the harmful effects of violence and crime films on kids were being studied, filmmakers and the studios were engaged in battles of their own with the state censors and the MPPDA's Studio Relations Committee (SRC) over the gangster genre. According to historian Stephen Prince, the crackdown on gangster films was due in part to the "increase in ferocity and vividness" of their violent content. Prince considers *Little Caesar* the least violent of the triumvirate, yet he points out that the Pennsylvania censors demanded cuts in not only the scenes with gunfire, but those in which characters brandish weapons, even if they are never used. However, the same restrictions did not apply to the police, who, for example, use a Tommy gun in the climactic shootout in *Little Caesar* (at the end of which Rico utters the famous line, "Mother of Mercy! Is this the end of Rico?")

By comparison, *The Public Enemy* is more "realistic" in terms of violence and its depiction of the underworld milieu, which, according to the opening title card, was the aim of the filmmakers:

> It is the ambition of the authors of *The Public Enemy* to honestly depict an environment that exists today in a certain strata of American life, rather than glorify the hoodlum or the criminal. While the story of *The Public Enemy* is essentially a true story, all names and characters appearing herein, are purely fictional.

What gives *The Public Enemy* its realistic edge is the added psychological dimension to the character of Tom Powers, who has a serious sadistic streak and seems to enjoy tormenting his victims, including his former mentor, Putty Nose (Murray Kinnell). Amidst the beer and bullets, the plot of *Enemy* also focuses on Tom's relationship with his family, who, at the end of the film, find it in their hearts to welcome him back into their home. Unfortunately, a rival gang gets to him first, and in the film's disturbing climax, his corpse is left at his family's doorstep. The closing title brings the film's message home: "'The Public Enemy' is not a man, nor is it a character—it is a problem that sooner or later WE, the public, must solve." In his report on the film, a member of the SRC praised it for showing "very clearly the effect gangster life has upon his immediate family" and believed the concluding title crawl was provocative and had "educational value."

The backlash against violence in films, gangster movies in particular, continued to gain ground. In the summer of 1931, the entire genre was banned from movie theatres in Syracuse, New York, and Worcester, Massachusetts. In Evanston, Illinois, the chief of police forbade "all underworld pictures" to be shown when a group of boys cheered during a gangster film. Meanwhile, back in Hollywood, producer Howard Hughes was ready to put his film version of Armitage Trail's novel *Scarface* into production. The film chronicles the career of Tony "Scarface" Camonte (Paul Muni), an ambitious and violent gangster based on Capone who seizes control of Chicago's bootlegging operations by killing off his rivals. Overly protective of his sister, Cesca (Ann Dvorak), Tony ruins her chance at happiness when he kills his right-hand man, Guino (George Raft), after discovering they have been sleeping together. But what Tony didn't know is that the couple tied the knot while he was out of town. In the climactic scene, a crazed Scarface and Cesca are holed up in his apartment by the police, who open fire. Cesca is shot and killed. When tear gas is thrown into the apartment, Scarface comes out crying and begging for his life. When he tries to make a run for it, the police riddle his body with bullets.

When Colonel Jason Joy, head of the Studio Relations Committee (the precursor to the PCA), reviewed the script, he was concerned that Scarface was being portrayed as a "home-loving man, good to his mother, and protecting his sister" and was glorified in the film's ending "when he deliberately walks into the police gunfire." In his notes on the script, Joy reminded Hughes's production team about the current backlash against the genre:

> In all my nine years of experience in our industry, no "cycle" has been criticized so severely and with such apparent feeling as is the cycle of crime pictures. Despite the fact that two or three of the more recent gang pictures have achieved more than average returns at the box office, I have been told emphatically by censors, chiefs of police, newspaper editors, exhibitors and leaders among the citizenry that there is a vast growing resentment against the continued production and exhibition of this type of picture.

Upon viewing footage of the film, Colonel Joy advised Hughes that state and local censors would prevent *Scarface* from playing in about

50 percent of the theatres in the country. Consequently, some major changes had to be made before the film could receive the MPPDA's approval. First, to appease the censors and make it clear the filmmakers did not intend to glorify the title character, the phrase "The Shame of the Nation" was added to the title. The film also took a strong position on gun control by blaming the federal government for failing to keep guns off the streets. With the approval of the MPPDA, two scenes were added to deliver an antigun message, which also, unfortunately, grinds the narrative to a screeching halt. In the first scene, the chief of detectives denounces the "morons in this country" who think gangsters are "colorful characters" and "demagogues" when innocent children are getting killed in the crossfire. The second scene involves a newspaper editor, Garston (Purnell Pratt), and a group of concerned citizens, who accuse the press of "glorifying the gangster" and blame the police for not controlling the violence. Garston fires back and tells them (and the audience) that it's up to them as American citizens to pressure the federal government to pass antigun laws, even "if we have to have martial law to do it!"

In his report to Will Hays, Colonel Joy was enthusiastic over the film's antigun position because it was "the direction in which many minds are going today." He also believed the new scenes give the film

> a right to live in spite of the prevalent, panicky opposition to gangster themes. That idea is simply this: As long as the gangster has access to guns, either pistols or machine guns, he is a bold, bad-man, menacing society and mocking at law and decency, but once robbed of his guns he is a yellow rat who will crawl into his hole.

The rise in gun violence during Prohibition led to the passing of the 1934 National Firearms Act, which imposed a tax on the transfer and manufacturing of Title II weapons, including the gangster's gun of choice, the M1928 Thompson Submachine Gun.

But the most contentious issue was the film's ending, which the PCA insisted must be altered in order to negate the character's heroism. In the alternate ending, which would be included at the time of the film's release, Scarface turns into a quivering coward when he is caught and taken away by the police. He stands before a judge, is sentenced to death by hanging, and is executed. After he is captured, Scarface is never again shown because a stand-in was used for Muni, who was reportedly not available. Scarface's absence and the fact that the audience doesn't see or hear the character during his sentencing or as he is climbs up the stairs to the gallows diminishes what the censors were trying to achieve in having moviegoers witness a legal system that assures Americans that crime does indeed not pay.

In the end, the Hollywood gangsters of the 1930s were defeated not by the cops or the courts, but by the censors. The morality police over at the PCA lowered the boom on the gangster genre in 1934, which led to the adoption in 1938 of "Special Regulations on Crime in Motion Pictures" (see appendix I). The remnants of the gangster genre could be see in a series of Warner Brothers crime dramas, such as *"G" Men* (1935), *Bullets or Ballots* (1936), and *San Quentin* (1937), in which Robinson and Cagney graduated to playing reformed gangsters or law enforcement agents. Thanks to the PCA, American moviegoers were on the right side of the law and their morals were, at least for the time being, out of the line of fire.

BLACKBOARD JUNGLE (1955): "A SHOCKING STORY OF TODAY'S HIGH SCHOOL HOODLUMS"

In 1953, a U.S. Senate subcommittee was formed to investigate the causes of juvenile delinquency in America and to assess the effectiveness of current laws designed to combat what the public was told had become a national epidemic. Statistically, juvenile crime was on the rise in post–World War II America, but as historian James Gilbert suggests, the increase may have been due to the lack of a uniform definition of juvenile delinquency by the FBI and state and local law enforcement agencies. For example, whether an underage teen caught drinking and/or breaking curfew was branded a "JD" depended on the state and county where he or she lived.

The hearings held by the subcommittee investigated the possible reasons why some kids go bad. The negative effects of comic books, specifically horror and crime comics with titles such as *Crime Patrol, The Vault of Horror,* and *Crypt of Terror,* were the subject of a 1955 subcommittee report. Based on the conflicting testimonies of experts, the subcommittee concluded it was unlikely that the reading of crime and horror comics would lead to delinquency in a well-adjusted and normally law-abiding child. However, the report did recommend that additional research needed to be done to determine the effects of comics on emotionally disturbed children.

Motion pictures, particularly those with excessive violence and sex, were also the subject of hearings conducted by the subcommittee's cochair, Senator Estes Kefauver (D-Tenn.), who traveled to the West Coast in June of 1955 to hear testimony from studio executives. One recent release Kefauver sharply criticized was MGM's *Blackboard Jungle*. Based on a bestseller by Evan Hunter, *Blackboard* is the story of an idealistic high school teacher named Richard Dadier (Glenn Ford), who accepts a job at an all-male vocational school in the inner city and has trouble controlling his class of delinquents, who only take orders from their ringleader, Artie West (Vic Morrow). Dadier believes the methods used by the other teachers, who are either too strict or too liberal, are ineffective. So he employs a "divide and conquer" strategy and develops a strong rapport with his brightest student, Greg Miller (Sidney Poitier), in hope he will challenge Artie's authority and lead the class against him.

MGM anticipated the film would be controversial, which is why *Blackboard Jungle* opens with a statement explaining the filmmakers' intentions:

> We, in the United States, are fortunate to have a school system that is a tribute to our communities and to our faith in American youth.
>
> Today we are concerned with juvenile delinquency—the cause—and its effects. We are especially concerned when this delinquency boils over into our schools.
>
> The scenes and incidents depicted here are fictional. However, we believe that public awareness is a first step toward a remedy for any problem. It is in this spirit and with this faith *Blackboard Jungle* is produced.

MGM's vice president in charge of production, Dore Schary, publicly defended the film to Kefauver, explaining, "We knew it would be controversial from the story, but with the increasing vandalism being reported in schools we thought that the picture would represent a dramatic report to the people. We are not frightened or intimidated by criticism of the picture." Senator Kefauver proceeded to question Schary about a recent news story in which a group of schoolgirls in Nashville admitted to setting a barn on fire after seeing *Blackboard Jungle*. Unaware of the incident, Schary responded, "There's no fire in the picture. They can't pin that on us." Although the executives who testified in the hearings admitted some of their films had perhaps gone too far in regards to violence and brutality, they would not concede to the suggestion that there was any link between the movies and the reported rise in teenage delinquency.

Unlike the majority of films about juvenile delinquents released in 1955 (mostly low-budget B-movies such as *Mad at the World, Teen-Age Crime Wave, Teenage Devil Dolls*, etc.) and in the years that followed, *Blackboard Jungle* is not an exploitation film. Writer/director Richard Brooks establishes with the opening crawl that his film is intended as a "message picture" about troubled teenagers living in the big city. Violence or, more precisely, the *threat* of violence that hangs over the adults in the film is presented—at least by 1955 Hollywood standards—as "real." There are three scenes in the film in which the adults are victims of teenage violence: the attempted rape of a female teacher, Lois Hammond (Margaret Hayes); the robbery of a newspaper delivery truck; and the violent beating of Dadier and another teacher in the street by their own students. When the Production Code Administration received the script in August of 1954, it approved the basic story, but found these three scenes unacceptable. It considered the assault of Miss Hammond unsuitable "for inclusion in that type of entertainment envisioned as being acceptable for general patronage" and the "brutality and violence" in the other two scenes to be "particularly spectacular and dramatized in unacceptable length and detail." The subsequent memos encouraged the studio to tone down these scenes, particularly the attack of Miss Hammond, which the filmmakers were directed to handle with "extreme care to avoid offensive sex-suggestiveness" so as not to "suggest an attempted rape, but rather that the boy is merely attempting to kiss the woman." (There is no doubt what occurs in the final film is an attempted rape.)

The Production Code Administration approved *Blackboard Jungle*. Pennsylvania's censorship board did so as well, but a provision was added to the contract that accompanied their seal:

> In the face of complete opposition on the part of officials of the Public and Parochial School Systems, the City Police, the Clergy, the Crime Prevention Association, and the Council of Churches, and because of certain legal limitations, we reluctantly issued a Seal of Approval of the film *Blackboard Jungle*.

> We call your attention to the Certification of Approval which carries "THE BOARD RESERVES THE RIGHT TO REVOKE THIS CERTIFI-CATION," and we advise that we will invoke this right if any instance directly connected to this film is reported.

Censor boards banned the film in Memphis and Atlanta, where the movie was declared "immoral, obscene, and licentious." Objections were also raised over Dadier's desegregated class, which included a mixture of Caucasian, African American, Hispanic, and Asian students, and the casting of an African American actor, Sidney Poitier, as the film's young hero. The film was also denounced by educators and prompted surprise inspections on two occasions of the Bronx Vocational High School, where Hunter briefly worked as a substitute and which served as the inspiration for his novel (inspectors reportedly gave the school glowing reviews). The Legion of Decency assigned the film a B rating, remarking that "its treatment contains morally objectionable elements (brutality, violence, disrespect for lawful authority) and tends to negate any constructive conclusion."

In the fall of 1955, *Blackboard Jungle* was at the center of an international scandal when the film was allegedly withdrawn from exhibition at the Venice Film Festival due to objections raised by the U.S. ambassador to Italy, Clare Boothe Luce. A playwright (*The Women*) and former Congresswoman (R-CT), Luce reportedly believed the film cast the American education system in an unfavorable light. In what he regarded as an act of "flagrant political censorship," Dore Schary was outraged that Mrs. Luce would "impose her personal authority" to prevent the film from being screened. Arthur Loew, President of Loews

International, which distributed the film, filed a formal complaint with the Secretary of State charging that Luce used her position to get the film withdrawn. The State Department denied that Luce had anything to do with the film being removed from the festival program, yet admitted she refused to attend a planned screening because she believed the film was not in the best interest of the United States. Still, *New York Times* critic Bosley Crowther said the entire incident smacked "suspiciously of federal censorship" and, ironically, piqued everyone's curiosity about the film. Crowther called *Blackboard Jungle* "the toughest, hardest hitting social drama the screen has had in years," yet he questioned if the filmmakers, even if they were sincere in their intentions to increase public awareness, exaggerated "the details" of some of the problems plaguing American schools. For him, such an act was "irresponsible and fraught with peril. . . . Certainly juvenile delinquency is a problem today. But it will not help to have it misrepresented and sensationalized."

Blackboard Jungle is perhaps best remembered for its theme song, "Rock Around the Clock," performed by Bill Haley and the Comets over the film's opening title sequence. The song, written by Max C. Freedman and Jimmy DeKnight (a pseudonym for James E. Myers), was first recorded by Sonny Dae and His Knights, but it was not until Haley's 1954 version was used on the film's soundtrack that it held the #1 spot on the Billboard Chart for seven weeks (July 9–August 20, 1955). After receiving national airplay (the first for a rock song), "Rock Around the Clock" became the bestselling single to date. An expression of teenage defiance and rebellion against authority, coupled with its link to a film about juvenile delinquency, "Rock Around the Clock" was adopted by teenagers around the world as their official anthem.

BONNIE AND CLYDE (1967): "THEY'RE YOUNG. THEY'RE IN LOVE. THEY ROB BANKS."

On May 23, 1934, twenty-five-year-old Clyde Barrow and his female companion, twenty-three-year-old Bonnie Parker, were ambushed by Texas Rangers and shot to death while the couple was traveling outside the small town of Gibsland, Louisiana. During their two-year crime spree, Barrow and his gang robbed banks, stores, and filling stations, killing a total of thirteen people along the way, eight of whom were policemen or guards.

Thirty-three years after their deaths, director Arthur Penn and actor/producer Warren Beatty finally gave Bonnie and Clyde the same big-screen treatment Hollywood had already bestowed on most of the A-list gangsters of the 1920s and 1930s. But anyone familiar with the couple's criminal record (few people were before the film's release) or feeling nostalgic for the Warner Bros. gangster films of the early '30s, was probably wondering what exactly the filmmakers were going for by portraying the duo as a pair of young, reckless (and at times sympathetic) free spirits. As the film's advertising tagline states, "They're young. They're in love. They rob banks." (A variation on the tagline substituted the line "They rob banks" with "and they kill people.")

When *Bonnie and Clyde* opened the 1967 Montreal Film Festival, the audience went wild—with the exception of one prominent film critic. Apparently the *New York Times*'s Bosley Crowther was expecting to see a gangster film in the same vein as *Little Caesar* and *Scarface*, but instead he saw (in his words) a "wild, jazzy farce melodrama" that "amusedly and sympathetically recounts the bank-robbing degradations" of Barrow and Parker. One week later, Crowther wrote a scathing review in which he berated the filmmakers for turning the lives of two cold-blooded killers into a "cheap piece of bald-face slapstick . . . loaded with farcical hold-ups, [and] screaming chases in stolen getaway cars that have the antique appearance and speeded up movement of the clumsy vehicles of the Keystone Cops." While he was not impressed by Beatty's portrayal of Clyde ("clowning broadly as the killer") and Faye Dunaway's Bonnie ("squirming grossly as his thrill-seeking sex-starved mole"), it was the "blending of farce and brutal killings" that he found "as pointless as it is lacking in taste, since it makes no valid commentary upon the already travestied truth."

Crowther's reviews sparked a national debate among critics, who were divided over the film. Like Crowther, many critics accused the filmmakers of glorifying the couple's violent, criminal lifestyle. *Time* magazine accused Beatty and Penn of reducing Bonnie and Clyde's story to a "strange and purposeless mingling of fact and claptrap that teeters easily on the brink of burlesque." In his review for *Films in Review*, Page Cook dismissed the film as "incompetently written, acted, directed and produced" and accused the filmmakers of promoting the idea that "sociopathology is art." *Newsweek*'s Joe Morgenstern initially panned the film, calling it "a squalid shoot 'em-up for the moron trade." But then he did something rare for a critic—he retracted his own review. His second review starts with an apology: "I am sorry to say I consider that review grossly unfair and regrettably inaccurate. I am sorrier to say that I wrote it." Although he still believed the film's "gore goes too far," he acknowledged the value of the film's violent content: "But art can certainly reflect life, clarify and improve life; and since most of humanity teeters on the edge of violence every day, there is no earthly reason why art should not turn violence to its own good ends, showing us what we do and why."

The critics who praised the film "read" *Bonnie and Clyde* "as a commentary on the rebellious spirit of today's youth and the prevalence of violence in contemporary society." While all the conventions and iconography (Tommy guns, hideouts, cars, etc.) of the '30s gangster are there, Bonnie and Clyde seem more like '60s renegades than '30s outlaws. They wage war on the "establishment," namely the banks and the law, yet, in a Robin Hood-esque gesture, show their sympathy toward the poor and downtrodden by never taking their money during a holdup. In their original treatment for the film, screenwriters Robert Benton and David Newman conceived the world of Bonnie and Clyde as a reflection of American life in the late 1960s:

> This is a movie about criminals only incidentally. Crime in the '30s was the strange, the exotic, the different. This is a movie about two people, lovers, movers, and operators. They're "hung up," like many people are today. They moved in odd, unpredictable ways which can be viewed, with an existential eye, as classic. . . . They are not Crooks. They are people, and this film is, in many ways, about what's going on now.

If *Bonnie and Clyde* had a critical cheerleader, it was the *New Yorker*'s Pauline Kael, who reveled in the "contemporary feeling" emanating from the "most excitingly American movie since *The Manchurian Candidate*," which "brings into the almost frightening public world of movies things that people have been feeling and saying and writing about." Kael compared the film to the gangster movies and crime dramas of the 1930s and 1940s (like Nicholas Ray's *They Live By Night* [1937]) to illustrate how the film deviates from the classical Hollywood mode, particularly in terms of its lack of a "secure basis for identification" for the audience, who "are made to feel but are not told how to feel." Kael's point is certainly a valid one. In classical gangster films, we identify with the "bad guy," who lives in a black-and-white, Manichaean world of good vs. evil. While morality dictates that Tommy Powers and Scarface must be eliminated in the end, there is a cloud of moral ambiguity that hovers over Bonnie and Clyde. The film's humor and stylization, particularly early in the film, gives us a window of time to identify with the couple, pledge our allegiance to them, and accept their values. But in the second half of the film, those values are called into question as the film's tone changes from comical to serious and people start to get shot and killed.

Kael also recognized the film's stylistic link to European art cinema, particularly the films of the French New Wave (François Truffaut was Beatty's first choice for director). What Kael could not have known is that *Bonnie and Clyde* would usher in a new wave of American moviemaking known today as "New Hollywood Cinema." Beginning in the late 1960s, a new generation of directors, film-school educated and heavily influenced by *auteurs* like Truffaut, Jean-Luc Godard, Michelangelo Antonioni, and Ingmar Bergman, infused American cinema with their own personal style and an "art film" sensibility. The list of "New Hollywood" filmmakers and films included such notable directors as Mike Nichols (*The Graduate* [1967], *Carnal Knowledge* [1971]); Martin Scorsese (*Mean Streets* [1973], *Taxi Driver* [1976]); Alan J. Pakula (*Klute* [1971], *The Parallax View* [1974]); and Francis Ford Coppola (*The Godfather* [1972], *The Conversation* [1974]).

Four months after panning the film, *Time* magazine featured Beatty and Dunaway on the cover (December 8, 1967) as part of their cover story on "The Shock of Freedom in Films." *Time* was now calling *Bonnie and Clyde* a "watershed picture" that signaled "a new style, a new trend" in the tradition of such American classics as *Birth of a Nation* (1915), *Citizen Kane* (1941), *Stagecoach* (1939), and *Singin' in the Rain* (1952).

One aspect of *Bonnie and Clyde* that most critics—both pro and con—addressed is the rapid shift in the film's tone from comical to serious.

Bonnie and Clyde's crime spree begins with a series of mishaps that call into question any notion that Clyde Barrow was some kind of criminal mastermind. The first bank Clyde tries to rob is literally empty, except for one lone teller who tells him the bank bailed three weeks ago (so Clyde makes the teller go outside and explain it to Bonnie, who bursts into laughter). When he tries to hold up a general store, he barely makes it out alive when a butcher comes after him with a meat cleaver. For their next job, C. W. Moss (Michael J. Pollard), a new addition to their team, is the duo's designated driver. Bonnie and Clyde hold up a bank and run out to their car, only to discover dimwitted C. W. has decided to park it. When a bank teller jumps on the car's riding board, Clyde shoots him point blank in the face. It's a disturbing, jarring moment because nothing prepares the audience for the radical shift in tone from comical to serious.

Bonnie and Clyde is best remembered for its harrowing climax, in which the couple is ambushed along a country road (the scene is historically accurate—over one thousand rounds were fired before the duo could even draw their guns). Penn shot the fifty-four-second montage sequence consisting of fifty-one shots using four cameras, each operating at a different speed (normal speed and varying rates of slow motion). The realism of an otherwise stylized sequence is enhanced by the blood we see pouring out of their bodies as they are riddled with bullets, an illusion created by squibs, small plastics bags containing red dye. As Stephen Prince observes, the sequence privileges the "mechanics of violent death . . . rather than the inner, emotional or psychological consequences of violent trauma." In an interview at the time of the film's release, Arthur Penn admitted he was not really concerned with the violent content while directing the film, adding that "the trouble with the violence in most films is that it is not violent enough. A war film that doesn't show the real horrors of war—bodies being torn apart and arms being shot off—really glorifies war."

Crowther's negative reviews and the critics' responses, both positive and negative, were a mixed blessing for the filmmakers. At the time of the film's release, Warner Brothers-Seven Arts did not have much faith in the film. As the studio's publicity executive Joe Hyams recalled, "they didn't understand the movie. On a scale of 1 to 10, 10 being the biggest culture shock for Warners, that might have been the end of it." After the initial reviews, the film was pulled from circulation, but the debate among the critics continued and the film received endorsements from critics like the *Village Voice*'s Andrew Sarris and the *New Yorker*'s Penelope Gilliat, who quipped the film "could look like a celebration of gangsters only to a man with a head full of head shavings" (guess which critic's head she was referring to?).

Bonnie and Clyde was nominated for ten Academy Awards, including nods for Best Picture and the five principal actors, and won two—for Estelle Parsons for supporting actress and cinematographer Burnett Guffey, who had won back in 1953 for *From Here to Eternity*. Although costume designer Theadora Van Runkle lost to John Truscott for *Camelot* (1967), her designs ushered in a revival of men's double-breasted suits and, for women, the maxiskirt and berets (also known as the "Bonnie beret"). In January of 1968, Ms. Dunaway was featured in a *Life* magazine photo spread entitled "Fashion That Rocked the World" wearing outfits from Bonnie's closet.

In terms of the younger generation, one wonders if they were capable of looking past the fashions, the Tommy guns, and Beatty and Dunaway's movie-star looks to really understand the film. In March of 1968, five teenagers thought it would be fun to go into the Westport Bank and Trust Company in Westport, Connecticut wearing *Bonnie and Clyde*–inspired outfits and create a disturbance. A half-dozen officers armed with shotguns and revolvers arrived on the scene and lined the youths up against the wall before bringing them down to headquarters. An editorial in the *Bridgeport Post* did not blame the incident on the youngsters or even the film, but interpreted the stunt as "another indication that *Bonnie and Clyde* is a misunderstood and misused movie" due to the "nonsense" surrounding the film, namely the "promotion and publicity," which opened the door for interpretation.

Perhaps a better testament to how the film spoke to the younger generation was a letter to the editor of the *New York Times* from Nancy Fisher, a teenager from Oklahoma City, Oklahoma. Fisher explained that she understood the real Bonnie and Clyde were "cold-hearted killers" and then goes on to describe how "Bonnie and Clyde fever" had taken over her high school and how she is playing Bonnie in the school assembly, but not the real Bonnie Parker, but Faye Dunaway as Bonnie Parker. "There will be posters of the Beatty and Dunaway Bonnie and Clyde used in the assembly," she added, "to clearly define that we are portraying their styles and influence." Along with her letter, the *Times* published a photo of blonde-haired Miss Fisher wearing a beret and '30s style dress sitting Bonnie-Parker-style on a vintage car—and holding a shotgun.

THE WILD BUNCH (1969): "IF THEY MOVE, KILL 'EM."

"If I'm so bloody that I drive people out of the theatres, then I've failed."
—Sam Peckinpah

When *The Wild Bunch* rode into theatres in the summer of 1969, director Sam Peckinpah was not a household name and his film seemed like just another old-fashioned shoot-'em-up Western. Even the film's stars—Hollywood veterans William Holden, Robert Ryan, and Ernest Borgnine—were holdovers from the studio era. There was no Dustin Hoffman or Warren Beatty or any of the young actors associated with the New Hollywood Cinema of the late 1960s. But any preconceived ideas audiences may have had going in to see *The Wild Bunch* were shattered in the film's first fifteen minutes.

In the opening sequence, a group of outlaws (the Bunch), posing as U.S. Cavalry soldiers, ride into San Rafael, a small Texas town. They intend to rob the railroad office, but their plan is thwarted by a group of bounty hunters waiting to ambush them. The shootout that erupts between the Bunch and the bounty hunters—the most violent and bloodiest to date in Hollywood history—stunned American audiences. Peckinpah literally transforms the streets of San Rafael into a battlefield with the townspeople, including the local Temperance Union, caught in the middle. Innocent men and women are among the casualties because, in Peckinpah's universe, no one is safe from the threat of violence and everyone, with the exception of children, is a potential victim (Peckinpah told a roomful of critics he was "constitutionally unable to show a child in jeopardy"). However, some children do witness the bloodbath while others are shown, in an allegorical moment, inflicting their own brand of violence on a scorpion by feeding it to an army of red ants.

It's also fitting (and clearly meant to be an inside joke) that Peckinpah's directorial credit appears on the screen when the Bunch take over the railroad office in San Rafael and are holding the staff at gunpoint. At that moment, Pike Bishop (Holden), the head of the Bunch, matter-of-factly orders his fellow bandits, "If they move, kill 'em!" which, judging from *The Wild Bunch*'s body count, seems to have been Peckinpah's watch-cry during the making of the film.

As in many Westerns of the post–World War II era, *The Wild Bunch* deviates from the classical Westerns of the 1930s and 1940s in which the hero (think John Wayne in *Stagecoach* [1939]) is a moral figure who serves as a social mediator between civilization, as represented by the Western town and its laws, and the uncivilized Western frontier. But audience demand for changes in the "classical Western formula" and the "sociopolitical realities" of postwar America redefined "the hero's motivation and mission." It was no longer viable that he would volunteer to clean up the town because it was the honorable or moral thing to do. So in the 1950s, the "professional Western" introduced moviegoers to a whole new breed of gunslingers who are "cynical, self-conscious, and even 'incorporated.'" But the real villains in *The Wild Bunch* are not the outlaws or the bounty hunters, but the oppressive, corrupt forces of corporate greed, progress, and power represented by the banks, the railroad company, and a fascist dictator-in-the-making— a sadistic Mexican general named Mapache (Emilio Fernández).

The bounty hunters who surprise the Bunch are being paid by the railroad company to kill Pike and his men. Like their intended victims, they have no regard for the law and are only interested in filling their own pockets (which they literally do after the San Rafael shootout when they start pillaging valuables off of still-warm corpses). Their leader, Deke Thornton (Ryan), is a convict with a personal investment in hunting down the Bunch. He must find them or get sent back to prison. Deke also used to ride with Pike until the law caught up with them. Pike managed to escape while Deke was sent to prison.

Like the bounty hunters, the Bunch are forced to become "guns for hire" when the robbery in San Rafael turns out to be a bust (the bags of money are filled with steel washers). Pike's dreams of early retirement are shattered, so he and his men agree to rob a train carrying guns and ammunition to the army of Mapache's nemesis, Pancho Villa. One of the Bunch, a Mexican named Angel (Jaime Sanchez), whose father was killed by Mapache, gives some of the weapons to the general's enemies. He is caught and brutally tortured by Mapache. Instead of simply walking away with their money (and perhaps to make up for abandoning Deke years ago), Pike and his men demonstrate their loyalty to one of their own by leading a suicidal assault on Mapache's army. In the end, the Bunch, Mapache, and his army are wiped out. Only Deke, who arrives after the show is over, survives.

The bloody climax between the Bunch and Mapache's soldiers, like the opening sequence, is excessive, chaotic, and visually stunning. As in *Bonnie and Clyde*, one device Peckinpah repeatedly and effectively uses for dramatic effect is slow motion, which *Time* magazine found to be particularly effective:

> Using a combination of fast cutting and slow motion, Peckinpah creates scenes of uncontrolled frenzy in which the feeling of chaotic violence is almost overwhelming. Where the slow-motion murders in *Bonnie and Clyde* were balletic, similar scenes in *The Wild Bunch* have agonizing effect of prolonging the moment of impact, giving each death its own individual horror.

Newsweek's Joseph Morgenstern also appreciated Peckinpah's use of beauty "as a tool for irony. The towns that these men destroy sit green and soft on the land." In his review in the *New York Times*, Vincent Canby pointed out that the "choreographed brutality" of the violence is what makes it both horrible and beautiful:

> Borrowing a device from *Bonnie and Clyde*, Peckinpah suddenly reduces the camera speed to slow motion, which at first heightens the horror of the mindless slaughter, and then—and this is what really carries horror—makes it beautiful, almost abstract, and finally into terrible parody.

The excessive violence did not go unnoticed by the MPAA, which, according to the *Los Angeles Times*, initially slapped the film with an X rating. Warner Brothers-Seven Arts subsequently cut and resubmit the film to the MPAA seven times before the X was reduced to an R. After the film was previewed, Peckinpah reportedly shortened the opening fight sequence to improve the pacing.

But the director tells a slightly different story. In a 1969 interview with Paul Schrader, Peckinpah said, "there was never danger of an X rating for violence. We had an R right from the beginning. I actually cut more than Warners requested. There were certain things Warners wanted cut, but I went farther. I had to make it play better."

The director's final cut of the movie was 145 minutes. The version that opened in theatres in June/early July and reviewed by the critics was 143 minutes, but if you went to see it in mid-July, the running time was 135 minutes. When Vincent Canby became aware that eight more minutes were cut out of the film, he telephoned producer Phil Feldman, who explained the cuts (or as he called them, the "lifts") were not in response to the negative response they received from some critics to the violence, but to accelerate the pace and shorten the running time so the theatres could add an extra screening. After seeing the second version of the film, Canby admitted one of the four cuts (a three-and-a-half minute sequence in which Pancho Villa's men attack Mapache's Mexican Federal Forces), did "ease the flow of the story," but the remaining changes altered the narrative, particularly the deletion of a flashback in which Deke and Pike are caught in an ambush in a bordello (we're told these men were friends, yet this is the only scene in which they appear together). Feldman claimed all of the cuts were made with the director's consent, but Peckinpah described the cuts as a "disaster" and stated in simple terms, "I do not agree with that in any way, shape, or form."

The British censors only required nine additional seconds to be cut, which was minor compared to the four and a half minutes demanded by the Canadian censors. Peckinpah traveled to Toronto to meet with O. J. Silverthorn, head of Canadian censorship, and convinced him to pass the film after cutting only twenty-four feet (a total of sixteen seconds). The film was subsequently banned in Alberta, where the censor said *The Wild Bunch*'s "repugnant barbarism" and "extreme brutality . . . made *Fistful of Dollars* look like *Mary Poppins*."

While the censors may have failed to understand (or chose not to consider) the message the director was relaying through the excessiveness and visual stylization of violence, the critics generally understood that Peckinpah was using violence in the context of the Western genre to comment on violence and government corruption during the Vietnam era. "Peckinpah's argument, if I understand him," wrote the *Los Angeles Time*'s Charles Champlin, "is that violence is a primal instinct in each of us. . . . And he suggests, in his gory, dramatic terms, that we have not merely a capacity for violence but a joy in violence, a blood lust." At a press junket prior to the film's opening, Feldman, Peckinpah, Holden, and Borgnine fielded questions from critics, who not surprisingly focused mostly on the violence. Peckinpah chose to let the film speak for itself, though he did remark that he wanted "to emphasize the horror and agony violence provides. Violence is not a game." When asked why he did not make a film about Vietnam, Peckinpah replied, "The Western is a universal frame within which it is possible to comment on today."

A letter written to the *New York Times* is a testament to how *The Wild Bunch* succeeded in tapping into the younger generation's fears over the prevalence of violence in contemporary society. The author, nineteen-year-old Tracy Hotchner, who, over a decade later, would be one of four screenwriters of the Joan Crawford biopic, *Mommie Dearest* (1981), responded to Vincent Canby's reading of the film's violence:

At 19, I am a member of that generation which has grown up surrounded by violence. In television we have been continually exposed to programs devoted to gun and fist fights. The knowledge and threat of riots in the cities has been ever present. And the war in Vietnam has had prominence in newspapers and newscasts for as long as I can recall. It has often been asked what effect this violence will have on my generation, and it was not until I saw "The Wild Bunch" that I began to have some insight into the possible effects of relentless violence on the people who are exposed to it.

Hotchner then makes a connection between the onscreen violence and a fight that apparently broke out within the theatre, implying that the film had a direct effect on their behavior (apparently the fisticuffs started when a woman purposely blew smoke into the face of another spectator who had complained about her cigarette). More importantly, she disagrees with Canby's assertion that slow motion "makes it [violence] beautiful, almost abstract, and finally into terrible par-ody." Instead, she found the violence to be all too real:

> Not at any time do the staggering men with shot-off faces seen close up, nor men with blood gushing from their groin, nor women with shot up breasts seem a parody. The realism is nauseatingly main-tained. . . . For most people there is *no* break in the realism, and thus the film is unbearable.

As Canby so rightfully explains in his reply, her revulsion to what she saw upon the screen was exactly the audience reaction Peckinpah was going for. The same can be said for the link Hotchner made between the violence happening onscreen and a few rows in front of her. While it is difficult to suggest that the violence in the film instigated what was happening in the theatre, the incident she witnessed certainly served the film's thematic exploration of violence by reinforcing that despite the expressive stylization, bullets and blood are indeed for real.

A CLOCKWORK ORANGE (1971): "A LITTLE OF THE OLD ULTRA-VIOLENCE"

Anthony Burgess's 1962 novel *A Clockwork Orange* is a morality tale set in a dystopian society ruled by a repressive regime and overrun by nasty youths with an unquenchable thirst for "ultra-violence." The story's narrator, fifteen-year-old Alex, is the authoritarian leader of a gang, which converses in its own brand of slang (Nadsat, which sounds like a cross between Russian and British English). One night, after break-ing into a house and terrorizing the female occupants, one of Alex's "droogies" (friends) turns on him. He is caught by the police and sent to prison, where, with some help from his cellmates, he beats another inmate to death. Alex is ordered to be a guinea pig for a form of aver-sion therapy, Ludovico's Technique, which is designed, through a com-bination of drugs and exposure to violent films, to trigger nausea when the subject is exposed to violence and hears the Ninth Symphony (last movement) of his favorite composer, Beethoven. The treatment's suc-cess results in his early release from prison, but once he is back in the outside world, Ludovico's Technique leaves him vulnerable to violence to the point where he is driven to attempt suicide by the husband of one of his victims, who locks him in a room and blasts the Ninth Symphony. In response to the experiment's failure, the government does some damage control and reverses Alex's condition. Back to his old self, Alex shows signs that he might resume his life of violence.

In the final chapter (chapter 21) of the British edition of Burgess's novel, Alex comes to the realization that it might be time for him to grow up and consider getting married and having children. Burgess explained he purposely divided the book into twenty-one chapters because "twenty-one is the symbol of human maturity, since at twenty-one you got the vote and assumed adult responsibility." According to Burgess, the last chapter was excluded from the American version because his New York publisher thought it was a "sellout" and "bland" and demonstrated an "unwillingness to accept that a human being could be a model of unregenerable evil." The American version served as the basis for Kubrick's film, which both end with the line "I was cured all right." In 1987, W. W. Norton & Company published a new edition of *A Clockwork Orange* that included chapter 21, which was also reprinted in *Rolling Stone* magazine (March 26, 1987).

In *A Clockwork Orange*, Burgess envisions a society in which citizens are robbed of their free will by a totalitarian government, which attempts to eradicate violence through mind control. As he explained in 1989, his book is not about violence, but free will and "the necessity to be free even if freedom is breaking the moral law." The inspiration for Alex and his droogies reportedly came from several sources, including the "Teddy Boy" youth subculture in post-war Britain, and his own encounter with a group of young rogues during a trip to Russia. Then there was a personal tragedy involving his pregnant wife, who was savagely attacked during World War II by four American deserters. She survived, but they lost their baby. Burgess fell into a deep depression and she became suicidal. He claims writing *A Clockwork Orange* was a way for him to deal with the tragedy. The veracity of the story of his wife's attack and Burgess's claim he was once mistakenly diagnosed with a cerebral tumor were challenged by biographer Roger Lewis in his book *The Life and Lies of Anthony Burgess*, published in 2002.

Then there is the question of Burgess's politics. Although a book like *A Clockwork Orange* may on the surface seems as if it is the product of a leftist imagination, Burgess was actually a staunch conservative who once noted that he "was always so conservative that my conservatism looked like Communism." He feared any form of government control, including the Socialist policies and programs of Britain, which he believed had turned his own country into a welfare state. The novel's title, which Burgess claims is derived from the Cockney expression ("He's as queer as a clockwork orange"), is a metaphor for what happens to Alex when he undergoes the Ludovico's Treatment, which deprives him of his ability to make moral choices:

> By definition a human being is endowed with free will. He can use this to choose between good and evil. If he can only perform good or only perform evil, then he is a clockwork orange—meaning that he has the appearance of an organism lovely with color and juice but is in fact only a clockwork toy to be wound up by God or the Devil or (since this is increasingly replacing both) the Almighty State. It is inhuman to be totally good as it is to be totally evil. The important thing is moral choice. Evil has to exist along with good, in order that moral choice may operate.

Kubrick's screenplay is faithful to Burgess's novel. Alex, who is a few years older in the film, also serves as the film's nihilistic narrator. He still has a penchant for "lovely, lovely Ludwig van" and his "Ninth Symphony" and converses in Nadstat with his droogies, who prowl the streets at night preying on innocent people and committing random, mindless acts of ultra-violence (though Alex's heinous attack on two ten-year-old girls is thankfully omitted from the film). Alex's moral universe is a black hole. He feels no guilt because he has no conscience and no soul.

Presented in a more stylized than realistic fashion, the scenes of sexual violence, particularly Alex's rape of Mrs. Alexander, are shocking and disturbing, yet effectively establish the amorality of our narrator. Alex croons the song "Singin' in the Rain" and performs a little tap dance as he kicks Mr. Alexander and cuts off his wife's cat suit until she is naked to the beat of the music (Gene Kelly's version is later played over the closing credits). The contrast between the song (an expression of joy) and what's happening on the screen makes the heinous act all the more difficult to watch. Some critics, such as Roger Ebert and Pauline Kael, read the scenes of sexual violence as nothing more than gratuitous. Ebert dismissed the film as an "ideological mess, a paranoid right-wing fantasy masquerading as an Orwellian warning" with a protagonist who is only violent "in order for this movie to entertain in the way Kubrick intends." Kael accused Kubrick of "sucking up to the thugs in the audience" in what amounts to an "abhorrent viewing experience" complete with violent scenes (such as the attack of the young woman by the rival gang) that are the "purest exploitation." Similarly, David Denby accused Kubrick of being "drawn to the images of violence themselves rather than any meaning which might emerge from them."

One critical jab that elicited a response from both Kubrick and his leading man Malcolm McDowell was a piece written by Fred Hechinger for the *New York Times* in response to a comment McDowell had made during an interview for the same paper. McDowell claimed liberals hated *A Clockwork Orange* "because they're dreamers and it shows them realities, shows 'em not tomorrow but now. Cringe, don't they, when faced with the bloody truth." In his response, Hechinger argues *A Clockwork Orange* is part of a recent trend in movies toward "a deeply anti-liberal totalitarian nihilism." "An alert liberal," Hechinger warns, "should recognize the voice of fascism." Kubrick was understandably not pleased and publicly criticized Hechinger for his lack of analysis and evidence to support his claim in what amounts to a "fuzzy and unfocussed . . . piece of alarmist journalism."

Upon its release in the United States, the film received an X rating from the MPAA, though later that year Kubrick agreed to cut the film in order to get the rating down to an R. In accordance with MPAA rules, the film was pulled from circulation for sixty days before re-release with the new rating. Ironically, it wasn't the rape sequences that were trimmed, but a few frames of the *ménage à trois* sequence (between Alex and the two girls, shown in fast motion to Rossini's "William Tell Overture") and frames from the filmed rape sequence Alex is forced to watch as part of his treatment.

The X was certainly a hindrance to the film receiving widespread distribution. Kubrick and Warner Brothers ran into another problem when thirty American newspapers agreed not to run ads for any X-rated films. The *Detroit Daily News* published an editorial outlining their rationale for supporting the ban:

> Some will fault us as "not with it," as defenders of a defunct moral code. Our answer is that, in our way, a sick motion picture industry is using pornography and an appeal to prurience to bolster theatre attendance; quite simply, we do not want to assist them in the process. . . . We anticipate no movie industry cleanup as a result of our decision. . . . Perhaps the only result will be in our own satisfaction in a modest declaration against the theory that makes hardcore sex, voyeurism and sadistic violence the prime ingredients of art and entertainment in the 1970s.

The editorial was reprinted in the *New York Times* along with Kubrick's response, in which the director draws an analogy between their policy and that of Adolf Hitler toward "degenerate art" ("we have set out to rid the nation and our people of all those influences threatening its existence and character") and questions whose interests they are serving:

> *The Detroit News* censors would indiscriminately defame and discredit all X films because they do not conform to what they judge to be the standards of their readers. . . . Many readers may find their purification program offensive. They may find that they are censoring their readers rather than their advertisers; that they are imposing their judgment in an arbitrary and exclusive fashion upon the right to be informed. . . . High standards of moral behavior can not be maintained by the coercive effect of the law. Or that of certain newspapers.

Surprisingly, the film was not banned in Britain, but released uncut and received an X classification (suitable for those 18 and over) by the British Board of Film Censorship (BBFC). Stephen Murphy, secretary of the BBFC at the time of the film's release, called it "one of the most brilliant pieces of cinema, not simply of this year, but possibly of the decade." His support essentially ended his career at the BBFC.

The controversy surrounding the film and its violent content continued to escalate and was being played out in the press even before the film hit the screens. Home Secretary Reginald Maudling expressed his concern over the connection between the rising crime rate in Britain and film violence and singled out *A Clockwork Orange* despite the fact that he hadn't seen it. "There is a new film out this week that I ought to go see," he told *The Sun*, "If things are being shown which one could reasonably suppose are contributing to the degree of violence, I think I ought to know." Maurice Edelman, Labour MP, warned the public that when "*A Clockwork Orange* is released, it will lead to a clockwork cult which will magnify teen violence. The phallic dress of the droogies with their codpieces will no doubt become widespread as the sub-Western gear in the High Street imitated from Western films." The implication that *A Clockwork Orange* is a direct cause for an escalation in teen violence was certainly open for debate, yet Edelman's warning proved to be prophetic when the papers begin to report a series of copycat crimes—violent attacks that mirrored those which occurred in the film. Defendants started to claim in court that the film incited them to commit violent crimes.

- A Dutch tourist was raped in Lancashire by a group of men chanting "Singin' in the Rain."
- A sixteen-year-old boy, dressed in white overalls and wearing a bowler hat and combat boots, was convicted of beating a young child.
- James Palmer, sixteen, beat a sixty-year-old homeless man to death. In typical tabloid style, *The Daily Mail* did not hesitate linking the crime with the film: "The terrifying violence of the film *A Clockwork Orange* fascinated a quiet boy from a Grammar School . . . and it turned him in to a brutal murderer." But Palmer had never seen the film and his only knowledge of it came from his friends. One judge stated, "We must stamp out this horrible trend which has been inspired by this wretched film."

A Clockwork Orange enjoyed a healthy run in theatres in Great Britain, but after a year the film seemed to have disappeared. Unbeknownst to the public, Kubrick pulled the film out of circulation without explanation. Technically, he did not have the right to ban it, but Warner Brothers, the studio which produced his last four films, honored his request. He never discussed his reasons publicly, though most assumed it was in reaction to the violent attacks that had taken place, though some speculated he and his family had received death threats. A few months after his death in 1999, his widow Christiane Kubrick told *Sight and Sound* magazine that her husband was "baffled" by the press's reaction to the film. "Because *A Clockwork Orange* played with the background of England," she said, "they blamed every crime in history on Stanley's film. That only happened here, nowhere else."

The director succeeded in keeping the film under lock and key for over twenty-five years. He even refused to allow the film to be shown at a 1979 retrospective of his work at the National Film Theatre. In 1993, Jane Giles, the manager of a London cinema, La Scala, was fined £1,000 for screening the film publicly. Giles had not seen the film before and claimed she was unaware it had been withdrawn. After Kubrick's death, there was speculation that the film would finally be back in theatres. Julian Senior, Vice President of Advertising and Publicity for Warner Brothers/Europe, confirmed that he had discussed the matter with him, though Kubrick had planned to wait until after *Eyes Wide Shut* was completed.

On March 17, 2000, one year and ten days after Kubrick's death, London audiences, many for the first time, had a chance to see *A Clockwork Orange*. As esteemed film critic Alexander Walker observed, "Whether one likes it or not, freedom of choice—the essential theme of the film—has at last regained its place on the screen."

SNUFF (1976): "THE BLOODIEST THING THAT EVER HAPPENED IN FRONT OF A CAMERA!"

One of the all-time great movie hoaxes played on American moviegoers occurred in February of 1976 when a low-budget, X-rated film called *Snuff* opened in Manhattan. The film was rumored to include footage of an actual, real-life, honest-to-God murder of one of the actresses in the film. By then *Variety* had already debunked the rumor that "the bloodiest thing that ever happened in front of a camera" did indeed not happen. But the fact that it was a hoax did not matter to the morally superior, who believed the film was yet another sign that American culture and morality were on a downward spiral, and feminists who objected to a film selling violence against women (real or fake) as entertainment. When *Snuff* was released, it also had a self-imposed X-rating, which by then had become synonymous with pornography.

Prior to the film's opening, the FBI and the New York City Police Department investigated rumors about 8mm color snuff films produced in South America that were allegedly being distributed in the U.S. According to New York Police Detective Joseph Horman, the films were reportedly screened in New York, Los Angeles, New Orleans, and Miami, though no law enforcement officer had ever seen one of the films. Horman, who described them as "the ultimate obscenity," believed organized crime was peddling the films for $1,500 each. One film was "reported to show an actress, unaware of the true nature of her role in the sex film, being stabbed to death and dismembered." That film was, of course, *Snuff*.

Snuff was shot in Argentina in 1970 under the title *The Slaughter* by filmmakers Michael and Roberta Findlay for $33,000. The cast consisted of mostly local actors whose voices were (poorly) postdubbed into English. The plot—if one can call it that—centers around a Charles Manson–like cult leader named Satan (pronounced "S'tan," I guess to avoid any confusion with that *other* Prince of Darkness) who has mental control over four hippie chicks, who bare their breasts for the camera in between stabbing, shooting, and mutilating their innocent victims, which include a sleazy producer, a grandmother, an elderly shopkeeper, and a little girl. S'tan has declared war on the wealthy, but instead of joining the Communist Party, he sends his girls to the home of a rich Argentine family. In a scene clearly "inspired" by the brutal murder of Roman Polanski's pregnant wife, actress Sharon Tate, and her friends, they slaughter (and in one instance castrate) the family and their friends. The last victim is a pregnant actress, who is stabbed to death.

Producer Allan Shackleton, who purchased the film from the Findlays, then tacked on a new ending. Suddenly, the camera pulls back to reveal that what we are watching is taking place on a movie set (but the actress in front of the camera is not the same one). The director compliments her on her performance and starts making out with her. She starts to panic when she realizes the camera is still rolling. He produces a knife and slashes her shoulder. Then, while the film crew holds her down, he cuts off her fingers and her arm with a buzz saw. He then opens her chest up with a razor and takes out her insides and holds them up to the camera. Cut to black (the absence of credits before and after the film only adds to its mystique).

The artwork for the film's advertising campaign featured a woman being decapitated by a movie clapboard with the film's title on it. Another ad with the same tagline ("The picture they said could never be shown. . . . The bloodiest thing that ever happened in front of a camera. . . . The film that only could be made in South America . . . where life is cheap!") included a pair of scissors with blood on it on top of a bloodied photograph of a woman cut at the head, breasts, and torso. Employing the same advertising techniques that have been used since the 1920s to sell exploitation films, the campaign titillates and teases the audience by implying they are going to see far more than what's actually in the film.

So did anyone who paid four dollars in 1976 to see a woman get dismembered think it was real? Answer: possibly. Shackleton was repeatedly asked by the press if the footage at the end of the film was real. He said he could not answer the question, explaining, "I'd be in jail in two minutes. . . . I'd be a damn fool to admit it. If it isn't real, I'd be a damn fool to admit it." Then again, Shackleton also denied in an interview that *Snuff* and *The Slaughter* were the same film. If anything, Shackleton deserves high marks for his impeccable timing (cashing in on the snuff film rumor that had been circulating for years prior to the film) and for making the last seven minutes seem as if they were part of the Findlays' film by using the same Z-grade special effects that would embarrass any NYU film student.

Although word eventually spread that the murder was a hoax, the backlash didn't diminish. *Snuff* was the first film banned by Maryland's state censorship board on the basis of violence. The board demanded the final scene be cut, but Barry Glasen, a spokesman for the film's distributor, Monarch Releasing, said the company would not authorize the cut because the film's "violence builds up to full blast" in the final scene and "it's the last five minutes when the film gets its novelty. To delete this portion would be suicide at the box office." George J. A.

Andreadakis, a member of the state censor board, told the *Baltimore Sun* that he believed the last five minutes were "genuine." "I'd have to see the woman in person before I'd believe otherwise. . . . I was so worked up about it that I got sick, I got excited. I called the FBI. I'd pay to see that girl just to put my stomach to rest." The ban was challenged in court, where the attorneys for the state argued that the film was designed to appeal to sadists and masochists and should be denied a seal because it might trigger deviants to commit similar acts of violence. Circuit Court Judge Harry A. Cole upheld the ban because the film passed the three-tier obscenity test established by the Supreme Court in *Miller v. California*, 413 U.S. 15 (1973): 1) the average person, applying community standards, finds the work, taken as a whole, appeals to the prurient interest; 2) the work depicts or describes, in a patently offensive way, sexual conduct or excretory functions specifically defined by applicable state law; and 3) the work, taken as a whole, lacks serious literary, artistic, political, or scientific value. Judge Cole also offered his interpretation of the film, stating that the sex scenes formed a frame for the acts of violence, which all led to the ultimate in psychotic sexual gratification—the dismemberment of the young woman. *Snuff* was slated to open at Baltimore's Hippodrome Theatre, but due to the ban, it was replaced with a double bill—*The Texas Chainsaw Massacre* (1974) and the Italian slasher movie *Torso* (1973)—which were advertised as "up to snuff in sheer terror."

In response to the film's release, a coalition of feminists calling themselves "Women Against Violence Against Women," was formed to protest the film's opening in major cities around the country, including Los Angeles, San Francisco, New York, Boston, and Washington. In Fullerton, a community in Orange County, California, the film was seized after a judge and members of the police department found it allegedly obscene due to violence. Eleanor Snow, director of the Feminist Women's Health Center, said films like *Snuff* "encourage and pander to deranged minds and perpetuate the fantasy that women are masochistic and 'ask for it'." Two theatres in neighboring Garden Grove and Santa Ana subsequently decided to cancel the film, though they claimed it was not because of the feminists' protest, but because "it's a trashy movie." Feminists were credited with getting the film withdrawn after a day in San Jose, California. They picketed a Philadelphia theatre, and the film was withdrawn and moved to a suburban drive-in. When feminists assembled in front of a theatre in Wilmington, Delaware, the manager didn't screen the last ten minutes and returned the three-dollar admission to the patrons (*Snuff* was replaced with Barbra Streisand in *Funny Lady* [1975], which no doubt appealed to a *very* different audience).

But the protestors were not limited to feminists. When the film opened in Hollywood, the Adult Film Association of America—the people who make porn—formed a picket line in front of Mann's Theatre. They were not protesting the content of the film, but the current ratings system and the X rating, which didn't differentiate between sex and violence. A spokesman for the organization felt the film's advertising campaign was a "rip-off" because "with the X rating people think they are going to see a sex film and instead will just see a violent film. We feel theatres have a right to show violent films, but we want them distinguished from the type of product our members show."

Meanwhile, in New York, where *Snuff* was playing, a group of prominent men and women that included authors Sol Yurick, Susan Sontag, and Eric Bentley; activists David Dellinger, Gloria Steinem, and Susan Brownmiller; and actors Ellen Burstyn, Shelley Winters, and Viveca Lindfors pressured Manhattan District Attorney Robert Morgenthau to shut the film down. But Morgenthau had no basis for honoring their request. After conducting a month-long investigation to determine if any women were harmed during the making of the picture, he confirmed it was a hoax and the actress who was allegedly murdered onscreen was alive and well (and "embarrassed by her performance" and wished to stay anonymous).

The fact that it was a hoax did not deter feminists, who believed *Snuff* exemplified violent trends not only in pornography, but also on album covers (the photo of a woman's clothed genital area on Montrose's *Jump on It* [1976]), billboards (a bound and bruised woman in an ad for the Rolling Stones' *Black and Blue* [1976]), and magazine fashion spreads. In July of 1977, a group of feminist leaders, including Steinem and Brownmiller, met to discuss the issue and outline ways to combat what Steinem characterized as the "acceptance of the idea that violence is a legitimate part of sexuality." Ironically, their participation aligned them with a campaign waged by moralists, political conservatives, and the Catholic Church against "smut," specifically pornographic magazines and films. They were opposed by groups like the American Civil Liberties Union, the American Library Association, and some members of the National Coalition Against Censorship, which believed the First Amendment includes all forms of expression.

Surprisingly, America was spared a sequel, though there's no doubt if *Snuff* were made today it would have been turned into a lucrative franchise with multiple sequels (*Snuff: The Next Day*, *Snuff Harder*, *Snuff III*) with increasingly higher body counts.

THE WARRIORS (1979): "THESE ARE THE ARMIES OF THE NIGHT . . ."

In Xenophon's *Anabasis*, an army of ten thousand Greek mercenaries is stranded in enemy territory when their leader, Cyrus the Younger, dies in battle. To return home, they must travel one thousand miles by foot through Persia to the Black Sea. When they reach their destination, they cry out, *Thalatta, thalatta* (Greek for "the sea, the sea") before boarding merchant ships and sailing for home.

Anabasis was the inspiration for Sol Yurick's 1965 novel *The Warriors*. One July 4th night, sometime in the future, Ismael, the leader of New York City's largest gang, summons all of the city's street gangs to a park in the Bronx. He calls for a truce and asks them to join forces together to fight "The Man." His speech is interrupted by a fight that escalates into gunfire when the police become involved. Ismael is killed in the crossfire. For the remainder of the novel, the reader follows one gang, the Dominators, as they make their way back through enemy territory to their home turf in Coney Island.

In adapting *The Warriors* to the screen, first-time director Walter Hill (who cowrote the screenplay with David Shaber) retained the basic premise of Yurick's novel but raised the stakes for the Dominators (renamed "The Warriors") as they try to make their way home. In the spirit of Xenophon's story, Ismael is renamed Cyrus (Roger Hill), who, as the leader of the most respected gang in New York, the Gramercy Riffs, summons representatives from the city's street gangs. He tells them if they form a united front, they will outnumber the police and take control of the city ("Can you count, suckers? I say the future is ours . . . if you can count!") His speech is cut short when Luther (David Patrick

Kelly), the crazy leader of the Rogues, shoots him dead and then blames it on Cleon (Dorsey Wright), the leader of the Warriors, who is killed by the mob. The police arrive and pandemonium breaks out. All of the gangs in the city, along with the entire New York City police force, are now after the Warriors, and it's up to the gang's second-in-command, Swan (Michael Beck), to lead them home.

The film builds to what one would expect to be a violent climax, but there's no major rumble. In the final scene, Luther and his Rogues have followed the Warriors back to Coney Island (that's where Luther, a total psycho menacingly played by Kelly, taunts them with the film's most memorable line, "Warriors, come out and play-ee-ay!") Luther tries to shoot Swan, who stops him by throwing his switchblade into his wrist. Then suddenly, the Gramercy Riffs, who now know Luther is the real killer, arrive on the scene. Their leader pays the Warriors a compliment ("You Warriors are good, real good." to which Swan replies, "The best.") We never see what the Gramercy Riffs actually do to Luther, but judging from his cries, it's not pretty.

Like the droogs in *A Clockwork Orange*, the identity of each gang is distinguished by its appearance. The shirtless Warriors wear brown leather vests with their gang's name on the back. The Punks wear overalls and bright-colored striped shirts and travel on roller skates. The Gramercy Riffs are first seen in *karategi*, but for their early-morning appearance on the beach the following day, they wear less stylish but more casual black jeans and t-shirts. But the "Best Costume" honors go to the Baseball Furies, who wear pinstriped baseball uniforms, cover their faces with multicolored paint (à la the rock group Kiss), and carry bats (between their outfits and makeup, these guys must need at least an hour before they can show themselves on the street at night).

Perhaps the biggest surprise about *The Warriors* is that for a film about gangs, it is not excessively violent or bloody. The fight sequences, such as the Warriors' battle in the park with the bat-wielding Baseball Furies or in the restroom with the Punks, are highly choreographed in the tradition of a Samurai movie. Instead of everyone pulling out a gun and blasting each other to bits, which is how it would be done in the movies today, the Warriors defend themselves the old-fashioned way—with their fists—even if much of it defies believability. Surprisingly, there is no racial tension between gang members, and some gangs, including the Warriors, are racially integrated.

The Warriors opened in 630 U.S. theatres on February 9, 1979, to respectable business, earning $3.4 million its first weekend, and would go on to earn a total of $10 million in its first two weeks. But the film's success at the box office was overshadowed by a series of tragic incidents.

On February 12, 1979, at a drive-in theatre in Palm Springs, California, a fight broke out between members of a black youth gang, the Blue Coats, and their white rivals, the Family, leaving eighteen-year-old Marvin Kenneth Eller dead from a .22 caliber bullet. On that same evening, eighteen-year-old Timothy Gitchel, along with his brother and two friends, attended the 10:10 p.m. show at the Esplanade triplex in Oxnard, California. When the film came on, fifteen youths, who were suspected of drinking and smoking grass during the previous show, attacked the teenagers. Gitchel died from a knife wound to his heart. Three days later, Martin Yakubowicz, a sixteen-year-old high school sophomore, was heading home on a Boston subway from his after-school job. Yakubowicz was stabbed to death by Michael Barrett, who, along with his two friends, had just sat through two screenings of *The Warriors*. Barrett, who was under the influence of drugs and alcohol, and Yakubowicz were members of rival youth gangs. Another incident attributed to the film involved twelve youths who allegedly harassed Manhattan subway passengers at the IND stop at 42nd Street and Eighth Avenue after seeing the film. Confrontations between New York youths also reportedly occurred in theatres in the Bronx and in Queens.

After the February 12 incidents, Paramount Pictures offered to pay for security guards to patrol the lobbies of the movie theatres where the film was being shown. The studio also canceled the national advertising campaign for the film, which consisted of television and radio spots and print ads. The artwork for the advertisement featured a drawing of the various gang members with the tagline "These are the Armies of the Night. They are 100,000 strong. They outnumber the cops five to one. They could run New York City. Tonight they are all out to get the Warriors." According to Frank Mancuso, Senior Vice President in Charge of Distribution, "Paramount did not want to exploit in any way a regrettable situation that has developed." The following week, *Variety* reported that the trailer for the film was continuing to play in 800–900 theatres and it was "'rougher' in content than either the radio or TV blurbs that were yanked. The article also noted that the subway posters containing the original tagline ("These Are the Armies of the Night") had never been changed or moved.

Citizen groups pressured Paramount to pull the movie. A South Central Los Angeles citizens' group claimed the film incited violence and racial strife between black and white youths. Dr. Ernest H. Smith, a pediatrician at the Charles H. Drew Medical School, denounced the film as "dangerous to all Americans regardless of race, color or creed." A Bronx-based "clean-up group" known as the "Rock Brigade" picketed in front of the Loews Theatre in Times Square. Carrying signs reading "Violence Begets Violence," they demanded the management enforce the film's R rating and prevent anyone under seventeen from seeing the film.

Director Walter Hill was reportedly surprised by the reaction to the film. In his mind, *The Warriors* was in some ways making "fun of the traditional youth film" and not meant to be a realistic treatment of gang life:

> I tried to do the motion picture as a comic book. The characters were comic-book characters, the relationships were comic-book relation-ships, the staging was comic-book staging. People say the characters are two-dimensional; *I* thought the characters were one-dimen-sional. I was trying to do something like the old EC comics, because ultimately I didn't think you could do a serious story about this sub-ject.

One device Hill employs that certainly counters the film's realistic elements (such as his use of New York City locations) is the comic-book transitions between scenes in which the image freezes and turns into comic-book artwork. One of the few critics who recognized what Hill was going for was Pauline Kael, who called *The Warriors* "a real moviemaker's movie: it has in visual terms the kind of impact that "Rock Around the Clock" did behind the titles of *Blackboard Jungle. The War-riors* is like visual rock." Kael likened Hill to a "fantasist, of a peculiarly

John Rice and May Irwin, stars of the stage play *The Widow Jones*, reenact their famous kiss for Edison's camera in *The May Irwin Kiss* (1896).

The Ku Klux Klan prepares to lynch Gus (Walter Long) in D. W. Griffith's *The Birth of a Nation* (1915).

Anna Magnani (center) stars as a peasant woman taunted by villagers for believing she has been touched by God in *Il miracolo* (The Miracle) (1948).

"Will you try to seduce me?" Patty O'Neill (Maggie McNamara) wonders what bachelor Donald Gresham (William Holden) is up to in director Otto Preminger's adult comedy *The Moon Is Blue* (1953).

Leach (Warren Finnerty) prepares for his next fix in *The Connection* (1962), directed by Shirley Clarke.

George (Richard Burton, left) pushes Martha (Elizabeth Taylor, right) over the edge as their guests, Nick (George Segal) and Honey (Sandy Dennis), look on in the screen version of Edward Albee's *Who's Afraid of Virginia Woolf?* (1966).

Antonio "Tony" Camonte (Paul Muni) faces off with the cops in the violent climax of
Scarface (1932).

"They're young. They're in love. They rob banks." Buck Barrow (Gene Hackman, left) helps Bonnie Parker (Faye Dunaway) and his brother Clyde (Warren Beatty) "stick up" a bank in *Bonnie & Clyde* (1967).

William Holden as aging gunslinger Pike Bishop in Sam Peckinpah's *The Wild Bunch* (1969).

"These are the armies of the night." The original poster for the controversial gang drama *The Warriors* (1979).

Mickey (Woody Harrelson) loves Mallory (Juliette Lewis) in Oliver Stone's satire on violence and the media, *Natural Born Killers* (1994).

Marlene Dietrich in her signature white tails and top hat in *Blonde Venus* (1932).

"The finest woman to ever walk the streets." Mae West strikes a sexy pose in a publicity still for *She Done Him Wrong* (1933).

"The most beautiful woman in the world." Austrian-born actress Hedy Kiesler, who would soon be known as Hedy Lamarr, swims au naturel in this censored scene from *Ekstase* (Ecstasy) (1933).

Fenton Bailey and Randy Barbato's *Inside Deep Throat* (2005) examines the cultural impact and controversy surrounding the popular "porno chic" flick of the 1970s.

Lena examines her past relationships with men in the Swedish import *Jag är nyfiken—en film i gult* (I Am Curious [Yellow]) (1967).

The degradation of innocent youth in Italian director Pier Paolo Pasolini's final and most controversial film, *Salò o le 120 giornate di Sodoma* (Salo, or the 120 Days of Sodom) (1975).

Al Pacino is an undercover cop on the trail of a serial killer in *Cruising* (1980).

The Fuehrer and the Filmmaker: Adolf Hitler and Leni Riefenstahl during the filming of *Triumph des Willens* (Triumph of the Will) (1935).

A miners' strike puts a strain on the marriage of Ramon (Juan Chacón) and Esperanza (Rosaura Revueltas) in *Salt of the Earth* (1954).

Mookie (Spike Lee), Sal (Danny Aiello), and his sons, Vito (Richard Edson) and Pino (John Turturro), outside Sal's Pizzeria in *Do the Right Thing* (1989).

Christian goody-goody Mercia (Elissa Landi) doesn't approve of the company her pagan suitor Marcus (Fredric March, center, standing) keeps in Cecil B. DeMille's *The Sign of the Cross* (1933).

Anthony Quinn stars as Hamza, the uncle of Mohammad, whose likeness, in accordance with Islamic law, could not be depicted in Moustapha Akkad's big-screen epic *Mohammad, Messenger of God* (1976).

"God is dead! Satan lives!" Rosemary (Mia Farrow) discovers she's the mother of Satan's child in *Rosemary's Baby* (1968).

The Pythoners—(front row, left to right) Michael Palin, John Cleese, Graham Chapman, Terry Gilliam, Terry Jones, and (back row) Eric Idle—on location in Tunisia shooting *Life of Brian* (1979).

Jesus (James Caviezel), assisted by Simon of Cyrene (Jarreth Merz), carries his cross through Calvary in Mel Gibson's *The Passion of the Christ* (2004).

violent yet abstract kind" and found the film's physical action "so stylized it has a wild cartoon kick to it like *Yojimbo* and the best kung-fu movies." The critic also did the filmmakers a terrific service by ending her review on a personal note. She saw *The Warriors* at an 11:15 p.m. show in a Broadway theatre. "The audience was so attentive to the movie it was hushed," Kael wrote. "It may have been the quietest late-night Broadway audience of my experience in recent years."

The Warriors continued to play in theatres around the country, and by the end of its run the film grossed over $22.4 million domestically. Paramount also found itself at the end of a civil action suit when Martin Yakubowicz's father sued Paramount Pictures and the Saxon Theatre Corporation, claiming they violated their duty of reasonable care to members of the public with respect to the producing, exhibition, and advertising of *The Warriors*. The Superior Court of Massachusetts ruled that the murder of Martin Yakubowicz could not be attributed to Paramount Pictures and Saxon Theatres through the production and exhibition of the film, which is protected by the First Amendment as free speech and does not incite "imminent lawless action" that would strip it of its First Amendment protection.

Another film about Spanish American gangs in the Los Angeles barrio, *Boulevard Nights* (1979), which opened in March of 1979 while *The Warriors* was still playing, was also linked to a series of incidents at theatres where both films were playing. Over the weekend of March 24–25, there were outbreaks of violence in San Francisco, Pomona, and San Juan Capistrano. Many of the incidents involved rival gang members. *Boulevard Nights* was subsequently pulled from many theatres, including San Francisco at the request of Mayor Dianne Feinstein.

Over ten years later, in 1991, the theatrical releases of two black urban dramas—Mario Van Peebles's *New Jack City* and John Singleton's *Boyz n the Hood*—were marred by reports of violence that occurred in and around theatres in several major cities around the country. In Los Angeles, Mann Theatres pulled *New Jack City*, a crime drama starring Wesley Snipes as a Harlem drug lord, from its Westwood Village theatre. On opening night, a riot broke out when hundreds of people who were turned away from the sold-out shows took to the streets and started vandalizing cars and looting stores. The incident occurred after the video of the Rodney King beating was made public, which some believed contributed to the tension. Four months later, *Boyz n the Hood*, a drama about the struggles of growing up in South Central Los Angeles, opened in nine hundred theatres. There were reportedly around twenty incidents, some gang related, around the country, including a fatal shooting outside of Chicago, a stabbing in Long Island, and an exchange of gunfire, presumably between rival gangs, just as the lights went down in a theatre in Universal City. Ironically, Singleton's drama, which earned the twenty-four-year-old filmmaker two Academy Award nominations for directing and writing, carries a strong antigang message.

NATURAL BORN KILLERS (1994): "THE MEDIA MADE THEM SUPERSTARS"

Writer/director Oliver Stone's *Natural Born Killers* is the story of Mickey Knox and Mallory Wilson, a pair of high-spirited, free-wheelin' killers in the tradition of Bonnie and Clyde and Charles Starkweather and Caril Ann Fugate, who were the inspiration for Terrence Malick's *Badlands* (1973). Very much in love, Mickey (Woody Harrelson) and Mallory (Juliette Lewis) are a pair of damaged souls. She was sexually abused by her hateful father while her mother turned a blind eye. As a young child, he was abused by both his mother and father. The abuse they suffered turned Mickey and Mallory into a pair of "natural born" killers with no conscience or feelings of remorse for any of their crimes.

As in *The Wild Bunch* and *A Clockwork Orange*, the excessive violence in *Natural Born Killers* is a cinematic strategy for critiquing contemporary society's desensitization to violence and the media's role in turning cold-blooded killers into media stars. Based on an original screenplay by Quentin Tarantino (who received story credit), Stone and his cowriters, David Veloz and Richard Rutowski, zero in on how the media (in the guise of a sleazy Australian tabloid TV host, played to the hilt by Robert Downey, Jr.) serves its own economic interests by exploiting the public's obsession with violence and turning murderers into media stars. Director Oliver Stone's hyperkinetic visual style is marked by rapid camera movements, quick cutting, and an array of cinematic "tricks" (slow motion, black-and-white inserts, etc.). Stone is at his best when his signature style enhances the film's dramatic content (as in *The Doors* [1991] and *JFK* [1991]), but when the subject matter doesn't warrant his "over the top" approach (*Talk Radio* [1988], *Any Given Sunday* [1999]), it can be excessive and distracting.

In *Natural Born Killers*, Stone's whips his audience into a frenzy by assaulting their senses with his use of rapid-fire editing, multiple film formats (video, 35mm, Super-8), front and rear projection, color filters, and a pulsating score. As Kimberly Owczarski observes, the film's visual excessiveness and stylized depiction of violence, as in the scene in which Mickey and Mallory blow away patrons at a roadside diner, "disrupt the flow of the narrative" and "foregrounds the gruesome effects of violence, breaking the illusion of violence as pleasurable spectacle within a non-critical (viewing) framework." Owczarski finds it ironic that a film like *Natural Born Killers*, which offers a social critique of violence, is demonized by the press and politicians, including 1996 Republican presidential candidate Bob Dole, while a film like Arnold Schwarzenegger's action-comedy *True Lies* (1994), in which violence "is a seamless part of the viewing experience," falls under the media's radar.

When Stone submitted his film to the MPAA, they returned it with an NC-17 rating. To get it down to a R he had to make 126 cuts, including a scene in which the prison warden, played by Tommy Lee Jones, is decapitated by the inmates, who then carry his head around on a stick, and another in which prisoners cut someone's legs off with a chainsaw. The R rating included a statement: "For extreme violence and graphic carnage, for shocking images, and for strong language and sexuality."

The critical backlash against the film and its violent content was immediate both at home and abroad. Oliver Stone faced the press at the Venice Film Festival, and he was greeted with "boos, hisses, and some scattered applause," yet the director was prepared to defend his film "as a joyride or a thrill ride because, horrible as it sounds, these two killers have fun. . . . The movie represents the cultural and social landscape of America in the '90s." When asked if he believed that if it "might influence some viewers to emulate that behavior," he replied "that anyone who would commit an act of violence (after seeing this film) is already predisposed to it."

This was not the last time this question would be posed to Stone. The release of *Natural Born Killers* in the United States and abroad was followed by a series of what the press called "copycat crimes" committed by individuals and male-female couples who were reportedly obsessed with the movie. Two high-profile cases involved two young French couples. On October, 4, 1994, twenty-three-year-old Audry Maupin and his nineteen-year-old girlfriend Florence Rey went on a shooting spree that left Maupin and four others dead. The press labeled the couple "France's natural born killers" after the police found a poster for the film in the apartment they were squatting. Rey was sentenced to twenty years in prison.

Three years later, twenty-year-old Veronique Herbert and her boyfriend, Sebastien Paindavoine, nineteen, were arrested in a Paris suburb for the murder of Herbert's former boyfriend, sixteen-year-old Abdeladim Ghabiche. On March 5, 1996, Herbert seduced Gahbiche by promising to sleep with him. Sebastien suddenly appeared and stabbed him in the back and neck, while Veronique stabbed him in the stomach. They buried his body in the garden at Paindavoine's house. Herbert, dubbed "Veronique la Diabolique" (after the 1955 French murder mystery *Les diaboliques*), had no apparent motive, but admitted there was a connection to *Natural Born Killers*: "The film coincided with my state of mind. Maybe I muddled up dream and reality. I wanted to eliminate someone, as if by magic. . . . The idea of killing invaded me." Herbert, who was considered the dominant half of the couple, was jailed for fifteen years, three more than Paindavoine.

In the United States, a double-murder committed by a couple of "natural born killers" made headlines. On March 5, 1995, Ben Darras and Sarah Edmondson spent the night at her family cabin, where they took LSD and watched *Natural Born Killers*. On the next day, they set out on a road trip. They stopped at a cotton mill south of Hernando, Mississippi. Sarah stepped out of the car and asked the mill's manager, Bill Savage, for directions. Darras appeared suddenly and shot him. They drove on to New Orleans where they spent the day and then headed north. They stopped at a convenience store off of a highway, where Edmondson shot a clerk, thirty-five-year-old Patsy Byers. She survived, but was paralyzed. In her statement, Edmondson said that when she looked into Byers's face before shooting her, she saw a "demon," echoing Mickey and Mallory's experience when visiting an Indian shaman while they are on hallucinogens (at one point the word "demon" also appears on Mickey's chest). But in an interview with *Vanity Fair*, Edmonson downplayed the comparison made by journalist Michael Shnayerson between her and Ben and Mickey and Mallory:

> Oh yeah, that's pushing it. As far as how much this case is leaning on *Natural Born Killers*, it is one of many elements. . . . It has its influence, but it is not as great as I would like to make it be. . . . And I wish I could say that it did. I wish I could point the finger at Hollywood completely. But that's not so, that's not honest.

Edmondson pleaded guilty and was sentenced to thirty-five years in prison. Darras received thirty-five years for his role in the Byers shooting and armed robbery. He was extradited to Mississippi where he was sentenced to life in prison for the murder of Savage.

Oliver Stone, along with Warner Brothers, was named in a lawsuit filed by Byers claiming their film inspired Edmondson and Darras's crime spree. In 2001, a Louisiana judge threw the suit out on the grounds that Stone and Warner Brothers were protected by the First Amendment and there was no evidence the director intended to incite violence (Byers had since died of cancer in 1998). The lawsuit sparked a heated debate between Stone and attorney/bestselling author John Grisham, who was a friend of their first victim, Bill Savage. One would expect Grisham to be defending a filmmaker's First Amendment rights, but he believed Stone should be held accountable:

> But the issue is responsibility: should Stone and his ilk be held responsible if, *and only if*, a direct causal link can be proven between a movie (or a book or a song) and the violence inspired by it? I'll admit this is a very difficult standard to meet, but when causation is *clearly* proven, then the "artist" should be held liable. And the "artist" should be required to share the responsibility along with the nut who actually pulled the trigger.

"Difficult standard" is an understatement. This is not to say a young killer's obsession with video games or even film could not have been a factor, though it may have more to do with *how*, rather than *why*, a crime was executed. Also, how can you prove a film "inspired" a killer, particularly when it had no such effect on the millions of other people who watched it? But popular culture—movies, television, music, video games, the Internet—have always been a popular target when there is a need to blame someone or something whenever a young person is accused of committing violent acts. There are more important and immediate questions that should be answered first, such as why is it so easy for young people to get their hands—legally or illegally—on a pistol or a shotgun in the United States? And who is being held accountable when a school shooter is able to get his hands on a semi-automatic rifle?

Since its release, *Natural Born Killers* has been linked to several other murders including the 1999 Columbine Massacre, in which Eric Harris and Dylan Klebold went on a shooting rampage at Columbine High School, killing twelve students and one teacher and injuring twenty-four others. Harris and Klebold were reportedly fans of the film and used the initials "NBK" as a code word for "attack." The murder of Brandon Murphy in 2004 by his roommates, Angus Wallen and Kara Winn, was reportedly modeled after the killing of Mallory's parents. Wallen and Winn watched the film before shooting Murphy and setting his apartment on fire.

In addition to *Natural Born Killers*, there have been several other films that have been credited as the "inspiration" for "real life" crimes.

NIGHTMARE ON ELM STREET (1984)

Freddy Krueger, the serial killer who invaded teenagers' dreams in eight *Nightmare* films, was the inspiration for Daniel Gonzalez's three-day murder spree in Britain in 2004. Wondering what it would be like to be Freddy for the day, he knifed four people to death and wounded two others. In 2006, he was sentenced to six consecutive sentences in a maximum psychiatric hospital. The next year, he committed suicide by slashing his wrists.

Another British Krueger fan, Jason Moore, attacked his friend John-Paul Skamarski after a night of drinking. Skamarski took a sleeping pill before going to bed and while he was sleeping. Moore used a home-made Freddy Krueger–style bladed glove to slash his friend's face and body. When sentencing Moore to life in prison, the judge said, "You are an extremely dangerous man."

THE BASKETBALL DIARIES (1995)

Leonardo DiCaprio stars in this film adaptation of writer Jim Carroll's autobiographical account of his teenage years growing up in the streets of New York in the 1960s and his early battle with drug addiction. With its dark, frank treatment of drugs and sexuality, *The Basketball Diaries* is one of those rare movies about teenagers made strictly for an older audience. A dream sequence in which Jim, dressed in black, walks into a classroom at his Catholic high school, takes out a gun, and starts firing at his classmates and his teacher, was linked to a 1997 school shooting in Paducah, Kentucky. In 1997, fourteen-year-old Michael Carneal walked into Heath High School on the morning of December and opened fire on a group of students holding a youth prayer meeting in the lobby of the school before the first bell. Carneal pled "guilty but mentally ill" and received life in prison with no possibility of parole for at least twenty-five years. The parents of his three victims, Nicole Hadley, fourteen; Jessica James, seventeen; and Kayce Steger, fifteen; filed a $33 million lawsuit against the makers of video games (Nintendo, Sega, Sony) and the producer and distributors of *The Basketball Diaries*, claiming they inspired him to kill. The U.S. Court of Appeals for the Sixth Circuit in Cincinnati affirmed the dismissal of the lawsuit by a lower court because the defendants could not have foreseen Carneal's "idiosyncratic" reaction and the video games and film were protected by the First Amendment.

THE MATRIX (1999)

In *The Matrix*, Keanu Reeves plays a computer hacker named Neo who discovers he has been living in a state of unconsciousness in a computer-generated false reality—the Matrix—controlled by machines that exist in the real world two hundred years in the future. The *Matrix* insanity-defense was used by defendants who claimed they were living in the Matrix and, therefore, were justified killing their victims.

In 2003, Tonda Lynn Ansley was found not guilty by reason of insanity for killing her landlord, Miami University professor Sherry Lee Corbett, who she claimed was part of a conspiracy to brainwash and kill her. "They commit a lot of crimes in *The Matrix*," she told a police detective, "That's where you go to sleep at night and they drug you and take you somewhere else. And then they bring you back and put you in bed, and when you wake up, you think that it's a bad dream."

On February 17, 2003, nineteen-year-old Josh Cooke walked down into the basement of his family home in Oakton, Virginia, and shot his father and mother, Paul and Margaret Cooke. Cooke was wearing the same style trench coat and carrying the same gun—a 12-gauge shotgun—as Neo. He then called the authorities and surrendered himself. He later described the murders to his lawyers as being "like a video game . . . like I was in a virtual reality. It was like I was watching myself." His lawyers pursued an insanity defense because Joshua "harbored a bona fide belief that he was living in a virtual reality of *The Matrix* at the time of the alleged offenses and thus could not distinguish right from wrong or understand the nature and character and consequences of his act." Although a psychologist determined he was mentally competent, his defense team raised the question of his mental health, along with his obsession with the film and violent video games. Cooke was an underachiever and a loner who preferred playing video games to socializing and failed out after his freshman year in college. Adoption records obtained by his lawyers revealed his father was a diagnosed paranoid schizophrenic and his mother had a history of mental illness. After interviewing Joshua, a clinical psychiatrist "testified that a combination of deep childhood trauma and failures in adolescence diagnosed him as being 'detached from himself'."

The Matrix was also linked to eighteen-year-old Lee Boyd Malvo's participation in the 2002 Washington, D.C. sniper attacks as well as the murder and dismemberment of a forty-seven-year-old San Francisco landlord by her tenant, Vadim Mieseges, who claimed he was "being sucked into 'The Matrix,' which he thought was real." A judge accepted Mieseges's plea of not guilty by reason of insanity and sentenced him to an institution.

CHAPTER 5

Sins of the Flesh: Sex and Nudity on Celluloid

The 1930 Production Code limited sex in motion pictures to pro-creative sexual intercourse performed offscreen between a fully clothed, legally married, monogamous heterosexual couple. No "excessive and lustful kissing." No "suggestive postures." No passionate love scenes that ran the risk of arousing "dangerous emotions" in the audience.

In other words—*no sex.*

During the Pre-Code Era (1930–34), when the Production Code was not yet fully enforced, Hollywood was overrun with an assortment of adulteresses, social climbers, prostitutes, and "fallen women," such as the desperate housewife (Tallulah Bankhead) with a gambling problem in *The Cheat* (1931), the gold digger (Jean Harlow) who seduces her boss in *Red-Headed Woman* (1932), the rich girl (Helen Twelvetrees) who falls for a lowlife in *Unashamed* (1932), and the poor girl (Constance Bennett) who exchanges her virtue for a modeling career in *The Easiest Way* (1931). Some of these gals used sex (or came pretty damn close) to get what they wanted or needed (like a man, money, or both). Yet, unlike the future "bad girls" of the Production Code era, they were not necessarily punished in the end for their folly, vices, or bad taste in men.

As part of their effort to clean up Hollywood's act, the Studio Relations Committee (SRC) (1929–34) and its successor, the Production Code Administration (PCA), started to "regulate" the content of motion pictures in regards to certain sex-related subjects and themes (adultery, prostitution, etc.), suggestive words and phrases, and the physical display of love, intimacy, and sex. As with violence, the curbing of sexual content in motion pictures occurred over a period of several years, though 1934 marked a turning point due to the enforcement of the Code by the newly formed PCA, and the expansion of the National Legion of Decency's campaign against immorality in the movies.

While the rules regulating sexuality in motion pictures pertained to both sexes, they were used by the censors throughout the 1930s to contain the behavior of transgressive female characters, who were overtly "sexual" and/or engaged in "impure love." It's no coincidence that by the end of the decade, the Code's list of forbidden words (see chapter 3) was comprised mostly of slang terms for "prostitute" or "a sexually promiscuous woman." These restrictions are evident in films featuring three of Paramount's leading ladies in the 1930s—a German chanteuse, an actress/writer whose name became synonymous with sex, and an animated, wide-eyed, jazz-Age flapper named Betty.

MARLENE DIETRICH: "IT TOOK MORE THAN ONE MAN TO CHANGE MY NAME TO SHANGHAI LILY"

Director Josef von Sternberg introduced Marlene Dietrich to the world when he cast her in *Der blaue Engel* (*The Blue Angel*—1930). Dietrich plays a sexy cafe singer named Lola Lola, whose marriage to a well-respected high-school teacher (Emil Jannings) leads to his tragic downfall. Shot simultaneously in English and German, *The Blue Angel* landed Dietrich a contract in Hollywood, though it wasn't released in the U.S. until after *Morocco* (1930), the first of six films she would make with von Sternberg for Paramount over the next five years.

Von Sternberg capitalized on Dietrich's exotic beauty by repeatedly casting her as a femme fatale who is icy and distant toward the opposite sex. Her characters are usually entertainers or some variation of a prostitute. In *Shanghai Express* (1932), she's a "coaster"—"a woman who lives by her wits on the Chinese coast"—who glibly explains to Captain Donald Harvey (Clive Brook), "It took more than one man to change my name to Shanghai Lily." But as critic Gaylyn Studlar points out, Dietrich was not your typical Hollywood sex symbol. Refusing to simply be reduced to a "passive object" for the gaze of the camera and her male admirers, she was usually in control while her suitors submitted to her seductive charms—sometimes to the point of masochism.

The Dietrich–Von Sternberg cycle (1930–35) coincided with the introduction and implementation of the Production Code. While her male costars may have been falling at her feet, Dietrich's charms did not seem to work on the boys over at the Hays Office, which had reservations about her "fallen women" characters and the wrong messages her films might be sending about adultery, promiscuity, and prostitution.

This was the case with *Blonde Venus* (1932), in which Dietrich stars as Helen Faraday, a devoted wife and mother who is forced to resume her stage career when her husband, Edward (Herbert Marshall), a scientist, is exposed to radiation and requires an expensive medical treatment. She receives "financial help" (prostitutes herself) from millionaire Nick Townsend (Cary Grant), with whom she falls in love. When Edward learns of Helen's affair, he leaves her. In the end, she gives up both her career and Nick to be with her husband and child. The plot posed major problems for the filmmakers and the studio due to objections raised by the Studio Relations Committee over Helen's adulterous affair with Nick. At one point Paramount suggested Edward have an affair with his housekeeper, thereby making it possible for Helen to marry Nick, but Lamar Trotti of the SRC objected to the idea of "tearing down the character of her husband, who, up to this point, has been a decent man who was deceived by his wife." Colonel Jason Joy approved the final draft of the script because "never are infidelity and prostitution themselves made attractive." But Helen's adulterous affair was too much for the PCA, which forced Paramount to pull the film from circulation in 1934.

But Dietrich's Helen Faraday—wife/mother/prostitute/adulteress—will always take a back seat to Helen's alter ego, the nightclub entertainer known as the Blonde Venus. Surrounded by chorus girls dressed as natives, she enters the stage wearing a gorilla suit and sings "Hot Voodoo." In her final number (now performing in Paris as Helen Jones), she dons what would become Dietrich's signature white tuxedo and a top hat and sings "I Couldn't Be Annoyed." Like Helen, Dietrich, whose career started in the theatre in Berlin, eventually returned to the stage, performing in nightclubs and theatres around the world.

MAE WEST: "GOODNESS HAD NOTHING TO DO WITH IT."

When Mae West arrived in Hollywood in the late 1920s, she was no stranger to censorship. In 1926, West wrote and starred on Broadway in her hit comedy-drama, *Sex*, which enjoyed a healthy run before the New York Police Department shut it down as part of the city's campaign against sex-themed plays. She was convicted of corrupting public morals, fined $500, and sentenced to ten days at the Women's Work-house on Welfare Island.

West returned to Broadway in 1928 in her hit sex comedy *Diamond Lil*, which landed her a contract with Paramount Pictures. She made her screen debut in a small role in the Prohibition drama *Night After Night* (1932), in which she utters one of her most famous lines, later used as the title for her autobiography.

Admiring West's jewelry, a hat-check girl remarks, "Goodness, what lovely diamonds."

"Goodness had nothing to do with it," West quips.

Maybe not—but talent certainly did. Mae West's rise to stardom in the early 1930s was meteoric. A major box-office draw, West's first pair of comedies, *I'm No Angel* (1933) and *She Done Him Wrong* (1933), were Paramount's highest-grossing films of the decade. However, her contribution to Hollywood history was not limited to saving her studio from bankruptcy during the Depression. In a male-dominated industry, West was a rarity: a female performer who wrote her own screenplays and/or the source material on which they were based. More importantly, the characters she created for herself were uninhibited females who guiltlessly attended to their own sexual needs and pleasure. Dressed in lavish gowns that emphasized her shapely form, West never hesitated to let a handsome man (like her *Angel* and *Wrong* costar, Cary Grant) know she was interested, usually by swaying her hips, rolling her eyes, and responding to a compliment with a bawdy double entendre about her sexual prowess ("When I'm good, I'm very good, and when I'm bad, I'm better."). She also never let men get the best of her, and there was never a question who was running the show when one of her many male admirers stepped into her boudoir.

When Universal Studios expressed interest in *Diamond Lil*, Colonel Jason Joy, the head of the SRC, advised the studio against purchasing it because it contained "vulgar dramatic situations" and "highly censorable dialogue." Paramount went ahead and secured the rights and put West under contract. Will Hays eventually gave his approval (with changes, of course) provided the advertising campaign did not associate the film with the play. The title was changed to *She Done Him Wrong* and the name of her character to "Lady Lou," yet the fact it was based on *Diamond Lil* was hardly a secret. The critic for the *New York Times* even jokingly noted in his review of *Wrong* that West gives "a remarkably suspicious impersonation of 'Diamond Lil.'"

Compared to *Wrong*, *I'm No Angel* ("A story about a gal who lost her reputation—and never missed it!") received minimal interference on the part of the censors. James Wingate, who took over as head of the SRC in 1932, found West's screenplay generally acceptable, though he required that the sexually suggestive song titles and lyrics to West's musical numbers be rewritten (for example, the song title "No One Does It Like That Dallas Man" was eventually changed to "Nobody Loves Me Like That Dallas Man").

The correspondence between the PCA and Paramount regarding West's subsequent films reflects the moral shift that occurred in Hollywood once the Code was being enforced. In her third vehicle, *Belle of the Nineties* (1934), West plays Ruby Carter, a nightclub singer with a shady past. Joe Breen strongly objected to Ruby's involvement in criminal activities, which resulted in what he described as the film's "general low tone" and "lack of sufficient compensating moral values." To appease the PCA, West cut the objectionable scenes and added a wedding at the end to make it clear Ruby was made an honest woman.

From a moral standpoint, Mae West embodied everything Joseph Breen thought was morally wrong with Hollywood. As with *Blonde Venus*, Breen denied seals to *She Done Him Wrong*, which had received an Academy Award nomination for Best Picture, and *I'm No Angel*, because "both pictures are so thoroughly and so completely in violation of the Code."

Fourteen years later, Paramount was denied permission to reissue *I'm No Angel*. At that time, Breen warned a Paramount executive of the danger re-releasing a Mae West picture would pose to their industry. "It would appear to me," Breen wrote, "that we would expose ourselves to the charge that we were 'letting down the bars'; that we were again making 'filthy pictures' as was the charge leveled against the industry, from a thousand sources, back in 1933–34."

As for West, by the late 1940s she had returned to the Broadway stage—her legacy as a sex symbol, a cultural icon, and "the finest woman to ever walk the streets" forever sealed in the annals of Hollywood history.

BETTY BOOP: "I WANNA BE LOVED BY YOU— BOOP-OOP-A-DOOP"

In the early 1930s, Betty Boop was *the* "It Girl" of the cartoon world— a wide-eyed, sexy, jazz babe with a devil-may-care attitude that left Depression audiences feeling nostalgic for the fun and frivolity of the 1920s. At first she was known only as "Betty," and like many Hollywood stars, she started her career as a supporting player, making her screen debut in 1930 in *Dizzy Dishes*, one of Fleischer Studios' Talkartoons produced for Paramount Pictures. She was originally conceived by legendary animator Myron "Grim" Natwick as a dog with floppy ears, which were eventually replaced with human ears complete with a stylish pair of hoop earrings, which complemented her signature low-cut black dress and garter. She landed her first starring role in *Betty Co-Ed* (1931). By the end of the decade, she was an international star appearing in over seventy-five cartoons (her male fans included philosophers Jean-Paul Sartre and Theodor Adorno).

Modeled after Clara Bow and baby-voiced singer Helen Kane, who coined one of Betty's favorite musical phrases, "Boop-Oop-A-Doop" (and unsuccessfully sued Paramount and Fleischer in 1934 for imitating her), Betty was more in touch with her sexuality than her contemporaries, Minnie Mouse and Olive Oyl. Deep down she was basically a "good girl," yet she also revealed her risqué side when she appeared topless, except for a lei covering her breasts, in *Betty Boop's Bamboo Isle* (1932). Men loved Betty, so she was often fighting off the unwelcome advances of male admirers (*Chess-Nuts* [1932], *Boop-Oop-A-Doop* [1932], *She Wronged Him Right* [1934]). When she wasn't running from the boys, she was competing against them in the political arena (*Betty Boop for President* [1932]) and on the car race track (*Betty Boop's Ker-Choo* [1933]).

194

Although one might assume cartoons were not the Hays Office's first priority, the censors did force her creator, Max Fleischer, to adhere to the Production Code and make Betty look and act more respectable. In 1934, Betty started to show less skin; her hemline was lowered (hiding her garter), her cleavage was now fully covered, and her dress grew sleeves. The new Betty was also less adventurous; she was spending more time at home than traveling through space or running from monsters and ghosts. As historian Karl F. Cohen explains, "the Code changed her into a rational adult, which destroyed most of her charm and her ability to venture very far from a realistic depiction of the world."

Betty retired from pictures in 1939, but based on her brief "return" in *The Romance of Betty Boop* (1985), *Betty Boop's Hollywood Mystery* (1989), along with a memorable cameo in *Who Framed Roger Rabbit?* (1988), time has indeed been kind to the saucy gal who will forever reign as "The Queen of Cartoons."

EKSTASE (ECSTASY—1933): "THE MOST TALKED ABOUT PICTURE IN THE WORLD"

Before it became available in a pill, ecstasy—that overpowering, euphoric rush—could be reached by experiencing some form of intense pleasure (sexual or otherwise) or attaining a heightened state of consciousness through nonchemical means.

Ecstasy is also the title of a controversial 1933 Czech-Austrian film starring nineteen-year old starlet Hedy Kiesler, who would soon be known to the world as Hedy Lamarr. The Austrian-born actress plays Eva, an unhappy young bride who finds herself in a sexless marriage with a much older man, Emil (Zvonimir Rogoz). She leaves him and files for divorce. Then, one day, while out riding her horse, Eva stops to swim nude in a pond. When her horse runs away with her clothes, she is forced to run naked through a field, where she encounters a young, handsome engineer named Adam (Aribert Mog), who helps her retrieve her horse. She can't stop thinking about him, so she pays a late night visit to his cottage. When Emil, who wishes to reconcile with Eva, learns of the affair, he becomes distraught. Later, at a local hotel,

Eva and Adam, who plan to run away together, dance and sip champagne. Meanwhile, in a nearby room, Emil commits suicide. When a guilty Eva learns of her ex-husband's tragic fate, she decides to leave without Adam and boards a train alone.

Highly controversial in its day, *Ecstasy* was branded "obscene" when distributor Samuel Cummins attempted to import the film into the United States in 1935. Ironically, the New York censors had passed the film (with deletions) the previous year, but the cuts were never made and it was never exhibited. Though the sight of Hedy Lamarr *au naturel* was sufficient reason for the New York Collector of Customs to seize the film under the 1930 Tariff Act, the scene in which she and Adam make love was regarded as equally objectionable.

During their love scene, director Gustav Machatý keeps the camera on a tight close-up of Eva's face, which clearly conveys through her expressions that she is having an orgasm (most likely her first). The close-up, along with the footage of her naked swim and romp through the field, would be excised from prints in order for the film to be shown in the United States. Nearly thirty years later, the Danish film *A Stranger Knocks* (1963) would be denied a license in New York in part because of a similar love scene in which the audience sees a close-up of a woman "with facial expressions indicative of orgasmic reaction."

Ecstasy was controversial on the other side of the Atlantic as well. A fan of the film, Italian dictator Benito Mussolini relaxed Italy's censorship law so it could be screened at the 1934 Venice Film Festival. However, the Vatican did not share Mussolini's enthusiasm, and the film was denounced by the Vatican's official publication, *L'Osservatore Romano*. In Germany, where it was released under the title *Symphonie der Liebe* (Symphony of Love), the film was praised by the critics and the public, yet denounced by the Nazis because it was "indecent" and Lamarr was part Jewish.

Meanwhile, back in the U.S., the film's distributor, Eureka Productions, not only lost its battle in court when a jury found *Ecstasy* "obscene and immoral," it lost its print when government agents burned it before the appeal could be heard. A second print imported into the U.S. contained major revisions, including an edited version of Eva's nude romp, an added voiceover stating she had been granted a divorce, and a new ending in which she and Adam are married. New York State still refused to grant the film a license, which Eureka unsuccessfully challenged in court.

Since 1936, the film's distributor had been trying to get approval from the PCA. After two members of the PCA staff saw the film, Breen sent a copy of their report to Will Hays, along with a note informing him that the film "is highly—even dangerously—indecent." The film eventually got its PCA seal and was finally granted a license by the New York censors in 1940 when the distributor, after being rejected six times, had the decision reversed by an appeals board. *Ecstasy* opened on Christmas Day at New York's Ambassador Theatre. By that time, Hedy Kiesler was known as Hedy Lamarr—"the most beautiful woman in the world."

THE NAKED AND THE NUDE

"Complete nudity is never permitted. This includes nudity in fact or silhouette."

—1930 Motion Picture Production Code

Thanks to the efforts of U.S. Customs agents, the PCA, and local and state censorship boards, American audiences didn't get to see Hedy Lamarr skinny dipping and running naked through the great outdoors. But if they had, it would not have been the first time a naked female appeared on an American movie screen.

During the silent era, several actresses bared it all for the screen: Annette Kellerman in *Daughter of the Gods* (1916), June Caprice in *The Ragged Princess* (1916), Lila Damita in *Red Heels* (1926), and Hope Hampton in *Lovers' Island* (1926). While a glimpse of a naked bodice could often get by the state and local censors, an extended view of the female anatomy would, in some instances, end up on the cutting room floor. One of the more controversial films was Lois Weber's *The Hypocrites* (1915), an allegorical drama about religious hypocrisy featuring a nude Margaret Edwards in the role of "The Naked Truth." The film opened to rave reviews and packed houses in New York, Detroit, and Washington, D.C., but was banned in Ohio, where the censor board decided the film was "vulgar" and accused the filmmakers of attempting to "commercialize the nude."

Another film released in that same year, *Inspiration*, featuring the famous sculptor's model Audrey Munson in the nude, was banned in New Rochelle, New York, where the local censors declared that while the film was not immoral, it was "highly suggestive and harmful to those between the age of 16 and 20 years." Munson played an artist's model in her next film, *Purity* (1916), which opens and ends with a Biblical quote: "To the pure all things are pure" (Titus 1:15). But everyone was not convinced, including New York City's censor board, which required the distributor to cut the number of nude scenes in half.

In the 1930s, some American producers tried to cash in on the burgeoning nudist movement with a series of low-budget exploitation films, such as *Back to the Sun* (1933), *This Nude World* (1933), *Nudist Land* (1937), and *Unashamed: A Romance* (1938). Although they did not contain full frontal nudity, some nudist films ran into problems with state censors. The most popular and widely distributed was *Elysia (Valley of the Nudes)* (1934), which was advertised in some cities as "Adults Only" and/or shown only at midnight. A screening at the Fox Theatre in Centralia, Washington included a special added attraction—nine members of the Elysia nudist camp, live, on stage, in their birthday suits.

Once the Hays Code was enforced, nudity in Hollywood films became a thing of the past. The restriction on nudity would not be lifted until the 1960s when the PCA granted a seal to Sidney Lumet's *The Pawnbroker* (1965). The film stars Rod Steiger as Sol Nazerman, a Jewish Holocaust survivor whose past has left him void of emotions. The brief nudity occurs toward the end of the film when a woman bares her breasts to Sol, triggering the memory of seeing his late wife naked and being raped by Nazi soldiers. When the film was submitted to the PCA, it was denied a seal due to the nudity. The producer, Ely Landau, was outraged by the "literal application of a thirty-five-year-old prohibition," considering the scenes in question are "highly moral" and "integral to the story." When Landau appealed to the MPPDA Board, the decision of the PCA was "upheld and affirmed," yet the board used its discretionary powers to grant the film a seal. The board noted that this exception was made for this film only, a point the Chairman of the Board of Paramount Pictures, Barney Balaban, thought was "meaningless" because it was inevitable that the film would set a precedent. The Legion of Decency initially condemned the film, stating it did not believe that the nudity was necessary, and expressed its concern that the introduction of nudity into the cinema "is open to the gravest of abuses."

In September of 1966, the new and improved Code was unveiled. The 1966 version prohibited the presentation of "indecent or undue exposure of the human body"—a rule that appeared in earlier versions of the Code, yet was more ambiguous that the earlier rule prohibiting "complete nudity, in fact or in silhouette."

JEAN GENET'S *UN CHANT D'AMOUR* (*SONG OF LOVE*—1947): "NOTHING MORE THAN CHEAP PORNOGRAPHY"

The only film by French novelist, playwright, and poet Jean Genet was groundbreaking for its frank treatment of homosexuality and inclusion of homoerotic imagery, male frontal nudity, and explicit scenes of male masturbation. Shot in black and white without sound, the experimental short was rarely shown publicly in France and not screened in the United States until the mid-1960s when Jonas Mekas, founder of the Film-Makers' Cooperative in New York City, smuggled a print into the country.

The story is set in a stone-walled French prison where two isolated, nameless prisoners, a young man with tattoos and a slightly older man, communicate with each other by knocking on the wall that separates them. In one of the film's sexually-charged moments, the older man blows cigarette smoke into the younger man's mouth with a straw through a hole in the cell wall. A guard, who voyeuristically looks in on the prisoners and watches them masturbate, appears to be turned on by the older prisoner. He enters his cell, beats him, and in another phallic, homoerotic moment, sticks his gun into the prisoner's mouth. Genet intercuts the scene with a fantasy sequence in which the two prisoners are seen frolicking in the woods, followed by shots of pairs of men having sex with their faces and body parts obscured by the shadowy lighting.

In 1965, Saul Landau obtained a print of the film from the cooperative and screened it in several venues on the West Coast. After a screening at University of California at Berkeley, the Berkeley Police

Department warned Landau not to screen the film again or he would be arrested and the print confiscated. Landau challenged the order in court. Although experts in the fields of literature, film, and criminology defended the film's artistic merits, a California court found it obscene, claiming the film lacked "any ideas of social importance" and that the "vividly revealed acts of masturbation, oral copulation, the infamous crime against nature (sodomy), voyeurism, nudity, sadism, masochism, and sex" made the film "nothing more than cheap pornography calculated to promote homosexuality, perversion, and morbid sex practices."

Landau appealed to the District Court of Appeal of California, which affirmed the lower court's ruling based on the court's opinion of what constitutes art:

> The fact that there is no text or dialogue accompanying the film contributes to its ambiguity and the absence of a dominant theme. . . . The erotic scenes recur with increasing intensity and without direction toward any well-defined, wholesome idea. . . . The various sexual acts are graphically pictured or emphatically suggested with nothing omitted except those sexual consummations which are plainly suggested but meaningfully omitted and thus by the very fact of omission emphasized.

Applying the "Roth Standard" ("whether to the average person, applying contemporary community standards, the dominant theme, taken as a whole, appeals to the prurient interest") from *Roth v. United States*, 354 U.S. 476 (1957), the District Court of Appeal concluded that "measured in terms of the sexual interests of its intended and probable recipient group or the average person, applying contemporary standards. . . the predominant appeal of the film taken as a whole is to the prurient interest." The following year, the case was heard before the U.S. Supreme Court (*Landau v. Fording*, 388 U.S. 456 [1967]), where the court of appeal's decision was confirmed without opinion.

Genet was never involved in the proceedings, and in an interview with Edward de Grazia, he seemed somewhat indifferent about the film and the controversy, claiming he made the film "to make money." But as critic Vito Russo explains, the film's importance in the annals of gay cinema is that it "gave the secret dreams of a hidden minority a small, avant-garde voice."

SEX AND AMOUR IN POST–WORLD WAR II AMERICA

In the 1950s, a series of French films released in the United States were targeted by state and local censors because of their frank and modern treatment of sexuality. These films played in "art house" cinemas so distributors were not required to obtain a seal from the PCA. But their popularity no doubt had a significant effect on how Americans perceived their own cinema, which seemed Victorian by comparison in terms of their treatment of sex.

La Ronde (1950)

La Ronde, Max Ophüls's adaptation of Arthur Schnitzler's 1903 comic play, *Reigen* (Hands Around), is comprised of a series of vignettes set in Vienna in 1900. The characters, who are from varied social and economic backgrounds, ride a "sexual merry-go-round" as they deceive and seduce each other in order to satisfy their own sexual desires. A prostitute seduces a sailor, who seduces a young girl, who is hired as a maid and seduces a young aristocrat, and so on . . . until the final episode, which involves a liaison between the prostitute and a count.

The French film made it through U.S. customs and played in movie houses in Los Angeles, San Francisco, and Washington, D.C. Only the New York censors denied *La Ronde* a license because the film was "immoral." The Legion of Decency agreed and condemned the film because "it condones and glorifies immoral actions and contains suggestive sequences." The ban was upheld by an appellate court, but reversed by the Supreme Court in 1954 based on "the *Miracle* decision" (see chapter 2), which stated that films were entitled to constitutional protection from state censorship. The film finally opened in New York in March of 1954. Forty-five years later, another work by Schnitzler, a novella entitled *Traumnovelle*, would be the source for another controversial film, Stanley Kubrick's *Eyes Wide Shut* (1999).

Le blé en herbe (*The Game of Love*—1954)

Based on the 1933 novel by Colette, *The Game of Love* is a coming-of-age tale about sixteen-year-old Philippe (Pierre-Michel Blanc) and his younger cousin, Vinca, who spend their summers together in Brittany. As Philippe is dealing with his burgeoning sexuality, he meets the beautiful, yet much older Madame Dalleray (Edwige Feuillère), who teaches the teenager about love and sex, which further complicates his relationship with his cousin.

The film was denied a permit in Chicago by the police commissioner on the grounds that it "arouses the sexual desires of normal people." After the mayor refused to overturn the decision, the distributor, Times Film Corp., took the matter to court, which ruled that Chicago's censorship ordinance was constitutional and their decision to ban the film was justified because it focused on "sexuality" including an "illicit relationship" between Philippe and an older woman. The U.S. Court of Appeals for the Seventh Circuit upheld the decision, but in *Times Film Corp v. City of Chicago*, 355 U.S. 35 (1957), the Supreme Court reversed the lower court's decision. The Supreme Court did not render a written decision, but cited the case of *Alberts v. California*, 354 U.S. 476 (1957), which was the companion case to *Roth v. United States*, 354 U.S. 476 (1957). According to DeGrazia, the decision was significant because it was "the first time the Supreme Court itself decided that a particular artistic work . . . was not obscene but was entitled to constitutional protection from suppression."

L'amant de Lady Chatterley (*Lady Chatterley's Lover*—1955)

First published in Italy in 1928, D. H. Lawrence's controversial novel about the illicit, passionate affair between a married noblewoman, Lady Chatterley, and a gamekeeper, Oliver Mellors, was still banned in the United States when this film version starring Danielle Darrieux crossed the Atlantic in 1957. In Lawrence's story, Lady Chatterley is trapped in a sexless marriage with an impotent baronet whose war injuries left him paralyzed below the waist. He encourages her to have an affair so she can produce an heir. She has a hot and heavy romance with Mellors, who releases her sexual inhibitions. But her husband objects to her choice because Mellors is from a lower social class.

When she becomes pregnant, her husband refuses to grant her a divorce, so she and Mellors run away.

Before issuing a license, the Motion Picture Division of the New York Education Department demanded the distributor cut three scenes, all involving Chatterley and Mellors's sexual affair (lying together on a cot, Mellors unzipping her dress and caressing her buttocks and body). When the distributor refused and petitioned the Regents of the University of the State of New York, the censors' decision was upheld because the film presents adultery as a "desirable, acceptable and proper pattern of behavior." After a series of appeals and reversals, the case went to the Supreme Court, which ruled that New York's refusal to grant the film a license because it "advocates an idea—that adultery under certain circumstances may be proper behavior" violates the First Amendment's basic guarantee of freedom to express ideas.

Et Dieu . . . créa la femme (. . . And God Created Woman—1956)

In . . . *And God Created Woman*, Brigitte Bardot plays Juliette Hardy, an eighteen-year-old nymphet caught in a love triangle between two brothers—one of whom she marries and the other whom she loves. The formulaic plot pales in comparison to the screen presence of the vivacious, curvy Bardot, who first-time director Roger Vadim positions as an erotic object, beginning with the opening scene in which the camera captures her lying face down and soaking in the St. Tropez sun, her nude body stretched straight across the screen. The film, which cost approximately $250,000 and grossed $4 million in the United States, made Bardot a hot commodity on the American art house circuit and marked the beginning of the New Wave movement in France.

But the actress, for whom the term "sex kitten" was coined, was too much for some Americans to handle. The Legion of Decency condemned the film, prompting one priest in Lake Placid, New York to impose a six-month ban on a movie theatre for showing the film. Rev. James T. Lynge offered to pay the theatre $350 in lieu of box-office receipts, but the theatre owner refused. Less than three months later, the substantial losses due to the ban forced the owners of the only movie theatre in town to close its doors.

In Cleveland, Tennessee, a theatre manager was charged with obscenity when he showed the film in his theatre. In Philadelphia, District Attorney Huette F. Dowling watched the "lewd and lascivious film" and decided it should not be shown in the city's movie houses. The distributor asked for an injunction so the film could be shown before the case went to trial. When a judge refused, the D.A. seized the prints and arrested the theatre managers. The distributor appealed to the Supreme Court of Pennsylvania, which reversed the lower court's decision.

Les amants (The Lovers—1958)

The French film that had the most significant impact on obscenity laws in the United States was a contemporary romantic drama based on *Point de lendemain*, a 1777 novel by Dominique Vivant. The story is about a romantic encounter between Jeanne (Jeanne Moreau), the unhappy wife of a rich publisher, and Bernard (Jean-Marc Bory), a young, handsome archeologist, who comes to her aid when her car breaks down and ends up spending the night at her estate. While Jeanne's husband is asleep, she and Bernard make love in a rowboat, a bathtub, and a bed. In the end, she decides to give up her husband, child, and bourgeois life to be with Bernard.

At the time of its release, the film was shocking because of its sensual, prolonged love scenes (with minimal skin) and the way director/cowriter Louis Malle and coscreenwriter Louise de Vilmorin "romanticize" the adulterous affair. In a moment similar to the controversial "orgasm shot" of Hedy Lamarr in *Ecstasy*, Malle keeps the camera on Jeanne's face and then follows her hand as she slowly moves it away from her body to her waist, where Bernard grasps it. She leaves with him in the morning, yet there is some hint of uncertainty about their future in her final narration ("Already, in the treacherous hours of dawn, Jeanne had her doubts. She was afraid, but regretted nothing").

The censors in New York, Virginia, and Maryland, and several cities, including Providence and Boston, required cuts during the twenty-minute lovemaking sequence at the end of the film, but the censors in Chicago and Ohio were not as accommodating. A judge lifted the ban in Chicago because members of the censor board apparently only watched the fifth reel of the film before making their decision. In Ohio, the manager of an arts theatre in Cleveland Heights named Nico Jacobellis was arrested and convicted by what a judge called "a major crime against society." Jacobellis appealed all the way to the Supreme Court (*Jacobellis v. Ohio*, 378 U.S. [1964]), which ruled *The Lovers* "was not obscene within the standards set in *Roth v. United States* and *Alberts v. California.*" In his opinion, Justice Potter stated that obscenity laws were limited to hardcore pornography; therefore, *The Lovers* was "entitled to the protection for free expression that is guaranteed by the First and Fourteenth Amendments." Potter also made the oft-quoted statement regarding the definition of pornography: "I shall not today attempt further to define the kinds of material I understand to be embraced within that shorthand description; and perhaps I could never succeed in intelligibly doing so. But I know it when I see it, and the motion picture involved in this case is not that."

BABY DOLL (1956): "19 YEARS OLD AND MARRIED . . . BUT NOT REALLY!"

When the audience first sees Baby Doll Meighan (Carroll Baker), it is from the point of view of her husband Archie (Karl Malden), who is watching his wife sleep through a peephole in the wall adjacent to her bedroom. The image is doubly disturbing. We are forced to look at something we obviously should not be seeing—a young adult woman sleeping in a crib, sucking her thumb like a baby. It's an appropriate introduction to one of Hollywood's most unconventional couples, who we soon learn are married, yet have never consummated their relationship because Archie promised her late father he would wait until her twentieth birthday, which is tomorrow.

In the meantime, Archie is facing financial ruin because his cotton mill, like the others in his small Mississippi town, has been forced out of business by a syndicate. He seeks revenge by burning down the syndicate's mill, thereby forcing the manager, Silva Vaccaro (Eli Wallach), to farm the work out to the local mills. While Archie is trying to deliver twenty-seven wagons of cotton at the end of day, Silva, who suspects Archie started the fire, tries to get the truth out of Baby Doll. He tries to charm her, but his demeanor becomes increasingly more sadistic as he forces her to sign a statement confirming her husband's guilt. Silva's behavior frightens Baby Doll, yet it also seems to awaken her sexuality. When Archie returns home, he sees Baby Doll walking down the stairs in her slip followed by Silva. Although Silva assures him nothing happened, Archie is enraged and goes after him with a gun. The police arrive in time to arrest Archie for setting the fires. When midnight strikes, Archie, who is being taken away by the police, laments, "It's my Baby Doll's birthday."

Tennessee Williams's screenplay of *Baby Doll* is based on his one-act play, *27 Wagons Full of Cotton*, which had a brief run in New York in 1955. When Joseph Breen read the first draft of Williams's script, he noted there is currently "very little relief as the story now stands from what might be called reasonably normal or healthy people, or those representing decency and sanity" (one wonders if Breen had ever seen a Tennessee Williams play). Breen's suggestion for remedying the problem was to turn one of the supporting characters into the "voice for morality vis-à-vis the sins and mistakes of the principals." But the biggest problem with the script for Breen is the adulterous affair between Silva and Baby Doll, which violated the Code.

When Breen read another draft of the script, he once again insisted it be clear there was no adulterous affair between Silva and Baby Doll. Director Elia Kazan assured Jack Warner that he "specifically did not want there to have been a 'sex-affair' between our characters." He hoped that the ending of the film, in which Silva leaves Baby Doll after Archie is driven away from the police, should make it clear that Silva is not at all interested in her. Kazan believed Archie was the "hero of the film," yet he is a "pathetic, misguided, confused, desperate man." But what Kazan could not change is the sexual frustration Archie is feeling over his nonsexual relationship with Baby Doll. "I will, you can be sure, handle it delicately and in good taste," Kazan assured Warner, "And it will all be done amusingly, the sordid side of it will be eliminated. . . . The audience will only feel how absurd his awkward and misarranged passion is. How funny! How sad!" Kazan also insisted that for motion pictures to compete with television, films had to start dealing with provocative themes and subject matter: "TV is improving fast, and getting bolder every day. . . . We got to break our own taboos and strike out for increasingly unusual material."

Upon seeing a rough cut of the film, the PCA was satisfied with Kazan's handling of Archie's sexual frustration, but it found the scene in which Silva "charms" Baby Doll as the two sit on a swing to be "extremely offensive" because it's clearly intimated that Silva is agitating the girl, and in a manner, seducing her, up to the point of suggesting that the girl is having physical reactions that are orgiastic. During the scene, one of Silva's hands is not in the frame, which led the censors to believe that he was putting his hand on her lower region. Kazan insisted they were wrong and proved his point by going over the footage frame by frame with a member of the PCA staff "showing why he could cut nothing and pleading that the texture of the fabric would be damaged." Kazan got his way and his film got a PCA seal.

Baby Doll was the first film condemned by the Legion of Decency to have received the approval of the Production Code Administration:

The subject matter of this film is morally repellent both in theme and treatment. It dwells almost without variation or relief upon carnal suggestiveness in action, dialogue and costuming. Its unmitigated emphasis on lust and the various scenes of cruelty are degrading and corruptive. As such, it is grievously offensive to Christian and traditional standards of morality and decency.

Cardinal Spellman of New York supported the Legion of Decency's decision to condemn the film. Upon his return from an overseas trip, he was disturbed by the posters plastered around New York City featuring the provocative shot of *Baby Doll* in her crib, especially a block-long billboard in Times Square that was 135 feet long and covered 15,600 square feet. On Sunday, December 16, 1956, Spellman read a prepared statement from the pulpit of St. Patrick's Cathedral during morning Mass:

The revolting theme of this picture, *Baby Doll,* and the brazen advertising promoting it, constitute a contemptuous defiance of the natural law, the observance of which has been the source of strength in our national life. . . . I exhort Catholic people to refrain from patronizing this film under pain of sin.

In other words, if you are Catholic and go to see *Baby Doll*, you are committing a sin.

Amen.

Both Kazan and Williams responded to the cardinal's review. The director emphasized that truth, not morality, dictates his vision as a filmmaker. "I made *Baby Doll* as I saw it . . ." he told the *New York Times*. "Not the way things should be, not the way they will someday be, but the way they appeared to me there and then. I wasn't trying to be moral or immoral, only truthful." In his autobiography, Kazan recalled how he was sure the "old windbag" (Cardinal Spellman) had not even seen the film, a fact a reporter from the *Herald Tribune* was able to confirm. Williams was more eloquent in his response: "The artist stares at life to the point of glaring at it, so fierce in his will to see it and understand it as clearly as he is able, but a censor covers his eyes with his hands, peeps between his fingers and cries 'shame.'"

The reviews from the secular critics were mixed. While some appreciated the direction, the acting, and, in some instances, what *Baby Doll* had to say, some found it difficult to get past the fact that the three main characters are not particularly likable people. *Time* magazine's review opens with the kind of quote you won't reprint in a newspaper ad: "*Baby Doll* is just possibly the dirtiest American-made motion picture that has been legally exhibited." A few lines down, the review states that it is also "almost puritanically moral" and the filmmaker's intentions was to "arouse disgust; not disgust with the film itself, but with the kind of people and the way of life it describes." At the same time, it questions if there is something voyeuristic about it as well because "long after it has made its moral point, to fondle a variety of sexual symbols and to finger the anatomical aspects of its subject, the moviegoer can hardly help but wondering if the sociological study has not generated into the prurient peep."

The repercussions of both the Legion of Decency and Cardinal Spellman's condemnation of the film were soon felt as the film was censored and banned in various parts of the country. In Providence, Rhode Island, the local censors demanded cuts before granting the film a license, while the city's bishop, the Most Rev. Russell J. McVinney, told Catholics to stay away from the controversial film. The management of the Esquire Theatre in Indianapolis canceled plans to open the film in the last week of December. A chain of twenty theatres owned by Joseph P. Kennedy (J.F.K.'s father) refused to show the film. The former ambassador to Britain (and a Catholic) stated, "I have been in the business forty-five years and I think this is the worst thing that has ever been done to the people and the industry. I think it should be banned everywhere."

The banning of *Baby Doll* was the focus of a citizens' meeting in Aurora, Illinois, where the Kane County Court honored city officials' request for an injunction to prevent the film being exhibited. One particular scene they found "scandalous, indecent, immoral, lewd, and obscene" (did they leave anything out?) was a shot of Baby Doll "lying on the floor or ground and her lover places his foot on her stomach, moving it about in circular motions and the wife displays an arousal of her sexual passion." A court affidavit stated that the "infidelity of an underaged wife is most dangerous and revolting" and the film as a whole is "an open and flagrant violation of public morals and decency." The court ruled in favor of the plaintiff, and an injunction prevented the film from opening in Aurora. Warner Brothers filed an appeal, but lost.

But Aurora, Illinois was not the only city where *Baby Doll* wasn't playing. Spellman's attack and the controversy surrounding it resulted in canceled bookings, affecting the film's take at the box office, which totaled around $3 million. Twenty-two years (and seven films) later, Kazan admitted he never made a profit from the film for which he had "considerable affection." "If you were to look at the film now," he writes, "you'd see a rather amusing comedy and wonder what all the fuss was about."

JAG ÄR NYFIKEN—EN FILM I GULT (I AM CURIOUS [YELLOW]—1967)

I Am Curious (Yellow) is the enigmatic title of a Swedish "art house" film that became the focus of several high-profile obscenity cases beginning in 1968. Shot in black-and-white in *cinéma vérité* style, *Yellow*'s highly fragmented "film-within-a-film" narrative alternates between two interrelated stories. The first involves *Yellow*'s writer/director Vilgot Sjöman and actress Lena Nyman, who are collaborating on a film about a young radical named Lena (played by Nyman). The second story is the plot of the fictional film the pair is shooting in which Lena (the radical) searches for meaning and truth in contemporary Swedish society. While Lena is concerned with current economic and social issues in Sweden, her "curiosity" also extends to her sexuality when she has a volatile affair with a married car salesman (Börje Ahlstedt). In the press kit for the film, Sjöman explains the connection between Lena's politics and her sexuality:

> She wants to be non-violent . . . but she has a lot of aggression inside her. Lena's development is a story of someone who becomes conscious of herself and her motives. And this consciousness is brought about by her deep sexual engagement with Börje. After their first happy time together, where no conflicts are apparent . . . demonstrating their contemporary sexual hypocrisy . . . Lena discovers all the hate and rage she has within her.

One unique aspect of *Yellow* is the inclusion of documentary footage in the fictional narrative. Lena's search for truth takes her out into the streets where she asks people passing by leading questions about Swedish politics, but she is more interested in expressing her personal views than searching for answers. The film also includes a brief interview with Dr. Martin Luther King, Jr. about the nonviolent movement in America. The footage was shot in 1966 during Dr. King's visit to Sweden to deliver a speech at Stockholm University.

In regards to the film's sexual content, *Yellow* contains both female and male frontal nudity and several simulated sex scenes between Lena and Börje (at one point it appears she is touching his penis with her lips), which is why a print of the film was seized by custom agents when it arrived in Kennedy Airport one day in December of 1967. The U.S. distribution rights were bought by Barney Rosset, publisher of Grove Press and an advocate of free speech and the First Amendment. In 1964, Rosset won a landmark Supreme Court case (*Grove Press, Inc. v. Gerstein*, 378 U.S. 577 [1964]) over the publication of Henry Miller's *Tropic of Cancer*. The Supreme Court overruled a Florida district court by declaring "material dealing with sex in a manner that advocates ideas, or that has literary or scientific or artistic value or any other form of social importance, may not be branded as obscenity and denied the constitutional protection."

On May 20, 1968, *I Am Curious (Yellow)* was put on trial in a New York district court. The presiding justice, Judge Thomas F. Murphy, had denied an earlier request to release the print of the film, which was still in the hands of company agents. "If this film has a message," Judge Murphy wrote, "I would suspect it is merely dross, providing a vehicle for portraying sexual deviation and hard core pornography." The defense called a series of expert witnesses to speak of its "social, political, artistic, and moral value," including Sjöman, Norman Mailer, three film critics, a minister, and two psychiatrists. Rosset and Grove Press lost their first round in court but won their appeal, in which the court ruled that while the "sexual content of the film is presented with greater explicitness than has been seen in any other film produced for general viewing," *I Am Curious (Yellow)* is not obscene "under the standards established in the Supreme Court" and thus, "the showing of the picture can not be inhibited."

The court's decision allowed the American public to finally see the film so much had been written about. The National Catholic Office for Motion Pictures was quick to condemn it, accusing the director of exploiting his star: "Sjöman's sensationalism only disillusions the viewer about his intentions as a social critic. [Lena's sexual problems] gradually become the focal point of the film that has gone out of control. By exploiting her, the film is as hypocritical as the society it has set out to condemn." The reviews from the mainstream press were generally negative. *Variety* found the sex "boring" and lacking a "political viewpoint." *Time* called it an "artistic failure" that "will certainly stand as a cultural curiosity." *Life* said it was a "fairly interesting, rather cold and clinical film emotionally, with quite a bit of sexy stuff in it." Rex Reed did not hold back, dismissing the film as a "vile and disgusting Swedish meatball in pseudo-pornography at its ugliest and least titillating, and pseudo-sociology at its lowest point of technical ineptitude" (and this from the critic who would appear the next year in one of the trashiest films of 1970s, *Myra Breckinridge* [1970]!)

While a U.S. court of appeals may have ruled in the film's favor, it did not bring an end to its legal troubles. When *Yellow* opened around the country, the distributor was dragged into court in several major cities (Cleveland, Denver, Atlanta, Detroit, and Philadelphia), and the film was banned in Boston, Spokane, Kansas City, and Baltimore. As Dawn Sova points out, if the U.S. Supreme Court, as opposed to an appeals court, had decided the film was not obscene, it would have no longer been an issue. *I Am Curious (Yellow)* did have its moment in the chambers of the U.S. Supreme Court when the Maryland Supreme Court upheld the state's board of censors' decision not to grant the exhibitor a permit to show the film on the basis that it was obscene. Grove Press took the case to the U.S. Supreme Court, which upheld the lower court's decision in a 4–4 split.

DEEP THROAT (1972): PORNO CHIC

In 1970, the National Commission on Obscenity and Pornography released a preliminary report of a two-year government study on the harmful effects of pornography on American society. Among the recommendations made by the commission was the repeal of all federal, state, and local laws prohibiting the exhibition of pornographic films and the selling of porn to adults. But as their report was being finalized, there was dissent among some of the commission's eighteen members over the issue of relaxing legal restrictions due to political changes in the White House.

The commission was created during the Johnson administration, so when President Nixon took office, he appointed conservative Charles Keating, a lawyer and antipornography activist, to the commission. In 1965, Keating produced a sensationalistic "educational" film, *Perversion for Profit*, which warned viewers about the "merchants of obscenity" and the "moral decay" that "weakens our resistance to the onslaught of the communist masters of deceit." Keating echoed President Nixon's objections to the commission's report as "morally bankrupt." "So long as I am in the White House," Nixon declared, "there will be no relaxation of the national effort to control and eliminate smut from our national life."

But the war against "smut" had only just begun in the United States thanks to beautician-turned-filmmaker Gerard "Jerry" Damiano. In 1972, Damiano, under the pseudonym Jerry Gerard, directed a low-budget porn film, *Deep Throat*, which revolutionized the porn industry by taking sex out of its plain brown wrapper. Shot in Miami in six days and financed with "mob money" for around $30,000, the film reportedly grossed anywhere from $25 to $100 million (the facts and figures surrounding the film's production, distribution, and exhibition are murky and hotly contested, which add to the film's mystique).

The plot (a term I use loosely) of *Deep Throat* revolves around a sexually unsatisfied woman (Linda Lovelace, as herself) who confesses to her roommate, Helen (Dolly Sharp), that she's "never gotten off." Helen lines up (literally) some guys to get Linda's "bells ringin'," but when that doesn't work, she seeks medical advice from Dr. Young (Harry Reems), who discovers her clitoris is actually located in the bottom of her throat. The solution? Deep throat. At last, Linda hears bells and skyrockets. She puts her talent to good use and becomes a nurse who makes house calls to Dr. Young's sexually troubled patients.

The film opened in New York City on June 12, 1972, at a time when the city's thriving sex exploitation business, under the control of organized crime, was targeted by Mayor John Lindsay as part of his campaign to rid Times Square of adult movie houses, massage parlors, peep shows, and streetwalkers. *Deep Throat* had been playing for twelve weeks when the police raided the New Mature World Theatre in Manhattan on August 29, 1972, and confiscated its print of the film. Mature Enterprises, which owned the theatre, was charged and found guilty of obscenity in March of 1973 and fined $2 million.

The verdict sent shock waves through the porn industry—and it was only the beginning. Between the years 1972 and 1981, obscenity trials were held in various cities in over twenty-two states. The most high-profile trial occurred in Memphis, Tennessee, where U.S Attorney Larry Parris filed charges against twelve individuals, including actor Harry Reems, and five corporations (and close to one hundred others) for their part in a "conspiracy" to transport "an obscene, lewd, lascivious, and filthy motion picture" over state lines. A federal judge granted Reems a new trial because the standards for obscenity applied in the case were based on the landmark *Miller v. California* decision, yet the film was produced prior to 1973. The election of Jimmy Carter in 1976 resulted in personnel changes in the U.S. Justice Department, which decided to drop the indictment against Reems, yet pursued the charges against those involved in the distribution of the film, several of whom were convicted for distributing the film across state lines.

Ironically, the legal battle to censor the film only fueled the public's interest in it. In a January 1973 article for *New York Times Magazine*, Ralph Blumenthal used the term "porno chic" to describe the crossover appeal of films like *Deep Throat*. Pornography had always been on the margins of popular culture, but *Deep Throat* was attracting a more diverse and "respectable" crowd (diplomats, celebrities, women, couples) than you would find in the average porn theatre. The phrase "Deep Throat" became part of the American lexicon, while Linda Lovelace, who later repudiated her career as an adult film actress, became a household name.

Deep Throat was followed by a host of other chic porno films, most notably *The Devil in Miss Jones* (1973), starring Georgina Spelvin as a virgin who commits suicide and receives an education in the art of sexual pleasure before moving on to the next world; and the surreal *Behind the Green Door* (1972), featuring former Ivory Snow box model Marilyn Chambers as a woman who is kidnapped and made to perform sexual acts in a private club before an audience. Both films cleaned up at the box office in states and cities where they were not banned.

SALÒ O LE 120 GIORNATE DI SODOMA (SALO, OR THE 120 DAYS OF SODOM—1975): SEXUAL ANARCHY

In the early 1970s, Italian director Pier Paolo Pasolini adapted three classical literary works for the screen: Boccaccio's *Il Decamerone* (*The Decameron*—1971), Chaucer's *I racconti di Canterbury* (*Canterbury Tales*—1972), and *Il fiore delle mille e una notte* (*Tales of a Thousand Nights*—1974). His "Trilogy of Life," as it would become known, was attacked by both right-wing and leftist critics. Those on the right were outraged by the films' explicit sexual content and nudity. In his defense, Pasolini explained how "the explicit sexuality of the trilogy was nothing less than a 'political protest' against the reification and alienation imposed by modern capitalism." When critics on the left complained about the lack of ideology in his films, he told them it was "really there, above their heads, *in the enormous cock on the screen.*"

Among the filmmakers who emerged in Italy after the Second World War (an impressive list that includes Fellini, Visconti, Antonioni, and Bertolucci), Pasolini was by far the most controversial. Having established himself in the 1950s as a poet and a novelist, the outspoken intellectual, committed Marxist, and homosexual utilized the language of the cinema to attack bourgeois capitalism and its "virtues," which he believed permeated all facets of post-War Italian society. In Pasolini's films, sexuality is politicized and political issues are sexualized. On a formal level, his films defied the codes and conventions of classical Hollywood cinema, relying heavily instead on allegory, symbolism, and ambiguity.

For example, in *Teorema* (*Theorem*—1968), a handsome, pansexual stranger (Terence Stamp) comes to stay in a bourgeois Italian household and sleeps with both the male and female members of the family, including the maid, temporarily liberating them from their bourgeois existence. But when he departs, their lives fall apart, while the maid is transformed into a saint with the power to levitate. The identity of Stamp's character is never made clear and is left open to interpretation. Is he the devil? God? Christ? Like many aspects of Pasolini's life and work, *Teorema* was at the center of a scandal when it received an award from the OCIC (the Catholic Film Office) and then was condemned by the Vatican's official newspaper, *L'Osservatore Romano*, which called the film "negative and dangerous." The film's release was blocked by a Roman public prosecutor, who claimed the film "contained various scenes and sequences offensive to decency" and described the scenes in which Stamp sleeps with each family member as "contrary to every moral, social, or family value." Pasolini appeared at the trial and succeeded in convincing the justices that the film was symbolic and, therefore, not pornographic.

But Stamp's bed hopping in *Teorema* is nothing compared to the sexual anarchy depicted in *Salo*, Pasolini's last and most controversial film loosely based on the Marquis de Sade's 1785 novel, *120 Days of Sodom or the School of Licentiousness*. In Sade's story, four aristocrats hold twenty-four teenagers hostage in a remote castle for six months and proceed to torture and violate them in every way imaginable for their own sexual pleasure. Written while the author was imprisoned in the Bastille by a royal order without the benefit of a trial, the book's shocking, detailed descriptions of the aristocrats' violent, perverse activities were meant to be metaphorical—a literary protest against the author's oppressors.

Pasolini's version is set in 1944 in an Italian villa in Salo, a town in Northern Italy that at the time was the capital for Mussolini's puppet regime. Although a film could only scratch the surface of the book's unfilmable acts of rape, degradation, mutilation, sodomy, and torture of children, Pasolini still manages to capture the perverse "flavor" of Sade's story. Four libertines—all powerful men—have chosen nine boys and nine girls, whose bodies essentially become their playthings as they are raped, sodomized, treated like dogs, forced to eat their own excrement, and in the film's climax, subjected to acts of unspeakable torture. There is nothing remotely erotic about all this debauchery, which Pasolini conceived as an attack on the corrupt, bourgeois capitalist society. In an interview during the making of the film, the director outlined his intentions:

My film is planned as a sexual metaphor, which symbolizes, in a visionary way, the relationship between exploiter and exploited. In sadism and in power politics human beings become objects. That similarity is the ideological basis of the story.

Unfortunately, Pasolini was not able to respond to the vicious critical attacks launched against his film. On November 2, 1975, the director was brutally murdered by a teenage hustler named Giuseppe Pelosi, who resembled the type of street kids Pasolini wrote about in his novels *Ragazzi di vita* (*Boys of Life*—1956) and *Una vita violenta* (*A Violent Life*—1959). Pelosi pleaded self-defense, claiming Pasolini became violent, yet he was convicted and imprisoned. Meanwhile, his friends and associates have speculated the director was killed by the Italian authorities, or the Mafia, or his many political adversaries, particularly the neofascists who certainly could not have been pleased with *Salo*. In 2005, Pasolini's case was reopened after Pelosi stated in a television interview that three other people were present at the time.

The film's release coincided with his death, so it became difficult for many people to separate the sadistic violence depicted in the film and the director's violent murder. As historian Naomi Greene observes, "it became virtually impossible to disassociate the sadomasochistic universe of *Salo* from the manner in which he lived his life and, above all, met his death." In the director's absence, producer Alberto Grimaldi was left to defend Pasolini's film when the commission of the Ministry of Tourism and Spectacle voted unanimously to censor it because "in all its tragedy, it brings the screen images that are so aberrant and repugnant of sexual perversion as certainly to offend community standards" (the ban was soon reversed by an appeals committee). In many countries, the film and the subsequent VHS and DVD releases have been edited and/or banned prior to release around the world. British audiences had to wait twenty-five years until a ban was finally lifted and it was approved for audiences eighteen years of age and older. The most unusual case has been in Australia, where *Salo* was banned for seventeen years (1976–93), until the film was finally reevaluated and the ban lifted (some local governments did override the decision, so the ban remained). Five years later, the ban was reinstated, which was a "triumph," in the opinion of one reporter, "of stupidity and anti-intellectualism, as well as a great victory for the unholy alliance of ratbag feminists and repressive Christian right."

CALIGULA (1979): *"ALMOST* BANNED IN BOSTON"

Caligula was the childhood nickname of Gaius Julius Caesar Augustus, the third Emperor of Rome, whose political career was cut short when he was assassinated in 41 A.D. at the age of twenty-nine. The most controversial of the ancient Roman rulers, Caligula is best remembered for his narcissistic tendencies, sadistic demeanor (he allegedly killed people for his own amusement), sexual excesses, and heavy spending. Some historians contend he was mentally ill, perhaps even insane, though his bizarre behavior has also been attributed to epilepsy and hyperthyroidism.

Caligula is also the title of a dirty movie with a $17.5 million price tag about the emperor's rise and fall produced by *Penthouse* publisher Bob Guccione, who conceived the project as an "adult film" with high art aspirations. Although it depends on which version you watch (between the various theatrical, VHS, laserdisc, and DVD releases there's close to ten), some prints of *Caligula*, including the first theatrical version released in the U.S. in 1980, contain hardcore sex footage in the Roman orgy sequence. Still, Guccione refused to label *Caligula* a "pornographic" film. "It's a question of definitions," he explained, "To me, pornography is a work of bad art, as opposed to good art. And I don't think *Caligula* qualifies under the heading of bad art . . . we wanted to make a serious statement."

With a script by Gore Vidal and a talented British cast that includes John Gielgud, Peter O'Toole, Malcolm McDowell, and Helen Mirren, *Caligula* certainly had the potential to be "good art." But any trace of artistry was overshadowed by director Tinto Brass and Guccione's mutual lack of good taste, which permeates every frame of this excessive mish-mash of ancient history, violence, sex, and debauchery. With its silly dialogue and hammy acting, *Caligula* qualifies as "camp," but not that "it's so bad it's good" brand of camp that make bad movies like Ed Wood's *Plan 9 From Outer Space* (1959) and *Valley of the Dolls* (1967) so enjoyable.

More entertaining than the film was the behind-the-scenes drama between the director, writer, producers, and stars, who were either wrangling for artistic control of the film or disassociating themselves from it. The film's original title was *Gore Vidal's Caligula*, but the bestselling author had his name removed from the title in exchange for his 10 percent of the profits (his screen credit reads "adapted from a screenplay by Gore Vidal," yet no one is credited for adapting it). Brass also removed his name as director, but he's credited for "Principal Photography" (not to be confused with the director of photography, Silvano Ippoliti). Giancarlo Lui and Guccione are also credited for directing and photographing "additional scenes," namely the hardcore sex scenes, which Guccione, dissatisfied with Brass's work, shot when principal photography was completed.

Adding to Guccione's troubles were the disparaging statements directed at him, Brass, and the film by Vidal and members of the cast, including McDowell, who, at the time of its release, regretted doing the film. "I was glad when the whole shambles was over," he told the press, "It was probably the most expensive amateur film ever made." Yet in a 2007 interview for *The Girls of Penthouse Magazine*, McDowell, who does the commentary on the most recent DVD release ("The Imperial Edition"), stated he was proud of his work in the film. "But there's all the raunchy stuff—the blatant, modern-day porno that Bob introduced into the film after we'd finished shooting," McDowell explained, "That to me was an absolutely outrageous betrayal. And quite unprecedented."

Guccione participated in the mudslinging as well. In the May 1980 issue of *Penthouse*, which was devoted exclusively to the making of the film, Guccione also offered his candid observations about Brass ("a megalomaniac"), McDowell ("A shallow person . . . stingier than anyone I have ever known"), and O'Toole ("I don't think I ever saw him sober").

An unrated *Caligula* opened in New York on February 1, 1980, without a press screening—a sure sign a film is expected to get negative reviews and a way to ensure they won't be published until after the opening weekend. Once the film was in theatres, the critical floodgates were opened. The *New York Times*'s Vincent Canby called it "the most expensive pornographic film ever made" that envisions ancient Rome as "some wildly overdecorated swingers' club where the floors are probably dirty." *Variety* called the film a "moral holocaust." The *Los Angeles Times*'s Kevin Thomas said the "X-rated orgies are far more frequently depressing than they are genuinely erotic." Michael Sragow of the *Herald-Examiner* wrote that sexuality in the film, which "could all be described in combination of two words ending in 'job,' are enacted with the passion of a casual golf game." But the reviews didn't bother Guccione, who dismissed the film critic as "a failed artist, an incomplete personality . . . a parasite, a remote observer."

Caligula made its Italian debut in Forli, a small northern town, where an obscenity complaint was filed with the local authorities but rejected. On November 11, 1979, the film opened in six theatres in Rome where it reportedly played to packed houses for a week until the prints were confiscated on the orders of Rome's district attorney Giancarlo Amati, who found scenes from the film to be "flagrantly obscene" under Penal Code 528. Under Italian law, a film seized in any part of Italy must be tried in the province where the national premiere was held. Six months later, a trial was held in Forli. Penthouse presumed the case would get thrown out of court because the local prosecutor had already said the film was not obscene, but the ban was upheld and producer Franco Rossellini and the Italian distributor were sentenced to four months in prison. A recut version was eventually released in Italy.

Meanwhile, across the Atlantic, a print of *Caligula* was seized when it entered customs, but charges were not filed, prompting the media watchdog group, Morality in Media, to file a class action lawsuit against the U.S. Attorney General's office for their failure "to perform their non-discretionary duty" by allowing the film to enter the country. It also served the owner of the Penthouse East theatre with an arrest warrant one hour after the film started its run. Although a judge threw the case out of court, Penthouse deposited a print of the film at the New York Federal Court. As Penthouse's counsel explained, "We'd rather have the obscenity question determined in this court than in 100 smaller towns where challenges won't be brought by object efforts to enforce the law, but with bad feelings and vigilante attitudes."

Morality in Media moved its campaign to Boston, where the print was seized by the vice squad of the Boston Police Department from the Saxon Theatre after breaking box-office records for four days. Confident the charges would not hold up in court, Guccione believed the Boston authorities were going after the film because it was playing in a theatre outside of the zone where the theatres that played X-rated films were located. After a two-week, high-profile trial, some of which aired on television, Chief Justice Harry J. Elam of the Boston Municipal Court found Saxon Theatres, Penthouse, and Penthouse's realty subsidiary, Newsconcorp (which leased the theatre), not guilty of disseminating obscene material. Using the three-pronged test applied by the Supreme Court in *Miller v. California*, Justice Elam said he found that the film appeals "to the prurient interests of the average person," yet the defense proved "a serious political theme ran through the film, namely that absolute power corrupts absolutely." When the picture reopened in Boston at the Cheri 3 theatre, the marquee read: "Almost Banned in Boston."

Over a twenty-one-month period (February 1980 through October 1981), *Caligula* grossed approximately $13.5 million. Guccione decided it was time to expand his market by cutting out the six minutes of hard-core footage and submitting it to the CARA, which granted the film an R rating. *Los Angeles Times* critic Kevin Thomas quipped that the R-rated version "would have to be better than in its original unrated form merely by virtue of being shorter." According to Guccione, the film grossed around $21 million in its initial release, but with video sales that amount rose to about $30 million.

Caligula didn't spark a wave of big-budget porn epics, though Guccione claimed he envisioned the film as "the first in a trilogy . . . to illustrate the axiom that power corrupts, and absolute power corrupts absolutely." In December 1980, he announced that the second film, a $25–$30 million biopic based on the life of Catherine the Great, was in the planning stage. Of course the Empress of Russia's sexual appetites would be part of the story, though Guccione assured the public that his production team was "going to be scrupulous about separating the truths from the legends," so an "aesthetic concession" had been made to deal with the legend that Catherine died while having intercourse with her stallion "philosophically." Fortunately, the project stalled at the planning stage, and the stallion remained in his stable.

CRUISING (1980): "YOU MADE ME DO THAT"

In October of 1961, the Production Code's ban on "sex perversion or any inference of it" was replaced by a less restrictive rule: "Restraint and care shall be exercised in presentations dealing with sex aberrations." The change coincided with the anticipated release of *The Children's Hour* (1962) and *Advise and Consent* (1962), both of which, as Vito Russo observes, treat homosexuality as a "dirty secret" and end tragically with the suicide of their respective gay characters. In other words, the change in the Code didn't mean Hollywood was ready to deal with the issue. In fact, around the same time the Code was amended, *Victim*, a British drama about a closeted lawyer who hunts down a man blackmailing homosexuals, was denied a seal. The PCA objected to the "psychology of homosexuality" being discussed "candidly and in such detail as to verge on clinical" and the film's "overtly expressed plea for an acceptance of homosexuality, almost to the point of suggesting that it may be made *socially tolerable*" (emphasis mine). The decision was upheld by the MPAA Appeals Board on December 11, 1961.

Over the next twenty years, there were few positive portrayals of gays and lesbians in American films, which is one reason why the gay and lesbian community was angry Paramount was planning to adapt Gerard Walker's novel *Cruising* into a movie. Having spent the 1970s battling antigay ballot measures and professional homophobes like singer Anita Bryant and Moral Majority leader Jerry Falwell, the community was certainly justified in raising objections to a film about a gay male serial killer who kills gay men.

Published in 1970, *Cruising* is the story of young undercover policemen assigned to act as decoys in order to catch a serial killer, a self-hating gay Columbia graduate student, whose victims are gay men. Walker, who was cultural editor of the *New York Times* at the time of the film's release, said he wrote the novel after witnessing the discovery of a mutilated body in an area of Central Park frequented by gays. Set against the backdrop of the New York gay leather scene, the novel exposes the homophobia within the New York Police Department and the mutual hatred between gay men and the police.

Academy Award–winning director William Friedkin, who, a decade earlier, had directed the film version of Mart Crowley's landmark gay play *The Boys in the Band*, became interested again in the project after there had been a series of unsolved killings in New York leather bars on the Lower West Side. Like Steve Burns (Al Pacino's character in the film), Randy Jurgensen, a friend of Friedkin's in the NYPD, went undercover in gay bars to help find the killer (and later served as a technical consultant on the film).

Friedkin and producer Jerry Weintraub's troubles started when location shooting began in New York City, where they were met with protestors who interfered with production by picketing, disrupting traffic, and making noise. After getting a copy of Friedkin's script, a coalition of gay activists vowed to halt production of the film because it "represents a gross distortion of the lives of gay men by portraying them as violent and sex-obsessed." On the evening of July 26, 1979, about one thousand protestors marched through Greenwich Village demanding Mayor Ed Koch withdraw the city's support of the film. He refused, claiming that would be censorship. Weintraub continued to defend *Cruising* on the grounds that it was only showing a "true segment" of the gay community and that it was not a "gay film" but "a murder mystery set in the gay community."

But while some gay men were on one side of the street protesting the film, there were others working as extras in the bar scenes (many of whom were harassed by the activists for participating in the film). John Devere, editor-in-chief of *Mandate* magazine, went "undercover" as an extra and wrote about his experiences on the set and his observations of Friedkin, who seemed intent to keeping everything real, urging "extras *not* to wear, say or do anything they would not ordinarily do in such a gay bar situation."

After production wrapped, the film's problems did not stop. When the film was submitted to the MPAA, it was given an X rating, but after two and a half minutes of sex and gore were cut out of the film, it was assigned an R. At least that is what was supposed to have happened. When Richard Heffner, chairman of CARA, saw the film in a New York theatre, it was clear the cuts were not made (another member of CARA confirmed an uncut print was playing in Los Angeles). When Heffner was ready to revoke the R, Jack Valenti pleaded with him not to raise the issue because he needed producer Jerry Weintraub, who had political connections and strong ties to celebrities, as an ally.

The General Cinema Corporation was also not satisfied with the R. It thought the film deserved an X, and as a policy, the theatre chain does not play films that in its judgment should be rated X. The chain pulled the film from twenty-six theatres. After rescreening the film, it stood by its decision. Other theatre chains included a warning in their advertisements and imposed their own age restrictions. The ads for the Sack and Redstone chains in Boston included this statement: "Warning! This motion picture is one of great artistic achievement; however, its subject matter is extremely sensitive and contains scenes of explicit violence. No one under 18 will be admitted to this motion picture."

Meanwhile, outside the theatre, protestors were picketing the film. When *Cruising* opened in New York, Los Angeles, and San Francisco, groups ranging from thirty to hundreds of people gathered in front of theatres. San Francisco Mayor Dianne Feinstein wanted the film's distributor, United Artists, to pick up the bill for the police overtime needed to control demonstrators in front of two theatres. In Los Angeles, *Cruising* protestors joined forces with lesbians and feminists who were protesting another film, *Windows* (1980), about a lesbian psychotic killer.

One suspects *Cruising* is not the film Friedkin set out to make (he reportedly cut forty minutes out of it). Murder mysteries align the audience with the detective, in this case Steve Burns, who is trying to figure out the identity and the motive of the killer. Friedkin puts the audience in the privileged position by allowing us to witness the horrific murders of gay men by an unidentifiable killer, who stabs his victims and then utters the line, "You made me do that." The killer is presumably captured, yet the audience is left wondering if Steve may have undergone such a severe identity crisis by going undercover that he may have killed his gay neighbor, Ted Bailey (Don Scardino). Besides being a total cop-out (no pun intended), the ending implies that Steve has essentially lost his mind and turned into a killer due to his immersion into the gay lifestyle.

THE "DIRTY" DOZEN: TWELVE MEMORABLE SEXUALLY CHARGED MOMENTS

Sex in the cinema, which basically boils down to what you can and can't show Person A doing to Person B, started changing in the early 1960s with the loosening and eventual demise of the Production Code. But as this list of twelve memorable "dirty" moments attests, the cinema never lost its ability—even to this day—to shock an audience when it came to s-e-x.

1. *Lolita* (1962): Humbert Humbert Meets Lolita
   "How did they ever make a movie of *Lolita*?" is the question posed by the trailer of Stanley Kubrick's film version of Vladimir Nabokov's controversial 1955 bestseller about a middle-aged man who falls in love with a twelve-year-old girl. By adding two years to Lolita's age and downplaying the novel's eroticism, Kubrick managed to get his script and the final cut of his film approved by the PCA "for persons over 18 only."
   The audience is first introduced to Dolores "Lolita" Haze (Sue Lyon) at the same time Humbert (James Mason) first lays his pedophilic eyes on the nymphet sitting on a blanket in the backyard wearing a two-piece bathing suit, a sunhat, and heart-shaped

sunglasses. Humbert gazes at Lolita. She takes off her glasses and returns his gaze.

The moment marks the beginning of one of the most unconventional love stories to come out of Hollywood since *Baby Doll*.

2. *Flaming Creatures* (1963): The Transvestite Orgy
Jack Smith's avant-garde classic is a polymorphously perverse homage to B-movie glamour-pusses (including the director's favorite starlet, Maria Montez) featuring a cast of "flaming creatures"—an assortment of drag queens, transvestites, and hermaphrodites. At one point, one performer, Delicious Dolores (Sheila Bick), is ravaged by the creatures. The scene erupts into a wild orgy, during which various male and female body parts and genitalia are exposed. Apparently this playful and delightfully trashy scene was too much for the Feds, who interrupted a screening at the New Bowery Theatre in New York and confiscated the print. The distributor and the projectionist were convicted of showing an "obscene, lewd, lascivious, filthy, indecent, sadistic, or masochistic picture." Their sixty-day sentences to the New York City Work House were suspended.

One of *Flaming Creatures'* devoted fans is the "Pope of Trash" himself—John Waters—who once declared, "I genuflect before Jack Smith."

3. *Trash* (1970): Holly Gets Off
Andy Warhol produced and Paul Morrissey directed this antidrug odyssey about an addict named Joe (Joe Dallesandro) and his girl-friend Holly (played by transgender actress Holly Woodlawn), who reside in the basement of a Lower East Side apartment building that's been furnished with trash Holly found on the street. In one unexpected, yet ultimately sad scene, a sexually frustrated Holly, who is unable to arouse a strung-out Joe, gets herself off by sub-stituting an empty Miller beer bottle for her lover. When she fin-ishes, she begs a teary-eyed Joe to get off drugs. "Tomorrow it's gonna be with you? Huh, Joe?" she asks, "You're better than that beer bottle."

4. *The Devils* (1971): The Rape of Christ

Set in seventeenth-century France, *The Devils* is based on the true story of an unscrupulous priest who was accused of witchcraft and burned at the stake. Ken Russell's most controversial film is an exercise in blasphemy complete with full-frontal nudity, scenes of masturbation, and Bible burning. In one legendary scene, commonly referred to as "The Rape of Christ," a group of hysterical, orgiastic, naked nuns straddle a statue of Christ. The scene was cut from the final version of the film and believed to be lost until it was discovered in 2002 by British film critic Mark Kermode and featured in his documentary, *Hell on Earth: The Desecration and Resurrection of "The Devils"*, which aired on Britain's Channel 4.

Even without the scene, film critic Alexander Walker was reportedly so offended by *The Devils* that he hit Russell over the head with a rolled up copy of the British newspaper *The Evening Standard*.

Throughout his long career, director Russell has always taken delight in shocking his audience, from the nude wrestling match in *Women in Love* (1969), to China Blue's sexual peccadilloes in *Crimes of Passion* (1984), to his portrait of a Los Angeles prostitute in the aptly titled *Whore* (1991)—all of which fell victim to the censors or were banned outright.

5. *Pink Flamingos* (1972): Sex with Poultry

No taboo is left unturned in director John Waters's early comedy about Divine's battle to retain the title of the "Filthiest Person Alive." In the sickest sex scene in American film history, Babs/Divine's son Crackers (Danny Mills) takes his date Cookie (Cookie Mueller) out to the shed where their chickens live. They get naked and start to have wild sex, in the middle of which Crackers starts putting live chickens in between their bodies. To top it off, he slits the throat of one of them and smears the bloody chicken between her legs. Meanwhile, Crackers's female friend, Cotton (Mary Vivian Pearce), is getting off by watching the action through a window.

In his aptly titled autobiography, *Shock Value*, Waters verified that a real chicken was killed in what is commonly referred to as the "chicken-fuck" scene, yet assured his readers that "the cast cooked and ate this same chicken immediately after the filming, therefore making it, well, morally ethical if you like."

6. *Last Tango in Paris* (1972): Paul "Butters" Jeanne
Two lonely and emotionally damaged strangers, a middle-aged man named Paul (Marlon Brando) and a young French woman named Jeanne (Maria Schneider), meet in an empty Paris flat. They begin a sexual relationship yet agree to keep their names and details about their personal lives a secret. The characters, particularly Paul, who is grief-stricken over his wife's suicide, use sex to express their inner turmoil. Some of the sex is rough and crude, particularly in one scene—explicit for its day—in which Paul anally penetrates Jeanne using butter as a lubricant.

The adult drama received an X rating for sexuality, nudity, and language in the United States, but was banned in Italy, where the two stars, along with director Bernardo Bertolucci, producer Alberto Grimaldi, and United Artists were brought up on obscenity charges. The charges were dropped, but the ban wasn't lifted until 1987.

7. *Ai no corrida* (*In the Realm of the Senses*—1976): The Big Cut
One of the first nonpornographic films to feature unsimulated sexual intercourse, Nagisa Oshima's *In the Realm of Senses* is a tale of obsessive love based on the legendary story of Sada Abe (played by Eiko Matsuda) who, in 1936, erotically asphyxiated her lover, Kichizo Ishida (Tatsuya Fuji), and, afterwards, cut off his penis and carried it around in her purse until she was apprehended by the police. In the film, the couple's relationship takes a sadomasochistic turn when she begins to hit him during sex, which he seems to enjoy. This leads to their final sexual encounter during which Sada, at Kichizo's request, asphyxiates him with a scarf, nearly killing him. When he passes out, she completely snaps and finishes the job.

The film was well received by critics at the 1976 Cannes Film Festival, but was heavily censored in Japan. In 1977, Oshima was charged with obscenity when a book containing stills from the film was published (he was acquitted in 1982). When it played in Japan, it was cut and some of the images were blurred—a technique also used for *Deep Throat* and *Behind the Green Door*. The film's debut in

Germany was delayed a year. A screening at the 1977 New York Film Festival was canceled after the film was previewed and U.S. Customs stepped in, resulting in a legal battle with the film's producer, which delayed its release (despite the fact that porn films were playing in theatres all along 42nd Street!).

Although the inclusion of "real sex" is not common in films, there have been a host of films featuring unsimulated intercourse, fellatio, and cunnilingus (thankfully, no castration) in recent years, including *The Brown Bunny* (2004), *9 Songs* (2004), *All About Anna* (2005), and *Shortbus* (2006)—all of which played in the U.S. without government interference.

8. *Basic Instinct* (1992): The Interrogation of Catherine Tramell
Prior to its release in theatres in March 1992, this tawdry thriller about a crime novelist/psycho killer made headlines due to objections raised by gay activists over its negative depiction of bisexual women and lesbians as oversexed, unstable, and in the case of Catherine Tramell (Sharon Stone), homicidal. The publicity generated by the protests that surrounded the film while it was shooting on location in San Francisco probably contributed to *Basic Instinct*'s success, though the credit for the film's $100-million-plus intake at the box office belongs to Stone and her star-turn performance.

One scene that qualifies *Basic Instinct* as a guilty pleasure occurs in a police interrogation room where Stone/Tramell manages to unnerve five middle-aged, male detectives with her blunt answers to their questions about her sex life with her murdered lover. At one point, she uncrosses her legs to reveals she is not wearing underwear under her dress. The men are shocked (and maybe even a little scared), but that's Catherine Tramell's M.O.—having a psychological hold on men by evoking pangs of castration anxiety and being in control of the film's narrative (the "killer" is using her novel as a guidebook).

9. *Kids* (1995): Telly Deflowers a Virgin
The label "teen movie" took on a whole new meaning when *Kids* opened in the U.S. in July 1995 following its premiere at the Cannes Film Festival. The drama follows a day in the life of two New York

City teenagers, Telly (Leo Fitzpatrick) and Casper (Justin Pierce), who only have sex and drugs on their mind. The opening scene sets the tone for the rest of the film: Telly succeeds in convincing a girl—a virgin—of going all the way with him. He then proceeds to share all the details ("the bitch was bleeding when I first put it in") to Casper. A teen movie for adults, *Kids* makes a convincing case for mandatory sex education classes in grammar schools.

10. *Crash* (1996): Post–Car Crash Love
James Spader stars in David Cronenberg's dark and disturbing adaptation of J. G. Ballard's novel about a film producer, James Ballard, whose involvement in a head-on crash leads to an introduction to a group of sexual fetishists who get turned on by car crashes (being in them, watching them, and reenacting famous ones, like the one that killed James Dean). James and his wife, Catherine (Deborah Kara Unger), have grown so far apart that they can only get aroused during sex by sharing the details of their extramarital affairs, but his association with the "auto-erotic" subculture eventually revives the couple's passion. In the film's final crash, James's car causes Catherine's car to go over an embankment. He is relieved to discover she's OK and then, aroused, starts feeling her up. (And who said romance in the movies is dead?)

Some audience members booed *Crash* after its world premiere at the 1996 Cannes Film Festival, where it won a Special Jury Prize "For Originality, For Daring, and For Audacity." When the film was passed by the British Board of Film Classification without cuts, the London newspaper *The Daily Mail* launched a campaign to have the film banned. The Westminster City Council succeeded in keeping the film off movie screens in central London. They were concerned that "sexually inexperienced people may look to the main characters as role models." ("Honey, let's crash the car tonight and have sex in the backseat like they did in that movie!")

11. *Team America: World Police* (2004): Puppet Sex
The writers/producers of *South Park* (Trey Parker, Matt Stone, and Pam Brady) created this satire about an incompetent counterterrorist organization inspired by the 1960s cult puppet series *The*

Thunderbirds. The comedy is the first film, and most likely the only, featuring an all-puppet cast that received an R rating from the MPAA—for "graphic, crude and sexual humor, violent images and strong language." Apparently the movie raters were not too thrilled with the sex scene involving a male and female puppet, who do it in almost every position imaginable and perform a few other unmentionable acts.

12. *Brokeback Mountain* (2005): Ennis and Jack Share a Tent
A gay love story like *Brokeback Mountain* was long overdue—but no one expected Hollywood to produce such a powerful and moving film about two ranchers who realize they have more in common than herding sheep. Ang Lee beautifully captures the subtlety of Annie Proulx's short story by taking his time in bringing Ennis and Jack together, which culminates with a sudden burst of passion as the two sleep side by side in the cold night air.

CHAPTER 6

A Hotbed of Controversy: Politics and Religion

I n polite company, there are two topics we are told to avoid: politics and religion.

They are both sensitive issues. They are also both inherently divisive and polarizing because people with strong political convictions or religious beliefs tend to have an "us vs. them" mentality. Many people believe if you are not with them (meaning share their convictions or beliefs), then you are against them. That was President George W. Bush's message after the 9/11 attacks. In his address to Congress on September 20, 2001, he spoke of the "War on Terror" and told the nations of the world, "either you are with us, or you are with the terrorists."

It's either them or us. Pick a side.

POLITICS

Throughout its long history, from *The Birth of a Nation* (1915) to Michael Moore's *Fahrenheit 9/11* (2004), the cinema has been an effective propaganda tool for the political right and left as well as for those who fall somewhere in between. The films and filmmakers discussed in the first part of this chapter all carry a strong political message, and for that reason they have been criticized, picketed, boycotted, censored, condemned and/or banned for what they say and, in some instances, how they say it.

Triumph des Willens (Triumph of the Will—1935): "History Becomes Theatre"

This Nazi propaganda film, "commissioned by the order of the Fuehrer," is director Leni Riefenstahl's love letter to Hitler and his regime on the occasion of the Sixth Congress of the National Socialist German Workers Party held in Nuremberg on September 5–8, 1934. The film opens with aerial shots presumably taken from inside of Hitler's plane as it sails through the clouds and descends, like a god from the heavens, and glides over the streets of Nuremberg, accompanied by music from *Die Meistersinger von Nürnberg* by Richard Wagner, the Fuehrer's favorite composer, and "Horst-Wessel-Lied," the anthem of the Nazi Party.

Over the next four days, Riefenstahl captured all the pomp and pageantry, from Hitler's arrival, to the opening ceremony, to the speeches by the top-ranking Nazi officials, and on the final day, the Fuehrer's address to one hundred fifty thousand SA and SS troops. The end result is a visually stunning film. Riefenstahl's direction, particularly the way she moves the camera, was regarded as highly innovative. For example, she built circular tracks around the podium so the camera could move around the Fuehrer while he was speaking and installed a lift on a 140-foot flagpole so she could move the camera vertically to capture the crowd from a high angle.

Triumph of the Will is pure spectacle—an aesthetic expression of fascist ideology and the grandeur, order, and power of the Third Reich. Critic Susan Sontag once described *Triumph of the Will* as an example of how "history becomes theatre." She believed anyone who defended *Triumph* as a documentary was being ingenuous because the film is in actuality a recording of a historical event staged for the camera "which was then to assume the character of an authentic documentary." "The document (the image) is no longer the record of reality," Sontag wrote. "'Reality' has been constructed to serve the image." "Fascinating Fascism," Sontag's critical essay on Riefenstahl's films and photography, was first published as a review of *The Last of the Nuba*, the German director's collection of color photographs of the Sudan taken over a forty-two year period. Sontag claimed Riefenstahl's photographs and Nazi art are linked by what she calls the "fascist aesthetic," which emphasizes the purity, beauty, and strength of the human body.

In her memoirs, published in the U.S. in 1993, Riefenstahl refutes Sontag's claim that the Nuremburg Party Rally of 1934 was staged for the camera. She also paints herself as an apolitical and naïve person who was essentially ordered by the Fuehrer to make the film. She makes it clear she did not become aware of the atrocities committed by Hitler and the Nazi Party until after Germany's defeat when she was shown photographs taken at the concentration camps. After the war, Riefenstahl was exonerated of all charges by the American and French governments, though her name would forever be associated with the Third Reich.

Triumph of the Will was shown commercially in the United States on June 27, 1960 at New York City's New Yorker Theatre as the first of a ten-picture summer series. An extra midnight showing had to be added to accommodate the crowd. The screening also featured *Dachau*, a six-minute compilation of newsreel footage depicting the atrocities committed at the concentration camp. Earlier that same year, Riefenstahl was invited by the British Film Institute to lecture at the National Film Theatre in London, but the government-subsidized BFI decided to withdraw its invitation due to protests.

Fourteen years later, Riefenstahl accepted an award at the first Telluride Film Festival in Colorado, where she was greeted by protestors. In an interview with the *New York Times*, Riefenstahl once again defended *Triumph of the Will* and her involvement in it. "I want to make it clear," she told the reporter, "I made the film not as propaganda; it is *documentary*. Everything you see is absolutely true. You can see the same thing in America, French, German newsreels. But the newsreel is not art—that is the difference." The following year, *Triumph of the Will* and *Olympia I & II* (1938), Riefenstahl's chronicle of the 1936 Olympic Games, were shown at the Festival of Women in the Arts in Atlanta, despite protests from the Anti-Defamation League and the Feminist Action Alliance. The screening was followed by a discussion, during which a panelist raised an issue that will forever plague films like *Triumph of the Will* and D. W. Griffith's *Birth of a Nation*: Is it possible to separate the skill of the filmmaker from a film's social content? In other words, should Riefenstahl's films be lauded as cinematic achievements, despite the fact they were propaganda for a fascist regime guilty of the worst genocide in modern history? Is it possible to appreciate a filmmaker's technical skills, yet at the same time ignore the subject the filmmaker is pointing his or her camera at?

Salt of the Earth (1953): "A New Weapon for Russia"

The effects of a labor strike on the daily lives of miners and their families is the focus of Salt of the Earth, a controversial drama based on the real events surrounding the 1950–51 strike by Mexican American miners in Hanover, New Mexico, against the Empire Zinc Company. The production, sponsored by the International Union of Mine, Mill, and Smelter Workers, featured men and women who participated in the actual strike. The creative team both behind and in front of the camera was comprised of mostly individuals who were blacklisted at the time from the Hollywood film industry because they were members of the Communist Party, were suspected of being communists, or refused to testify or "name names" when subpoenaed by the House Un-American Activities Committee.

Salt of the Earth is told from the point of view of Esperanza Quintero (Rosaura Revueltas), a housewife whose husband, Ramón (Juan Chacón), is beaten up by the local deputies when someone fingers him as the ringleader of the striking miners. When the strikers are served with an injunction prohibiting them from picketing, their wives take their places on the picket line, while their husbands do the housework. The situation puts a strain on Ramón and Esparanza's marriage, but when he orders her to stay home, she refuses and chastises him for his sexist attitude, equating him with the miners' racist bosses. Law officers try to evict Ramón and his family from their home, but with the help from their neighbors, the officers back down, as does the mining company, which eventually gives in to their demands.

The leftist politics of director Herbert J. Biberman, writer Michael Wilson, and producer Paul Jarrico permeates every aspect of this progressive film, which was way ahead of its time in terms of how the narrative links social, economic, racial, and gender-related issues. Told from the point of view of its female protagonist (a rarity at the time in Hollywood), the narrative equates the miners' fight for higher wages and better working conditions with their wives' struggle for "equality" in their private lives. By the end of the story, Ramón's consciousness is

234

raised. He understands that he and Esparanza are in this together. "You were right," he concedes, "Together we can push everything with us as we go."

Ramón could also have been speaking about the makers of *Salt of the Earth*, who had to overcome some major obstacles to complete the film. Putting a crew together was especially difficult because Roy M. Brewer, head of the International Alliance of Theatrical and Stage Employees Union (IATSE) and chairman of the conservative Motion Picture Alliance for the Preservation of American Ideals, encouraged union members not to work on the film. Brewer admitted he did permit some union members to work on the crew in New Mexico in order to keep track of the production's "Red-Tainted Activities." On February 24, 1953, Congressman Donald Jackson (R-California), a member of the House Un-American Activities Committee, stood on the floor of the House and publicly denounced the film as racist, and falsely claimed it was "deliberately designed to inflame racial hatreds and to depict the United States of America as the enemy of all colored people." "If this picture is shown in Latin America, Asia and India, it will do incalculable harm not only to the United States but to the cause of free people everywhere," Jackson declared, "In effect, this picture is a new weapon for Russia." Screenwriter Wilson responded to Jackson's allegations and threats by simply stating, "There is not one shred of truth in his description of the subject or intent of this motion picture. . . . He is lying." Two days after Jackson's speech, actress Revueltas was arrested for being in the country illegally, despite the fact that she had a passport and a work visa, which had not been stamped by immigration officials when she entered the country.

Meanwhile, the crew started running into problems when the citizens of Silver City, New Mexico started to interfere with the production. Like a scene out of an old Western, a citizens group warned them to get out of town "by noon tomorrow—or go out in black boxes." By the last day of shooting, thirty state patrolmen had to be called in to keep the peace. As for Revueltas, she decided to return to Mexico voluntarily, so a stand-in was used for some scenes. The filmmakers traveled to Mexico to shoot her remaining scenes under the pretense they were doing a screen test (that just happened to be her remaining scenes from the film). Then, once *Salt of the Earth* was "in the can," the filmmakers had trouble finding a laboratory in Hollywood that would process the film. The union boycott also extended to projectionist members, some of whom refused to run the film.

The makers of *Salt of the Earth* fired back by filing a $7.5 million lawsuit against sixty-two film companies, two trade associations, and sixteen individuals for boycotting and blacklisting the film in violation of the Sherman and Clayton Acts. The list of names included Howard Hughes, who advised Senator Jackson on how to stop the film during postproduction. The case dragged on in court for eight years until the last twenty-five of the remaining defendants were acquitted in November of 1964 by a New York Federal Grand Jury.

Salt of the Earth played in theaters in New York, Los Angeles, and San Francisco, while projectionists in Chicago refused to run it. Fortunately, some critics were able to forget what they heard (much of it inaccurate) and judge the film on its own merits. In his review for the *New York Times*, Bosley Crowther admitted "in light of its agitated history, it is somewhat surprising that *Salt of the Earth* is, in substance, simply a strong pro-labor film with a particularly sympathetic interest in the Mexican-Americans with whom it deals." Roy Ringer of the *Los Angeles Daily News* went a step further and commended the film and the relevance of its theme to every American. "If there is propaganda in this picture," Ringer writes, "it is not an alien one, but an assertion of principles no thoughtful American can reject."

Salt of the Earth is not only a testament to the dignity and strength the miners displayed in their struggle against the system to improve the quality of their lives, but the commitment of its makers. Despite the attempts by members of the U.S. government and their own industry to silence them, the filmmakers remained true to their vision and demonstrated the American cinema's potential for tackling social, political, and economic issues within the confines of narrative filmmaking.

Peter Watkins's *The War Game* (1965): Fictional Reality

What if Great Britain were the target of a nuclear attack?

That's the hypothetical question filmmaker Peter Watkins poses and answers in *The War Game*, a harrowing and all-too-realistic docudrama that envisions what could happen if a limited nuclear war broke out between the Soviets and European NATO countries.

The film opens with the narrator setting the political stage for the fictional international crisis that will lead to the attack. Chinese troops have invaded South Vietnam, and the United States is planning to use tactical nuclear weapons in retaliation. To show their "collective Communist support" for their Chinese comrades, Russia and East Germany have sealed off access to Berlin and threaten to invade the western half of the city unless the U.S. withdraws its weapons. When NATO troops are unable to enter Berlin, the U.S. has no choice but to release nuclear warheads to NATO forces, which leads to an exchange of missiles between the Soviets and European NATO countries, including Britain.

But *The War Game* is not so much concerned with Cold War tensions as it is with the inevitable, immediate death of thousands (as well as the aftermath) if such a tragedy were to occur. In this regard, the film is a wake-up call to British citizens, who are portrayed as apathetic or ignorant about nuclear weapons and the threat they pose to mankind. To drive his message home, Watkins enhances the reality of the fictional events by shooting his film *"cinéma vérité* style" in black-and-white with a handheld 16mm camera. He also uses other documentary conventions, such as a nondiegetic "Voice of God" male narrator and interviews with experts, government officials, and clergymen (all played by actors), whose nonsensical and, at times, callous remarks about nuclear weapons and war are based on actual quotes or published information. Watkins also added to what he describes as the film's "documentary authenticity" by shooting on location in the county of Kent and using nonprofessional and amateur actors, whose real responses to Watkins's "man/woman-on-the-street" questions reveal their lack of understanding of nuclear weapons and the devastation they would cause if launched by either side. Although we know what we are witnessing is not authentic, it doesn't diminish the emotional impact of seeing a little boy crying hysterically as the heat from a nuclear explosion burns his retinas, people suffering from severe burns and gasping their last breath during a firestorm, and police officers putting the victims classified as "hopeless" out of their misery by shooting them in the head.

The film's "documentary authenticity" was also a factor in the BBC's decision not to broadcast the film, which the government-chartered station considered "too horrifying for the medium of broadcasting." The official statement made it clear that there was no "outside pressure of any kind," yet media critics and historians continue to debate the role the Home Office and the Ministry of Defense played in banning the program from the airwaves due in part to the doubts it raised about deterrence strategy.

As one would expect, the banning of the film left Watkins feeling angry and betrayed. The public was eventually given the opportunity to see *The War Game* for the price of a movie ticket when it was released theatrically in Britain in April of 1965 and in the U.S. in February of 1967. Peter Watkins received a special prize at the 1966 Venice Film Festival and in the following year took home two British Academy Awards (for Best Short and the U.N. Award) and the Oscar for Best Feature Documentary—the only time the statue was given to a fictional film in that category.

In 1966, British critic Kenneth Tynan called *The War Game* "the most important film ever made." "We are always being told that works of art cannot change the course of history," Tynan wrote, "Given wide enough dissemination, I believe this one might." Twenty years after it was banned, *The War Game* was finally broadcast on British television (on BBC2) as one in a series of programs commemorating the fortieth anniversary of the Hiroshima and Nagasaki bombings.

Ironically, the much-deserved awards and critical praise bestowed on the film were no doubt due in part to the ban. The BBC's *Radio Times* agreed: "It's clear that *The War Game*—unbroadcast—has played a more pivotal role in the nuclear debate than if Sir Hugh [Green, BBC's Director-General in the 1960s] had approved its screening in 1965."

Titicut Follies (1967): Reality Fiction

Titicut Follies is not a musical, but it opens with a song—"Strike Up the Band"—performed by a group of men dressed in white shirts and bowties holding a pom-pom in each hand. We soon learn this odd performance is part of a variety show featuring the inmates and staff of the Bridgewater Hospital for the Criminally Insane in Massachusetts, which is the subject of filmmaker Frederick Wiseman's first, and most controversial, documentary.

Over the course of a career that has spanned over four decades and thirty-seven films, Wiseman developed his own unique "observational" style of filmmaking. In an article published in 2001 in the journal *Social Research*, he outlined his basic methodology:

> I make documentary films based on unstaged events using the photographs and voices of people who are not actors and who are not asked to do anything other than give their permission to be included in the film. . . . Many but not all of my films are about public institutions. They are public in the sense that they are supported by tax money collected by public authorities—city, state, or federal—and exist to provide services such as education, health care, welfare, and police to the community.

In addition to Bridgewater Hospital, Wiseman's camera has observed the daily activities of a Philadelphia high school (*High School* [1968]); the Kansas City, Missouri police department (*Law and Order* [1968]); a New York City hospital (*Hospital* [1970]); and more recently, a shelter for battered women (*Domestic Violence* [2001]) and the Idaho legislature (*State Legislature* [2006]).

His distinct shooting style is designed to minimize the filmmaker's presence. Wiseman does not interact with his subjects on camera and there is no narration or nondiegetic music on the soundtrack. The action itself is "un-staged" and "un-manipulated," yet, as the director explains, the process of shooting (what the camera shows, how the action is shot) and editing (the footage shot vs. the footage used) are both highly manipulative. For *Titicut*, Wiseman shot 80,000 feet/37 hours of film, which was edited down to 3,200 feet/84 minutes. The term "reality fiction" has been applied to Wiseman's films to emphasize they are not objective renderings of social reality, but a reality that has been "constructed" in the editing process when the footage is organized and given a dramatic structure.

The reality Wiseman constructed from his footage of Bridgewater Hospital is a deeply disturbing portrait of a public institution where mentally ill inmates are mistreated, neglected, and stripped of their clothes and dignity by the guards and staff. Many of them are shown walking around naked in a state of confusion. While there are moments in which staff members display some compassion, they are overshadowed by the cruelty of the guards and the hospital's obvious neglect of its residents.

For example, for their own amusement, the guards taunt a disturbed patient named Jim by bombarding him with questions and badgering him for not keeping his room clean. In one of the film's most disturbing sequences, an older man who refuses to eat is stretched out naked on a table and force fed through a greased tube that is placed through his nose. A doctor smoking a cigarette stands nearby; his ashes look as if they are about to fall into the funnel of food. The sequence is intercut with shots of the corpse of the same man being prepared for burial. In a 2007 interview, Wiseman admitted he showed "too heavy an editorial hand in that sequence" and regretted cutting the two sequences together.

Wiseman's uncompromising portrait of life in Bridgewater set off a legal battle between the filmmaker and his company, Bridgewater Films, and the Commonwealth of Massachusetts over several issues, including whether Wiseman breached an oral contract he had made with Bridgewater Hospital regarding his intentions. On the witness stand, Bridgewater Superintendent Charles Gaughan accused Wiseman of tricking him by giving him the impression the film's "primary theme" would be the hospital's treatment of alcoholism. "I don't think, as it now stands, the film has benefit to anyone." Gaughan said, "It appeals to offbeat, hippie types. A reasonable man would get nothing from it. It is not even an authentic document." Gaughan and Commissioner of Correction John Gavin claimed Wiseman had given the state's final approval of the film prior to its release. The director denied any such agreement was made.

A far more complex issue involved the public's right to know versus the right of privacy of the inmates, who were legally wards of the state. In the case of *Commonwealth v. Wiseman*, Superior Court Judge Harry Kalus ruled that Wiseman had not only misrepresented his purposes but had violated the privacy of its participants. In his decision, Judge Kalus also assumed the role of film critic by attacking the director's shooting style and the film's lack of a cohesive structure:

The film is 80 minutes of brutal sordidness and human degradation. It is a hodge-podge of sequences, with the camera jumping, helter-skelter, from the showing of an inmate in an act of masturbation to scenes depicting mentally ill patients engaged in repetitive, incoherent and obscene rantings and ravings. The film is excessively preoccupied with nudity, with full exposure of the privates of these persons. There is no narrative accompanying the film, nor are there any subtitles, without which the film is a distortion of the daily routine and conditions of the Institution. Each viewer is left to his own devices as to just what is being portrayed and in what context.

As part of Judge Kalus's decision, *Titicut Follies* was banned from public exhibition—the only American film censored for reasons other than obscenity or national security. In 1969, an appeals court amended the decision to allow the film to be shown in Massachusetts, but only to "legislators, judges, lawyers, doctors, psychiatrists, students in those related fields, and organizations dealing with the social problems of custodial care and mental infirmity." Otherwise, Wiseman was prohibited from showing the film both inside and outside the state. This restriction remained in effect until 1991. Two years later, *Titicut Follies* was shown on PBS.

Frederick Wiseman continued to defend his film: "I have always taken the position that what goes on in a public institution should be transparent. And once it grants access to that institution, the state cannot assert a right to privacy." The film did indeed accomplish what Wiseman set out to do—improve the conditions of the hospital. As a title after the closing credits states, the Supreme Judicial Court of Massachusetts ordered the following statement to be added to the film: "Changes and improvements have taken place at Massachusetts Correctional Institution Bridgewater since 1966."

Do the Right Thing (1989): "Fight the Power"

In the summer of 1989, amidst the studio big-budget blockbusters like *Batman*, *Indiana Jones and the Last Crusade*, *Lethal Weapon 2*, and *Ghostbusters II*, Universal Studios released a comparatively low-budget film ($6.5 million) with no major stars. Although Spike Lee had made a name for himself as a writer/director with *She's Gotta Have It* (1986) and *School Daze* (1988—both of which he also appeared in), and as a spokesman for Nike, nothing prepared critics and summer audiences for *Do The Right Thing*.

Lee's film, which had its world premiere at the Cannes Film Festival in May, is set on the hottest day of the summer on a street in the Bedford-Stuyvesant section of Brooklyn. Lee plays Mookie, a pizza delivery guy who works for Sal's Pizzeria, the neighborhood pizza joint owned and operated by its Italian American namesake, Salvatore Frangione (Danny Aiello) and his two sons, Pino (John Turturro), a bigot who hates the family business and the neighborhood, and his younger brother, Vito (Richard Edson), whom Mookie considers a friend. Over the course of a day, Mookie interacts with an assortment of characters in his neighborhood. As the day grows hotter, tempers flare, along with racial tensions, culminating with Sal destroying the boom box of one of his patrons, Radio Raheem (Bill Nunn). An argument turns into a brawl, and when the police arrive they unnecessarily put Radio Raheem in a chokehold, which kills him (a Brooklyn graffiti artist, Michael Stewart, met the same fate in 1980). An angry Mookie picks up a trashcan, yells "Hate," and hurls it through Sal's window. The crowd completely destroys Sal's place.

Do the Right Thing succeeded in opening up a long overdue dialogue about race relations in America without advocating any solutions or reducing racism to strictly a black vs. white issue. One effective device Lee employs in the film is a montage in which several characters, including Mookie, Pino, and the local Korean grocer, spout racial epithets against Italians, African Americans, Koreans, Puerto Ricans, and Jews. As Lee explained in a *New York Times* interview at the time of the film's release, "I wanted to generate discussion about racism because too many people have their head in the sand about racism. . . . As far as I am concerned, racism is the most pressing problem in the United States; and I wanted to bring the issue into the forefront where it belongs." Lee also admitted he didn't have the answer, and to get people thinking and talking, he ended the film with two contradictory quotations—one from Martin Luther King, Jr., repudiating violence, and the other by Malcolm X, advocating violence as a defensive measure. The soundtrack, featuring Public Enemy's "Fight the Power," echoed the film's message of standing up for what's right.

While the majority of critics praised *Do the Right Thing* (Siskel and Ebert devoted an entire show to it), Lee and his film were also criticized for their message. *New York* magazine critic David Denby interpreted the film as "a demonstration of the pointlessness of violence that is also a celebration of violence."

But the film hardly "celebrates" violence. Mookie throws the garbage can through the window because he just witnessed the police kill his friend. He is angry—and justifiably so. In another piece for the same magazine, political columnist Joe Klein suggested the film could potentially cause race riots and lose David Dinkins, an African American New York City mayoral candidate, the election. "If they react violently—which can't be ruled out—," Klein wrote, "the candidate with the most to lose will be David Dinkins." (There were no reports of violence linked to the film, and Dinkins was indeed elected mayor in 1990.)

Nearly nineteen years after *Do the Right Thing* hit the theatres, Spike Lee evoked the title (and message) of his film for an entirely new cause. He told a crowd at the University of Dayton, Ohio, to "do the right thing" and support Senator Barack Obama for president.

Michael Moore: First-Person Provoc-auteur

Peter Watkins's *The War Game* is a "what if?" enactment of events based on the filmmaker's extensive research on the death and devastation that could occur if Britain engaged in a limited nuclear war. In *Titicut Follies*, Frederick Wiseman uses his camera to record and reveal reality, which he then assembles to reflect what he observed. The films of Michael Moore follow a completely different set of rules. He clearly does not subscribe to the belief that the filmmaker should be invisible. He is literally at the center of his films, appearing on camera and serving as the narrator. In this regard, his films are first-person essays, exposing the greed of corporate capitalism (*Roger and Me* [1989]), investigating institutionalized violence and the prevalence of guns in American society (*Bowling for Columbine* [2002]), criticizing George W. Bush's so-called War on

Terror (*Fahrenheit 9/11* [2004]), and demonstrating the failure of the American health care system (*Sicko* [2007]). Unlike Wiseman, whose audience, to quote Judge Kalus, is "left to its own devices" to draw its own conclusions about what it is watching, Moore guides his audience through his argument. It is not surprising that Wiseman is not a fan of Moore, whom he considers an "entertainer" with a viewpoint that is "extremely simplistic and self-serving."

The entertainment value of Moore, particularly his satirical edge, have certainly contributed to his films' appeal to mainstream American audiences—even those who associate the word "documentary" with long, boring films that air on public television about the Louisiana Purchase or the mating habits of the blister beetle. As for the politically minded who were growing tired of sitting quietly on the sidelines while the Rush Limbaughs and Bill O'Reillys continued to clog up the airwaves with their mindless jawing, Moore was a godsend. He was, after all, every right-wing nut job's worst nightmare: a rich, successful, talented, Oscar-winning, in-your-face provocateur, who, unlike the corporate-controlled news media and press, didn't seem to think twice about going after the big guns like General Motors, the National Rifle Association, and the Bush Administration. Whether or not you buy Moore's argument that the Bush Administration took advantage of the tragic events of September 11, 2001, to launch the Iraq War (does anyone still not get it?), it's difficult to dispute that the director did get America talking and asking questions about what the government is telling us vs. the so-called truth.

Fahrenheit 9/11 grossed $119 million at the box-office—an unprecedented amount for a documentary—which gave his critics and political adversaries even more reason to discredit him, mostly by pointing out the inaccuracies, untruths, and distortions of facts that they claim permeate his films. His work has even spawned a whole new subgenre of anti-Moore documentaries, with titles like *Michael and Me* (2004), *Michael Moore Hates America* (2004), *Fahrenhype 9/11* (2004), and *Manufacturing Dissent* (2007), all of which aim to discredit (and, in some instances, satirize) Moore, who seems to enjoy the attention and has no problem defending his position on any subject.

RELIGION

Throughout the ages, religion has been one of the great dividers of mankind.

Religion is rooted in faith, not science, yet many people defend their religious beliefs as truth. In their minds, the world is divided between those who believe (in what they believe) and those who don't. Many "believers" even consider themselves to be closer to God and therefore on a higher spiritual and moral plane than nonbelievers. Their spiritual and moral superiority is based on a fundamental belief that their god is *the* one true god and their religion *the* one true religion.

The men who wrote the Production Code (including one Jesuit, Father Daniel Lord), as well as its primary enforcer, PCA Director Joseph Breen (a Catholic), understood that religion is an inherently controversial subject. Consequently, they believed the cinema must treat religion and the clergy with care and respect (see appendix D, section VIII).

One of the first religious films to make waves came from an unlikely source. During the silent era, Cecil B. DeMille directed two highly revered, morality-laden Biblical epics: *The Ten Commandments* (1923) and *The King of Kings* (1927). Set in ancient Rome, the third part of his religious trilogy, *The Sign of the Cross* (1932), contrasts the holier-than-thou, morally superior Christians with the paganistic, hedonistic Romans. DeMille devotes equal screen time to the Romans' vices and "immoral" behavior, which was met at the time of the film's release with strong opposition from some clergymen and religious leaders, who branded the film "indecent" and "immoral."

The Sign of the Cross (1932): Virtue vs. Vice

In 1932, director Cecil B. DeMille scored at the box office with his big-screen adaptation of Wilson Bartlett's play about the persecution of the Christians by the Romans. The year is 64 AD and the Roman Empire is under the rule of the tyrannical Emperor Nero (Charles Laughton). His wife, Empress Poppaea (Claudette Colbert), is in love with her husband's chief magistrate, Marcus Superbus (Fredric March), who has fallen for a virtuous Christian girl named Mercia (Elissa Landi). The empress's jealousy and Mercia's refusal to denounce her faith drive Marcus and Mercia apart. She decides to join her fellow Christians in the Coliseum, where they are to be fed to hungry lions in front of a standing-room-only crowd. Although he remains a nonbeliever, Marcus decides he can't live without Mercia and accompanies her into the arena, where they presumably meet their fate.

DeMille was certainly the right choice for turning this otherwise dull story into a full-blown spectacle, which would have never made it past the PCA if the film had been released two years later. In one of several objectionable scenes, Poppaea takes a bath in a pool of ass's milk, during which Colbert's breasts are partially exposed. When her friend Dacia (Vivian Tobin) arrives to deliver the latest gossip on Marcus, Poppaea invites her to join her ("Dacia, you're a butterfly with a sting," Poppaea says, "Take off your clothes. Get in here and tell me all about it.") Cut to Dacia's dress falling to the floor.

There is another hint of lesbianism during the Roman orgy hosted by Marcus, who coaxes sexy Ancaria (Joyzelle Joyner) to do her "Dance of the Naked Moon" for Mercia in hope of breaking through her virginal Christian shell. But Ancaria's Sapphic dance has the opposite effect and sends Mercia straight back to her Christian friends. In his autobiography, DeMille recalls Will Hays phoning and asking him what he was going to do about the controversial scene. DeMille's reply: "Not a damn thing." Colonel Jason Joy, the head of the Studio Relations Committee, actually felt the film's overall message was moral and approved the scene because Ancaria's "kootch" dance fails to entice Mercia. Although the film demonizes the pagan Romans, they are having a much better time than the Christians, who, by comparison, are portrayed as a dull bunch who spend most of the film praying, singing, and accepting their role as victims with little, if any, resistance.

One part of the film Joy was concerned about was the Coliseum sequence, where hundreds of Romans (large crowds of extras were one of DeMille's trademarks) gather to watch gladiators battle, Barbarian women fight pygmies from Africa, and for the finale, one hundred Christians thrown to lions (this happens offscreen). In between, we see a man's head get crushed by an elephant, a scantily clad woman fed to alligators, and another woman tied to a stake and presumably raped by a gorilla.

While some states censored Poppaea's milk bath and the gorilla rape, others made no cuts at all. In an effort not to offend its audience, one theatre in Victoria, Texas showed two versions of the film. A newspaper ad explained "due to criticism of the scenes in *The Sign of the Cross* we eliminated them during our regular Thursday and Friday shows, but Saturday night we will show *The Sign of the Cross* just as it was produced—nothing cut!"

Many members of the clergy were far less forgiving and hurled every negative critical word in the book at the film: "intolerable," "highly offensive," "repellent and nauseating," and "cheap . . . disgusting, suggestive, and unclean." But DeMille and Paramount didn't care because, based on box-office receipts, audiences around the country weren't listening. There were also clergymen in New York; Portland, Oregon; Michigan; and New Orleans who endorsed the film and recommended it to their parishioners. In Abilene, Texas, a special matinee screening was held for local schoolchildren and their teachers.

Many historians cite *The Sign of the Cross* as one of the films that contributed to the formation of the Catholic Legion of Decency in 1933. Like *She Done Him Wrong*, the film was pulled from circulation in 1934 when the PCA reviewed all current releases and refused to give it a seal. When the film was re-released ten years later, the Legion of Decency rated the film a "B, or objectionable in part" due to "suggestive sequences and costumes and some suggestive dialogue." Some editing was reportedly done to satisfy the Hays Office, and a prologue was added in which a Protestant and Catholic chaplain aboard an American bomber fly over the city of Rome and begin to discuss Nero's persecution of the Christians in ancient Rome.

Martin Luther (1953): The Monk of Wittenberg

On October 31, 1517, Martin Luther (1483–1546), a German monk and theologian, forever changed the course of organized religion by nailing his *Ninety-five Theses*—a list of complaints against the Roman Catholic Church—to the door of the *Schlosskirche* (Castle Church) in the town of Wittenberg. Luther, a friar in the Catholic Order of St. Augustine, challenged the moral authority and greed of Pope Leo X and the church's selling of indulgences (absolution for one's sins). "Every truly repentant

Christian has a right to full remission of penalty and guilt," Luther wrote, "even without letters of pardon." Excommunicated from the church on January 3, 1521, his defiance sparked the start of the Protestant Reformation, which resulted in the creation of various Protestant denominations, including the Lutheran Church, which is based on his teachings.

In 1953, documentarian Louis De Rochemont and the Lutheran Church of America coproduced *Martin Luther*, a biopic starring Irish-born actor Niall MacGinnis in the title role. The film opened to generally favorable reviews and received a pair of Academy Award nominations for Art Direction and Cinematography. *Time* magazine described the "action and dialogue, drawn mostly from Luther's own written words" as "accurate and edifying." The *New Yorker* noted that the film—already a box-office success—could only have been made by industry outsiders because Luther, neglected by Hollywood, "is too controversial a figure to be advertised in a democracy whose basic notions in a good many instances derive from doctrines he enunciated four centuries ago." *New York Times* critic Bosley Crowther praised *Martin Luther* as a "scholarly religious film"—a refreshing departure from the "previous gaudy spectacles" of most religious-themed films. "It carefully and patiently—one might even say documents," Crowther wrote, "the mental steps of Martin Luther in arriving at his shattering doctrine of the individuality of Christian faith." While the biopic is certainly on par with most Hollywood films in terms of its production values, modern audiences are likely to find the direction a bit stiff, the narration running throughout the film excessive, and the theological exchanges and debates between Luther and both his followers and critics to be more didactic than dramatic.

The film's criticism of the Roman Catholic Church posed a problem for the National Legion of Decency, which ran the risk of exposing its Catholic bias by condemning the film. It chose instead to place the film in the "Special Classification" category and warn Catholics it "offers a sympathetic and approving representation of the life and times of Martin Luther, the 15th century figure of religious controversy. It contains theological and historical references and interpretations which are unacceptable to Roman Catholics." But as historian Gregory Black points out, the Catholic Press did what the Legion could not and condemned the film for its historical inaccuracies. Meanwhile, Lutherans in Ironwood, Michigan responded to similar attacks made against the film in an advertisement published in a local newspaper, the heading of which reads "A Note from Lutherans About the Film *Martin Luther*." The ad asserts that the film "is not only technically excellent but factual throughout," and lists the titles of the both Protestant and Roman Catholic books consulted by the nine writers who worked on the script. It also refutes the statement made in a Catholic ad that their church is "unchanging in its teachings" by giving examples to the contrary.

The kind of controversy the Legion of Decency was trying to avoid in the United States erupted in Canada in December of 1953 when the Quebec Film Censorship board banned the film in the predominantly Catholic province "because it was felt it would be against the real interests of the population to show a film that would cause undue antagonistic sentiments." The ban was opposed by Lutheran and Protestant groups in the U.S. and Canada as well as by Canadian political leaders, who sent letters of protest to Prime Minister Louis St. Laurent. The Montreal District of the Presbyterian Church denounced the ban, which they believed was a sign Quebec was "headed for a control of thought, communication, and action which is absolutely dictatorial in the tradition of Communist dominated countries." As the ban only applied to public performances, the film was eventually shown in eleven churches in Montreal.

The situation in Catholic Quebec was not an isolated case. *Martin Luther* was also banned in several other predominantly Catholic countries, including Brazil, Cuba, and Peru.

The influence of the Catholic leaders in the United States was not only limited to theatrical releases. In 1956, WGN-TV in Chicago announced plans to air *Martin Luther*, but the station caved under pressure from the Catholic Church and pulled the film from its schedule. Ward L. Quaal, vice president and general manager, said the station elected to cancel the showing "not wanting to be party to the development of any misunderstanding or ill will among persons of the Christian faith in the Chicago area." A group of Protestant ministers were joined by rabbis in calling the cancellation "a violation of civil and religious liberty as defined by the press," adding that the film was "far less controversial" than other shows that aired on WGN-TV.

Rosemary's Baby (1968): "God Is Dead! Satan Lives!"

Polish director Roman Polanski's film adaptation of Ira Levin's best-selling novel is an example of how a great book can be turned into a great movie. Twenty-three-year-old Mia Farrow, one of Hollywood's most underrated actresses, stars as Rosemary Woodhouse, a New York housewife who, along with her actor-husband Guy (John Cassavetes), moves into an apartment building on the Upper West Side of Manhattan. They befriend the eccentric older couple next door, Roman and Minnie Castevet (Sidney Blackmer and Ruth Gordon, who won an Oscar for her performance), who a pregnant Rosemary slowly suspects may be witches who are after her unborn baby. When her child is born, her worst fears come true: the dream she had about being raped by the devil wasn't a dream and her newborn son is indeed the son of Satan.

Although *Rosemary's Baby* deals with Satanism and the occult, and even gives us a glimpse of the devil in Rosemary's Fellini-esque rape dream, the most horrific aspect of the story is the realization Rosemary (and we) make that Satan may be living amongst us and his followers could be the kindly old couple next door. Polanski makes it seem all too real, which makes it all the more frightening.

While working on the film, Polanski made it clear to the PCA and Paramount that he did not want any interference, a request the studio honored to keep him on the project. Producer William Castle assured Paramount and the PCA that he would have complete control of the finished product and make cuts dictated by the Code. But when the PCA instructed Castle to eliminate Cassavetes's unscripted, "throw away" exclamation of "Oh, shit" (one of the first in a major studio film), the director and the producer refused, claiming Paramount wanted the phrase in.

When *Rosemary's Baby* was released in June of 1968, the MPAA classified the film as "Suggested for Mature Audiences" (once the new ratings system went into effect at the end of the year, the rating was changed to R). As expected, the Legion of Decency, now known as the National Catholic Office for Motion Pictures, condemned *Rosemary's Baby*:

> Because of several scenes of nudity, this contemporary horror story about devil worship would qualify for a condemned rating. Much

more serious, however, is the perverted use which the film makes of fundamental Christian beliefs, especially the events surrounding the birth of Christ, and its mockery of religious persons and practices. The very technical excellence of the film serves to intensify its defamatory nature.

Twenty years previously, a C from the Legion of Decency would have had a major studio like Paramount running scared like poor Rosemary. Although the studio would not officially comment on the rating, it was evident the Catholic Office's influence had declined significantly and no longer had the same impact on box-office receipts. A Paramount spokesman did point out that another Paramount release, Otto Preminger's *Hurry Sundown* (1967), was condemned for its "prurient and demeaning . . . approach to sex," yet was a "moderate success."

By December 31, 1968, *Rosemary's Baby* was the seventh-highest grossing movie of the year, taking in a total of $12.3 million. In the end, evil triumphed over good at the box office, while the Catholic Church's thirty-five-year reign of terror had at last come to an end.

The Exorcist (1973): "What an Excellent Day for an Exorcism."

New York Times critic Vincent Canby called it the "biggest thing to hit the industry since Mary Pickford, popcorn, pornography, and *The Godfather*."

Like *Rosemary's Baby*, *The Exorcist* elevated the status of the horror genre, which up to then had been generally regarded as a B genre, by approaching the supernatural (in this case, demonic possession) and making it all seem very real. Based on the bestseller by William Peter Blatty, *The Exorcist* is the story of twelve-year-old Regan MacNeil (Linda Blair), who begins to exhibit odd and violent behavior. When doctors are unable to help her, her mother, Chris (Ellen Burstyn), turns to a Roman Catholic priest, Father Karras (Jason Miller), who elicits the help of an older priest, Father Merrin (Max von Sydow), to perform an exorcism, an ancient religious ritual to evict demons from someone believed to be possessed.

As Canby asserts, the film, directed by Academy Award winner William Friedkin (*The French Connection* [1971]) was a cultural phenomenon when it opened in December of 1973. In its first five weeks, *The Exorcist* took in over $10 million at the box office. In New York, Boston, and several other cities, moviegoers waited for up to four hours in the freezing cold to see the film. What the film promised (and delivered) were horrific scenes of demonic possession the likes of which had never been seen before on the screen, ranging from the truly gross (Regan vomits pea soup) to the shocking (Regan's head spins around) to the disturbing (Regan masturbates with a cross). The mixed reviews, which included pans from such influential critics as Canby ("a chunk of elegant occultist claptrap . . . establishes a new low for grotesque special effects"), *Time* magazine's Jay Cocks ("vile and brutalizing . . . the explicitness amounts to nothing more than a shill, a come-on"), and *New Yorker*'s Pauline Kael ("a faithful adaptation—and that's not a compliment"), certainly did not deter folks from lining up. The film profited from word-of-mouth and stories, most unsubstantiated, that audience members were running out of the theatre in terror, passing out in the aisles, and having heart attacks.

In her review, Kael also raised a question over the suitability of the film's R rating (under seventeen required accompanying parent or adult guardian), which she believed the film received because the MPAA would never give a film with a budget that skyrocketed from $4 million to $10 million an X. In a piece for the *New York Times*, Washington, D.C. critic Roy Meacham questioned the integrity of the ratings board, which he believed "wasn't thinking about the youngsters and the possibility of traumatic damage to them from the movie's unremitting and violent assault upon the emotions." MPAA President Jack Valenti stood by the board's decision, claiming the film contained no overt sex and excessive violence and the strong language "is rationally related to the film's theme and is kept to the minimum." But the morals division of the Washington, D.C. Police Department did not agree. Acting in response to complaints received by its office, it imposed a "no one under 17" restriction on the film, which is comparable to an X rating. According to the obscenity clause of the D.C. Omnibus Crime Bill, it is unlawful to show films depicting "sado-masochistic abuse" and "masturbation" to minors (under seventeen). The owners of the D.C. theatre where the film was in its second week not only complied, but agreed the film should have been rated X.

An attempt to ban the film in Boston failed when a judge ruled it did not meet the U.S. Supreme Court's guidelines for obscenity. Prosecutors were more successful in Hattiesburg, Mississippi, where theatre owners were convicted and fined $100. The conviction was overturned on appeal and the Mississippi Supreme Court declared the antiobscenity law unconstitutional.

The Exorcist generated public interest in the subject of exorcisms as well as a minor wave of hysteria over demonic possession. While the rite of exorcism is still part of the Catholic dogma (a revised version was released in 1999), many Catholics, including clergymen, do not believe Satan is a person and understand the behaviors once attributed to demonic possession were actually undiagnosed medical conditions, such as epilepsy, Tourette syndrome, autism, and schizophrenia. As some predicted, the film planted in the minds of people who saw the film that they or someone they knew was possessed.

Mohammad, Messenger of God (1977): The Story of Islam

The makers of this film honour the Islamic tradition which holds that the impersonation of the prophet offends against the spirituality of his message. Therefore, the person of Mohammad will not be shown.

The 1977 drama *Mohammad, Messenger of God* opens with the above message, informing the audience that Islamic law forbids any representation (by image or sound) of the prophet Mohammad. This restriction posed a major challenge for Moustapha Akkad, the director/producer of this $17 million, three-hour epic chronicling the adult life of the founder of what is currently the second largest religion in the world (approximately 1.5 billion and growing). Akkad aimed to do for Islam what religious spectacles like *The Ten Commandments* (1956), *Ben-Hur* (1959), and *King of Kings* (1961) had done for Christianity. But how does one tell the story of a prophet of God, who would one day be the leader of the second largest religion in the world, without him ever being seen? (Imagine *King of Kings* or *The Greatest Story Ever Told* (1965) without Jesus Christ!)

Not only does Mohammad not appear on screen, the audience never hears his voice. Most of what the prophet says is relayed through other characters, namely his Uncle Hamza (Anthony Quinn) and his adopted son, Zaid (Damien Thomas). If his presence is required for a scene, Akadd shoots it from Mohammad's point of view, so when the other characters converse with him, they must look directly into the camera (this takes some getting used to for the audience, because it also appears as if they are conversing with us). Akkad also uses offscreen space, so characters look at and talk to him as if he was standing on the other side of the edge of the frame, out of our view.

In an interview at the time of the film's release, Akkad was well aware the film would be controversial, yet admitted he made the film (actually two films—one in Arabic, the other in English, with two sets of actors) to educate non-Muslims about his faith and its history. He correctly predicted he and his film would be criticized by Muslim groups. An ad hoc committee of twelve groups in the New York area released a statement around the time of *Mohammad*'s opening claiming the film "contains historical inaccuracies and creates misleading impressions about Prophet Mohammad." For the London release, Akkad gave in to pressure from Muslims to remove the name "Mohammad" from the title.

Mohammad opened in theatres in March of 1977, though screenings in New York and Los Angeles were shut down (in some theatres in the middle of the film) when a hostage crisis erupted on March 10 in Washington, D.C. Hanafi leader Khalifa Hamaas Abdul Khaalis and a group of armed terrorists held more than one hundred hostages in three locations—the Islamic Center; the headquarters of B'nai B'rith, the world's largest and oldest Jewish service organization; and the District Building. Their demands included the release of the three Black Muslim prisoners convicted of murder, and the banning of *Mohammad, Messenger of God* from all theatres on the grounds that it was sacrilegious. After thirty-eight hours, the hostages were set free, the gunmen surrendered, and by March 12, the film resumed playing in theatres in New York, New Jersey, and California.

While the film was not a moneymaker, Akkad found success as a producer of the *Halloween* film franchise. He did return to the desert in the early 1980s to direct *Lion of the Desert* (1981), which told the story of Omar Mukhtar, a Libyan resistance leader who fought against the Italian fascists during Mussolini's reign.

Akkad's story ended tragically when he and his daughter, Rima Akkad Monla, were killed in the lobby of the Grand Hyatt Hotel in Amman by a suicide bomber who was a member of Al-Qaeda. It is also an ironic ending for someone who was dedicated to teaching the world about his Muslim faith.

Life of Brian (1979): "Always Look on the Bright Side of Life"

"An act of blasphemy," "a crime against religion," and "a crude and rude mockery," were some of the unsolicited responses from religious organizations when Monty Python's *Life of Brian*, the British comedy troupe's parody of Biblical epics, opened in the United States in August of 1979.

Instead of doing a parody of the Christ story (Jesus, seen only from a distance, makes a very brief cameo appearance in *Brian*), the Pythons chose to focus instead on Brian, the Baby Jesus's next door neighbor. The Jewish bastard son of a Roman soldier, Brian (Graham Chapman) hates the Romans. He falls in love with Judith, a member of one of Judea's many underground anti-Roman rebel groups who spend most of their time sitting around voting on meaningless measures and bad-mouthing their rival groups. Through a series of circumstances, Brian is mistaken for the Messiah, a role he has no interest in filling. But his career as a prophet is short-lived when he is caught by the Romans and crucified. Abandoned by his mother, his followers, Judith, and his fellow radicals, Brian is left all alone, though his spirits get a lift when he joins the others who have been left to die in a chorus of "Always Look on the Bright Side of Life."

The fact that the film is about Brian, not Jesus, did not stop religious leaders from airing their complaints. A spokesman for the Archdiocese of New York, Msgr. Eugene V. Clark, called the film an "act of blasphemy" and criticized the entertainment industry for promoting antireligious sentiments. Speaking on behalf of the Rabbinical Alliance of America and the Union of Orthodox Rabbis of the United States and Canada, Rabbi Abraham B. Hecht denounced *Brian* as a "vicious attack upon Judaism and the Bible." "This film," Hecht warned, "is so grievously insulting that we are genuinely concerned that its continued showing could result in serious violence." He believed it would move people to violence because "it's such a bad movie." Robert A. Lee, communications director of the U.S. Lutheran Council, called the film a "crude and rude mockery" that is "grossly offensive to those who accept Jesus Christ as Lord and Savior . . . and it should be equally offensive to any others who believe that religious faith should not be scoffed at or demeaned by overt and perverse sacrilege."

The Pythons were surprised by the extreme reaction the film received when it opened in the U.S. in August of 1979. Terry Jones, who directed the film, explained they believed they made "a very moral, religious film" that didn't "diminish" religion as such but rather *organized* religion. Ultimately, there were attempts to get the film banned. In Boston, a judge refused to issue a criminal complaint against the film because it was not in violation of the city's blasphemy statute, which was no longer enforced. Realizing he could never get the film banned on religious grounds, an attorney in Valdosta, Georgia representing ten church groups succeeded in getting a Superior Court Judge to issue a temporary restraining order prohibiting the showing of the film on the grounds it was obscene due to a "lewd exhibition of genitals." The order was reversed the next day after the judge saw the film. A controversy over the film erupted in Columbia, South Carolina, when seventy-six-year-old Republican Senator Strom Thurmond intervened on behalf of a local minister who succeeded in getting a theatre to withdraw the film, charging that the movie ridiculed his faith, was anti-Semitic, and "not art." When the theatre manager pulled the film at Thurmond's request, 150 people picketed the theatre, carrying signs that read "Resurrect Brian, Crucify Censors" and "Strom Doesn't Pay for My Movie Ticket." Similar incidents occurred throughout the United States and were not limited to the Bible Belt. Religious groups staged demonstrations in Massachusetts, Maine, Michigan, New York, and California.

As with most controversial films, it's difficult to determine the effect all the cries of "blasphemy" had on ticket sales, which totaled approximately $19 million in the U.S. *Life of Brian* was back in theatres briefly in May of 2004 to cash in on *The Passion of the Christ*. The ads read: "The Second Coming of *The Life of Brian*."

The Gospels According to Marty and Mel

In a world in which Christianity ranks #1 among organized religions in terms of number of followers, and in a nation in which Christianity permeates many aspects of popular culture, it's not surprising that "The Greatest Story Ever Told" is also "The Greatest Story *Most Often* Told."

Since the silent era, the story of Jesus Christ—his birth, Crucifixion, death, and resurrection—has been the subject of silent epics, widescreen spectacles, musicals, and TV miniseries. While they each have their own respective "take" on the life of Christ, Jesus biopics essentially tell the same story based on one or more of the four gospels of the New Testament. To attract the widest audience, the general rule of thumb when making a film about Jesus Christ (or, for that matter, any religious-themed film) is not to stray too far from the Holy Book. Give the people what they want, meaning give them what they already know. Two filmmakers, both raised Catholic, chose not to "play it safe" when they brought their respective renditions of the "The Greatest Story" to the screen. The end results were two very different films, both controversial, yet for very different reasons.

The Last Temptation of Christ (1988)

Nikos Kazantzakis's novel *The Last Temptation of Christ* was first published in the author's native Greece in 1953 (the English translation in the U.S. in 1960). Both the novel and the film, directed by Martin Scorsese, were denounced by devout Christians who found Kazantzakis's characterization of Christ a direct assault on the teachings of the church.

In most films about the life of Jesus, he is portrayed as a man who accepts his fate, predetermined by God, with no questions asked. In *Last Temptation*, Jesus (Willem Dafoe) is fraught with human emotions—full of self-doubt and fearful of what lies ahead. While dying on the cross, he is rescued by an archangel sent by God who tells him his father is pleased with him, yet he is not the Messiah. God allows Jesus to live a mortal life. He marries Mary Magdelene (Barbara Hershey), and when she dies, he remarries and has children. Judas (Harvey Keitel) visits Jesus on his deathbed and reveals to him that the archangel was really

Satan. Jesus returns to his cross to fulfill his destiny. At the moment of his death, he cries out, "It is accomplished! It is accomplished!"

Kazantzakis was surprised by the adverse reaction to his book because his "primary motive" for writing it was not to challenge church doctrine, but, in his words, to "reincarnate the essence of Jesus, setting aside the dross—falsehoods and pettiness which all the churches and all the cassocked representatives of Christianity have heaped up on His figure, thereby distorting it." But while Kazantzakis's narrative may contain all of the evidence that Christ was the Messiah (his teachings, miracles, Crucifixion, etc.), the text he is rewriting and reinterpreting is not Shakespeare, Dickens, or Tolstoy, but the Bible, the Holy Book Christians believe is the "Word of God." Therefore, probing into the psyche of Jesus Christ was seen by Christians as nothing short of blasphemy. One year after *Last Temptation* was published, Kazantzakis was excommunicated from the Eastern Orthodox Church, and his novel was put on the Catholic Church's "Index of Forbidden Books," which includes works by Voltaire, Erasmus, Balzac, and Sartre. When the author died in 1957, the Archbishop of Athens refused to give him Christian rites, although he was given a Christian burial in his native Crete.

A film version of *Last Temptation* was first announced in February of 1971 with director Sidney Lumet attached, but the project never materialized. Scorsese brought *Last Temptation* to Paramount in the early 1980s. The film was budgeted at $16 million and was slated to begin shooting in 1983. But when Paramount announced its plans to turn Kazantzakis's book into a movie, the studio and Paramount's parent company, Gulf and Western, were flooded with letters from evangelical Christians protesting the project. The corporate heads got cold feet, so Paramount withdrew its support from the project, which Scorsese shopped around until it landed at Universal Studios.

To prepare for the inevitable backlash, Universal hired Tim Penland, a born-again Christian, to serve as a liaison between the studio and fundamentalist Christian groups. In March of 1988, an article appeared in *Christianity Today* in which Penland stated that Universal was flying evangelical leaders out to Hollywood to see an advanced screening of the film. "I'm hopeful they will be able to embrace a film that shows the human side of Christ," Penland explained, "But if the movie is blasphemous, or if Christian leaders feel it would be damaging to the cause of Christ, that will be the end of my involvement with the project." When the screening was abruptly canceled reportedly due to problems in post-production, Penland quit his job and joined the campaign against the film spearheaded by Rev. Donald Wildmon, the head of the American Family Association, who had received a copy of an early draft of Paul Schrader's script. When Scorsese invited evangelical leaders to a rescheduled screening in New York in July, they declined because Universal had broken its promise to screen the film far in advance of the film's opening. A document entitled "The Last Temptation of Christ—Facts," which accompanied a letter dated July 6, 1988, and signed by Larry Pond, president of Mastermedia International, a Christian consulting firm, outlined the specific reasons why the film is offensive to Christians, most of which pertains to Jesus's sexual relationship to Mary Magdelene as well as his depiction as someone suffering from "brain fever," "struggling over his sins," "lust driven," "bedeviled by 'nightmares and hallucinations'," and "unable to answer basic questions about his identity." Their evaluation is based on two versions of the script (including the "shooting script") and "an eyewitness account of the film as shown to Universal 'insiders'." The Mastermedia mailing also lists ways Christians can participate in the protest, including praying for the top executives and Christians employed at MCA-Universal, putting pressure on key figures to stop the release, contacting heads of divisions of MCA-owned businesses, organizing a prayer vigil at the theatre, and if you are an employee of MCA-Universal, protesting "to your superiors about this film and, if led to do so, threaten resignation if the film is released."

Universal Studios did not back down when fundamentalist leaders started attacking the film, sight unseen. In a press release dated July 12, 1988, they invoked the U.S. Constitution:

In America we have a long tradition of freedom of the press, speech and religion. Each individual has a right to express his own religious beliefs through books, film, and art. The opponents of this film are attempting to prevent its release. This is censorship. People have a right to choose for themselves whether or not to see this movie and to form their own opinions about it. Universal Pictures and Cineplex Odeon Films stand behind the principle of freedom of expression and hope that the American public will give the film and the filmmaker a good chance.

On Thursday, August 11, 7,500 picketers showed up at the front of Universal Studios in Hollywood to protest the film. On the following day, *The Last Temptation of Christ* opened in nine cities across the country to positive reviews and strong box-office returns.

So *Last Temptation* was released in theatres. The world did not come to an end. The earth continued to spin. California did not sink into the ocean. As the number of demonstrators started to dwindle outside the theatre, so did the audience inside.

On a more personal note: While I was standing on line to see the film in Los Angeles on opening weekend, a protester handing out leaflets told me not to go see the film because it was blasphemous. I asked him if he had seen it. He replied he had not. When I offered to give him my ticket and judge for himself, he refused. I questioned him about how he could protest against a film he had not even seen. He gave me a deer-in-the-headlights look. I gave him back his leaflet.

The Passion of the Christ (2004)

Nine years after winning a pair of Oscars for his Scottish epic *Braveheart* (for Best Picture and Best Director), actor Mel Gibson returned to the director's chair to make *The Passion of the Christ*. Cowritten by Gibson and Benedict Fitzgerald, *Passion* is a major departure from other Christ films, which typically devote their first half to Jesus's teachings, miracles, and the events leading up to his arrest. In Gibson's film, this is where the story begins. Since the film starts *in medias res*, it is presumed the audience is familiar with Christ and his teachings. There is also an absence of movie stars. Instead, Gibson cast a relatively unknown actor, Jim Caviezel, who appeared in *The Thin Red Line* (1998), to play Jesus, and Italian actress Monica Bellucci, best known for her work in *The Matrix Reloaded* (2003) and *The Matrix Revolutions* (2003), as Mary Magdelene. Finally—and certainly Gibson's boldest move—was to have the characters speak in Aramaic, Hebrew, and Latin, because he felt if they spoke English it would distance the audience from them and detract from the authenticity he was striving to achieve.

Gibson's film strives to be "authentic"—to transport his audience back in time so they can bear witness to the suffering Christ endured for "our" sins. Consequently, Gibson's Christ is not your typical kind-hearted and loving Jesus, but a masochistic figure, whose body is whipped beyond recognition and then nailed (reportedly by Gibson's own hand) to the cross. The excessive violence, for which the film was criticized, can be traced to the writings of a nineteenth-century Roman Catholic Augustinian nun, Anne Catherine Emmerich (1774–1824). She was a stigmatic who had visions of Christ's Passion, which she told to poet Clemens Brentano, who wrote them down. The first volume was published in 1833 under the title of *The Dolorous Passion of Our Lord Jesus Christ*. Gibson admitted he was influenced by her imagery. In an interview with ABC-TV's Diane Sawyer, Gibson discussed openly how he intended for the film to be shocking, extreme, and violent so it "pushes one over the edge so that they can see the enormity . . . of that sacrifice." In the same interview, he answered to the charges that the film is anti-Semitic. "To be anti-Semitic is a sin," he said. "It's been condemned by one papal council after another. To be anti-Semitic is to be un-Christian, and I'm not."

Many Jewish leaders and scholars accused Gibson of being anti-Semitic because *Passion* clearly blames the Crucifixion of Jesus Christ on the Jews, rather than the Romans. The scene in which Jesus appears in front of the Jewish temple elders is particularly disturbing. Rabbi Marvin Hier, Dean of the Simon Wiesenthal Center in Los Angeles, was "horrified" by the way the elders, in their black robes and beards, were portrayed as villainous, much "like Rasputin." By comparison, Pontius Pilate is portrayed in a more sympathetic light. He seems generally conflicted about sentencing Jesus to death, which furthers the film's anti-Semitic characterization of the Jews. As Michael Parenti points out, the irony is that Jews may have plotted against him, but they also followed him, so "to say therefore that 'the Jews killed Jesus' makes as much sense as to say 'the Jews loved and followed Jesus.'"

The lack of a box-office star, the film's dark tone, the excessive violence, the dialogue in ancient languages, and even the charges of anti-Semitism didn't keep audiences away from *The Passion of the Christ,* which took in over $300 million at the box office, making it the highest-grossing Jesus film of all time and the highest-grossing independently made film in Hollywood history.

Postscript: On Friday, July 28, 2006, Mel Gibson was arrested in Malibu, California on suspicion of drunk driving. According to the published reports, he stated during his arrest that, "The Jews are responsible for all the wars in the world" and asked the arresting officer, "Are you a Jew?"

The following week, Gibson issued an apology: "There is no excuse, nor should there be any tolerance, for anyone who thinks or expresses any kind of anti-Semitic remark. I want to apologize specifically to everyone in the Jewish community for the vitriolic and harmful words that I said."

AFTERWORD

Over 112 years have passed since John Rice planted a big wet one on May Irwin's lips, and what one critic back then described as "absolutely disgusting" seems today like a harmless, innocent display of public affection. Over time, our cultural standards for what we consider *obscene, indecent, immoral,* and *offensive* have certainly changed. Still, while the controversy that once swirled around most films has been reduced to a piece of trivia on an imdb.com page, some titles are still banned and remain unavailable (at least legally) on DVD in parts of the world.

Here's a few that come to mind: *Cannibal Holocaust* (1980), a faux documentary once banned in many countries for featuring what was once believed to be the slaughtering of human beings can still not be shown in some countries because it depicts the real live slaughtering of animals on camera; *Borat: Cultural Learnings of America for Make Benefit Glorious Nation of Kazakhstan* (2006), Sacha Baron Cohen's cross-cultural mockumentary, which did not amuse Middle Eastern censors and Russia's Federal Agency for Culture and Cinematography; *Ken Park* (2002), a teen drama with explicit sex from the creative team behind *Kids*, writer Harmony Korine and Larry Clark (who codirected with Edward Lachman), which was banned in Australia and never released theatrically in the United States; and *The Da Vinci Code* (2006) and *The Golden Compass* (2007), screen adaptations of religious-themed bestsellers that both had the Vatican in a tizzy for their anti-Catholic content.

Violence, sex, and religion—they are all here to stay.

Fortunately, so is cinema.

"The Thirteen Points" Adopted by NAMPI (1921)

In its efforts to self-regulate the content of motion pictures, the National Association of the Motion Picture Industry (NAMPI) adopted the following thirteen resolutions, which are essentially a list of forbidden subject matter, themes, stories, and scenes. The resolutions were never enforced because NAMPI failed to create a board to oversee the self-regulation of motion pictures.

The "Thirteen Points" condemned the production and exhibition of certain kinds of motion pictures. They were pictures:

1. Which emphasize and exaggerate sex appeal or depict scenes therein exploiting interest in sex in an improper or suggestive form or manner

2. Based upon white slavery or commercialized vice or scenes showing the procurement of women or any of the activities attendant upon this traffic

3. Thematically making prominent an illicit love affair which tends to make virtue odious and vice attractive

4. With scenes which exhibit nakedness or persons scantily dressed, particularly suggestive bedroom and bathroom scenes and scenes of inciting dancing

5. With scenes which unnecessarily prolong expressions or demonstrations of passionate love

6. Predominantly concerned with the underworld of vice and crime, and like scenes, unless the scenes are part of an essential conflict between good and evil

7. Of stories which make gambling and drunkenness attractive, or of scenes which show the use of narcotics and other unnatural practices dangerous to social morality
8. Of stories and scenes which may instruct the morally feeble in methods of committing crimes or, by cumulative processes, emphasize crime and the commission of crime
9. Of stories or scenes which ridicule or deprecate public officials, officers of the law, the United States Army, the United States Navy, or other governmental authority, or which tend to weaken the authority of the law
10. Of stories or scenes or incidents which offend religious belief or any person, creed or sect, or ridicule ministers, priests, rabbis, or recognized leaders of any religious sect, and also which are disrespectful to objects or symbols used in connection with any religion
11. Of stories or with scenes which unduly emphasize bloodshed and violence without justification in the structure of the story
12. Of stories or with scenes which are vulgar and portray improper gestures, posturing and attitudes
13. With salacious titles and subtitles in connection with their presentation or exhibition, and the use of salacious advertising matter, photographs, and lithographs in connection therewith

Source: Jowett 465.

"The Formula" (1924)

The following statement was approved by the Motion Picture Producers and Distributors of America, Inc. on February 26, 1924:

Whereas, The Members of the Motion Picture Producers and Distributors of America, Inc., in their continuing effort 'to establish and maintain the highest possible moral and artistic standards of motion picture production' are engaged in a special effort to prevent the prevalent type of book and play from becoming the prevalent type of picture; to exercise every possible care that only books or plays which are of the right type are used for screen presentation; to avoid the picturization of books or plays which can be produced after such changes as to leave the producer subject to a charge of deception; to avoid using titles which are indicative of a kind of picture which should not be produced, or by their suggestiveness seek to obtain attendance by deception, a thing equally reprehensible; and to prevent misleading, salacious or dishonest advertising:

Now, therefore, be it resolved by the board of directors of the Motion Picture Producers and Distributors of America, Inc., That said Association does hereby reaffirm its determination to carry out its purposes above set out; and does hereby repledge the best efforts of the members of the Association to that end; and does hereby further declare that they will not produce or promote the production, distribute or promote the distribution, exhibit or promote the exhibition, or aid in any way whatsoever in the production, distribution or exhibition by the members of this Association or by companies subsidiary

to said members or by any other person, firm, or corporation producing, distributing, or exhibiting pictures, of any picture or pictures by
whomsoever produced, distributed, or exhibited, which because of
the unfit character of title, story, exploitation or picture itself, do not
meet the requirements of this preamble and resolution or hinder the
fulfillment of the purposes of the Association set out herein.

Source: Moley 58–59.

The "Don'ts and Be Carefuls" of the MPPDA (1927)

The "Don'ts and Be Carefuls" were included as Rule 21 of the Code of the Motion Picture Industry adopted at a trade practice conference by the Federal Trade Commission in New York City in October 1927:

Resolved, That those things which are included in the following list shall not appear in pictures produced by the members of this Association, irrespective of the manner in which they are treated:

1. Pointed profanity—by either title or lip—this includes the words "God," "Lord," "Jesus," "Christ" (unless they be used reverently in connection with proper religious ceremonies), "hell," "damn," "Gawd," and every other profane and vulgar expression however it may be spelled;
2. Any licentious or suggestive nudity—in fact or in silhouette; and any lecherous or licentious notice thereof by other characters in the picture;
3. The illegal traffic of drugs;
4. Any inference of sex perversion;
5. White slavery;
6. Miscegenation (sex relationships between the white and black races);
7. Sex hygiene and venereal diseases;
8. Scenes of actual childbirth—in fact or in silhouette;
9. Children's sex organs;
10. Ridicule of the clergy;
11. Willful offense to any nation, race, or creed;

And be it further resolved, That special care be exercised in the manner in which the following subjects are treated, to the end that vulgarity and suggestiveness may be eliminated and that good taste may be emphasized:

1. The use of the flag;
2. International relations (avoiding picturizing in an unfavorable light another country's religion, history, institutions, prominent people, and citizenry);
3. Arson;
4. The use of firearms;
5. Theft, robbery, safe-cracking, and dynamiting of trains, mines, buildings, etc. (having in mind the effect which a too-detailed description of these may have upon the moron);
6. Brutality and possible gruesomeness;
7. Technique of committing murder by whatever method;
8. Methods of smuggling;
9. Third-degree methods;
10. Actual hangings or electrocutions as legal punishment for crime;
11. Sympathy for criminals;
12. Attitude toward public characters and institutions;
13. Sedition;
14. Apparent cruelty to children and animals;
15. Branding of people or animals;
16. The sale of women, or of a woman selling her virtue;
17. Rape or attempted rape;
18. First-night scenes;
19. Man and woman in bed together;
20. Deliberate seduction of girls;
21. The institution of marriage;
22. Surgical operations;
23. The use of drugs;
24. Titles or scenes having to do with law enforcement or law-enforcing officers;
25. Excessive or lustful kissing, particularly when one character or the other is a "heavy."

Source: Moley 240–41.

The Motion Picture Production Code (1930)

The following excerpt is from the Motion Picture Production Code as approved and signed by the Board of Directors of AMPP on February 17, 1930 and the Board of Directors of the MPPDA on March 31, 1930.

Code

TO GOVERN THE MAKING OF
TALKING, SYNCHRONIZED AND SILENT MOTION PICTURES
Formulated by
Association of Motion Picture Producers, Inc. and
The Motion Picture Producers and Distributors of America, Inc.

[PREAMBLE]
Motion picture producers recognize the high trust and confidence which have been placed in them by the people of the world and which have made motion pictures a universal form of entertainment.

They recognize their responsibility to the public because of this trust and because entertainment and art are important influences in the life of a nation.

Hence, though regarding motion pictures primarily as entertainment without any explicit purpose of teaching or propaganda, they know that the motion picture within its own field of entertainment may be directly responsible for spiritual or moral progress, for higher types of social life, and for much correct thinking.

During the rapid transition from silent to talking pictures they realized the necessity and the opportunity of subscribing to a Code to govern the production of talking pictures and of reacknowledging this responsibility.

On their part, they ask from the public and from public leaders a sympathetic understanding of their purposes and problems and a spirit of cooperation that will allow them the freedom and opportunity necessary to bring the motion picture to a still higher level of wholesome entertainment for all people.

GENERAL PRINCIPLES

1. No picture shall be produced which will lower the moral standards of those who see it. Hence the sympathy of the audience shall never be thrown to the side of crime, wrong-doing, evil or sin.
2. Correct standards of life, subject only to the requirements of drama and entertainment, shall be presented.
3. Law, natural or human, shall not be ridiculed, nor shall sympathy be created for its violation.

PARTICULAR APPLICATIONS

I. CRIMES AGAINST THE LAW

These shall never be presented in such a way as to throw sympathy with the crime as against law and justice or to inspire others with a desire for imitation.

1. *Murder*
   a. The technique of murder must be presented in a way that will not inspire imitation.
   b. Brutal killings are not to be presented in detail.
   c. Revenge in modern times shall not be justified.
2. *Methods of crime* should not be explicitly presented.
   a. Theft, robbery, safe-cracking, and dynamiting of trains, mines, buildings, etc., should not be detailed in method.
   b. Arson must be subject to the same safeguards.
   c. The use of firearms should be restricted to essentials.
   d. Methods of smuggling should not be presented.
3. *Illegal drug traffic* must never be presented.

4. *The use of liquor* in American life, when not required by the plot or for proper characterization, will not be shown.

II. *SEX*

The sanctity of the institution of marriage and the home shall be upheld. Pictures shall not infer that low forms of sex relationship are accepted or common thing.

1. *Adultery*, sometime necessary plot material, must not be explicitly treated, or justified, or presented attractively.
2. *Scenes of Passion*
   a. They should not be introduced when not essential to the plot.
   b. Excessive and lustful kissing, lustful embraces, suggestive postures and gestures, are not to be shown.
   c. In general passion should so be treated that these scenes do not stimulate the lower and baser element.
3. *Seduction or Rape*
   a. They should never be more than suggested, and only when essential to the plot, and even then never shown by explicit method.
   b. They should never be the proper subject for comedy.
4. *Sex perversion* or any inference to it is forbidden.
5. *White-slavery* shall not be treated.
6. *Miscegenation* (sex relationships between the white and black races) is forbidden.
7. *Sex hygiene* and venereal diseases are not subjects for motion pictures.
8. Scenes of *actual child birth*, in fact or in silhouette, are never to be presented.
9. *Children's sex organs* are never to be exposed.

III. *VULGARITY*. The treatment of low, disgusting, unpleasant, though not necessarily evil, subjects should be subject always to the dictate of good taste and a regard for the sensibilities of the audience.

IV. *OBSCENITY*. Obscenity in word, gesture, reference, song, joke or by suggestion (even when likely to be understood only by part of the audience) is forbidden.

V. *PROFANITY*

Pointed profanity (this includes the words, God, Lord, Jesus, Christ—unless used reverently—Hell, S.O.B., damn, Gawd), or every other profane or vulgar expression however used, is forbidden.

VI. *COSTUME*

1. *Complete nudity* is never permitted. This includes nudity in fact or in silhouette, or any lecherous or licentious notice thereof by other characters in the picture.
2. *Undressing scenes* should be avoided, and never used save where essential to the plot.
3. *Indecent or undue exposure* is forbidden.
4. *Dancing costumes* intended to permit undue exposure or indecent movements in the dance are forbidden.

VII. *DANCES*

1. Dances suggesting or representing sexual actions or indecent passion are forbidden.
2. Dances which emphasize indecent movements are to be regarded as obscene.

VIII. *RELIGION*

1. No film or episode may throw *ridicule* on any religious faith.
2. *Ministers of religion* in their character as ministers of religion should not be used as comic characters or as villains.
3. *Ceremonies* of any definite religion should be carefully and respectfully handled.

IX. *LOCATIONS*

The treatment of bedrooms must be governed by good taste and delicacy.

X. *NATIONAL FEELINGS*

1. *The use of the Flag* shall be consistently respectful.
2. *The history*, institutions, prominent people and citizenry of other nations shall be represented fairly.

XI. *TITLES*

Salacious, indecent, or obscene titles shall not be used.

XII. *REPELLENT SUBJECTS*

The following subjects must be treated within the careful limits of good taste:

1. *Actual hangings* or electrocutions as legal punishments for crime.
2. *Third Degree* methods.
3. *Brutality* and possible gruesomeness.
4. *Branding* of people or animals.
5. *Apparent cruelty* to children or animals.
6. *The sale of women*, or a woman selling her virtue.
7. *Surgical operations*.

Source: Richard Maltby, "Documents on the Genesis of the Production Code," *Quarterly Review of Film and Video* 15.4: 53–59.

Supplement to the Motion Picture Production Code (1930)—Reasons for the Code

The following statement was written in 1930 by Father Daniel Lord and Martin Quigley, publisher of the *Motion Picture Herald*. It was added to the Production Code whenever it appeared in print, beginning in 1934.

REASONS SUPPORTING PREAMBLE OF CODE

1. Theatrical motion pictures, that is, pictures intended for the theatre as distinct from pictures intended for churches, schools, lectures halls, educational movements, social reform movements, etc., are primarily to be regarded as ENTERTAINMENT.

   Mankind has always recognized the importance of entertainment and its value in rebuilding the bodies and souls of human beings.

   But it has always recognized that entertainment can be of a character either HELPFUL or HARMFUL to the human race, and in consequences has clearly distinguished between:

   a. *Entertainment which tends to improve* the race, or at least to re-create and rebuild human beings exhausted with the realities of life; and

   b. *Entertainment which tends to degrade* human beings, or to lower their standards of life and living.

Hence the MORAL IMPORTANCE of entertainment is something which has been universally recognized. It enters intimately into the lives of men and women and affects them closely; it occupies their minds and affections during leisure hours; and ultimately touches the whole of their lives. A man may be judged by his standard of entertainment as easily by the standard of his work.

So *correct entertainment* raises the whole standard of a nation.

Wrong entertainment lowers the whole living conditions and moral ideals of a race.

Note, for example, the healthy reactions to healthful, moral sports, like baseball, golf; the unhealthy reactions to sports like cock-fighting, bull-fighting, bear-baiting, etc.

Note, too, the effect on ancient nations of gladiatorial combats, the obscene plays of Roman times, etc.

2. Motion pictures are very important as ART.

Though a new art, possibly a combination art, it has the same object as the other arts, the presentation of human thought, emotion, and experience, in terms of an appeal to the soul through the senses.

Here, as in entertainment:

Art *enters intimately* into the lives of human beings.

Art can be *morally good*, lifting men to higher levels. This has been done through good music, great painting, authentic fiction, poetry, drama.

Art can be *morally* evil in its effects. This is the case clearly enough with unclean art, indecent books, suggestive drama. The effect on the lives of men and women is obvious.

Note: It has been argued that art in itself is unmoral, neither good nor bad. This is perhaps true of the THING which is music, painting, poetry, etc. But the thing is the PRODUCT of some person's mind, and the intention of that mind was either good or bad morally when it produced the thing. Besides, the thing has its EFFECT upon those who come into contact with it. In both these ways, that is, as a product of a mind and as the cause of definite effects, it has a deep moral significance and an unmistakable moral quality.

Hence: The motion pictures, which are the most popular of modern arts for the masses, have their moral quality from the intention of the minds which produce them and from their effects on the moral lives and reactions of their audiences. This gives them a most important morality.

1. They *reproduce* the morality of the men who use the pictures as a medium for the expression of their ideas and ideals.

2. They *affect* the moral standards of those who, through the screen, take in these ideas and ideals.

   In the case of motion pictures, this effect may be particularly emphasized because no art has so quick and so widespread an appeal to the masses. It has become in an incredibly short period *the art of the multitudes*.

3. The motion picture, because of its importance as an entertainment and because of the trust placed in it by the peoples of the world, has special MORAL OBLIGATIONS.

A. Most arts appeal to the mature. This art appeals at once to *every class*, immature, developed, undeveloped, law abiding, criminal. Music has its grades for different classes; so has literature and drama. This art of the motion picture, combining as it does the two fundamental appeals of looking at a *picture* and *listening to a story*, at once reaches every class of society.

B. By reason of the mobility of a film and the ease of picture distribution, and because of the possibility of duplicating positives in large quantities, this art reaches places unpenetrated by any other forms of art.

C. Because of these two facts, it is difficult to produce films intended for only certain classes of people. The exhibitor's theatres are built for the masses, for the cultivated and the rude, the mature and the immature, the self-respecting and the criminal. Films, unlike books and music, can with difficulty be confined to certain selected groups.

D. The latitude given to film material cannot, in consequence, be as wide as the latitude given to *book material*. In addition:

   a. A book describes; a film vividly presents. One presents on a cold page; the other by apparently living people.

   b. A book reaches the mind through words merely; a film reaches the eyes and ears through the reproduction of actual events.

   c. The reaction of a reader to a book depends largely on the keenness of the reader's imagination; the reaction to a film depends on the vividness of presentation.

Hence many things which might be described or suggested in a book could not possibly be presented in a film.

E. This is also true when comparing the film with the newspaper.
   a. Newspapers present by description, films by actual presentation.
   b. Newspapers are after the fact and present things as having taken place; the film gives the events in the process of enactment and with the apparent reality of life.
F. Everything possible in a *play* is not possible in a film:
   a. Because of the *larger audience of the film*, and its inconsequential mixed character. Psychologically, the larger the audience, the lower the moral mass resistance to suggestion.
   b. Because through light, enlargement of character, presentation, scenic emphasis, etc., the screen story is *brought closer* to the audience than the play.
   c. The enthusiasm for and interest in the film actors and actresses, developed beyond anything of the sort in history, makes the audience largely sympathetic toward the characters they portray and the stories in which they figure. Hence the audience is more ready to confuse actor and actress and the characters they portray, and it is most receptive of the emotions and ideals presented by their favorite stars.
G. *Small communities*, remote from sophistication and from the hardening process which takes place in the ethical and moral standards of groups in larger cities, are easily and readily reached by any sort of film.
H. The grandeur of mass settings, large action, spectacular features, etc., affects and arouses more intensely the emotional side of the audience. In general, the mobility, popularity, accessibility, emotional appeal, vividness, straightforward presentation of fact in the film make for more intimate contact with a larger audience and for greater emotional appeal.

Hence the larger moral responsibilities of the motion pictures.

REASONS SUPPORTING THE GENERAL PRINCIPLES
1. No picture shall be produced which will lower the moral standards of those who see it. Hence the sympathy of the audience should never be thrown on the side of crime, wrong-doing, evil or sin.

This is done:

1. When *evil* is made to appear *attractive* or *alluring*, and good is made to appear *unattractive*.
2. When the *sympathy* of the audience is thrown on the side of crime, wrong-doing, evil, sin. The same thing is true of a film that would throw sympathy against goodness, honor, innocence, purity, or honesty.

Note: Sympathy with a person who sins is not the same as sympathy with the sin or crime of which he is guilty. We may feel sorry for the plight of the murderer or even understand the circumstances which led him to his crime. We may not feel sympathy for the wrong which he has done.

The presentation of evil is often essential for art or fiction or drama: This in itself is not wrong provided:

a. That evil is *not presented alluringly*. Even if later in the film the evil is condemned or punished, it must not be allowed to appear so attractive that the audience's emotions are drawn to desire or approve so strongly that later the condemnation is forgotten and only the apparent joy of the sin remembered.
b. That throughout, the audience feels sure that *evil is wrong* and *good is right*.

2. Correct standards of life shall, as far as possible, be presented.

   A *wide knowledge of life and of living* is made possible through the film. When right standards are consistently presented, the motion picture exercises the most powerful influences. It builds character, develops right ideals, inculcates correct principles, and all this in the attractive story form.

   If motion pictures consistently *hold up for admiration high types of characters* and presents stories that will affect lives for the better, they can become the most powerful natural force for the improvement of mankind.

3. Law, natural or human, shall not be ridiculed, nor shall sympathy be created for its violation.

By *natural law* is understood the law which his written in the hearts of all mankind, the great underlying principles of right and justice dictated by conscience.

By *human law* is understood the law written by civilized nations.

1. *The presentation of crimes* against the law is *often necessary* for the carrying out of the plot. But the presentation must not throw sympathy with the crime as against the law nor with the criminal as against those who punish him.
2. *The courts of the land* should not be presented as unjust. This does not mean that a single court may not be represented as unjust, much less that a single court official must not be presented this way. But the court system of the country must not suffer as a result of this presentation.

REASONS UNDERLYING PARTICULAR APPLICATIONS

1. *Sin and evil* enter into the story of human beings and hence in themselves *are dramatic* material.
2. In the use of this material, it must be distinguished between *sin which repels* by its very nature and *sins which often attract.*
   a. In the first class come murder, most theft, many legal crimes, lying, hypocrisy, cruelty, etc.
   b. In the second class come sex sins, sins and crimes of apparent heroism, such as banditry, daring thefts, leadership in evil, organized crime, revenge, etc.

The first class needs far less care in treatment, as sins and crimes of this class are naturally unattractive. The audience instinctively condemns all such and is repelled.

Hence the important objective must be to avoid the hardening of the audience, especially of those who are young and impressionable, to the thought and fact of crime. People can become accustomed to even murder, cruelty, brutality, and repellent crimes, if these are sufficiently repeated.

The second class needs real care in handling, as the response of human nature to their appeal is obvious. This is treated more fully below.

3. A careful distinction can be made between films intended for *general distribution*, and films intended for use in theatres restricted to a *limited audience*. Themes and plots quite appropriate for the latter would be altogether out of place and dangerous in the former.

Note: In general the practice of using a general theatre and limiting its patronage during the showing of a certain film to "Adults Only" is not completely satisfactory and is only partially effective.

However, maturer minds may easily understand and accept without harm subject matter in plots which do younger people positive harm.

Hence: If there should be created a special type of theatre, catering exclusively to an adult audience, for plays of this character (plays with problem themes, difficult discussions and maturer treatment) it would seem to afford an outlet, which does not exist, for pictures unsuitable for general distribution but permissible for exhibitions to a restricted audience.

I. CRIMES AGAINST THE LAW

The treatment of crimes against the law must not:

1. *Teach methods* of crime.
2. *Inspire potential criminals* with a desire for imitation.
3. *Make criminals seem heroic* and justified.

Revenge in modern times shall not be justified. In lands and ages of less developed civilization and moral principles, revenge may sometimes be presented. This would be the case especially in places where no law exists to cover the crime because of which revenge is committed.

Note: When Section I, #3 of the Production Code was amended by resolution of the Board of Directors (September 11, 1936), the following sentence became applicable:

Because of its evil consequences, the drug traffic should not be presented in any form. The existence of the trade should not be brought to the attention of audiences.

The use of liquor should never be excessively presented, even in picturing countries where its use is legal. In scenes from American life, the necessities of plot and proper characterization alone justify its use. And in this case, it should be shown with moderation.

II. SEX
Out of regard for the sanctity of marriage and the home, the *triangle*, that is, the love of a third party for one already married, needs careful handling. The treatment should not throw sympathy against marriage as an institution.

Scenes of passion must be treated with an honest acknowledgment of human nature and its normal reactions. Many scenes cannot be presented without arousing dangerous emotions on the part of the immature, the young or the *criminal classes*.

Even within the limits of *pure love*, certain facts have been universally regarded by lawmakers as outside the limits of safe presentation.

In the case of *impure* love, the love which society has always regarded as wrong and which has been banned by divine law, the following are important:

1. Impure love must *not* be presented as *attractive and beautiful.*
2. It must *not* be the subject of *comedy or farce*, or treated as material for *laughter*.
3. It must *not* be presented in such a way as to *arouse passion* or morbid curiosity on the part of the audience.
4. It must *not* be made to seem *right and permissible*.
5. In general, it must *not* be *detailed* in method or manner.

III. VULGARITY; IV. OBSCENITY; V. PROFANITY; hardly need further explanation than is contained in the Code.

VI. COSTUME
General principles:
1. The effect of nudity or semi-nudity upon the normal man or woman, and much upon the young and immature persons, has been honestly recognized by all lawmakers and moralists.
2. Hence the fact that the nude or semi-nude body may be *beautiful* does not make its use in the films moral. For, in addition to its beauty, the effect of the nude or semi-nude body on the normal individual must be taken into consideration.

3. Nudity or semi-nudity used simply to put a *"punch"* into a picture comes under the head of immoral actions. It is immoral in its effect on the average audience.

4. Nudity can never be permitted as being *necessary for the plot*. Semi-nudity must not result in undue or indecent exposure.

5. *Transparent or translucent materials* and silhouette are frequently more suggestive than actual exposure.

VII. DANCES

Dancing in general is recognized as an *art* and as a *beautiful* form of expressing human emotions.

But dances which suggest or represent sexual actions, whether performed solo or with two or more, dances intended to excite the emotional reaction of an audience, dances with movement of the breasts, excessive body movements while the feet are stationary, violate decency and are wrong.

VIII. RELIGION

The reason why ministers of religion may not be comic characters or villains is simply because the attitude taken toward them may easily become the attitude taken toward religion in general. Religion is lowered in the minds of the audience because of the lowering of the audience's respect for a minister.

IX. LOCATIONS

Certain places are so closely and thoroughly associated with sexual life or with sexual sin that their use must be carefully limited.

X. NATIONAL FEELINGS

The just rights, history, and feelings of any nation are entitled to consideration and respectful treatment.

XI. TITLES

As the title of a picture is the brand on that particular type of goods, it must conform to the ethical practices of all such honest business.

XII. REPELLENT SUBJECTS

Such subjects are occasionally necessary for the plot. Their treatment must never offend good taste nor injure the sensibilities of an audience.

Source: Moley 243–48.

The Legion of Decency

THE LEGION OF DECENCY PLEDGES

The original pledge was written by the head of the Legion of Decency, Archbishop John T. McNicholas, and first administered in 1934.

Legion of Decency Pledge (1934)

I wish to join the Legion of Decency, which condemns vile and unwholesome moving pictures. I unite with all who protest against them as a grave menace to youth, to home life, to country and to religion.

I condemn absolutely those salacious motion pictures, which, with other degrading agencies, are corrupting public morals and promoting a sex mania in our land.

I shall do all that I can to arouse public opinion against the portrayal of vice as a normal condition of affairs, and against depicting criminals of any class as heroes and heroines, presenting their filthy philosophy of life as something acceptable to decent men and women.

I unite with all those who condemn the display of suggestive advertisements on billboards, at theatre entrances, and the favorable notices given to immoral motion pictures.

Considering these evils, I hereby promise to remain away from all motion pictures except those which do not offend decency and Christian morality. I promise further to secure as many members as possible for the Legion of Decency.

I make this protest in a spirit of self-respect and with the conviction that the American public does not demand filthy pictures, but clean entertainment and educational features.

Legion of Decency Pledge (1958)

I condemn indecent and immoral motion pictures, and those which glorify crime of criminals.

I promise to do all that I can to strengthen public opinion against the production of indecent and immoral films, and to unite with all who protest against them.

I acknowledge my obligation to form a right of conscience about pictures that are dangerous to my moral life. As a member of the Legion of Decency, I pledge myself to remain away from them. I promise, further, to stay away altogether from places of amusement which show them as a matter of policy.

Legion of Decency Pledge (1960)

I promise to promote by word and deed what is morally and artistically good in motion-picture entertainment.

I promise to discourage indecent, immoral, and unwholesome motion pictures especially by my good example and always in a responsible and civic-minded manner.

I promise to guide those under my care and influence in their choice of motion pictures that are morally and culturally inspiring.

I promise not to co-operate by my patronage with theatres which regularly show objectionable films.

I promise as a member of the Legion of Decency to acquaint myself with its aims, to consult its classifications, and to unite with all men of good will in promoting high and noble standards in motion-picture entertainment.

I freely make these solemn resolutions to the honor of God for the good of my soul and for the welfare of my country. Amen.

THE LEGION OF DECENCY RATINGS SYSTEM

Original Classification (1936)

A-1: Morally Unobjectionable for General Patronage

These films are considered to contain no material which would be morally dangerous to the average motion picture audience, adults and children alike.

A-2: Morally Unobjectionable for Adults

These are films which in themselves are morally harmless but which, because of subject matter or treatment, require maturity and experience if one is to witness them without danger or moral harm. While no definite age limit can be established for this group, the judgment of parents, pastors, and teachers would be helpful in determining the decision in individual cases.

B: Morally Objectionable in Part for All

Films in this category are considered to contain elements dangerous to Christian morals or moral standards.

C: Condemned

Condemned films are considered to be those which, because of theme or treatment, have been described by the Holy Father as "positively bad."

Separate Classification

This is given to certain films which, while not morally offensive, require some analysis and explanation as a protection of the uninformed against wrong interpretations and false conclusions.

Revised Classification (1957)

A-1: Morally Unobjectionable for General Patronage
A-2: Morally Unobjectionable for Adults and Adolescents
A-3: Morally Unobjectionable for Adults
B: Morally Objectionable in Part for All
C: Condemned

The Legion of Decency offered the following rationale for the new classifications:

(a) The Legion recognizes that in connection with motion-picture attendance the average adolescent of our day will not infrequently consider himself more than a child and hence will seek out pictures with more adult content and orientation. In keeping with the sound principles of modern Catholic educational psychology, it seems desirable that the Legion aid the adolescent in this quest for more mature movie-subjects and thereby contribute to his intellectual and emotional maturation. To this end the new A-2 classification has been adopted; it is hoped that this classification, while providing the necessary reasonable moral controls upon the adolescent, will at the same time aid him in his "growing up."

(b) The A-3 classification is an attempt on the part of the Legion to provide for truly adult subject matter in entertainment motion pictures, provided that the themes in question and their treatment be consonant with the moral law and with traditionally-accepted moral standards.

(c) Although the B and C classifications remain unchanged, it is to be recognized that the new triple A classification is intended to strengthen the meaning of the B category. Henceforth, there will be no doubt that a B film is one adjudged to contain material which in itself or in its offensive treatment is contrary to traditional morality and constitutes a threat not only to the personal spiritual life of even an adult viewer, but also to the moral behavior-patterns which condition public morality. Catholic people are urged to refrain from attendance at all B pictures, not only for the sake of their consciences, but also in the interest of promoting the common good.

Source: Harold C. Gardiner, *Catholic Viewpoint on Censorship* (Rev. Edition) (Garden City, New York: Doubleday, 1961), 92–93, 97–99.

The Motion Picture Ratings System (1968)

This Code is designed to keep in close harmony with the mores, culture, the moral sense and change in our society.

The objectives of the Code are: (1) To encourage artistic expression by expanding creative freedom; and (2) To assure that the freedom which encourages the artist remains responsible and sensitive to the standards of the larger society.

Censorship is an odious enterprise. We oppose censorship and classification by governments because they are alien to the American tradition of freedom.

Much of the nation's strength and purpose is drawn from the premise that the humblest of citizens has the freedom of his own choice. Censorship destroys this freedom of choice.

It is within this framework that the Motion Picture Association continues to recognize its obligations to the society of which it is an integral part.

In our society parents are the arbiters of family conduct. Parents have the primary responsibility to guide their children in the kind of lives they lead, the character they build, the books they read, and the movies and other entertainment to which they are exposed.

The creators of motion pictures undertake a responsibility to make available pertinent information about their pictures which will assist parents to fulfill their responsibilities.

But this alone is not enough. In further recognition of our obligation to the public, and most especially to parents, we have extended the Code operation to include a nationwide voluntary film rating program which has as its prime objective a sensitive concern for children. Motion pictures will be reviewed by a Code and Rating Administration which, when it reviews a motion picture as to its conformity with the standards of the Code, will issue ratings. It is our intent that all motion pictures exhibited in the United States will carry a rating. These ratings are:

(G)—SUGGESTED FOR GENERAL AUDIENCES
This category includes motion pictures that in the opinion of the Code and Rating Administration would be acceptable for all audiences, without consideration of age.

(M)—SUGGESTED FOR MATURE AUDIENCES—ADULTS & MATURE YOUNG PEOPLE
This category includes motion pictures that in the opinion of the Code and Rating Administration, because of their theme, content, and treatment, might require more mature judgment by viewers, and about which parents should exercise their discretion.

(R)—RESTRICTED—Persons under 16 not admitted, unless accompanied by parent or adult guardian.
This category includes motion pictures that in the opinion of the Code and Rating Administration, because of their theme, content or treatment, should not be presented to persons under 16 unless accompanied by a parent or adult guardian.

(X)—PERSONS UNDER 16 NOT ADMITTED
This category includes motion pictures submitted to the Code and Rating Administration which in the opinion of the Code and Rating Administration are rated X because of the treatment of sex, violence, crime or profanity. Pictures rated X do not qualify for a Code Seal. Pictures rated X should not be presented to persons under 16.

The program contemplates that any distributors outside the membership of the Association who chose not to submit their motion pictures to the Code and Rating Administration will self-apply the (X) rating. . . .

STANDARDS FOR PRODUCTION

In furtherance of the objectives of the Code to accord with the mores, the culture, and the moral sense of our society, the principles stated above and the following standards shall govern the Administrator in his consideration of motion pictures submitted for Code approval:

- The basic dignity and value of human life shall be respected and upheld. Restraint shall be exercised in portraying the taking of life.
- Evil, sin, crime and wrong-doing shall not be justified.
- Special restraint shall be exercised in portraying criminal or anti-social activities in which minors participate or are involved.
- Detailed and protracted acts of brutality, cruelty, physical violence, torture and abuse shall not be presented.
- Indecent or undue exposure of the human body shall not be presented.
- Illicit sex relationships shall not be justified. Intimate sex scenes violating common standards of decency shall not be portrayed.
- Restraint and care shall be exercised in presentations dealing with sex aberrations.
- Obscene speech, gestures or movements shall not be presented. Undue profanity shall not be permitted.
- Religion shall not be demeaned.
- Words or symbols contemptuous of racial, religious or national groups, shall not be used as to incite bigotry or hatred.
- Excessive cruelty to animals shall not be portrayed and animals shall not be treated inhumanely.

Source: "The Revised MPAA Code of Self-Regulation," *Variety* 8 October 1968: 6.

The Motion Picture Production Code: Revisions of the Profanity Clause

1. THE 1939 AMENDMENT (ADOPTED NOVEMBER 1, 1939)

V. PROFANITY

Pointed profanity or every other profane or vulgar expression, however used, is forbidden.

No approval by the Production Code Administration shall be given to the use of words and phrases in motion pictures including, but not limited to, the following:

Alley cat (applied to a woman); bat (applied to a woman); broad (applied to a woman); Bronx cheer (the sound); chippie; cocotte; God, Lord, Jesus, Christ (unless used reverently); cripes; fanny; fairy (in a vulgar sense); finger (the); fire, cries of; Gawd; goose (in a vulgar sense); "hold your hat" or "hats"; hot (applied to a woman); "in your hat"; louse; lousy; Madam (relating to prostitution); nance; nerts; nuts (except when meaning crazy); pansy; razzberry (the sound); slut (applied to a woman); SOB.; son-of-a; tart; toilet gags; tom cat (applied to a man); traveling salesman and farmer's daughter jokes; whore; damn; hell (excepting when the use of said last two words shall be essential and required for portrayal, in proper historical context, of any scene or dialogue based upon historical fact or folklore, or for the presentation in proper literary context of a Biblical, or other religious quotation, or a quotation from a literary work provided that no such use shall be permitted which is intrinsically objectionable or offends good taste).

Source: Cobbett Steinberg, *Reel Facts: The Movie Book of Records* (New York: Vintage Books, 1978) 462–63.

2. The following words and phrases are invariably deleted by political censor boards:

Bum	in England
Bloody	in England
"Cissy" or "Sissy"	in England
Gigolo	in England
Poisons (specific names of)	in United States
Punk	in England
Sex appeal	in England
Sex life	in England
Shag	in British Empire
Shyster	in England
"Stick'em up"	in United States and Canada

Source: *The 1941–42 Motion Picture Almanac* (New York: Quigley Publishing Company, 1942), 879. Part (2) appears in subsequent editions of the Almanac through the 1944–45 edition.

2. 1945 AMENDMENT (ADOPTED SEPTEMBER 12, 1945)

In the administration of Section V of the Production Code, the Production Code Administration may take cognizance of the fact that the following words and phrases are obviously offensive to the patrons of motion pictures in the United States and more particularly to the patrons of motion pictures in foreign countries:

Chink, Dago, Frog, Greaser, Hunkie, Kike, Nigger, Spic, Wop, Yid.

Source: Steinberg 463.

3. The following words and phrases were deleted from the list in 1951:

Alley cat	Cocotte
Bat	Slut
Broad	

3. EXCERPTS FROM 1956 MOTION PICTURE PRODUCTION CODE (ANNOUNCED DECEMBER 11, 1956)

IV. VULGARITY:

Vulgar expressions and double meanings having the same effect are forbidden. This shall include but not be limited to such words and expressions as chippie, fairy, goose, nuts, pansy, s.o.b., son-of-a. The treatment of low, disgusting, unpleasant, though not necessarily evil, subjects should be guided always by the dictates of good taste and a proper regard for the sensibilities of the audience.

V. OBSCENITY

1. Dances suggesting or representing sexual actions or emphasizing indecent movements are to be regarded as obscene.
2. Obscenity in words, gesture, reference, song, joke or by suggestion, even when likely to be understood by only part of the audience, is forbidden.

VI. BLASPHEMY AND PROFANITY

1. Blasphemy is forbidden. Reference to the Deity, God, Lord, Jesus, Christ, shall not be irreverent.
2. Profanity is forbidden. The words "hell" and "damn," while sometimes dramatically valid, will if used without moderation be considered offensive by many members of the audience. Their use shall be governed by the discretion and prudent advice of the Code Administration.

X. NATIONAL FEELINGS

3. No picture shall be produced that tends to incite bigotry or hatred among peoples of differing races, religions, or national origins. The use of such offensive words as chink, dago, frog, greaser, hunkie, kike, nigger, spig, wop, yid, should be avoided.

XI. TITLES

The following titles shall not be used:

1. Titles which are salacious, indecent, obscene, profane or vulgar.
2. Titles which violate any other clause of this Code.

Source: "Revised MPAA Production Code," *Hollywood Reporter*, 12 December 1956: 6.

4. EXCERPTS FROM 1966 MOTION PICTURE PRODUCTION CODE (ADOPTED SEPTEMBER 20, 1966)

Standards for Production (excerpt)

Obscene speech, gestures, or movements shall not be presented. Undue profanity shall not be permitted.

Religion shall not be demeaned.

Words or symbols contemptuous of racial, religious or national groups shall not be used so as to incite bigotry or hatred.

Standards for Titles

A salacious, obscene, or profane title shall not be used on motion pictures.

Source: "Motion Picture Assn. Code of Self-Regulation," *Daily Variety*, 21 September 1966: 9.

Special Regulations on Crime in Motion Pictures (1938)

Resolved, that the Board of Directors of the Motion Picture Association of America, Inc., hereby ratifies, approves, and confirms the Interpretations of the Production Code, the practices thereunder, and the resolutions indicating and confirming such interpretations heretofore adopted by the Association of Motion Picture Producers, Inc., all effectuating regulations relative to the treatment of crime in motion pictures, as follows:

1. Details of crime must never be shown and care should be exercised at all times in discussing such details.
2. Actions suggestive of wholesale slaughter of human beings, either by criminals, in conflict with police, or as between warring factions of criminals, or in public disorders of any kind, will not be allowed.
3. There must be no suggestion, at any time, of excessive brutality.
4. Because of the increase in the number of films in which murder is frequently committed, action showing the taking of human life, even in the mystery stories, is to be cut to the minimum. These frequent presentations of murder tend to lessen regard for the sacredness of life.
5. Suicide, as a solution of problems occurring in the development of screen drama, is to be discouraged as morally questionable and as bad theatre—unless absolutely necessary for the development of the plot.

6. There must be no display, at any time, of machine guns, submachine guns or other weapons generally classified as illegal weapons in the hands of gangsters, or other criminals, and there are to be no off-stage sounds of the repercussions of these guns.

7. There must be no new, unique or trick methods shown for concealing guns.

8. The flaunting of weapons by gangsters, or other criminals, will not be allowed.

9. All discussions and dialogue on the part of gangsters regarding guns should be cut to the minimum.

10. There must be no scenes, at any time, showing law-enforcement officers dying at the hands of criminals. This includes private detectives and guards for banks, motor trucks, etc.

11. With special reference to the crime of kidnapping—or illegal abduction—such stories are acceptable under the Code only when the kidnapping or abduction is (a) not the main theme of the story; (b) the person kidnapped is not a child; (c) there are no details of the crime of kidnapping; (d) no profit accrues to the abductors or kidnappers; and (e) where the kidnappers are punished.

    It is understood, and agreed, that the word kidnapping, as used in paragraph 11 of these Regulations, is intended to mean abduction, or illegal detention, in modern times, by criminals for ransom.

12. Pictures dealing with criminal activities, in which minors participate, or to which minors are related, shall not be approved if they incite demoralizing imitation on the part of youth.

Addendum (Adopted December 3, 1947)

13. No picture shall be approved dealing with the life of a notorious criminal of current or recent times which uses the name, nickname, or alias of such notorious criminal in the film, nor shall a picture be approved if based upon the life of such a notorious criminal unless the character shown in the film be punished for crimes shown in the film as committed by him.

Source: Steinberg 472–73.

L'amant de Lady Chatterley (*Lady Chatterley's Lover*—1955)
Director/Writer: Marc Allégret. Play: Philippe de Rothschild, Gaston Bonheur. Based on the novel by D. H. Lawrence. Producers: Gilbert Cohen-Seat, Claude Ganz. Cast: Constance Chatterley (Danielle Darrieux), Oliver Mellors (Erno Crisa), Sir Clifford Chatterley (Leo Genn).

Les amants (*The Lovers*—1958)
Director: Louis Malle. Writer: Louise de Vilmorin. Based on the novel *Point de lendemain* by Dominique Vivant. Cast: Jeanne Tournier (Jeanne Moreau), Henri Tournier (Alain Cuny), Bernard Dubois-Lambert (Jean-Marc Bory).

Anatomy of a Murder (1959)
Director/Producer: Otto Preminger. Writer: Wendell Mayes. Based on the novel by John Voelker (Robert Traver). Cast: Paul Biegler (James Stewart), Laura Manion (Lee Remick), Lt. Frederick Manion (Ben Gazzara), Maida Rutledge (Eve Arden), Mary Pilant (Kathryn Grant), Asst. State Attorney General Claude Dancer (George C. Scott), Judge Weaver (Joseph N. Welch).

Baby Doll (1956)
Director/Producer: Elia Kazan. Writer/Producer: Tennessee Williams, based on his play *27 Wagons Full of Cotton*. Producers: Kazan, Williams. Cast: Archie Lee Meighan (Karl Malden), Baby Doll Meighan (Carroll Baker), Silva Vacarro (Eli Wallach), Aunt Rose Comfort (Mildred Dunnock).

Birth Control (1917)
Writer/Director/Producer: Margaret Sanger. Producer: Frederick A. Blossom.

The Birth of a Nation (1915)

Director/Cowriter/Producer: D. W. Griffith. Writer: Frank E. Woods. Based on the novels *The Clansman: An Historical Romance of the Ku Klux Klan* and *The Leopard's Spots,* and the play *The Clansman* by Thomas F. Dixon, Jr. Cast: Elsie Stoneman (Lillian Gish), Flora Cameron (Mae Marsh), Col. Ben Cameron (Henry B. Walthall), Margaret Cameron (Miriam Cooper), Lydia Brown (Mary Alden), Silas Lynch (George Siegmann).

Blackboard Jungle (1955)

Director/Writer: Richard Brooks. Based on the novel by Evan Hunter. Producer: Pandro S. Berman. Cast: Richard Dadier (Glenn Ford), Anne Dadier (Anne Francis), Jim Murdock (Louis Calhern), Joshua Y. Edwards (Richard Kiley), Gregory W. Miller (Sidney Poitier), Artie West (Vic Morrow).

Le blé en herbe (*The Game of Love*—1954)

Director/Cowriter: Claude Autant-Lara. Writers: Jean Aurenche, Pierre Bost. Based on the novel by Colette. Cast: Phil (Pierre-Michel Beck), Vinca (Nicole Berger), La dame en blanc (Edwige Feuillère).

Blonde Venus (1932)

Director: Josef von Sternberg. Writers: Jules Furthman and S. K. Lauren. Cast: Helen Faraday (Marlene Dietrich), Edward Faraday (Herbert Marshall), Nick Townsend (Cary Grant).

Bonnie and Clyde (1967)

Director: Arthur Penn. Writers: David Newman and Robert Benton. Producer: Warren Beatty. Cast: Clyde Barrow (Warren Beatty), Bonnie Parker (Faye Dunaway), C. W. Moss (Michael J. Pollard), Buck Barrow (Gene Hackman), Blanche (Estelle Parsons).

Caligula (1979)

Director: Tinto Brass. Additional footage by Bob Guccione and Giancarlo Lui. Adapted from a screenplay by Gore Vidal. Producers: Guccione, Franco Rossellini, and Jack H. Silverman. Cast: Caligula (Malcolm McDowell), Drusilla (Teresa Ann Savoy), Nerva (John Gielgud), Tiberius (Peter O'Toole), Caesonia (Helen Mirren).

Un chant d'amour (*Song of Love*—1947)

Director/Writer: Jean Genet. Producer: Nikos Papatakis. Cast: Java, André Reybaz, Lucien Sénémaud.

The Connection (1962)
> Director/Producer: Shirley Clarke. Writer: Jack Gelber, based on his play. Producer: Lewis M. Allen. Cast: Leach (Warren Finnerty), Solly (Jerome Raphael), Ernie (Garry Goodrow), Sam (James Anderson), Cowboy (Carl Lee), J. J. Burden (Roscoe Lee Browne), Jim Dunn (William Redfield).

Cruising (1980)
> Director/Writer: William Friedkin. Based on the novel by Gerald Walker. Producer: Jerry Weintraub. Cast: Steve Burns (Al Pacino), Capt. Edelson (Paul Sorvino), Stuart Richards (Richard Cox), Ted Bailey (Don Scardino), Nancy (Karen Allen).

Deep Throat (1972)
> Director/Writer: Gerard Damiano (as Jerry Gerard). Producers: William J. Links, Lou Perry, Phil Perry. Cast: Linda Lovelace (Herself), Dr. Young (Harry Reems), Helen (Dolly Sharp), the Nurse (Carol Connors).

Do the Right Thing (1989)
> Director/Writer/Producer: Spike Lee. Producers: John Kilik, Monty Ross. Cast: Mookie (Spike Lee), Sal (Danny Aiello), Pino (John Turturro), Vito (Richard Edson), Da Mayor (Ossie Davis), Mother Sister (Ruby Dee), Radio Raheem (Bill Nunn).

Ekstase (*Ecstasy*—1933)
> Director/Cowriter: Gustav Machatý. Writers: Frantisek Horký, Jacques A. Koerpel. Based on the book by Robert Horky. Cast: Eva Hermann (Hedy Lamarr, as Hedy Kiesler), Adam (Aribert Mog), Emile (Zvonimir Rogoz).

Et Dieu . . . créa la femme (. . . *And God Created Woman*—1956)
> Director/Cowriter: Roger Vadim. Writer: Raoul Lévy. Producers: Lévy, Claude Ganz. Cast: Juliette Hardy (Brigitte Bardot), Eric Carradine (Curd Jurgens), Michel Tardieu (Jean-Louis Trintignant).

The Exorcist (1973)
> Director: William Friedkin. Writer: William Peter Blatty, based on his novel. Producers: Blatty, Noel Marshall, David Salven. Cast: Chris MacNeil (Ellen Burstyn), Father Merrin (Max von Sydow), Father Karras (Jason Miller), Regan (Linda Blair), Sharon (Kitty Winn), Lt. Kinderman (Lee J. Cobb).

Fahrenheit 9/11 (2004)

Director/Writer/Producer: Michael Moore. Producers: Jim Czarnecki, Kathleen Glynn. Editors: Kurt Engfehr, T. Woody Richman, Chris Seward.

Fit to Win (1919)

Director/Writer: Lieut. Edward H. Griffith. Production Company: U.S. Public Health Service, American Social Hygiene Association, War Department Commission on Training Camp Activities in cooperation with the Medical Department of the Army. Cast: Billy Hale (Serg. Raymond McKee), Chick Carlton (Harry Gripp), Hank Simpson (Paul Kelly).

The Hand That Rocks the Cradle (1917)

Codirectors/Cowriters/Producers: Phillips Smalley and Lois Weber. Cast: Dr. Broome (Phillips Smalley), Mrs. Broome (Lois Weber), Mrs. Graham (Priscilla Dean), Mr. Graham (Wedgwood Nowell), Sarah (Evelyn Selbie), Sarah's husband (Harry De More).

The Inside of the White Slave Traffic (1913)

Director/Cowriter: Frank Beal. Writer: Samuel H. London. Producer: Samuel H. London. Cast: Immigrant (Ninita Bristow), Procurer (Edwin Carewe), Victim (Virginia Mann), Procurer's sweetheart (Jean Thomas).

Jag är nyfiken—en film i gult (*I Am Curious [Yellow]*—1967)

Director: Vilgot Sjöman. Producer: Lena Malmsjö. Cast: Anna Lena Lisabet Nyman/Lena (Lena Nyman), Vilgot Sjöman (Himself), Börje (Börje Ahlstedt).

Jeffries-Johnson World's Championship Boxing Contest, Held in Reno, Nevada, July 4, 1910 (1910)

Producer: J. Stuart Blackton.

The Last Temptation of Christ (1988)

Director: Martin Scorsese. Writer: Paul Schrader. Based on the novel by Nikos Kazantzakis. Producers: Barbara De Fina, Harry J. Ufland. Cast: Jesus Christ (Willem Dafoe), Judas (Harvey Keitel), Mary Magdalene (Barbara Hershey).

Life of Brian (1979)

Director/Cowriter: Terry Jones. Writers: Graham Chapman, John

Cleese, Terry Gilliam, Eric Idle, Michael Palin. Producers: Tarak Ben Ammar, John Goldstone, George Harrison, Denis O'Brien. Cast: Brian Cohen (Graham Chapman), Mandy Cohen (Terry Jones), Judith (Sue Jones-Davies).

Little Caesar (1931)

Director: Mervyn LeRoy. Writers: Robert N. Lee, Francis Edward Faragoh. Based on the novel by W. R. Burnett. Producers: Hal B. Wallis, Darryl F. Zanuck. Cast: Little Caesar (Edward G. Robinson), Joe Massara (Douglas Fairbanks, Jr.), Olga Stassoff (Glenda Farrell).

Martin Luther (1953)

Director: Irving Pichel. Writers: Allan Sloane, Lothar Wolff, Jaroslav Pelikan, Theodore G. Tappert. Producers: Louis De Rochemont, Lothar Wolff. Cast: Martin Luther (Niall MacGinnis), Vicar von Staupitz (John Ruddock).

The May Irwin Kiss (1896)

Director: William Heise. Producer: Edison Manufacturing Company. Cast: May Irwin, John C. Rice.

Il miracolo (*The Miracle*—1948) (released as second segment of *L'amore* [1948])

Director/Producer: Roberto Rossellini. Writer: Tullio Pinelli. Story: Federico Fellini. Cast: Nanni (Anna Magnani), The Stranger (Federico Fellini).

Mohammed, Messenger of God (1977)

Director/Producer: Moustapha Akkad. Writers: H. A. L. Craig, Tewfik El-Hakim, A. B. Jawdat El-Sahhar, A. B. Rahman el-Sharkawi, Mohammad Ali Maher. Producers: Harold Buck, Mohammad Sanousi. Cast: Hamza (Anthony Quinn), Hind (Irene Pappas), Abu Sofyan (Michael Ansara).

The Moon Is Blue (1953)

Director/Producer: Otto Preminger. Writer: F. Hugh Herbert (based on his play). Cast: Donald Gresham (William Holden), Patty O'Neill (Maggie McNamara), David Slater (David Niven), Cynthia Slater (Dawn Addams), Michael O'Neill (Tom Tully).

Natural Born Killers (1994)

Director/Cowriter: Oliver Stone. Writers: Richard Rutowski, David Veloz. Story: Quentin Tarantino. Producers: Jane Hamsher, Don Murphy, Clayton Townsend. Cast: Mickey Knox (Woody Harrelson), Mallory Knox (Juliette Lewis), Det. Jack Scagnetti (Tom Sizemore), Wayne Gale (Robert Downey, Jr.).

The Outlaw (1943)

Director/Producer: Howard Hughes. Writer: Jules Furthman. Cast: Billy the Kid (Jack Buetel), Rio McDonald (Jane Russell), Pat Garrett (Thomas Mitchell), Doc Holliday (Walter Huston).

The Passion of the Christ (2004)

Director/Cowriter/Producer: Mel Gibson. Writer: Benedict Fitzgerald. Producers: Bruce Davey, Stephen McEveety, Enzo Sisti. Cast: Jesus (James Caviezel), Mary (Maia Morgenstern), Mary Magdalene (Monica Belluci).

The Public Enemy (1931)

Director: William A. Wellman. Writers: Kubec Glasmon, John Bright, Harvey F. Thew. Cast: Tom Powers (James Cagney), Gwen Allen (Jean Harlow), Matt Doyle (Edward Woods), Mamie (Joan Blondell), Mike Powers (Donald Cook), Kitty (Mae Clark).

La Ronde (1950)

Director/Cowriter: Max Ophüls. Writers: Louis Ducreux, Kurt Feltz, Jacques Natanson. Based on the play *Reigen* by Arthur Schnitzler. Producers: Ralph Baum, Sacha Gordine. Cast: Raconteur (Anton Walbrook), Leocadie (Simone Signoret), Franz (Serge Reggiani), Marie (Simone Simon), Alfred (Daniel Gélin).

Rosemary's Baby (1968)

Director/Writer: Roman Polanski. Based on the novel by Ira Levin. Producer: William Castle. Cast: Rosemary Woodhouse (Mia Farrow), Guy Woodhouse (John Cassavetes), Minnie Castevet (Ruth Gordon), Roman Castevet (Sidney Blackmer), Edward Hutchins (Maurice Evans), Dr. Sapirstein (Ralph Bellamy).

Salò o le 120 giornate di Sodoma (*Salo, or the 120 Days of Sodom*—1975)

Director/Cowriter: Pier Paolo Pasolini. Writer: Sergio Citti. Based on the novel by the Marquis de Sade. Producers: Alberto Grimaldi, Alberto De Stefanis, Antonio Girasante. Cast: The Duke (Paolo

Bonacelli), The Bishop (Giorgio Cataldi), The Magistrate (Umberto Paolo Quintavalle), The President (Aldo Valletti).

Salt of the Earth (1954)

Director: Herbert J. Biberman. Writers: Michael Biberman, Michael Wilson. Producers: Adolfo Barela, Sonja Dahl Biberman, Paul Jarrico. Cast: Esperanza Quintero (Rosaura Revueltas), Sheriff (Will Geer), Barton (David Wolfe), Ramon Quintero (Juan Chacón).

Scarface (1932)

Codirectors: Howard Hawks and Richard Rosson. Writer: Ben Hecht. Based on the novel by Armitage Trail. Continuity and Dialogue: Seton I. Miller, John Lee Mahin, W. R. Burnett. Cast: Antonio "Tony" Camonte (Paul Muni), Francesca Camonte (Ann Dvorak), Johnny Levo (Osgood Perkins), Guino Rinaldo (George Raft).

She Done Him Wrong (1933)

Director: Lowell Sherman. Writers: Harvey F. Thew, John Bright. Producer: William LeBaron. Cast: Lady Lou (Mae West), Capt. Cummings (Cary Grant).

The Sign of the Cross (1932)

Director/Producer: Cecil B. DeMille. Writers: Waldemar Young, Sidney Buchman. Based on the play by Wilson Barrett. Cast: Marcus Superbus (Fredric March), Mercia (Elissa Landi), Empress Poppaea (Claudette Colbert), Emperor Nero (Charles Laughton), Ancaria (Joyzelle Joyner).

Snuff (1976)

Codirectors/Cowriters: Michael Findlay, Roberta Findlay. Codirector: Horacio Fredriksson. Writer: A. Bochin. Producers: Jack Bravman, Allan Shackleton. Cast: Angelica (Margarita Amuchástegui), Ana (Ana Carro), Susanna (Liliana Fernández Blanco), Carmela (Roberta Findlay), Satan (Enrique Larratelli).

Titicut Follies (1967)

Director/Producer/Coeditor: Frederick Wiseman. Cinematography: John Marshall. Coeditor: Alyne Model.

Traffic in Souls (1913)

Director/Cowriter: George Loane Tucker. Writer: Walter MacNamara. Cast: Mary Barton (Jane Gail), Lorna Barton (Ethel Grandin),

Isaac Barton (William Turner), Officer Burke (Matt Moore), William Trubus (William Welsh), Bill Bradshaw (William Cavanaugh).

Triumph des Willens (Triumph of the Will—1935)
Director/Cowriter/Producer: Leni Riefenstahl. Writer: Walter Ruttmann.

The Unwritten Law: A Thrilling Drama Based on the Thaw-White Case (1907)
Production Company/Distributor: Lubin Manufacturing Company.

The War Game (1965)
Director/Writer/Producer: Peter Watkins.

The Warriors (1979)
Director/Cowriter: Walter Hill. Writer: David Shaber. Based on the novel by Sol Yurick. Producers: Lawrence Gordon, Frank Marshall. Cast: Swan (Michael Beck), Ajax (James Remar), Cleon (Dorsey Wright), Mercy (Deborah Van Valkenburgh), Luther (David Patrick Kelly).

Where Are My Children? (1916)
Codirectors/Cowriters/Coproducers: Lois Weber and Phillips Smalley. Story by Lucy Payton and Franklin Hall. Cast: District Attorney Richard Walton (Tyrone Power Sr.), Mrs. Walton (Helen Riaume), Roger (A. D. Blake), Lillian (Rena Rogers), Waltons' Housekeeper (Cora Drew).

The Wild Bunch (1969)
Director/Cowriter: Sam Peckinpah. Writer/Story: Walon Green. Story: Roy N. Sickner. Producer: Phil Feldman. Cast: Pike Bishop (William Holden), Dutch Engstrom (Ernest Borgnine), Deke Thornton (Robert Ryan).

Who's Afraid of Virginia Woolf? (1966)
Director: Mike Nichols. Writer/Producer: Ernest Lehman. Based on the play by Edward Albee. Cast: Martha (Elizabeth Taylor), George (Richard Burton), Nick (George Segal), Honey (Sandy Dennis).

All Production Code Administration (PCA) case files (designated by "[title of film] PCA File") are from the Department of Special Collections, Margaret Herrick Library, Academy of Motion Picture Arts and Sciences, Beverly Hills, California.

Code

HR = *Hollywood Reporter*

LA Times = *Los Angeles Times*

NY Times = *New York Times*

CHAPTER 1

Censorship and Silent Cinema, or Why a Kiss Is No Longer *Just* a Kiss

1 According to a: "Edison's Vitascope Cheered," *NY Times* 24 Apr. 1896: 5. Although the Vitascope was promoted as Edison's invention, it was actually invented by Charles Francis Jenkins and Thomas Armat.

1 Over the next: Charles Musser, *The Emergence of Cinema: The American Screen to 1907* (Los Angeles: University of California Press, 1990) 120, 122.

1 The article, entitled: "Anatomy of a Kiss," *New York World* 26 April 1896: 21.

2 "Of the 10 pictures": "Keith's New Theatre," *The Boston Herald* 19 May 1896: 9, as qtd. in Charles Musser, "The May Irwin Kiss: Performance and the Beginnings of Cinema," *Visual Delights—Two: Exhibition and Reception*, ed. Vanessa Toulmin and Simon Popple (Eastleigh, United Kingdom: John Libbey Publishing, 2005) 103.

2 "The famous kissing": "Hopkin's South Side Theatre," *Chicago Tribune* 5 July 1896: 36.

2 "In San Francisco": "About the Theatres," *LA Times* 5 July 1896: 8.

3 "Now I want to": John Sloan, "Notes," *Chap-Book* 15 (July 1896): 239–40, as qtd. in Terry Ramsaye, *A Million and One Nights* (New York: Simon and Schuster, 1986) 259. Ramsaye erroneously attributes the quote to Herbert S. Stone, publisher of *Chap-Book*.

3 One can safely: Ramsaye 259.

4 They were in: *Newark Daily News* 17 July 1894, as qtd. in Gordon Hendricks, *The Kinetoscope* (New York: The Beginnings of the American Film, 1966) 77.

4 The senator didn't: As qtd. in Hendricks 78.

4 Both men agreed: Ibid.

5 After having a: Ramsaye 256.

5 A spokesman for: As qtd. in Hendricks 78.

5 According to the *Brooklyn*: *Brooklyn Daily Eagle* 30 July 1897: 1.

5 The transcript of: Samuel Smith, *Hansard* 85 (13 July 1900), col. 1549, as qtd. in Katherine Mullin, *James Joyce, Sexuality and Social Purity* (New York: Cambridge University Press, 2003) 147.

5 Surviving stills: Musser, *The Emergence of Cinema* 188.

6 "One of the perils": Dr. John Joseph Munro, "Picture Galleries of Hell," *New York Evening Journal* 28 November 1899: 9, as qtd. in Dan Streible, "Children at the Mutoscope," *CiNéMas* 14.1: 99.

6 The *Journal* accused: Streible 97.

6 The paper also: As qtd. in Streible 99.

6 But as historian: Streible 104.

7 One reporter chose: As qtd. in Streible 98.

7 Streible believes the: Streible 104.

7 "Most of them are evil": "The Five Cent Theatres," *Chicago Daily Tribune* 10 April 1907: 8.

7 The editorial proposed: Ibid.

7 The *Tribune* continued: "Nickel Theatres Crime Breeders," *Chicago Daily Tribune* 13 April 1907: 3.

8 Although they tackled: Garth Jowett, *Film: The Democratic Art* (Boston: Little, Brown and Company, 1976) 77.

8 As Michael G. Aronson explains: "Pennsylvania Movie Censorship in the Progressive Era," *Turning the Century: Essays in Media and Cultural Studies*, ed. Carol A. Stabile (Boulder, CO: Westview Press, 2000) 81.

8 Another proposed ordinance: "Social Workers to Censor Shows," *Chicago Daily Tribune* 3 May 1907: 3.

8 Addams supported: Ibid.

8 She tried to prove: Lee Grieveson, *Policing Cinema: Movies and Censorship in Early-Twentieth-Century America* (Los Angeles: University of California Press, 2004) 68.

9 To prevent the: *Proceedings of the City Council of the City of Chicago*, 4 November 1907: 3052, as qtd. in Grieveson 73.

9 Historian Lee Grieveson regards: Grieveson 72.

9 The constitutionality: *Block v. City of Chicago*, 87 N.E. 1011, 239 Ill. 251 (1909), as qtd. in Edward de Grazia and Roger K. Newman, *Banned Films:*

Movies, Censors and the First Amendment (New York: R.R. Bowker Co., 1982) 180.

9 Block's lawyers also: John Wertheimer, "Mutual Film Reviewed: The Movies, Censorship, and Free Speech in Progressive America," *The American Journal of Legal History* 37.2 (April 1993): 167–68.

9 As John Wertheimer observes: Wertheimer 168.

10 According to Section 1,481: "All Sunday Shows Declared Illegal," *NY Times* 4 December 1907: 1.

10 Judge O'Gorman's decision: Ibid.

10 A spokesman for: "Bingham to Close Sunday Theatres," *NY Times* 5 December 1907: 16.

10 In the "Amusements" section: *NY Times* 6 December 1907: 18.

11 The *New York Times* reported: "Police Get Orders to Enforce Blue Law," *NY Times* 6 December 1907: 3.

11 Their lawyers claimed: "Pictures Shows to Test Blue Law," *NY Times* 7 December 1907: 12.

11 The Duoll ordinance: "One More Sunday Under Blue Laws," *NY Times* 11 December 1907: 1.

11 After a series: *People v. Hemleb* (1908), 127 App. Div 356, 111 N.Y. Supp. 690.

12 William C. Chase of the: "Say Pictures Shows Corrupt Children," *NY Times* 24 December 1908: 4.

12 Another man of: Ibid.

12 Episcopal Bishop David R. Greer: Ibid.

12 Exhibitors also claimed: Ibid.

12 Speaking on behalf: Ibid.

12 "'I do further'": "Picture Shows All Put Out of Business," *NY Times* 25 December 1908: 1.

13 What evidence did: "War on Moving Pictures," *NY Times* 2 June 1907: C1; "Eyes and Moving Picture Shows," *NY Times* 7 October 1907: 8; "Moving Pictures as Helps to Crime," *NY Times* 21 February 1909: SM6.

13 The *New York Times* featured: "Show Made Boy a Burglar," *NY Times* 21 June 1908: 6.

13 In July of 1910: "Turned to Arson by Moving Pictures," *NY Times* 15 July 1910: 16.

13 An even more: "Jersey Boy Slayer Remanded to Jail," *NY Times* 21 July 1909: 14.

13 The annual report: "Shows Schools of Crime," *NY Times* 14 February 1909: 8.

13 Costumes, make-up, and: "Diluted Vaudeville To-Day's Show Menu," *NY Times* 27 December 1908: 1, 2.

13 Alleged violators were: "Mayor Makes War on Sunday Vaudeville," *NY Times* 29 December 1908: 3.

14 "At Hammerstein's Victoria": Ramsaye 479.

14 Collier was the author: John Collier, "Cheap Amusements in Manhattan: Preliminary Report of Investigation," 31 January 1908: 2, 3, as qtd. in Daniel Czitrom, "The Politics of Performance: From Theater Licensing to Movie Censorship in Turn-of-the-Century New York," *American Quarterly* 44.4 (December 1992): 538.

14 Since 1907, its: Czitrom 545.

15 At its first: Frank Miller, *"Censored Hollywood: Sex, Sin and Violence on Screen* (Atlanta: Turner Publishing, Inc., 1994) 25; "Moving Pictures Censored," *NY Times* 26 March 1909: 2.

15 Distributors sent: Nancy J. Rosenbloom, "Between Reform and Regulation: The Struggle Over Censorship in Progressive America, 1909–1922," *Film History* 1.4 (1987): 310.

15 In a letter to: Walter Storey, "Limits of Censorship" (Letter to the Editor), *NY Times* 1 October 1910: 12.

15 There was also: Charles V. Tevis, "Censoring the Five-Cent Drama," *World Today* October 1910, as reprinted in Gerald Mast, ed., *The Movies in Our Midst: Documents in the Cultural History of Film in America* (Chicago: University of Chicago Press, 1982) 66.

15 He is apprehended: Tevis 68.

16 In 1910, *Vogue* editor: Nancy Rosenbloom, "Between Reform and Regulation" 312.

16 She also believed: "Say Motion-Picture Censorship Is Lax," *NY Times* 8 November 1911: 8.

16 The board fired back: "Picture Film Board Attacks Its Critics," *NY Times* 9 November 1911: 8.

16 It stated that the board: "Women Tell of Snub by Censors of Films," *NY Times* 10 November 1911: 18.

17 But one Alderman: "Pass Film Bill with Censorship Clause," *NY Times* 18 December 1912: 9.

17 "Our founders did away": "Gaynor Against Censor," *NY Times* 25 December 1912: 15.

18 The commissioner of: Ford H. MacGregor, "Official Censorship Legislation," *Annals of the American Academy of Political and Social Science* (November, 1926): 172–73.

18 One thing local: Ellis Paxson Oberholtzer, *The Morals of the Movies* (Philadelphia: Penn Publishing Company, 1922) 121–22.

18 It also objected: Mast 192.

18 "Awakened public opinion": Mast 193.

19 According to state law: Federal Motion Picture Commission, *Hearings Before the Committee on Education, House of Representatives, 64th Congress, First Session on H.R. 456* (New York: Arno Press, 1978) 293.

19 In addition, all: *Hearings Before the Committee on Education* 295, 298.

19 To ensure that: "Will Assist Censors," *Gazette and Bulletin* 26 October 1915: 6.

19 In 1915, sixty-four: "Collect Fines for Proscribed Pictures," *New Castle News* 8 January 1916: 5.

19 *"Barroom Scenes, Drinking, and Drunkenness"*: "Hearings Before the Committee on Education" 299–301.

20 "The rough treatment": *Hearings Before the Committee on Education* 301.

21 Among the list: "Ban Is Placed on Indecent Pictures," *New Castle News* 9 December 1916: 7; "Film Safe Crackers Banned," *Indiana Evening Gazette* 21 December 1916: 5.

21 If an applicant: MacGregor 163–74.

21 They describe Pennsylvania: Morris L. Ernst and Pare Lorentz, *Censored: The Private Life of the Movie* (New York: Jonathan Cape and Harrison Smith, 1930) 52.

21 The efforts of: Ramsaye 482.

21 In May of 1922: Benjamin De Casseres, "Virtue Made in Pennsylvania," *NY Times* 21 May 1922: 52.

21 "The board marries": Ibid.

22 The board had: 103 Ohio Laws 399 (1913), as qtd. in Ira H. Carmen, *Movies, Censorship and Law* (Ann Arbor: University of Michigan Press, 1967) 11.

22 That's exactly: "Williams Has Picture Man Under Arrest," *Coschocton Morning Tribune* 8 April 1915: 1.

22 When the Ohio: "Censor Board to Begin to Work" *The Mansfield News* 4 September 1913: 3.

22 "One thing is certain": Ibid.

22 The law violated: *Mutual Film Corp v. Industrial Commission of Ohio*, 236 U.S 230 (1915) *Find Law*, 24 Jan. 2008 <http://laws.findlaw.com/us/236/230.html>.

23 "It can not be": Ibid.

24 The introduction to: *Federal Motion Picture Commission: Hearings Before the Committee on Education on H.R. 456*, 13–19 January 1916 (New York: Arno Press, 1978) 5.

24 The bill contends: *Federal Motion Picture Commission* 5.

24 Also, the Board: Ibid.

24 Consequently, the state: Ibid.

24 "The commission shall": *Federal Motion Picture Commission* 6.

25 He then made: *Federal Motion Picture Commission* 44.

25 In response to: "Oppose Federal Censors," *NY Times* 10 March 1915: 13.

25 "The greatest peril": "Film Land History Told in Exposition," *NY Times* 7 May 1916: E3.

26 Afterwards, the league: "President Leaves on Trip to Omaha," *NY Times* 4 October 1916: 1.

26 "The pictures are": Senator Henry L. Myers, *Congressional Record* 62: 9657, June 29, 1922, as qtd. in *Selected Articles on Censorship of the Theatre and Motion Pictures*, ed. Lamar T. Beman (New York: H. W. Wilson Company, 1931) 176.

26 The Upshaw Bill: MacGregor 165.

27 As Upshaw declared: As qtd. in Steven Alan Carr, *Hollywood and Anti-Semitism: A Cultural History Up to World War II* (New York: Cambridge University Press, 2001) 74.

27 The Bill went as far: MacGregor 15.

27 Despite the verdict: "Arbuckle Banished from Film by Hays," *NY Times* 19 April 1922: 27.

27 According to her: Stephen Michael Shearer, *Patricia Neal: An Unquiet Life* (Lexington, KY: University of Kentucky Press, 2006) 391, n.17.

28 His health deteriorated: "Wallace Red Dies in Fight on Drugs," *NY Times* 19 January 1923: 17.

28 She later denied: "Press Film Star for Taylor Clew," *NY Times* 7 February 1922: 1.

29 It publicly condemned: "Picture Makers to Censor Films," *NY Times* 28 April 1919: 12.

29 NAMPI never followed: Jowett 465.

30 He became the voice: Ruth A. Inglis, *Freedom of the Movies* (Chicago: University of Chicago Press, 1947) 90.

30 Miller explained: "Movie Censor Law Signed by Miller," *NY Times* 15 May 1921: 1.

30 One year later, censorship bills: Jowett 169.

30 "The principle of freedom": "Hays Says Public Censors Will Fail," *NY Times* 25 July 1922: 18.

30 Hays's plan: Ibid.

31 To test the: Inglis 104–05.

32 As Inglis: Inglis 113.

32 In January of 1929: Moley 66–67.

32 As for the: Moley 67.

32 The transition to sound: Ibid.

32 The Vitagraph Company tried: "Will Censor Vitaphone," *NY Times* 1 July 1928: 20.

33 The state supreme court: "Upholds Censorship of 'Talking' Movies," *NY Times* 5 February 1929: 14.

33 When Thaw's wife: "Features of Harry K. Thaw Trial," *Chicago Daily Tribune* 13 April 1907: 2.

34 As his defense attorney: "Thaw's Plea is Unwritten Law," *NY Times* 10 April 1907: 1.

34 The summary of: As qtd. in *"The Unwritten Law: A Thrilling Drama Based on the Thaw-White Case,"* AFI Catalog, <http://www.afi.com/members/catalog/AbbrView.aspx?s=1&Movie=28674&bhcp=1>.

35 In Houston, Texas: "Houston Authorities Object to Picture of Thaw-White Tragedy," *Moving Picture World* 20 April 1907: 102.

35 In Chicago: "Evil Pictures Taken Out," *Chicago Daily Tribune* 6 May 1907: 3.

35 In Superior, Wisconsin: *Moving Picture World* 27 April 1907: 119.

35 Upon discovering: *Moving Picture World* 11 May 1907: 153.

35 Henry Hemleb was arrested: "To Enjoin Police from Interfering with Show," *Brooklyn Standard Union* 3 May 1907.

35 In its review: "Rev. of *The Unwritten Law,*" *Variety* 30 March 1907.

35 *Moving Picture World*: "The Film Manufacturer and the Public," *Moving Picture World* 25 May 1907: 179.

36 "The exhibition of": Ibid.

36 "Mr. Thaw has requested": *Moving Picture World* 25 May 1907: 180.

36 The story was also: *"A Millionaire's Revenge* Tonight," *The Fort Wayne Evening Sentinel* 22 December 1906: 10; *"A Millionaire's Revenge,"* *The Lowell Sun* 10 October 1908: 20; "Academy—*A Millionaire's Revenge,"* *The Washington Post* 14 February 1909: Magazine sect., 3.

36 A production at: *"A Millionaire's Revenge* Actors Jailed," *NY Times* 10 March 1908: 1.

37 In response to news: "A Shame to a Christian Nation," *NY Times* 28 January 1894: 3.

37 The most successful: Musser, *The Emergence of Cinema* 195.

37 According to historian: Musser, *The Emergence of Cinema* 200.

37 On July 6, the: "Bar Fight Pictures to Avoid Race Riots," *NY Times* 6 July 1910: 3.

38 In New Orleans: "Fight Cause of Riots," *Gettysburgh Times* 6 July 1910: 3.

38 African Americans were nearly: "Outbreak at Clarksburgh, W.Va.," *Gettysburgh Times* 6 July 1910: 3; "Third Lynching Is Narrowly Averted," *LA Times* 5 July 1910: 3.

38 The film was banned: "Bar Fight Pictures to Avoid Race Riots" 3.

38 New York City Mayor: Ibid.

38 The film was also: "Fight Pictures on Monday," *NY Times* 12 July 1910: 14.

38 The *Times* also reported: Ibid.

38 William Morris: "Fake Fight Pictures in Theatre," *NY Times* 10 July 1910: 4.

38 The crowd was: "Theatre Wrecked in Fight Pictures Row," *NY Times* 12 July 1910: 14.

38 The following year: "'Jack' Johnson Is Reindicted," *NY Times* 1 May 1913: 5.

39 She also would: Grieveson 139.

39 More recently, an interview: Stephanie Reitz, "Black Boxer's Musings Turned into Memoir," *LA Times* 13 November 2007: E10.

39 This was the second: "Showing of *Birth of a Nation* Canceled," *LA Times* 10 August 2004: E2.

42 As historian V. F. Calverton: V. F. Calverton, "Current History in the World of Fine Arts: Cultural Barometer," *Current History* 49 (1938): 45.

42 Griffith once drew: D. W. Griffith, Letter to the Editor, *The American* 8 April 1915.

42 "The time will come": D. W. Griffith, "Five Dollar 'Movies' Prophesied," *The Editor* 24 April 1915: 409.

42 As Robert Lang observes: Robert Lang, "*The Birth of a Nation*: History, Ideology, Narrative Form," *The Birth of a Nation* (Films in Print series), ed. Lang (New Brunswick, NJ: Rutgers University Press, 1994), 4.

43 In her analysis: Janet Staiger, "*The Birth of a Nation:* Reconsidering Its Reception," Lang 203.

43 The NAACP: Arthur Lenning, "Myth and Fact: The Reception of *The Birth of a Nation*," *Film History* 16.2 (2004): 120.

43 Before the film opened: Thomas Cripps, *Slow Fade to Black* (Cary, NC: Oxford University Press, 1977) 53.

43 "I am hot": "Censors Edit *The Clansman*," *LA Times* 31 January 1915: VII12.

44 "The unexpected opposition": "Despite Council, Clune will Produce Clansman," *LA Times* 6 February 1915: P. II6.

44 The NAACP turned next: Lenning 120.

44 The film was approved: Bosley Crowther, "The Birth of *The Birth of a Nation*," *NY Times* 7 February 1965: 84.

44 *The Birth of a Nation* also: Arthur Link, *Wilson: The Road to the White House* (Princeton, NJ: Princeton University Press, 1947) 502.

44 According to the *New York Times*: "President Resents Negro's Criticism," *NY Times* 13 November 1914: 1.

44 Upon seeing the film: Lenning 122.

45 The NAACP next moved: Lenning 126.

45 On the fiftieth anniversary: Lenning 128.

45 There was a confrontation: Lenning 128–29.

45 The film was banned: Dawn B. Sova, *Forbidden Films* (New York: Checkmark Books, 2001) 48–50.

46 Prior to that time: Kevin Brownlow, *Behind the Mask of Innocence* (New York: Alfred A. Knopf, Inc., 1990) xviii–xix.

46 Their report found: Ruth Rosen, *The Lost Sisterhood: Prostitution in America, 1900–1918* (Baltimore: John Hopkins Press, 1982) 124.

47 Although the law: Mark Thomas Connelly, *The Response to Prostitution in the Progressive Era* (Chapel Hill, NC: University of North Carolina Press, 1980) 129.

47 The film was passed: "The Theatres," *Syracuse Herald* 31 December 1913: 14.

47 In its final analysis: De Grazia and Newman 12–13.

47 The film, which opened: "White Slavery in Films," *The Racine Journal-News* 17 December 1913: 5.

48 In the end: Brownlow 80–82.

48 According to the *New York Times*: "Moving Picture Show in Court," *NY Times* 5 March 1914: 2.

48 "MOTHERS! Can you afford": As reprinted in Nancy F. Cott, *No Small Courage: A History of Women in the United States* (New York: Oxford University Press, 2000) 402.

48 But the film's opening: As qtd. in De Grazia and Newman 187.

49 A New York State: *Message Photo-Play Co. v. Bell*, 166 N.Y.S. 338 (1917).

49 The judge's ruling: *Universal Film Manufacturing Co. v. Bell*, 166 N.Y.S. 344 (1917).

49 Under the law: *Griswold v. Connecticut*, 381 U.S. 479 (1965); De Grazia and Newman 188.

49 According to historian: Brownlow 54.

50 The newly formed: "A Film Controversy," *NY Times*, 18 May 1919: 52.

50 A U.S. Circuit Court: *Silverman v. Gilchrist*, 260 F 564 (1919).

CHAPTER 2

Movies, Morality, and the (Self-)Regulation of the Hollywood Film Industry

51 As chair of: Gerald R. Butters, *Banned in Kansas: Motion Picture Censorship, 1916–1966* (Columbia, Missouri: University of Missouri Press, 2007) 149–50.

51 "It is our job": Ernst and Lorentz 50.

52 She decided the film: Ernst and Lorentz 51.

53 Throughout most of: Gerard B. Donnelly, S. J., "The Bishops Rise Against Hollywood," *America* 25 May 1934: 152, as qtd. in Gregory D. Black, *The Catholic Crusade Against the Movies* (New York: Cambridge University Press, 1997) 22.

55 The PCA then: Geoffrey Shurlock, "The Motion Picture Production Code," *Annals of the American Academy of Political and Social Science* 254 (November 1947): 143.

55 In addition, distributors: Shurlock 144.

55 In 1946, the PCA approved: Ibid.

56 After reading the play: Geoffrey Shurlock, "Memo for the Files," 6 June 1955, *Cat on a Hot Tin Roof* PCA File.

56 In Schary's proposed: Geoffrey Shurlock, "Memo for the Files," 23 June 1955, *Cat on a Hot Tin Roof* PCA File.

56 If an MPPDA member: As qtd. in Moley 83.

57 "In general, the mobility": As qtd. in Moley 245.

57 Breen was also: Gregory D. Black, *Hollywood Censored: Morality Codes, Catholics, and the Movies* (New York: Cambridge University Press, 1994) 38.

57 "Motion pictures, I need": Joseph Breen, Letter to Dr. Arthur E. DeBra, 20 November 1944, MPPDA Correspondence.

58 The Natural Law, which: St. Thomas Aquinas, *Summa Theologia*, Q.94 A.2 <http://www.newadvent.org/summa/2094.htm#2>.

58 In a letter to: Joseph Breen, Letter to Otto Preminger, 29 April 1954, *Carmen Jones* PCA File.

59 As Preminger explained: Otto Preminger, Letter to Joseph Breen, 8 May 1954, *Carmen Jones* PCA File.

59 Consequently, Twentieth-Century Fox: William Michel, Telegram to Frank McCarthy, 9 June 1954, *Carmen Jones* PCA File.

59 Although it was: Joseph Breen, Letter to Eric Johnston, 23 April 1954, *On the Waterfront* PCA File.

59 Wallis was forced: Joseph I. Breen, Letter to Hal Wallis, 25 September 1953, *Cease Fire* PCA File.

59 His studio, Paramount: Barney Balaban, Letter to Eric Johnston, 12 October 1953, *Cease Fire* PCA File.

59 As Wallis explained: Hal Wallis, Letter to Clifford Forster, 23 November 1953, *Cease Fire* PCA File.

60 "Political censor boards": Joseph Breen, Letter to David O. Selznick, 28 April 1939, *Gone with the Wind* PCA File.

60 "The suggestion that Ilsa": Joseph Breen, Letter to Jack Warner, 21 May 1945, *Casablanca* PCA File.

60 "Page 122: We presume": Joseph Breen, Letter to Samuel Goldwyn, 1 April 1945, *Best Years of Our Lives* PCA File.

60 "With regard to": Geoffrey Shurlock, Letter to Walter M. Mirisch, 3 August 1960, *West Side Story* PCA File.

60 "Page 43: In scene 53": Geoffrey Shurlock, Letter to Sam Spiegel, 8 March 1962, *Lawrence of Arabia* PCA File.

60 "Granted that this": Geoffrey Shurlock, Letter to Edward Schellhorn, 16 May 1962, *Tom Jones* PCA File.

62 In 1940, at the age: Lloyd Shearer, "Long Vacation Ended," *NY Times* 27 August 1950: X6.

62 As Hawks explained: Joseph Breen, "Memo for the Files," 19 April 1940, *The Outlaw* PCA File.

62 Breen was optimistic: Joseph Breen, Letter to Howard Hawks, 3 December 1940, *The Outlaw* PCA File.

62 In a five-page letter: Joseph Breen, Letter to Howard Hughes, 27 December 1940, *The Outlaw* PCA File.

63 He informed Hughes: Joseph Breen, Letter to Howard Hughes, 28 March 1941, *The Outlaw* PCA File.

63 "In my more": Joseph Breen, Letter to Will Hays, 29 March 1941, *The Outlaw* PCA File.

63 "In recent months": Joseph Breen, Letter to Will Hays, 28 March 1941, *The Outlaw* PCA File.

64 The notification letter: Carl E. Milliken, Letter to Howard Hughes, 16 May 1941, *The Outlaw* PCA File.

64 The film was: Censorship reports for Kansas (9/12/41), Pennsylvania (4/10/42), and Ohio (11/16/42), *The Outlaw* PCA File.

64 Articles with titles: Dee Lowrance, "Publicity's Lucky Star," *The Montana Standard* 30 August 1942: 26; "Provocative Poser Muffled to Calm Censors," *Oakland Tribune* 2 November 1941: Human Interest: 1; "Will Hollywood's Jane Russell Be a Dark-Haired Harlow?" *Oakland Tribune* 9 February 1941: Human Interest: 1.

64 "Jane, as publicity material": Lowrence 26.

65 Hughes transported via train: "Hughes's Western," *Time* 22 February 1943: 85–86.

65 The film was preceded: Edwin Schallert, "*Outlaw* Dubbed Weird Among Movie Experiences," *LA Times* 8 February 1943: 22.

65 *Time* magazine described: "Hughes's Western" 85–86.

65 The review also described: "Hughes's Western" 86.

65 Syndicated Hollywood columnist: Erskine Johnson, "In Hollywood," *Dunkirk Evening Observer* 16 February 1943: 9.

65 Fellow columnist Robbin Coons: Robbin Coons, "*The Outlaw* Is So Bad That It Might Be Good," *The Big Spring Herald* 1 March 1943: 6.

65 Wood Soanes of: Wood Soanes, "*The Outlaw* Has Premiered at the Geary After Long Battle," *Oakland Tribune* 6 February 1943: 6.

65 *Los Angeles Times*'s Edwin Schallert dubbed: Schallert 22.

65 A letter addressed: Mrs. May E. Miller, Letter to Will Hays, 21 April 1943, *The Outlaw* PCA File.

66 Apparently word about: Geoffrey Shurlock, "Memo for the Files," 7 April 1943, *The Outlaw* PCA File.

66 A complaint was filed: "San Francisco Bans Showing of *The Outlaw*," *The Yuma Daily Sun and Arizona Sentinel* 24 April 1946: 3.

66 The judge in: "Freed of Indecent Film Charge," *NY Times* 18 May 1946: 11; "That Outlaw," *Time* 10 June 1946.

66 "I cannot bring": As qtd. in Gregory D. Black, *The Catholic Crusade* 41.

66 The advertising campaign: "*The Outlaw* Condemned," *NY Times* 22 February 1943: 19.

66 Hughes never provided: F. S. Harmon, "Memo for the Files," 4 March 1943, *The Outlaw* PCA File.

67 "Stupid; no changes could": Ibid.

68 Perhaps the lowest point: James M. Skinner, *The Cross and the Cinema* (Westport, CT: Praeger, 1993) 75–76.

68 Darryl F. Zanuck, Vice President: Darryl F. Zanuck, Letter to Joseph Breen, 2 April 1946, *The Outlaw* PCA File.

68 Zanuck was certainly not: Moley 235–36.

69 Hughes filed a lawsuit: "Howard Hughes Sues on 'Boycott' of Film," *NY Times* 23 April 1946: 27.

69 Hughes's request for: "Film Injunction Denied," *NY Times* 18 June 1946: 28.

69 Surprisingly, Eric Johnston: Peter Dart, "Breaking the Code: A Historical Footnote," *Cinema Journal* 8.1 (Autumn 1968): 41.

69 As historian Ruth Inglis: Inglis 141–42.

69 While Hughes's legal team: A. H. Weiler, "Random Notes on the Film Scene," *NY Times* 19 May 1946: X3.

69 Baltimore Judge E. Paul Mason: Peter Harry Brown and Pat H. Broeske, *Howard Hughes: The Untold Story* (Cambridge, MA: Da Capo, 2004) 208.

70 A judge refused: "Court Won't Lift *The Outlaw* Ban," *NY Times* 24 October 1946: 27.

70 The film opened on: E. J. B. "At the Broadway [rev. of *The Outlaw*]," *NY Times* 12 September 1947: 18.

72 Geoffrey Shurlock rejected each draft: Geoffrey Shurlock, Memo to MGM, 25 March 1955, *Tea and Sympathy* PCA File.

74 "I believe the time has come": "Code Change Pressure Grows," *HR* 29 December 1953: 9.

75 Goldwyn also believed: "Code Change Pressure Grows" 9.

75 In a press release: As qtd. in Walsh 281; "Production Code Liberalized," *HR* 12 December 1956: 1.

75 In 1945, an average: Joel W. Finler, *The Hollywood Story* (New York: Crown Books, 1988) 15.

75 The introduction of: Dorothy Hamilton, *Hollywood's Silent Partner: A History of the Motion Picture Association of America Movie Rating System*, Unpublished Dissertation, U of Kansas, 1999: 19.

77 Both men believed: Black, *Hollywood Censored* 166.

77 "An example in": "Catholic Leaders Call for Battle Against Want in New Social Era," *NY Times* 2 October 1933: 5.

77 Their strategy was: Black, *Catholic Crusade* 22.

78 When the Catholic: "Three Drives on Films Under Way," *NY Times* 23 June 1934: 14; "Protestants Map Clean-Film Drive," *NY Times* 26 June 1934: 22.

78 "A very great": "Cardinal Dougherty Orders Film Boycott Through the Diocese of Philadelphia," *NY Times* 9 June 1934: 3.

78 In his correspondence: As qtd. in Black, *Hollywood Censored* 171.

78 He also suggested: Ibid. For a reevaluation of Breen's anti-Semitism, see Thomas Doherty, *Hollywood's Censor* (New York: Columbia University Press, 2007).

79 In New York, an interfaith: "2,000,000 Pledges Aim of Film Drive," *NY Times* 24 July 1934: 19.

79 Chicago's Michigan Boulevard: "50,000 March in Film War," *NY Times* 28 September 1934: 27.

79 Archbishop John T. McNicholas: "Asks Film Boycott By All Catholics," *NY Times* 9 December 1934: 38.

79 One theologian claimed: As qtd. in Harold C. Gardiner, *Catholic Viewpoint on Censorship* (New York: Doubleday & Co, 1961) 93.

80 The group consisted: Skinner 45.

80 "The character of": "Legion of Decency Condemns Movie," *NY Times* 14 August 1947: 29.

81 "The film is of": "*Rififi* is Condemned," *NY Times* 21 June 1956: 33.

81 "Both in theme": *National Catholic Office for Motion Pictures Film Catalogue 1936–65* (New York: National Catholic Office for Motion Pictures, 1966) 230.

81 "The grossly indecent": *National Catholic Office for Motion Pictures Film Catalogue* 30.

81 "The theme of": "Legion of Decency Hits Film," *NY Times* 12 January 1962: 31.

81 "Brilliance of camera": "Catholic Agency Rejects Blow-up," *NY Times* 28 December 1966: 28.

81 "This science fiction": *1968 Films: A Comprehensive Review of the Year in Motion Pictures* (New York: National Catholic Office for Motion Pictures, 1969) 129.

82 But as historian: Walsh 151.

82 He also accused: Black, *The Catholic Crusade* 49.

82 From his pulpit: Black, *The Catholic Crusade* 50.

82 The Legion issued: "*Duel* Rating Clarified," *NY Times* 10 May 1947: 9.

83 He also added that: Thomas F. Brady, "Hollywood Wire," *NY Times* 20 November 1949: X5.

83 "As the director": Elia Kazan, "Pressure Problem," *NY Times* 21 October 1951: 101.

83 "My picture has": Kazan, "Pressure Problem" 101.

85 Consequently, the *Miracle*: Sova 200–01.

86 "*The Miracle* is a despicable": "Spellman Urges *Miracle* Boycott," *NY Times* 8 January 1951: 1.

86 The Catholic Cinematographic: "*The Miracle*," *Time* 19 February 1951.

86 A review that: Marjorie Heins, "*The Miracle*: Film Censorship for Contemporary Thought," Free Expression Policy Project (online), 28 October 2002 (rev. October 6, 2003) <http://www.fepproject.org/commentaries/themiracle.html>.

87 In fact, in 1949: "The Miracle," *Time*.

87 The film had: Richard H. Parke, "Rossellini Film Is Halted by City: *The Miracle* Held 'Blasphemous'," *NY Times* 24 December 1950: 1.

87 It was certainly: "*Miracle* Banned Throughout City," *NY Times* 25 December 1950: 21.

87 Greenberg considered: "M'Caffrey, Warned of Injunction, Drops *Miracle* Ban in 5 Minutes," *NY Times* 30 December 1950: 1.

87 One week later: "Court, Disallowing *Miracle* Ban, Denies City Has Censorship Powers," *NY Times* 6 December 1951: 1.

88 But the courts: "*Miracle* Picketed by 1,000 Catholics," *NY Times* 15 January 1951: 31; "Threat Made to Bomb St. Patrick's; *Miracle* Theatre Gets New Scare," *NY Times* 28 January 1951: 1; "Bomb Hunt Routs 570 at Theatre Showing *Miracle*, But All Return," *NY Times* 21 January 1951: 1.

88 Martin Quigley fanned: Martin Quigley, Jr. "*The Miracle*: An Outrage," *Motion Picture Herald* 6 January 1951: 1.

88 "In *The Miracle*, men": "Rossellini Appeals to Spellman on Film," *NY Times* 13 January 1951:10.

88 Although the: Joseph I. Breen, Letter to Kenneth Clark, 11 January 1951, *The Miracle* PCA File.

88 When the State: "More Groups Fight a Ban on *Miracle*," *NY Times* 16 January 1951: 34; "Protestants Back Showing of *Miracle*," *NY Times* 30 January 1951: 20; "Right to See a Film Held 'Guaranteed'" *NY Times* 5 February 1951: 23.

89 "In this country": "Text of Regents' Report Banning *Miracle*," *NY Times* 17 February 1951: 20.

89 A *New York Times* editorial: "Decision on *The Miracle*," *NY Times* 17 February 1951: 9.

89 The ban was upheld: *Joseph Burstyn, Inc. v. Wilson*, 104 NYS 2d 740 (1951), as qtd. in "Supreme Court Upholds Ban on *The Miracle*," *The Tablet* 12 May 1951: 1, 19.

89 After losing an appeal: "Court Guarantees Films Free Speech; Ends *Miracle* Ban," *NY Times* 27 May 1952: 1.

89 Valenti arrived in: Peter Bart, "Hollywood: New Riches, New Doubts," *NY Times* 12 December 1966: 1.

90 In September of 1966: "Motion Picture Assn. Code of Self-Regulation," *Variety* 21 September 21 1966: 9.

91 According to Jack Valenti's: "How It All Began" <http://www.mpaa.org/Ratings_HowItAllBegan.asp>

94 More importantly, some: Stephen Farber, *The Movie Ratings Game* (Washington, D.C.: Public Affairs Press, 1972) 17.

94 His staff of five: Vincent Canby, "For Better or Worse, Film Industry Begins Ratings," *NY Times* 1 November 1968: 41.

94 The appeal cases: Stephen Vaughn, *Freedom of Entertainment: Rating the Movies in the Age of New Media* (New York: Cambridge University Press, 2006) 28.

94 The *New York Times* and: "Rating the Movies," *NY Times* 9 October 1968: 46; "A Ratings System for Films," *LA Times* 11 October 1968: B4.

94 By its first birthday: Vincent Canby, "Why Do They Laugh at 'G' Movies?" *NY Times* 2 November 1969: D1.

94 A joint report issued: Charles Champlin, "Churches Challenge Film-Rating System," *LA Angeles Times* 23 May 1970: A8.

95 In regards to: Howard Thompson, "Film Rating System Attacked by Two Major Church Groups," *NY Times* 30 May 1970: 11.

95 One year later: "Churches Drop Support for Movie Ratings," *LA Times* 19 May 1971: 1.

95 Jack Valenti disputed: "Churches Drop Support for Movie Ratings" 11.

95 The change in: Farber 21–22.

95 In addition, the M (Mature) rating: Charles Champlin, "'Mature' Rating Dropped in Movie Code Revision," *LA Times* 28 January 1970: 1.

95 In 1972, Farber chronicled: Farber 21.

96 MGM, which was: *"Ryan's Daughter* to Be Advertised Without Rating," *NY Times* 13 November 1970: 25.

97 At the same time : Farber 77.

97 As part of their: Hamilton 167.

97 In an apologetic letter to Redford: Frank Segers, "Does 'President's' Re-rating to a PG Open the Door for More Film-Lingo Leniency?" *Variety* 3 March 1976: 18.

97 "This judgment applies": As qtd. in Segers 18.

98 However, according to Heffner: Vaughn 48–49.

98 A PG rating for *Poltergeist*: Aljean Harmetz, "Film Rating System Under Fire," *NY Times* 2 June 1982: C21.

99 Aware their film: Aljean Harmetz, *"Indiana Jones* Stirs Ratings Debate, *NY Times* 21 May 1984: C12.

99 Acknowledging there were PG-rated: Vaughn 117.

99 He believed: Harmetz, *"Indiana Jones* Stirs Ratings Debate" C12.

99 Vincent Canby found: Vincent Canby, "As a Rating, PG Says Less Than Meets the Eye," *NY Times* 10 June 1984: H16.

99 A film buyer in: Aljean Harmetz, "Hollywood Plans New Rating to Protect Children Under 13," *NY Times* 20 June 1984: C23.

99 However, Valenti succeeded: Aljean Harmetz, "Some Groups Unhappy with PG-13 Film Rating," *NY Times* 13 August 1984: C20.

100 Consequently, the distributors: Andrew L. Yarrow, "Almodóvar Film's X Rating is Challenged in Lawsuit," *NY Times* 24 May 1990: C14.

100 In his thirteen-page: Glenn Collins, "Judge Upholds X Rating for Almodóvar Film," *NY Times* 20 July 1990: C12.

100 Of course Valenti denied: Ibid.

101 Over thirty Hollywood: David J. Fox, "Valenti Agrees to Talk to Critics of Movie Ratings," *LA Times* 26 July 1990: Calendar sec. 7.

101 In a joint statement: Ari L. Goldman, "Rating the Raters," *NY Times* 6 October 1990: 7.

101 Although the critics: Peter Rainer, "Wispy *Henry & June* All Soul, No Body," *LA Times* 4 October 1990: Calendar sec. 1; Hal Hinson, "*Henry & June*: Hot & Daring, *The Washington Post* 5 October 1990: D01; Jay Carr, "Gorgeous *Henry & June* Fails to Heat Up the Screen" *The Boston Globe* 5 October 1990.

101 The film opened: Jack Mathews, "Sell-out Crowds for *Henry & June*," *LA Times* 8 October 1990: F1.

101 In Bedham, Massachusetts: "First Film Rated NC-17 Is Banned Near Boston," *LA Times* 5 October 1990: 10.

101 Meanwhile, Kaufman: Matthew Gilbert, "Behind the X Appeal Spirit, Sexuality Lured Kaufman Into His Film *Henry & June*," *The Boston Globe* 5 October 1990.

102 Miramax owner Harvey: Richard Corliss, "Murder Gets an R; Bad Language Gets NC-17," *Time* 29 August 1994.

102 "It's a first-amendment issue": As qtd. in Lou Lumenick, "Local Filmmaker May Debut with a NC-17 Rating," *The Record* (Bergen County, NJ) 10 August 1994 <http://www.highbeam.com/doc/1P1-22553066.html>.

102 The appeal was: As qtd. in John Brodi, "*Clerks* Wins Rating Appeal," *Chicago Sun-Times* 13 October 1994: 40.

CHAPTER 3

%@!%!#@#—A Few Choice Words About Bad Language

103 "Still, I declared": Will H. Hays, *The Memoirs of Will H. Hays* (Garden City, New York: Doubleday & Co., 1955) 436.

103 The philosopher believed: Aristotle, *Politics*, trans. Benjamin Jowett (Kitchner, Ontario: Batoche Books, 1999) 179.

104 What constituted profanity: "Profanity on Stage Puzzles Aldermen," *NY Times* 28 February 1911: 6.

104 *Profanity* literally means: Edward Sagarin, *The Anatomy of Dirty Words* (New York: Lyle Stuart, 1962) 126–27.

104 *Blasphemy* expresses: Timothy Jay, *Cursing in America* (Philadelphia: John Benjamins Publishing Co., 1992) 3–4.

104 *Obscenity* is a: Jay 5.

104 The FCC also uses: Ibid.

106 But playwrights Anderson: "Broadway Shows Chastened Before Police Interfere," *NY Times* 25 September 1924: 1.

106 Consequently, no arrests: "Censor *What Price Glory*," *NY Times* 25 September 1925: 21.

106 The profanity was: "Along with the Introduction of Talkies Came Bad Language," *The Literary Digest* 5 March, 1927; 1 October, 2007 <http://www.1920-1930.com/movies/bad-language.html>.

106 *Variety* predicted: "Rev. of *What Price Glory*," *Variety* 1 January 1926.

106 *The Hollywood Spectator* was: "Along with the Introduction of Talkies" 2.

108 The PCA had strong: Joseph Breen, Letter to Harry M. Cohn, 30 January 1936, *Hell-Ship Morgan* PCA File.

108 Schenck wanted to: Will Hays, Letter to Nicholas Schenck, 28 October 1935, *Hell-Ship Morgan PCA File.*

108 Hays also listed: Ibid.

109 Colonel Jason Joy was: Jason S. Joy, Letter to Samuel Goldwyn, 18 November 1931, *Arrowsmith* PCA File.

109 Joy and Will Hays eventually: James Wingate, Letter to Will H. Hays, 16 December 1932, *Cavalcade* PCA File; James Wingate, "Memo for the Files," 15 January 1933, *Cavalcade* PCA File.

109 After seeing the film: James Wingate, Letter to Will H. Hays, 16 December 1932, *Cavalcade* PCA File.

110 While Hays believed the word *hell*: Will Hays, Letter to James Wingate, 20 December 1932, *Cavalcade* PCA File.

110 "Each time this": Ibid.

110 "Here again it": Will H. Hays, Letter to James Wingate, 6 January 1933, *Cavalcade* PCA File.

111 "David seems to think": Joseph Breen, Letter to Will Hays, 21 October 1939, *Gone with the Wind* PCA File.

111 "It is my contention": David O. Selznick, Letter to Will Hays, 20 October 1939, reprinted in *Memo from David O. Selznick*, ed. Rudy Behlmer (New York: Viking Press, 1972) 222.

111 The PCA justified: Will Hays, Letter to Joseph Breen, 28 October 1937, *The Gorgeous Hussy* PCA File.

112 But apparently everyone: "News of the Screen," *NY Times* 5 January 1938: 17.

112 In a chapter: Olga J. Martin, *Hollywood's Movie Commandments* (New York: H. W. Wilson, Co., 1937) 218–20.

113 Forbidden Words/Expressions/Sounds [Table B]: Sources: J. Louis Kuethe, "Johns Hopkins Jargon," *American Speech* Vol. 7, No. 5 (June 1932), 327–38; Jonathan Green, *Cassell's Dictionary of Slang* (London: Weidenfeld & Nicolson, 2005).

114 Upon hearing the news: Joseph Kesselring, *Arsenic and Old Lace* (New York: Dramatists Play Service, 1995) 91. There is an asterisk next to the line "Your mother came to us as a cook—and you were born about three months afterwards." The note at the bottom reads: "Directors who may wish to modify the situation mentioned by Abby may add the following text after the words 'three months afterward': . . . 'her poor husband had just died, and she was such,' etc. Then add, 'So we adopted the baby and brought him up ourselves.' Mortimer's line 'I'm a bastard' will, in this case, be omitted."

114 When Columbia Pictures studio chief: Joseph I. Breen, Letter to Harry Cohn, 24 January 1941, *Arsenic and Old Lace* PCA File.

115 The change did not go: "Rev. of *Arsenic and Old Lace*," *HR* 1 September 1944: 3.

115 An editorial in: As qtd. in *New York Herald Tribune* 29 November 1942.

115 While the word might: Ibid.

115 On the floor of: "It's Just a Difference in U.S., British Languages," *The Hammond Times* 10 December 1942: 16.

116 Furthermore, there is: "Memorandum in Opposition to Production Code Administration's Ruling That Certain Deletions Be Made from the Dialogue of the Photoplay," n.d., *In Which We Serve* PCA File.

116 As evidence, their written: Ibid.

116 "The function of the": "Report of the Appeals Board Regarding the United Artists Appeal," n.d., *In Which We Serve* PCA File.

116 In appealing the decision: "Outline of Argument in Support of Appeal by the March of Time from the Rule of the Production Code Administration Order the deletions from the film *We Are the Marines*," 17 December 1942, *We Are the Marines* PCA File.

117 More specifically, in regards: Ibid.

117 "*Bastard* as a word": Ibid.

118 Seven months later: Michael Balcon, Wire to Production Code Administration, 9 January 1950, *The Blue Lamp* PCA File.

118 The film received a seal: "Massachusetts Territory Report," n.d., *The Blue Lamp* PCA File.

118 The play was first submitted: Will H. Hays, Letter to Joseph M. Schenck, 18 July 1935, *Saint Joan* PCA File.

118 When the play was submitted again: Joseph Breen, Letter to Gabriel Pascal, 19 March 1943, *Saint Joan* PCA File.

120 Mickey Mouse's motorcycle: Karl F. Cohen, *Forbidden Animation: Censored Cartoons and Blacklisted Animators in America* (Jefferson, NC: McFarland, 1997) 24.

121 Among the illustrations: "Hollywood Censors Its Animated Cartoons," *Look* 17 January 1939: 19.

121 According to the *New York Times*: "Bronx Cheer and Razzberry Demonstrated for Benefit of Court in Murder Trial," *NY Times* 19 November 1933: E6.

121 A second demonstration: Ibid.

121 As for the judge: Ibid.

121 The judge stated that he: "Bronx Cheer Okeyed By New York Judge," *Oshkosh Daily Northwestern* 2 November 1939: 2.

121 The *New York Times* reported: Debate Fails to Decide If U.S. Got 'Bronx Cheer'," *NY Times* 2 August 1936: S1, S3.

121 One of the cartoon's writers: Cohen 24–25.

123 The producers of both: Joseph Breen, Letter to Dore Schary, 20 September 1954, *Blackboard Jungle* PCA File; Joseph Breen, Letter to Samuel Goldwyn, 1 October 1954, *Guys and Dolls* PCA File.

125 The real issue is: Joseph Breen, Letter to Otto Preminger, 2 January 1953, *The Moon is Blue* PCA File.

125 According to Jack Vizzard: Jack Vizzard, *See No Evil: Life of a Hollywood Censor* (New York: Simon & Schuster, 1970) 153.

126 "Not only as": Otto Preminger, Letter to Joseph Breen, 13 April 1953, *The Moon Is Blue* PCA File.

126 "On the contrary": Ibid.

126 Preminger, who had: "Filming *The Moon Is Blue* in Both English and German," *NY Times* 22 February 1953: X5.

126 The director also: "Preminger's 'Hypocrisy in Antiquated' Code's *Blue* Nix; 'Let Public Decide,'" *Variety* 10 June 1953: 3.

127 It gave the film: PCA Report, 2 July 1953, *The Moon Is Blue* PCA File.

127 "The picture is": "Condemned Movie Overrides Moral Law, Cardinal Asserts," n.d., *The Moon Is Blue* PCA File.

127 Meanwhile, out on: "Cardinal McIntyre Directly Asks L.A. Catholics Not to See *Moon*," *Variety* 6 July 1955: 1, 4.

127 Critic Richard Hayes: "*Moon Is Blue*; Face is Red," *Variety* 14 July 1953.

127 There were attempts: "St Paul Tries to Ban *Moon* As 'Don't Blush Easy' Critic Attacks Pic He Hasn't Seen," *Weekly Variety* 22 July 1953; "St. Paul Critic Stirs City Dads Into Drive to Ban Blue, Altho Nobody's Seen Film," *Variety* 20 July 1953: 1, 7.

128 As for Diehl: "St. Paul City Fathers, After Peek at *Moon*, Drop Move to Ban Film; Paper Suspicious," *Variety* 27 July 27 1953.

128 He limited admission: "Hullabaloo Over *Moon Is Blue*," *Life* 13 July 1953: 71, 73–74.

128 They told Chief Brown: "*Moon*, Cab Scene Cut, Plays Alabam'; St. Paul Solons Hold Nose, O.K. It," *Weekly Variety* 29 July 1953: 4, 25.

128 When asked about his: Ibid.

128 When the public: "*Moon* Furor Creates an Alabama Censor Board,'" *Weekly Variety* 5 August 1953: 46.

128 Meanwhile, as the: As qtd. in Sova 211.

129 But Holmby Productions won: As qtd. in De Grazia and Newman 240.

129 The board appealed: *Holmby Productions v. Vaughn*, 350 U.S. 970 (1955); "Film Censor Law in Kansas Killed," *NY Times* 25 October 1955: 26.

129 "Every believer in freedom": "Kansas to Halt Film Censorship," *NY Times* 8 April 1955: 16.

130 "It's not only the *look*": As qtd. in Richard Griffith, *Anatomy of a Motion Picture* (New York: St. Martin's Press, 1959) 25–26.

131 As for his performance: Timothy Hoff, "*Anatomy of a Murder*," *Legal Studies Forum* 24, Nos. 3 & 4 (2000), 665, 2 January 2007 <http://tarlton.law .utexas.edu/lpop/etext/lsf/hoff24.htm>.

131 When Otto Preminger: Geoffrey Shurlock, Letter to Otto Preminger, 8 December 1958, *Anatomy of a Murder* PCA File.

132 He also complained: Ibid.

132 "He does not": Otto Preminger, Letter to Geoffrey Shurlock, 28 April 1959, *Anatomy of a Murder* PCA File.

132 He also reminded: Geoffrey Shurlock, Letter to Otto Preminger, 30 April 1959, *Anatomy of a Murder* PCA File.

132 Echoing Shurlock's: "Rev. of *Anatomy of a Murder*," *Variety* 1 July 1959.

132 Perhaps even more: Ibid.

132 An editorial in the: "Too Much Anatomy," *The Richmond News Ledger* 5 August 1959: 10.

133 The board, composed of: "Ban on *Anatomy* in Chicago Fought," *NY Times* 4 July 1959: 9.

133 "Taken as a whole": "Judge Voids Ban on *Anatomy* Film," *NY Times* 9 July 1959: 24.

133 As authors: De Grazia and Newman 258–59.

134 Preminger's contract: "Writ to Keep Film Off TV Refused," *NY Times* 14 October 1965: 53.

134 During the trial: "'We Live By Contract, Not Custom' Sez Preminger at 'Anti-TV' Trial," *Variety* 1 December 1965: 29.

134 Later that same year: "Preminger Gets No-Cut Pact for *Golden Arm* on TV," *NY Times* 28 December 1966: 75.

135 He understands: Howard Taubman, "Rinse Its Mouth," *NY Times* 24 September 1961: X1.

135 The filmmaker, Shirley Clarke: "The First Statement of the New American Cinema Group," *Film Culture Reader*, ed. P. Adams Sitney (New York: Praeger, 1970) 80.

136 Under Section 122: "Court Upsets State's Obscenity Ban on *Connection*," *NY Times* 3 July 1962: 15.

136 The decision stated: Ibid.

137 Before the third show: William Specht, "Court Halts Showing of *The Connection*," *Film Daily* 4 October 1962: 1, 7.

137 The case was heard: "*The Connection* Ruled Not Obscene by Appeals Court," *NY Times* 2 November 1962: 33.

137 "The controversy is over": Stanley Kauffman, "What Connection?" *New Republic* 27 October 1962.

138 The effects of: A. D. Murphy, "Process of Elimination Code Authority Dilemma," *Variety* 24 May 1968: 1.

138 The PCA tried to excise: Morris V. Murphy, "Memo to the File," 29 February 1968, *Rosemary's Baby* PCA File.

139   "As discussed over": Geoffrey Shurlock, Letter to Jack Warner, 20 March 1963, *Who's Afraid of Virginia Woolf?* PCA file.

139   Five days later: Geoffrey Shurlock, Letter to Jack Warner, 26 March 1963, *Who's Afraid of Virginia Woolf?* PCA File.

139   As the playwright explains: As qtd. in Mel Gussow, *Edward Albee: A Singular Journey* (New York: Simon & Schuster, 1999) 153.

140   The title, a variation: Ibid.

140   Ironically, the song: "Title of Albee's Work Sung to Different Tune," *NY Times* 15 October 1962: 33.

140   "Could Edward Albee's play": "Pulitzer Prizes, Minus One," *NY Times* 7 May 1963: 42.

140   The reviews for Albee's: As qtd. in Gussow 179.

140   Once again, Geoffrey Shurlock: Geoffrey Shurlock, Letter to Jack Warner, 27 May 1966, *Virginia Woolf* PCA File.

141   "1. The film is not designed": Press Release, Motion Picture Association of America, n.d., *Virginia Woolf* Production PCA File. According to Frank Miller, the press release was issued on June 10, 1966. See Miller 203.

141   "The play was undoubtedly": "Jack Warner Remarks Re: Woolf," *Variety* 1 May 1955.

CHAPTER 4

Guns, Gangs, and Random Acts of Ultra-Violence

144   "*Racket*: An apparently:" "Well, Pupils, Tell Us What Is a 'Racket'?" *Chicago Daily Tribune* 22 September 1928: 1.

144   In the same month: James P. Kirby, "Racketeering—The New 'Big Business,'" *Appleton Post-Crescent* 11 September 1928: 18.

144   His first article: Ibid.

144   According to statistics: James P. Kirby, "215 Gang Murders in Two Years, Not One Conviction, Is Chicago's Crime Record," *The Olean Evening Times* 7 September 1928: 15.

145   The censor boards in: Brownlow 211.

145   Cormack's play: "Chicago Bars The Racket," *NY Times* 5 January 1928: 33; Brownlow 210.

146   In 1931, two eighteen-year-olds: "Young Gunmen Lay Crimes to Movies," *NY Times* 4 August 1931: 4.

146   "The moving picture industry": Ibid.

146   While sixteen-year-old: "Boy Kills Chum, 12, Enacting Gang Film," *NY Times* 24 June 1931: 22.

147   The mayor of East Orange: "Hays Calls Gang Film a Crime Deterrent," *NY Times* 27 June 1931: 23.

147   Hays also added: Ibid.

147 Italian-American organizations: "Resents Depicting Italians as Gunmen," *NY Times* 19 April 1931: 23; Will Hays, Letter to Generoso Pope, 29 June 1931, *Scarface* PCA file.

147 The Patrolmen's Benevolent: "Policemen Ask Ban on Movies Glorifying Gangsters' Lives," *NY Times* 13 May 1931: 52.

147 The author claims: Henry James Forman, *Our Movie Made Children* (New York: Macmillan Company, 1933) 203–4, 212.

147 Testifying on behalf: "Movies Stir Row at Crime Hearing," *NY Times* 25 November 1933: 32.

148 According to historian: Stephen Prince, *Classical Film Violence* (New Brunswick, NJ: Rutgers University Press, 2003) 94.

148 However, the same: Prince 91.

148 What gives *The Public Enemy*: Prince 96.

148 In his report: August Vollmer, Letter to Will H. Hays, 20 April 1931, *The Public Enemy* PCA File.

149 In the summer: "Rochester Theatre Heads See Humor in Gang Film Ban," *Syracuse Herald* 6 July 1931: 4; Thomas Doherty, *Pre-Code Hollywood: Sex, Immorality and Insurrection in American Cinema, 1930–1934* (New York: Columbia University Press, 1999) 150.

149 In Evanston, Illinois: "Evanston Banishes Gangster Pictures," *The News-Palladium* 17 June 1931: 6.

149 When Colonel Jason Joy: Jason Joy, Letter to E. B. Derr, 4 June 1931, *Scarface* PCA File.

149 "In all my nine years": Ibid. Jason Joy, "Memo to the Files," 20 August 1931, *Scarface* PCA File.

149 Upon viewing: Jason Joy, "Memo to the Files," 20 August 1931, *Scarface* PCA File.

150 In his report: Jason Joy, "Memo to the Files," 20 September 1931, *Scarface* PCA File.

150 He also believed: Jason Joy, Letter to Will Hays, 20 September 1931, *Scarface* PCA File.

151 Statistically, juvenile crime: James Gilbert, *A Cycle of Outrage: America's Reaction to the Juvenile Delinquent in the 1950s* (New York: Oxford University Press, 1986) 69–71.

152 However, the report: "Comic Books and Juvenile Delinquency," Interim Report of the Committee on the Judiciary, 1954 <http://www.geocities.com/Athens/8580.kefauver.html>

152 MGM's vice president: "Impact of Movies on Youth Argued," *NY Times* 17 June 1955: 24.

153 Unaware of the incident: Thomas M. Pryor, "Hollywood Test," *NY Times* 26 June 1955: X5.

153 Although the executives: Ibid.

153 When the Production Code: Joseph Breen, Letter to Dore Schary, 20 September 1954, *Blackboard Jungle* PCA File.

153 The susequent memos: Joseph Breen, Letter to Dore Schary, 22 October 1954, *Blackboard Jungle* PCA File.

154 "In the face": "Confidential," 27 April 1955, *Blackboard Jungle* PCA File.

154 Censor boards in: "*Blackboard Jungle* Banned," *NY Times* 29 March 1955: 33.

154 The film was: "2 Reports Clear School in Bronx," *NY Times* 17 July 1955: 39.

154 The Legion of Decency: Legion of Decency Report, *Blackboard Jungle* PCA File.

154 In what he: Thomas M. Pryor, "U.S. Film Dropped at Fete in Venice," *NY Times* 27 August 1955: 9.

154 Arthur Loew, President of: Ibid.

155 The State Department: "Mrs. Luce Denies Censoring Movie," *NY Times* 3 September 1955: 8.

155 Still, *New York Times* critic: Bosley Crowther, "Festival Frustration," *NY Times* 4 September 1955: X1.

155 Crowther called *The Blackboard Jungle*: Bosley Crowther, "The Exception or the Rule?" *NY Times* 27 March 1955: X1.

155 For him, such: Ibid.

155 During their two-year: John Toland, "Sad Ballad of the Real Bonnie and Clyde," *NY Times* 8 February 1968: 29.

156 Apparently the *New York Times*'s: Bosley Crowther, "Shoot-em-up Film Opens World Fete," *NY Times* 7 August 1967: 32.

156 One week later: Bosley Crowther, "Screen: *Bonnie and Clyde* Arrives," *NY Times* 14 August 1967: 36.

156 While he was: Ibid.

156 *Time* magazine accused: "Low-Down Hoedown," *Time* 25 August 1967: 13.

156 In his review: Page Cook, Rev. of *Bonnie and Clyde, Films in Review* 18.8 (October 1967): 504.

157 *Newsweek*'s Joe Morgenstern: Joseph Morgenstern, "Two or a Tommy Gun," *Newsweek* 21 August 1967: 65.

157 His second review: Joseph Morgenstern, "The Thin Red Line," *Newsweek* 28 August 1967: 82.

157 Although he still: Ibid.

157 "This is a movie": As qtd. in David Newman, "What's It Really About?" *Arthur Penn's Bonnie and Clyde*, ed. Lester D. Friedman (New York: Cambridge University Press, 2000) 40.

157 If *Bonnie and Clyde*: Pauline Kael, Rev. of *Bonnie and Clyde, The New Yorker* 21 October 1967: 147.

157 Kael compared: Kael, Rev. of *Bonnie and Clyde* 154.

158 The film's humor: William J. Free, "Aesthetic and Moral Value in *Bonnie and Clyde*," *Focus on* Bonnie and Clyde (Englewood Cliffs, NJ: Prentice-Hall, 1973) 101.

158 Kael also recognized: Kael, Rev. of *Bonnie and Clyde* 160.

158 *Time* was now: "The Shock of Freedom in Films," *Time* 8 December 1967.

159 As Stephen Prince: Stephen Prince, "The Hemorrhaging of American Cinema," Friedman 135.

159 As the studio's publicity: Patrick Goldstein, "Bonnie & Clyde & Joe & Pauline," *LA Times* 25 August 1997: F4.

160 After the initial: Penelope Gilliat, Rev. of *Bonnie and Clyde*, *The New Yorker* 18 August 1967.

160 Although costume designer: Judy Klemesrud, "It's the Great Hat Revival and the Young are Setting the Pace," *NY Times* 2 May 1968: 50.

160 In January of 1968: "Fashion That Rocked the World," *Life* 12 January 1968.

160 In March of 1968: "5 Teen-agers Held in '30's Bank Caper," *NY Times* 23 March 1968: 25.

160 An editorial in : "Bonnie and Clyde Clowns," *The Bridgeport Post* 28 March 1968: 28.

160 Fisher explained: Nancy Fisher, Letter to the Editor, *NY Times* 21 April 1968: SM21.

160 "There will be posters": Ibid.

161 "If I'm so bloody": As qtd. in Laurent Bouzereau, *Ultraviolent Movies: From Sam Peckinpah to Quentin Tarantino* (New York: Citadel Press, 2000) 131.

161 Innocent men: "Press Violent About Film's Violence; Prod Sam Peckinpah Following *Bunch*," *Variety* 24 June 1969: 15.

162 But audience demand: Thomas Schatz, *Hollywood Genres* (New York: McGraw-Hill, 1981) 58.

162 So in the 1950s: Schatz 59.

163 "Using a combination": "Man and Myth," *Time* 20 June 1969.

163 *Newsweek*'s Joseph Morgenstern: Joseph Morgenstern, "The Bloody Bunch," *Newsweek* 14 July 1969: 85.

163 "Borrowing a device": Vincent Canby, "Violence and Beauty in *The Wild Bunch*," *NY Times* 26 July 1969: 45.

163 After the film: Wayne Warga, "*The Wild Bunch*'s Fight Against the Censor's Scissors," *LA Times* 11 September 1969: E1.

164 In a 1969 interview: As qtd. in Paul Schrader, "Sam Peckinpah Going to Mexico," *Doing It Right: The Best Criticism of "The Wild Bunch*," ed. Michael Bliss (Carbondale, IL: Southern Illinois University, 1994) 22.

164 When Vincent Canby: Vincent Canby, "Which Version Did *You* See?" *NY Times*, 20 July 1969: D1, 7.

164 The film was subsequently: Warga E1.

165 "Peckinpah's argument": Charles Champlin, "Violence Runs Rampant in *The Wild Bunch*," *LA Times* 15 June 1969: O1.

165 Peckinpah chose to: "Press Violent About Film's Violence; Prod Sam Peckinpah Following *Bunch*" 15.

165 "At 19, I am a member": Tracy Hotchner, Letter to the Editor, *NY Times*, 20 July 1969: D16.

166 "Not at any": Hotchner 21.

167 Burgess explained he: Anthony Burgess, "*A Clockwork Orange*: The Missing Chapter," *Rolling Stone* 26 March 1987: 74–75.

167 According to Burgess: Burgess, "*A Clockwork Orange*: The Missing Chapter" 75.

167 As he explained: James Christopher, "Blood," *Time Out* 6 December 1989: 19.

167 He claims writing: Vincent Lobrutto, *Stanley Kubrick: A Biography* (New York: Da Capo Press, 1999) 336.

167 The veracity of: John Cornwell, "Anthony Burgess: His Dark Materials," *The Sunday Times* 13 March 2005; Richard Brooks, "*Clockwork Orange* Author Invented 'Fantasy Life of Lies,'" *The Sunday Times* 7 April 2002; Roger Lewis, *Anthony Burgess: A Biography* (New York: St. Martin's Press, 2004) 304.

168 Although a book: As qtd. in Lewis 143.

168 He feared any: Anthony Lewis London, "I Love England, But I Will No Longer Live There," *NY Times* 3 November 1968: 52.

168 "By definition a human": Burgess, "*A Clockwork Orange*: The Missing Chapter" 75.

169 Ebert dismissed the film: Roger Ebert, rev. of *A Clockwork Orange*, *Chicago Sun-Times* 11 February 1972 <http://rogerebert.suntimes.com/apps/pbcs .dll/article?AID=/19720211/REVIEWS/202110301/1023>.

169 Kael accused Kubrick: Pauline Kael, "*A Clockwork Orange*: Stanley Strangelove," *New Yorker* 1 January 1972: 50–53.

169 Similarly, David Denby accused: David Denby, "Pop Nihilism at the Movies," *Atlantic Monthly* 229.3 (March 1972): 102.

169 McDowell claimed: Tom Burke, "Malcolm McDowell: The Liberals, They Hate Clockwork," *NY Times* 30 January 1972: D13.

169 "An alert liberal": Fred M. Hechinger, "A Liberal Fights Back," *NY Times* 13 February 1972: D1.

169 Kubrick was understandably: Stanley Kubrick, "Now Kubrick Fights Back," *NY Times* 27 February 1971: D1.

169 Ironically, it wasn't: "Kubrick Subs 30 Seconds of Film and *Clockwork* Sheds X, Gets R," *Variety* 25 August 1972: 1, 8.

170 "Some will fault": As qtd. in Stanley Kubrick, "A Newspaper Says No to *Orange*," *NY Times* 23 April 1971: D11.

170 "*The Detroit News*": Kubrick, "A Newspaper Says No to *Orange*" D11, 25.

170 Stephen Murphy, secretary of the BBFC: Julian Petley, "Clockwork Crimes," *Index on Censorship* 6 (1995): 48.

171 "There is a new film": As qtd. in Christian Bugge, "The Clockwork Controversy," The Kubrick Site <http://www.visual-memory.co.uk/amk/doc/0012.html>.

171 Maurice Edelman, Labour MP: As qtd. in Alexander Walker, "The Winding Road to *A Clockwork Orange*," *Evening Standard* 1 March 2000 <http://www.highbeam.com/doc/1P2-5266230.html>.

171 A Dutch tourist: Dick Polman, "Banned in Britain—Kubrick Refuses to Allow *A Clockwork Orange* to Be Shown," *Chicago Tribune* 14 November 1993: 26.

171 A sixteen-year-old boy: Bugge, "The *Clockwork* Controversy."

171 James Palmer, sixteen: Ibid.

171 But Palmer had never: Ibid.

172 "Because *A Clockwork Orange* played": As qtd. in James Howard, "UK Clock Ticks Again for Kubrick's *Orange*," The Kubrick Site <http://www.visual-memory.co.uk/amk/doc/0088.html>.

172 Giles had not seen: James Landale, "Cinema Breached Kubrick Copyright," *The Times* 24 March 1993.

172 Julian Senior, Vice President: James Howard, "UK Clock Ticks Again for Kubrick's *Orange*."

172 As esteemed film critic: Walker, "The Winding Road to *A Clockwork Orange*."

172 By then *Variety*: "Snuff (Sex Murders) Film Now Thought Hoax from Argentina," *Weekly Variety* 17 December 1975: 4.

173 One film was "reported": "FBI Probes Reports of Mutilation, Death Films," *LA Times* 2 October 1975: 2.

174 Employing the same: Eithne Johnson and Eric Schaefer, "Soft Core/Hard Gore: *Snuff* as a Crisis in Meaning," *Journal of Film and Video* Vol. 45 Nos. 2–3 (Summer/Fall 1993), 43.

174 He said he could: "Snuff (Sex Murders) Film" 4.

174 Then again, Shackleton: "*Snuff*: It Just Might Be Nothing But a P.R. Hoax," *Daily Variety* 17 December 1975.

174 The board demanded: "*Snuff* Okay Refused by Maryland Censors," *Box Office* 1 March 1976.

175 "I'd have to see": "*Snuff* Spawns More Controversy in Several Eastern Localities," *Box Office* 15 March 1976.

175 Judge Cole also offered: "Maryland Bans *Snuff* Based on Its 'Psychotic Violence,'" *Weekly Variety* 7 April 1976.

175 *Snuff* was slated: Ibid.

175 Eleanor Snow, director: Jeffrey Perlman and George Getze, "Judge Bans *Snuff* Movie in County," *LA Times* (OC Edition) 24 March 1976: A1.

175 Two theatres in neighboring: "Hearing Scheduled on X-rated Movie," *LA Times* 22 March 1976: A7.

175 Feminists were credited: "Femmes Snuff out *Snuff* in Frisco," *Variety* 23 November 1977.

175 They picketed: "Paper Deplores Film Gore; Lauds Pickets at *Snuff*," *Boxoffice* 1 March 1976.

176 When feminists assembled: "*Snuff* Spawns More Controversy . . ."

176 A spokesman for: "Adult Film Association Pickets *Snuff*," *Hollywood Reporter* 18 March 1976.

176 After conducting: "Victim in *Snuff* Says She Prefers Anonymity," *Boxoffice* 22 March 1976.

176 The fact it was: "Feminist Leaders Join Anti-Smut Campaign Despite Reservations," *NY Times* 2 July 1977: 31; "Record Albums Come Under Attack for Portraying Crimes on Women," *NY Times* 1 January 1977: 28.

177 They were opposed: "Feminists Leaders Join . . . ."

179 On February 12, 1979: "The Flick of Violence," *Time* 19 March 1979.

179 On that same evening: "A Street-Gang Movie Called *The Warriors* Triggers a Puzzling, Tragic Wave of Audience Violence and Death," *People* 12 March 1979: 38.

179 Three days later: Sandra Hochel, "Using Court Cases on Freedom of Speech Issues in the College Classroom," *The National Forensic Journal*, VIII (Fall, 1990): 206.

179 Another incident: "Ads Resumed for a Gang Movie After Sporadic Violence at Theatres," *NY Times* 23 February 1979: A18.

179 Confrontations between: "2 Deaths Linked to Showings of Gang War Movie," *Chronicle-Telegram* 18 February 1979: B-8.

179 After the February 12th: "Exhibs Report Par Request for Added *Warriors* Security," *Daily Variety* 15 February 1979.

179 According to Frank Mancuso: "Par Cancels *Warriors* Ads, Tells Exhibs They Can Halt Film If Violence Feared," *Variety* 20 February 1979: 1.

180 The following week: "Trailer Rougher Than *Warriors*?" *Variety* 28 February 1979.

180 The article also: Ibid.

180 Dr. Ernest H. Smith: Mary Beth Murrill, "Gang War Film Recall Requested," *L.A. Herald-Examiner* 17 February 1979.

180 A Bronx-based: "*Warriors* Spurs Violence: Protestors," *Chronicle-Telegram* 18 February 1979: B-8.

180 "I tried to do": Dave Marsh, "*The Warriors*: Murders Baffle Director Walter Hill," *Rolling Stone* 5 April 1979: 40.

180 One of the few: Pauline Kael, "Rumbling," *New Yorker* 5 March 1979: 108.

180 Kael likened Hill: Kael 111.

181 She saw *The Warriors*: Kael 114.

181 The Superior Court: *William V. Yakubowicz v. Paramount Pictures Corporation*, 404 Mass. 624 (1989). See <http://masscases.com/cases/sjc/404/404mass624.html>.

181 Over the weekend: Louise Sweeney, "Can Screen Violence 'Inspire' the Masses?" *Chronicle-Telegram* 11 May 1979: 6.

181 The incident occurred: Elaine Wood and Irene Chang, "Rampage in Westwood: Hundreds Loot Stores Riot," *LA Times* 10 March 1991: 1.

182 Four months later: "An Anti-gang Movie Opens to Violence," *NY Times* 14 July 1991: 10.

183 As Kimberly Owczarski: Kimberly A. Owczarski, "Articulating the Violence Debate: *True Lies*, *Natural Born Killers*, and the Terms of 'Cultural Contamination'," *CineAction* 1 January 2006 <http://www.highbeam.com/doc/1G1-141588744.html>.

183 Owczarski finds it ironic: Owczarski, Ibid.

183 When Stone submitted: "Stone's Cuts Produced Kinder, Gentler Killers," *Hollywood Reporter* 1 September 1994.

183 Oliver Stone faced: James Ulmer, "Stone Answers *Killers* Critics," *Hollywood Reporter* 12 September 1994: 4.

183 When asked if he believed: Ibid.

184 On October 4, 1994: Sharon Waxman, "Paris Reels from Cinema Verite," *The Washington Post* 8 October 1994: C04; Isabelle Monnin, "The Big Extract," *Nouvel Observateur*, as reprinted in *The Guardian* 10 October 1998: 012.

184 Herbert, dubbed 'Veronique la Diabolique': Stephen Moss, "Real Lives," *The Guardian* 7 October 1998: T4.

184 Herbert, who was: Karen Boyle, "What's Natural About Killing? "Gender, Copycat Violence and *Natural Born Killers*," *Journal of Gender Studies* 10.3. (2001): 313.

185 "Oh, yeah, that's pushing it": Michael Shnayerson, "Natural Born Opponents," *Vanity Fair* (July 1996): 142.

185 In 2001, a Louisiana: "Filmmaker Cleared in Shooting Trial," *Times-Picayune* 13 March 2001: 1.

185 "But the issue is": As qtd. in Shnayerson 143–44.

186 Harris and Klebold: Kevin Simpson, Ann Schrader, Howard Pankratz, and Kieran Nicholson, "Inside Teen Killers' Minds," *Denver Post* 7 July 2006: 1.

186 The murder of: Shannan Bowen, "Jacksonville Pair Found Guilty in Roommate's Death," *The Times-Union* 15 July 2006 <http://www.jacksonville.com/tu-online/stories/071506/met_22335790.shtml>.

186 Wondering what it: Pat Clarke, "'Freddy Krueger' Copycat Found Guilty of Murder," *Independent.ie* 17 March 2006; Owen Bowcott, "Killer Who Wanted Fame Murdered Four in Random Attacks," *The Guardian* 17

March 2006; Martin Wainwright, "Serial Killer is Found Dead at Broadmoore," *The Guardian* 11 August 2007; James Watson, "Serial Killer Found Dead," *The Independent* 10 August 2007.

187 When sentencing Moore: Andrew Barrow, "Krueger Slasher Gets Life for Horror Attack," *Independent.ie* 5 April 2007.

187 The parents of his three victims: "Media Companies Are Sued in Kentucky Shooting," *NY Times* 13 April 1999: A19.

187 The U.S. Court of Appeals: "National Briefing," *NY Times* 17 August 2002: A8.

188 In 2003, Tonda: Janice Morse, "*Matrix* Influence Examined in Slayings," *The Cincinnati Enquirer* 3 June 2003 <http://www.enquirer.com/editions/2003/06/03/loc_matrix03.html>.

188 "They commit a": Ibid.

188 After interviewing Joshua: Peter Perl, "'I Don't Think They Deserved It'," *Washington Post* 30 November 2003 <http://www.washingtonpost.com/wp-dyn/content/article/2006/11/28/AR2006112800742.html?nav=emailpage>.

188 *The Matrix* was also: Morse, "*Matrix* Influence Examined in Slayings."

CHAPTER 5

Sins of the Flesh: Sex and Nudity on Celluloid

189 Some of these: Doherty, *Pre-Code Hollywood* 103.

190 But as critic: Gaylyn Studlar, *In the Realm of Pleasure: Von Sternberg, Dietrich, and the Masochistic Aesthetic* (New York: Columbia University Press, 1992) 48.

191 At one point: Lea Jacobs, *The Wages of Sin: Censorship and the Fallen Woman Film* (Berkeley: University of California Press, 1997) 93.

191 Colonel Jason Joy: Sova 55.

192 In 1926, West: "Police Raid Three Shows, *Sex*, *Captive* and *Virgin Man*; Hold Actors and Managers," *NY Times* 10 February 1927: 1.

192 She was convicted: "Mae West Jailed with Two Producers," *NY Times* 20 April 1927: 1; "Mae West Departs from Workhouse," *NY Times* 28 April 1927: 27.

192 When Universal: Colonel Jason Joy, "Col. Joy's Resume," 11 January 1930, *She Done Him Wrong* PCA File.

193 The critic for: "Diamond Lil" (rev. of *She Done Him Wrong*), *NY Times* 10 February 1933: 12.

193 James Wingate, who: A. M. Botsford, Letter to James Wingate, 6 July 1933, *I'm No Angel* PCA File.

193 Joe Breen strongly objected: As qtd. in Miller 96.

193 To appease the PCA: Miller 96.

193 As with *Blonde Venus*: Joseph Breen, Letter to Will Hays, 1 October 1935, *I'm No Angel* PCA File.

193 "It would appear": Joseph Breen, Letter to Luigi Luraschi, 2 September 1949, *I'm No Angel* PCA File.

194 She landed her: Norman M. Klein, *7 Minutes: The Life and Death of the American Animated Cartoon* (New York: Verso, 1996) 9.

195 As historian Karl F. Cohen: Cohen.

196 Nearly thirty years: De Grazia and Newman 280.

196 However, the Vatican: Sova 117.

196 In Germany, where: "Germany Also Excludes Czech Film Barred Here," *NY Times* 11 January 1935: 13.

196 A second print: Sova 117.

197 New York State still: *Eureka Productions v. Lehman*, 17 F. Supp. 259 (1936), affirmed 302 U.S. 634 (1937), as qtd. in De Grazia and Newman 211.

197 After two members: Gerald Gardner, *The Censorship Papers: Movie Censorship Letters from the Hays Office to 1934 to 1968* (New York: Dodd, Mead & Company, 1987) 74.

197 During the silent: Patrick Roberts, *Film Facts* (New York: Watson-Guptill, 2001) 64–65.

197 The film opened: Anthony Slide, *Lois Weber: The Director Who Lost Her Way in History* (Westport, CT: Greenwood Press, 1996) 70–76; "Hypocrites Film," *The Mansfield News* 14 September 1915: 2.

198 Another film: "*Inspiration* is Censored," *Middletown Daily Times-Press* 24 January 1915: 5.

198 But everyone: Sova 244–45.

198 A screening at: "Nudists Will Come to Town Sunday," *The Centralia* 1 February 1934: 5.

198 The producer, Ely Landau: Ely A. Landau, Letter to Geoffrey M. Shurlock, 29 January 1965, *The Pawnbroker* PCA File.

198 The board noted: Barney Balaban, Letter to Ralph Hetzel, 29 March 1965, *The Pawnbroker* PCA File.

199 The Legion of Decency: "Legion of Decency's Hesitation but Finally 'C's' Pawnbroker," *Variety* 12 May 1965.

199 Shot in: Jonas Mekas, "A Note on Genet's film, *Un Chant D'Amour*," *The Brooklyn Rail* (February 2006) <http://www.brooklynrail.org/2006/02/express/a-note-on-genet-s-film-un-chant-d-amour->.

200 Although experts: As qtd. in Sova 79–80.

200 "The fact that there": *Landau v. Fording*, 245 Cal. App. 2d 820 (1966).

200 Applying the "Roth Standard": Ibid.

200 Genet was never: Edward de Grazia, "An Interview with Jean Genet," *Cardozo Studies in Law and Literature* 5.2 (Autumn, 1993): 321.

200 But as critic: Vito Russo, *The Celluloid Closet* (New York: New York University Press, 1987) 98.

201 Only the New York: "State Court Hears Censors Challenge, " *NY Times* 8 January 1953: 33.

201 The Legion of Decency agreed: "Legion Bans *La Ronde*,' *NY Times* 5 November 1951: 26.

202 The film was denied: "Film Immoral, O'Connor Says in Court Case," *Chicago Daily Tribune* 12 October 1955:20.

202 After the mayor: Sova 142.

202 According to De Grazia: De Grazia and Newman 246.

203 When the distributor: Sova 165.

203 After a series: De Grazia and Newman 253.

203 Less than three: "Church Ban Shuts Theatre Upstate," *NY Times* 14 October 1958: 39.

204 In Cleveland, Tennessee: "Movie Manager Arrested," *The Daily Courier* (Connellsville, PA) 17 May 1958: 2.

204 In Philadelphia: "Move to Prevent Controversial Movie Showing," *The Daily Courier* 13 February 1958: 8; De Grazia and Newman 257.

204 A judge lifted: "Movie Censor Board Hit for Lax Viewing," *Chicago Daily Tribune* 21 June: A9.

204 In Ohio, the manager: "Man Convicted in Lewd Movie Trial," *The Coshocton Tribune* 9 June 1960: 22.

206 When Joseph Breen read: Joseph Breen, letter to Jack Warner, 1 August 1952, *Baby Doll* PCA File.

206 Breen's suggestion: Ibid.

206 But the biggest problem: Ibid.

206 Director Elia Kazan: Elia Kazan, Letter to Jack Warner, 15 November 1955, *Baby Doll* PCA File.

206 "I will, you can": Ibid.

206 Kazan also insisted: Ibid.

207 Upon seeing the rough cut: Jack Vizzard, "Memo for the Files," 25 July 1956, *Baby Doll* PCA File.

207 Kazan insisted: Vizzard, *See No Evil: Life Inside a Hollywood Censor* 207.

207 "The subject matter": *Classifications 1936–1965.* (New York: National Catholic Office for Motion Pictures, n.d.) 13.

207 Upon his return: Meyer Berger, "About New York," *NY Times* 22 October 1956: 23.

207 "The revolting theme": Claire Cox, "Spellman Calls *Baby Doll* Film Evil, Immoral," *Panama City News* 17 December 1956: 1.

208 "I made *Baby Doll*": "New Kazan Movie Put on Blacklist," *NY Times* 28 November 1956: 32.

208 In his autobiography: Elia Kazan, *A Life* (New York: Alfred A. Knopf, 1988) 564.

208 Williams was more: Cox 1.

208 *Time* magazine's: "New Picture," *Time* 24 December 1956.

208 In Providence, Rhode Island: *"Baby Doll* Ordered Cut to Get License for Exhibition to Providence Theatre," *NY Times* 5 January 1957: 11.

208 The management: *"Baby Doll* Canceled," *NY Times* 20 December 1956: 36.

209 The former ambassador: "Kennedy's Chain Bars *Baby Doll,"* NYT 27 December 1956: 21.

209 One particular scene: De Grazia and Newman 243–44.

209 A court affidavit: Sova 29.

209 Twenty-two years: Kazan 564.

210 "She wants to be": *I Am Curious (Yellow)* Pressbook, *I Am Curious (Yellow)* Production File, Margaret Herrick Library, Academy of Motion Picture Arts & Sciences, Beverly Hills, California.

210 The Supreme Court: As qtd. in Nicholas J. Karolides, Margaret Bald, and Dawn B. Sova *100 Banned Books* (New York: Facts on File, 199) 327.

211 "If this film": "U.S. Judge Refuses to Clear Swedish Film Seized in 1967," *NY Times* 4 May 1968: 44.

211 Rosset and Grove Press: Sova 151.

211 The National Catholic: "Catholic Group Condemns *I Am Curious (Yellow),"* *NY Times* 22 March 1969: 24.

211 The reviews from: "About as Far as A Swede Can Go?" *Variety* 1 November 1967:7; "Dubious *Yellow,"* *Time* 14 March 1969: 98; Richard Schickel, "It Hides Nothing but the Heart," *Life* 21 March 1969; Rex Reed, *"I Am Curious (No),"* *NY Times* 23 March 1969: D1.

212 As Dawn Sova: Sova 153.

212 *I Am Curious (Yellow)* did: *Wagonheim v. Maryland*, 258 A. 2d 240 (1969).

212 Grove Press: *Grove Press v. Maryland Board of Censors*, 401 U.S. 480 (1971).

212 But as their report: Richard Halloran, "Federal Commission on Pornography is Now Divided on the Easing of Legal Controls," *NY Times* 6 September 1970: 42.

212 In 1965, Keating: *Perversion for Profit* can be viewed on the web in the Prelinger Archives (www.archive.org).

212 "So as long as I": Warren Weaver, "Nixon Repudiates Obscenity Report as Morally Void," *NY Times* 25 October 1970: 1.

213 *Deep Throat* had been: "N.Y. Court Holds 'Throat' Obscene; Slaps $2 Mil Fine," *Variety* 2 March 1973: 1.

213 A federal judge: Matty Brescia, "Reems Wins New Trial on *Throat* Obscenity Charges," *Variety* 28 March 1977, 1, 11; Matty Brescia, "Sentences Handed Down in Second Throat Trial," *Variety* 9 March 1979.

214 Ironically, the legal: Ralph Blumenthal, "Porno Chic," *NY Times* 21 January 1973: 272.

214 His "Trilogy of Life": Naomi Greene, *Pier Paolo Pasolini: Cinema as Heresy* (Princeton, NJ: Princeton University Press, 1990) 181–82.

214 Those on the right: As qtd. in Greene 183.

214 When critics on the left: Ibid.

215 Like many aspects: As qtd. in Barth David Schwartz, *Pasolini Requiem* (New York: Pantheon, 1992) 524.

215 The film's release: As qtd. in Schwartz 525.

215 Pasolini appeared: Schwartz 525–26.

216 "My film is planned": As qtd. in Gideon Bachman, "Pasolini on de Sade," *Film Quarterly* Vol. 29, No. 2 (Winter 1975–76) 40.

216 Pelosi pleaded: Aidan Lewis, "30 Years After Italian Director Pier Paolo Pasolini's Slaying, Calls for Fresh Probe," *AP Mainstream* 9 May 2005 <http://www.highbeam.com/doc/1P1-108535974.html>.

216 As historian: Greene 218.

217 In the director's: Schwartz 668.

217 In many countries: A comparison of the various DVD versions in terms of their quality and content can be found online at http://www.dvd-beaver.com/film/DVDCompare/salo.htm.

217 British audiences: "James Ferman; To Come," *The Economist* 4 January 2003.

217 Five years later: Terry Lane, "*Salo* Is Rebanned," *The Sunday Age* 1 March 1998.

217 Although it depends: For background on *Caligula*, its various incarnations on video, laser disc, and DVD, as well as the works of Tinto Brass, visit http://rjbuffalo.com/index/html.

218 "It's a question": "*Penthouse* Interview [with] Bob Guccione," *Penthouse* (May 1980).

218 Giancarlo Lui and: Ibid.

218 "I was glad": Roderick Man, "Tit for Tat," *LA Times* 18 February 1980.

219 "But there's all": Eric Danville, "Caligula Speaks: An Audience with Malcolm McDowell," *The Girls of Penthouse* (November/December 2007): 19, 26.

219 In the May: "*Penthouse* Interview: Bob Guccione."

219 The *New York Times*'s Vincent Canby: "Film: Malcolm McDowell in Bob Guccione *Caligula*," *NY Times* 2 February 1980: 9; Vincent Canby, "Of Coercion, *Caligula* and Cloisters," *NY Times* 10 February 1980: D17.

219 *Variety* called it: Werb, "Rev. of *Caligula*," *Variety* 23 November 1979: 3.

219 The *Los Angeles Times*'s Kevin Thomas: "A $7.50 Wallow in Roman Decadence" *LA Times* 21 April 1980: G3.

219 Michael Sragow: Michael Sragow, "This Caligula Diddled While Rome Churned," *Herald-Examiner* 22 April 1980: B1–B2.

219 But the reviews: "*Penthouse* Interview [with] Bob Guccione."

219 On November 11, 1979: "Guccione, Rossellini *Caligula* seized as 'Flagrantly Obscene,'" *Variety* 21 November 1979.

219 Six months later: "Italian Court Bans *Caligula*; Sentence Distrib Rep, Prod.," *Variety* 14 May 1980.

220 It also served: "Sue Attny-Gen. For Not Prosecuting *Caligula*," *Variety* 6 February 1980.

220 As Penthouse's counsel: "Morality in Media Loses; Kraft Seeks Obscenity Test in N.Y. City as Most Favorable for *Caligula*," *Variety* 13 February 1980: 5.

220 Confident the charges: "Penthouse Plans Broadside Against Hub 'Combat Zone,'" *Variety* 24 June 1980: 1, 11.

220 Using the three-pronged test: "X-Rated Film *Caligula* Adjudged Not Obscene," *NY Times* 2 August 1980: 12.

220 When the picture: Guy Livingston, "Cleared of Obscenity charges, *Caligula* Shows Again in Hub,"' *Variety* 22 August 1980.

220 *Los Angeles Times* critic: Kevin Thomas," *Caligula* Back, Trimmed Down," *LA Times* 11 February 1982.

221 According to Guccione: Ted Loos, "But Is the World Ready for More of *Caligula*?" *NY Times* 19 September 1999: AR29.

221 *Caligula* didn't spark: "*Catherine the Great* Will Get That *Caligula* Touch in Penthouse Pic," *Variety* 5 December 1980.

221 Of course the: Ibid.

221 The change coincided: Russo 120–22.

221 The PCA objected: Geoffrey M. Shurlock, Letter to Michael O'Hare, n.d., *Victim* PCA File.

221 The decision: Press Release, Motion Picture Association of America, 18 December 1961, *Victim* PCA file.

222 Walker, who was: Clarke Taylor, "Gay Drama Offscreen on *Cruising*," *LA Times* 19 August 1979: N32.

222 After getting a copy: "Protestors Call the Film *Cruising* Antihomosexual," *NY Times* 26 July 1979: B7.

222 On the evening: Les Ledbetter, "1,000 in 'Village' Renew Protest Against Movie on Homosexuals," *NY Times* 27 July 1979: B2.

222 Weintraub continued: "Protestors Call the Film *Cruising* Antihomosexual" B7.

223 John Devere, editor-in-chief: John Devere, "On the Set," *Mandate* (February 1980) 6.

223 When Heffner was ready: Vaughn 60–61.

223 After rescreening the film: "GCC Still Won't Play *Cruising* After Rescreening," *Hollywood Reporter* 6 February 1980.

223 San Francisco Mayor: "S.F. Mayor: Send Bill to United Artists," *Los Angeles Herald Examiner* 22 February 1980: A3.

223 In Los Angeles: "Gays, Feminists Protest Movie," *LA Times* 25 January 1980: F7.

225 The distributor: Sova 131.

226 In his aptly titled autobiography: John Waters, *Shock Value* (Philadelphia: Running Press, 2005) 7.

227 The adult drama: "Italy Acquits Brando of Obscenity in Film," *LA Times* 3 March 1973.

227 The film was well received: Joan Mellen, *In the Realm of the Senses* (London: BFI Publishing, 2004) 76–77.

227 When it played: "Oshima, Disappointed at Barring of His Film as Obscene, Says He Expected 'Some Reaction'," *NY Times* 3 October 1976: 25.

228 A screening: Ibid.

CHAPTER 6

A Hotbed of Controversy: Politics and Religion

232 Critic Susan Sontag: Susan Sontag, "Fascinating Fascism," *Movies and Methods*, ed. Bill Nichols (Los Angeles: University of California Press, 1976) 36.

232 "The document": Ibid.

232 Sontag claimed: Sontag 40–41.

233 In her memoirs: Leni Riefenstahl, *Leni Riefenstahl: A Memoir* (New York: St. Martin's Press, 1992) 622–23.

233 She also paints: Riefenstahl 158.

233 She makes: Riefenstahl 311–12.

233 The screening also: "Nazi Movie Draws Throng at Theatre," *NY Times* 28 June 1960: 26.

233 Earlier that same year: Walter H. Waggoners, "British Group Withdraws Its Invitation to Friend of Hitler," *NY Times* 9 January 1960: 2.

233 "I want to make it": Rena Andrews, "Hitler's Favorite Filmmakers Honored at Colorado Festival," *NY Times* 15 September 1974: 15.

233 The following year: Sam Lucchese, "Protest of Nazi Films Erupts at Women's Fest," *Boxoffice* 20 October 1975: SE-2.

233 The screening was: Sam Lucchese, "Nazi Film Screening Applauded in Atlanta," *Boxoffice* 3 November 1975.

235 Brewer admitted: "Coast AFL Film Council Trying to Halt *Salt*," *Variety* 22 July 22 1953.

235 On February 24, 1953: "Jackson Brands Silver City Film 'A New Weapon for Russia,'" *Daily Variety* 25 February 1953.

235 "If this picture is shown" Ibid.

235 Screenwriter Wilson: "*Salt* Scribe Blasts Speech by Jackson," *Variety* 25 February 1953.

235 Two days after: "Mexican Actress Faces Deportation Quiz Today for Role in 'Red' Film," *Daily News* 26 February 1953: 2.

235 Meanwhile, the crew: "Cameramen Run Out of New Mexico Town," *Hollywood Citizen-News* 3 March 1953; "Citizens Balk Crew Making Leftist

Picture," *LA Times* 3 March 1953: 1; "Fist Fight Routs Crew of 'Red' Movie Makers," *Los Angeles Examiner* 4 March 1953.

235 Like a scene: "Film Leftists Get Death Warning," *LA Times* 4 March 1953: 6.

235 By the last day: "Police Keep Order in Row Over Union Film," *Hollywood Citizen-News* 5 March 1953.

235 As for Revueltas: As qtd. in Deborah Silverton Rosenfelt, "Commentary on *Salt of the Earth*," in Michael Wilson, *Salt of the Earth* (screenplay) (Old Westbury, NY: The Feminist Press, 1978) 132–33.

236 The union boycott: "Taking No Official Responsibility But Acting 'Phantom' Style, Union Hampers Indie *Salt of the Earth*," *Variety* 17 March 1954: 3, 17.

236 The list of names: Howard Hughes, letter to Congressman Donald L. Jackson, 18 March 1953, reprinted in James J. Lorence, *The Suppression of "Salt of the Earth"* (Albuquerque: University of New Mexico Press, 1999) 205–6.

236 The case dragged: "Jury Acquits 25 Defendants, Reduced from 110, in $6-Mil 1956 Suit on *Salt of the Earth*," *Variety* 18 November 1964.

236 In his review: Bosley Crowther, "*Salt of the Earth* Opens at the Grande—Filming Marked by Violence," *NY Times* 15 March 1954: 20.

236 "If there is": Roy Ringer, "*Salt* Deals with Human Issues," *Los Angeles Daily News* 4 June 1954.

237 Watkins also added: Alan Rosenthal, *New Challenges for Documentary* (Second Edition), ed. Alan Rosenthal and John Corner (Manchester: Manchester University Press, 2005) 119.

238 The film's "documentary authenticity": See Tony Shaw, "The BBC, the State and Cold War Culture: The Case of Television's *The War Game* (1965)," *English Historical Review* Vol. CXXI, No. 494 (December 2006): 1351–84; Patrick Murphy, "*The War Game*—The Controversy," *Film International* 1 January 2003: 25–28; James Chapman, "The BBC and the Censorship of *The War Game*," *Journal of Contemporary History* Vol. 41.1 (2006): 75–94; Mike Wayne, "Failing the Public: The BBC, *The War Game* and Revisionist History: A Reply to James Chapman," *Journal of Contemporary History* 42.4 (2007): 627–37; James Chapman, *The War Game*—Again, *Journal of Contemporary History* 43.1: 105–12.

238 In 1966, British critic: Kenneth Tynan, "A Film That Could Alter History," *LA Times* 20 February 1966: O8.

238 Twenty years after: Shaw 1383.

238 The BBC's *Radio Times*: Ibid.

239 "I make documentary": Frederick Wiseman, "Privacy and Documentary Filmmaking," *Social Research* 68.1 (2001) 41.

239 The action itself: Kaleem Aftab and Alexandra Weltz, "Fred Wiseman," <http://www.iol.ie/~galfilm/filmwest/40wiseman.htm>.

239 For *Titicut*: Carolyn Anderson and Thomas W. Benson, *Documentary Dilemmas: Frederick Wiseman's Titicut Follies* (Carbondale, IL: Southern Illinois University Press, 1991) 120.

239 The term: Thomas W. Benson and Carolyn Anderson, *Reality Fictions: The Films of Frederick Wiseman* (Carbondale, IL: Southern Illinois University Press, 1989) 1–2.

240 In a 2007 interview: Jesse Walker, "Let the Viewer Decide: Documentarian Frederick Wiseman on Free Speech, Complexity, and the Trouble with Michael Moore," *Reason* 1 December 2007 <http://www. reason.com/news/show/123022.html>.

240 On the witness: Loring Swaim, Jr., "Demands Hearing—Wiseman Wants to Answer Critics," *The Lowell Sun* 19 October 1967: 35.

240 Gaughan and Commissioner: Anderson and Benson, *Documentary Dilemmas* 92–93.

241 "The film is 80 minutes": *Commonwealth v. Wiseman*, 249 N.E. 2d 610 (1969).

241 In 1969: De Grazia and Newman 313.

241 Frederick Wiseman continued: Walker, "Let the Viewer Decide."

242 As Lee explained: Michael T. Kaufman, "In a New Film, Spike Lee Tries to Do the Right Thing," *NY Times* 25 June 1989: H1.

243 *New York* magazine: As qtd. in W. R. Grant, *Post-Soul Black Cinema: Discontinuities, Innovations, and Breakpoints, 1970–1995* (New York: Routledge, 2004) 58.

243 "If they react": As qtd. in Donald Bogle, *Toms, Coons, Mulattoes, Mammies, and Bucks: An Interpretive History of Blacks in American Films* (Fourth Edition) (New York: Continuum Publishing, 2006) 319.

243 Nearly nineteen years: Associated Press, "Spike Lee Is Backing Barack Obama," ABC News 17 February 2008 <http://abcnews.go.com/Entertainment/Vote2008/wireStory?id=4309292>.

244 It's not surprising: Walker, "Let the Viewer Decide."

246 In his autobiography: As qtd. in Black, *Hollywood Censored* 69.

246 Colonel Jason Joy: Black, *Hollywood Censored* 68.

246 One part of the: Ibid.

247 While some states: Black, *Hollywood Censored* 69.

247 A newspaper ad: Advertisement, *Victoria Daily Advocate* 5 May 1933: 2.

247 Many members of: Black, *Hollywood Censored* 68.

247 But DeMille and Paramount: Black, *Hollywood Censored* 69.

247 There were also: Ibid.

247 In Abilene, Texas: "Sign of the Cross Will Be Shown for Student Matinee," *The Abilene Daily Reporter* 28 February 1933: 4.

247 Many historians cite: Black, *Hollywood Censored* 163; Sova 273; Walsh 78–80.

247 "When the film": Thomas M. Pryor, "By Way of Report," *NY Times* 20 August 1944: X3.

247 Some editing: Ibid.

248 *Time* magazine: "The Reformer," *Time* 14 September 1953.

248 The *New Yorker* noted: John McCarten, "The Monk of Wittenberg," *New Yorker* 19 September 1953: 108–09.

248 *New York Times* critic: Bosley Crowther, "Religious Film," *NY Times* 13 September 1953: X1.

248 It chose instead: As qtd. in Black, *The Catholic Crusade Against the Movies* 130.

249 Meanwhile, Lutherans in: Advertisement, *Ironwood Daily Globe* 27 April 1954: 8.

249 The kind of controversy: "Quebec Movie Board Bars *Martin Luther*," *NY Times* 31 December 1953: 10.

249 The ban was opposed: "Protestant Editors Regret Luther Ban," *NY Times* 6 January 1954: 26.

249 The Montreal district: "Luther Film Ban Protested," *Ironweed Daily Globe* 15 January 1954: 9.

249 As the ban only: "Montreal Churches Will Show *Luther*," *NY Times* 31 May 1955: 24.

249 *Martin Luther* was also banned: "3 Nations Put Ban on *Martin Luther*," *NY Times* 30 April 1955: 11; "Brazil Bans *Luther*," *NY Times* 8 September 1955: 28; "Havana Bans *Martin Luther*," *NY Times* 26 September 1955: 19.

249 Ward L. Quaal, vice president: "Luther Film Ban Explained by WGN-TV," *Chicago Daily Tribune* 20 December 1956: B9.

249 A group of Protestant: Ibid; "Canceling of Film TV Protested," *NY Times* 20 December 1956: 34

250 Producer William Castle: Morris V. Murphy, "Memo to the File," 14 August 1967, *Rosemary's Baby* PCA File.

250 But when the PCA: Morris V. Murphy, "Memo to the File," 29 February 1968, *Rosemary's Baby* PCA File.

250 "Because of several": "*Rosemary's Baby* Given a 'C' Rating By Catholic Office," *NY Times* 21 June 1968: 45.

251 A Paramount spokesman: Ibid; "Hurry Sundown Gets Catholic 'C'," *NY Times* 8 March 1967: 52.

251 *New York Times* critic Vincent Canby: Vincent Canby, "Why the Devil Do They Dig *The Exorcist?*" *NY Times* 13 January 1974: 107.

252 The mixed reviews: Vincent Canby, "Blatty's *The Exorcist* Comes to the Screen," *NY Times* 27 December 1973: 46; Jay Cocks, "Beat the Devil," *Time* magazine 14 January 1974; Pauline Kael, "Back to the Ouija Board," *New Yorker* 7 January 1974: 59–62.

252 In a piece: Roy Meacham, "How Did *The Exorcist* Escape an X Rating?" *NY Times* 3 February 1974: 109.

252 MPAA President: Jack Valenti, "Three Movie Men Tell Their Side of the Story" ("Letter to the Editor"), *NY Times* 24 February 1974: 105.

252 But the morals division: Tom Shales, "*Exorcist*: No One Under 17 Admitted," *Washington Post* 3 January 1974: E1.

252 An attempt to ban: Laurent Bouzereau, *Cutting Room Floor: Movie Scenes Which Never Made It to the Screen* (New York: Citadel Press, 1994): 160–61.

252 Prosecutors were more: "Conviction Is a First," *Delta Democrat-Times* 3 May 1974: 2.

253 The conviction: Sova 123–24.

254 In an interview: C. Gerald Fraser, "*Mohammad* Director Says Film Is Meant to Inform Non-Moslems," *NY Times* 11 March 1977: 13.

254 An ad hoc committee: Ibid.

254 For the London release: Gene Siskel, "Controversy Follows *Mohammad* Film, *The Times Record* 10 March 1977: 3.

254 Their demands included: "The 38 Hours: Trial By Terror," *Time* magazine 21 March 1977: 16–20.

254 After thirty-eight hours: "Showings to Resume on Mohammed Film," *NY Times* 12 March 1977: 9.

255 A spokesman for: Eleanor Blau: "Catholics Deplore New Python Movie," *NY Times* 30 August 1979: C13.

255 "This film": "Three Jewish Groups Condemn *Monty Python's Life of Brian*," *NY Times* 28 August 1979: C8.

256 He believed: Ibid.

256 Robert A. Lee: "*Life of Brian* labeled 'crude and rude mockery'," *The Daily Herald* 8 September 1979: Section 1: 9.

256 The Pythons were: The Pythons, *The Pythons Autobiography* (New York: St. Martin's Press, 2003) 299–300.

256 Terry Jones, who: Clarke Taylor, "Members of Monty Python Defend *Life of Brian*," *LA Times* 23 October 1979: F14.

256 In Boston: "*Life of Brian* OK'd in Boston," *Pacific Stars and Stripes* 24 November 1979: 6.

256 Realizing he could: "Georgia City Bans Monty Python Film," *Indiana Evening Gazette* 1 November 1979: 29.

256 The order was: Robert Hewison, *Monty Python: The Case Against* (New York: Grove Press, 1981) 83.

256 A controversy over: "*Life of Brian* Stirs Carolina Controversy," *NY Times* 24 October 1979: A14.

256 Similar incidents: Hewison 83.

258 Kazantzakis was surprised: Karolides, Bald & Sova 220.

258 When the author died: Nancie Matthew, "In the Town of Nazareth," *NY Times* 7 August 1960: BR4.

258 "I'm hopeful": Steve Rabey, "Producer Tries to Dim Fears Over Movie," *Christianity Today* 4 March 1988.

259 A document entitled: Letter from Larry W. Pond, 6 July 1988, 5, *Last Temptation of Christ* Production File, Margaret Herrick Library, Academy of Motion Picture Arts and Sciences, Beverly Hills, California.

259 "In America": Universal News, Press Department, 7 July 1988, 2, *Last Temptation of Christ* Production File, Margaret Herrick Library, Academy of Motion Picture Arts and Sciences, Beverly Hills, California.

260 On Thursday, August 11: Aljean Harmetz, "7,500 Picket Universal Over Movie About Jesus," *NY Times* 12 August 1988: C4.

261 Gibson admitted: Peter J. Boyer, "The Jesus War: Mel Gibson's Obsession," *New Yorker* 15 September 2003: 71.

261 In an interview: "Gibson Defends Film on *Primetime*," *NY Times* 16 February 204: E2.

261 "To be anti-Semitic": Ibid.

261 Rabbi Marvin Hier: "*Passion* Film is Incendiary, 2 Jewish Leaders Report," *NY Times* 23 January 2004: A12.

261 As Michael Parenti: "Jesus, Mel Gibson & the Demon Jew," *The Humanist* 64.5 (September–October 2004): 22.

262 "There is no excuse": <http://www.cnn.com/2006/SHOWBIZ/Movies/08/01/gibson.statement/index.html>.

SELECTED BIBLIOGRAPHY

Black, Gregory D. *The Catholic Crusade Against the Movies, 1940–1975*. New York: Cambridge University Press, 1998.

_____. *Hollywood Censored: Morality Codes, Catholics, and the Movies*. New York: Cambridge University Press, 1994.

Bouzereau, Laurent. *Ultraviolent Movies: From Sam Peckinpah to Quentin Tarantino*. New York: Citadel Press, 2000.

Brownlow, Kevin. *Behind the Mask of Innocence*. New York: Alfred A. Knopf, 1990.

Butters, Jr., Gerald R. *Banned in Kansas: Motion Picture Censorship, 1915–1986*. Columbia: University of Missouri Press, 2007.

Carmen, Ira H. *Movies, Censorship and the Law*. Ann Arbor: University of Michigan Press, 1967.

Cohen, Karl F. *Forbidden Animation: Censored Cartoons and Blacklisted Animators in America*. Jefferson, North Carolina: McFarland & Company, Inc., 1997.

De Grazia, Edward and Roger K. Newman. *Banned Films: Movies, Censors, and the First Amendment*. New York: R. R. Bowker Company, 1982.

Doherty, Thomas. *Pre-Code Hollywood: Sex, Immorality, and Insurrection in American Cinema 1930–1934*. New York: Columbia University Press, 1999.

Farber, Stephen. *The Motion Picture Ratings Game*. Washington, D.C.: Public Affairs Press, 1972.

Federal Motion Picture Commission. *Hearings Before the Committee on Education*. House of Representatives, Sixty Fourth Congress, First Session on H.R. 456. Washington: Government Printing Office, 1916, reprinted by New York: Arno Press, Inc., 1978.

Gardner, Gerald C. *The Censorship Papers: Movie Censorship Letters from the Hays Office, 1934 to 1968*. New York: Dodd, Mead, and Company, 1987.

Grieveson, Lee. *Policing Cinema: Movies and Censorship in Early Twentieth-Century America*. Los Angeles: University of California Press, 2004.

Index on Censorship. 24.6 Issue 167 (December 1995). London: Writers & Scholars International Limited, 1995.

Inglis, Ruth A. *Freedom of the Movies*. Chicago: University of Chicago Press, 1947.

Jacobs, Lea. *The Wages of Sin: Censorship and the Fallen Woman Film, 1928–1942.* Madison: University of Wisconsin Press, 1991.

Jowett, Garth. *Film: The Democratic Art.* Boston: Little, Brown & Company, 1976.

Karolides, Nicholas J., Margaret Bald, and Dawn B. Sova. *100 Banned Books.* NY: Checkmark Books, 1999.

Kuhn, Annette. *Cinema, Censorship, and Sexuality, 1909–1925.* New York: Routledge, 1988.

Leff, Leonard J. and Jerold L. Simmons. *The Dame in the Kimono: Hollywood Censorship and the Production Code.* Lexington: University Press of Kentucky, 2001.

Lorence, James J. *The Suppression of "Salt of the Earth."* Albuquerque: University of New Mexico Press, 1999.

Martin, Olga J. *Hollywood's Movie Commandments.* New York: Arno Press, 1970.

Mast, Gerald, ed. *The Movies in Our Midst.* Chicago: University of Chicago Press, 1982.

Miller, Frank. *Censored Hollywood: Sex, Sin, & Violence on Screen.* Atlanta: Turner Publishing, Inc., 1994.

Musser, Charles. *The Emergence of Cinema: The American Screen to 1907.* Los Angeles: University of California Press, 1990.

Prince, Stephen. *Classical Film Violence: Designing and Regulating Brutality in Hollywood Cinema, 1930–1968.* New Brunswick, New Jersey: Rutgers University Press, 2003.

_____. *Sam Peckinpah's "The Wild Bunch."* Cambridge: Cambridge University Press, 1999.

Russo, Vito. *The Celluloid Closet.* Revised Edition. New York: New York University Press, 1987.

Schatz, Thomas. *Hollywood Genres.* New York: McGraw-Hill, 1981.

Skinner, James M. *The Cross and the Cinema: The Legion of Decency and the National Catholic Office for Motion Pictures, 1933–1970.* Westport, Connecticut: Praeger, 1993.

Sova, Dawn B. *Forbidden Films: Censorship Histories of 125 Motion Pictures.* New York: Checkmark Films, 2001.

Vaughn, Stephen. *Freedom and Entertainment: Rating the Movies in the Age of New Media.* New York: Cambridge University Press, 2006.

Vizzard, Jack. *See No Evil: Life Inside a Hollywood Censor.* New York: Simon and Schuster, 1970.

Walsh, Frank. *Sin and Censorship: The Catholic Church and the Motion Picture Industry.* New Haven: Yale University Press, 1996.

Wilson, Michael. *Salt of the Earth.* Old Westbury, NY: Feminist Press, 1978.

INDEX

Index

Index